TEXAS
REAL
ESTATE
APPRAISAL

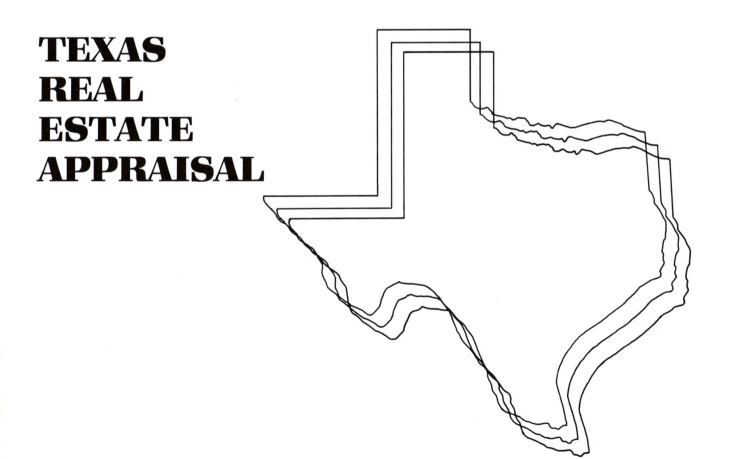

THE JOHN WILEY TEXAS REAL ESTATE SERIES

Under the consulting editorship of

Dr. Edgar J. Manton

East Texas State University

J. B. FEATHERSTON
Merrill Lynch Real Estate Advisory and Appraisal Group

J. DON JONES
Houston Community College

an adaptation of
BASIC REAL ESTATE APPRAISAL
by **RICHARD BETTS** and **SILAS J. ELY**

TEXAS
REAL
ESTATE
APPRAISAL

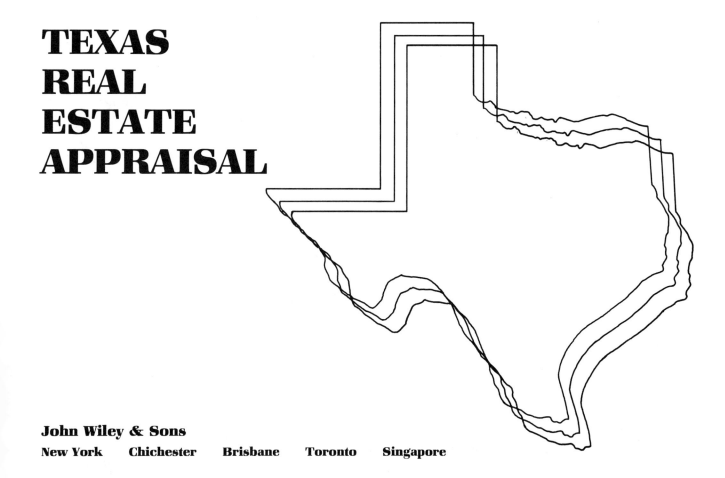

John Wiley & Sons
New York   Chichester   Brisbane   Toronto   Singapore

Library of Congress Cataloging in Publication Data:

Featherston, J. B.
  Texas real estate appraisal.

  (Wiley series in Texas real estate)
  "An adaptation of Basic real estate appraisal by
Richard Betts and Silas J. Ely."
  Includes index.
  1. Real property—Valuation—Texas. I. Jones,
J. Don. II. Betts, Richard M., 1935–   Basic
real estate appraisal. III. Title. IV. Series.

HD266.T4F4 1986   333.33'2'09764   85-26479
ISBN 0-471-82299-X

Printed in the United States of America

10 9 8 7 6 5 4 3 2

My contributions to this book are dedicated to the memory of my first real estate instructor, my father, Solon R. Featherston. He is best described in the words of a plaque signed by his numerous former students and associates as:

"Realtor - Teacher - Friend."

J.B. Featherston

To Tina Jones, my seven-year-old daughter, whose analytical mind and inquisitive personality is the envy of any appraiser.

J. Don Jones

ABOUT
THE
AUTHORS

J. B. FEATHERSTON

Mr. Featherston is currently National Director of Special Projects for the Merrill Lynch Real Estate Advisory and Appraisal Group, a subsidiary of Merrill Lynch & Co. Residing in Dallas, Mr. Featherston is a Senior Vice President of his company and has previously served as manager of the Dallas district office of Merrill Lynch Commercial Real Estate.

Mr. Featherston has 31 years experience in the real estate industry, most of that time as head of his own appraisal and consulting business. In 1962 he was elected to membership in the American Institute of Real Estate Appraisers, awarded the designation MAI (Member, Appraisal Institute). He has served the Appraisal Institute in a number of capacities, including President of the North Texas Chapter in 1968, National Chairman of Professional Ethics in 1971 and 1972, National Chairman of Education in 1978, First Vice President in 1979, and National President in 1980. He has taught appraisal courses throughout the United States and has contributed numerous articles to the *Appraisal Journal*. In November 1985, Mr. Featherston was invited to membership in the prestigious American Society of Real Estate Counselors and awarded the designation of CRE (Counselor in Real Estate).

Mr. Featherston received a Bachelor of Arts degree in 1950 from Hardin Simmons University in Abilene. He has completed most of the professional courses offered by the American Institute of Real Estate Appraisers and has done graduate work in real estate and financial subjects at Midwestern State University.

J. DON JONES

J. Don Jones is a professor in the Real Estate Department at Houston Community College. He received a BA degree from the University of

Texas. He has taught real estate courses at Houston Community College, at the University of Houston, and at several proprietary schools in the Houston area for over 9 years. He has been active in the Houston real estate market for 12 years, having owned a large residential brokerage firm for 7 years, served as a senior appraiser for both the City of Houston and the Harris County Appraisal District for 3 years, and worked as an independent fee appraiser doing primarily right-of-way and eminent domain appraisals. Mr. Jones is active in the Houston market as an appraiser and real estate consultant for investors of apartment buildings and shopping centers. He holds the GRI, CRB, and CRS designations. He is a member of the National Association of Realtors (NAR), Real Estate Educators Association (REEA), and the Texas Real Estate Teacher's Association (TRETA).

RICHARD M. BETTS

Mr. Betts is an independent real estate appraiser and consultant in Berkeley, California. He was educated at the University of California, Berkeley, earning B.S. and MBA degrees in Business Administration. Subsequent educational work includes a Real Estate Certificate; AIREA courses/exams I, II, IV, and VIII; SREA Course 301 and Educare Course I. Mr. Betts has extensive experience as a fee appraiser, including expert-witness appraisals before various superior courts and assessment appeals boards. He has taught extensively for Merritt Community College; the University of California, Berkeley, Extension Division; and SREA (Courses 101 and 201). He has also taught for AIREA (Course IB), IAAO (Courses 1, 2, and 3), the University of Southern California College of Continuing Education and the University of California, Berkeley, School of Business. Mr. Betts holds the professional designations MAI, SRPA, and ASA (Real Estate), is a past president of East Bay Chapter 54 of SREA, an officer of Northern California Chapter 11 of AIREA, and a member of the National Editorial Board, *The Appraisal Journal,* AIREA. He is the coauthor of *The Essentials of Real Estate Economics,* 2nd ed., published by John Wiley & Sons, Inc., New York, in *1980.*

SILAS J. ELY

Born in Texas, Mr. Ely is an independent real estate appraiser, instructor, and educational consultant, who resides in Van Nuys, California. He is a graduate of the University of California at Los Angeles, holding the B.A. degree in political science and a Certificate in Real Estate. He also holds a full-time California Community College Instructor teaching credential. For many years, Mr. Ely was a Principal Appraiser and Regional Manager for the Los Angeles County Assessor. He is currently an instructor at Santa Monica College, where he has taught both the beginning and advanced appraisal courses since 1966. He was also a senior faculty member in appraisal for the University of Southern California College of Continuing Education. Mr. Ely was the 1978 Chairman of the California Association of Real Estate Teachers. Currently a member of the Real Estate Educators Association, Mr. Ely is also a past president of the Los Angeles County Chapter of the IAAO. He holds the RECI Designation of the California Association of Realtors and was recipient of the Teacher of the Year Award for 1979 from the California Association of Real Estate Teachers.

PREFACE

We have written *Texas Real Estate Appraisal* to meet two goals. The first is to provide a text for the beginning college-level appraisal course. The second is to provide a clearly written and practical guide to real estate appraisal for brokers and salespeople, as well as appraisal trainees, investors, and consumers.

Texas Real Estate Appraisal is a thorough outline of generally accepted theory and practice today. Both simple and complex subjects are covered in terms that are easy to understand yet accurate. Although this is an entry-level text, advanced appraisal techniques such as statistical analysis are briefly introduced.

This text is based on the authors' years of teaching at both the community college and university levels, as well as on years of practical appraisal experience. As to the format of the book, the chapters are subdivided into sections, usually three. Each chapter starts with a preview paragraph and statement of learning objectives. These should help the reader to identify the important elements in the chapter. The major sections of the text material follow. Each chapter concludes with a comprehensive summary and a list of important terms and concepts. A group of chapter review questions is provided to help readers review their understanding. The answers to these questions are provided at the end of the book.

Finally, we wish to stress our view that appraisal concepts and techniques are important tools, which are useful to people in *every* field of real estate. We hope that our presentation will provide many ideas and skills for use in your daily real estate endeavors.

J. B. Featherston
J. Don Jones
Richard M. Betts
Silas J. Ely

ACKNOWLEDGMENTS

We want to express our deep appreciation to the many people who have played a part in the preparation of this book. Valued technical contributions were made by Professor Nicholas Ordway, Department of Finance and Real Estate, University of Texas at Arlington; Sam Derobertis, San Antonio College; Ted Jones, Texas Real Estate Research Center, Texas A & M University; Ray Woodard, Independent Fee Appraiser; and Richard Nowack, Houston Institute of Real Estate. Many other people have helped; the students in our appraisal classes who have shared their insights with us, the appraisal colleagues and friends with whom we have exchanged and debated ideas over the years, the authors of earlier appraisal texts from which we have learned, and the lecturers at the appraisal courses and seminars at which we have been students.

We also acknowledge the use of valuable resource materials from the Texas Real Estate Research Center and the technical advice of Mr. Charles Carnahan in finalizing the manuscript. Mr. Tom Brodnax was most helpful in developing figures and illustrations for the text.

We are indebted to Paul Metzger and Katherine Tyra of Houston Community College for their assistance in the project. Dennis McKenzie's leadership, guidance, and encouragement are truly appreciated. We are also indebted to Karen Martin for preparing the glossary. Finally, we would like to acknowledge the able and dedicated team at John Wiley—Carole O'Keefe, Pat Fitzgerald, Kevin Murphy, Elizabeth Doble, Barbara Mele, and Cindy Funkhouser.

This book could not have been produced without the dedicated help of Donna Johnson and Debbie Isaacks in typing and proofing the manuscript. We are also especially indebted to our families for their understanding.

J. B. F.
J. D. J.

TABLE OF CONTENTS

TEXAS
REAL
ESTATE
APPRAISAL

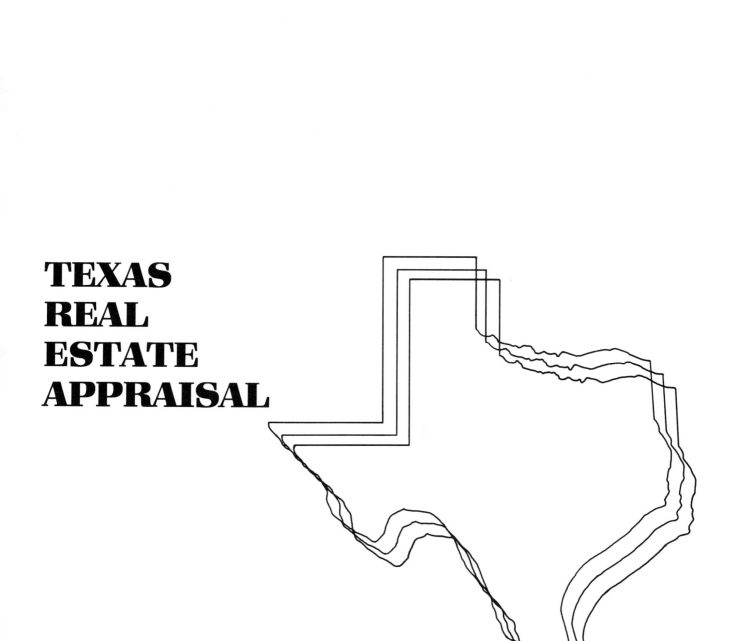

CHAPTER
ONE

REAL
ESTATE
APPRAISAL
AND YOU

PREVIEW

As you begin reading this book, you may already have some general ideas about real estate appraisal. Perhaps you have taken classes, read books, or have had prior real estate experience. On the other hand, maybe you have had no experience with real estate appraising and are simply interested in finding out what it is all about. In either case you will find the information in this book very useful.

Appraisal involves making accurate estimates of value. Since value is the central concern for most real estate decisions, knowing how to make good estimates of value is important to the entire real estate community. This chapter will explain what an appraisal is, who makes appraisals, and how appraisals are useful to our society. In particular, we shall point out that most of us make decisions every day that use basic appraisal skills. The goal of this book is to help you develop the appraisal skills that you already have so that you can make better real estate decisions, with more successful results.

When you have completed this chapter, you should be able to:

1.   Define the term appraisal.
2.   Explain the difference between a formal and an informal appraisal.
3.   List the main uses of appraisals.
4.   List the four reasons for studying appraisal.

SECTION 1.1
APPRAISING—WHAT IS IT?

Very simply, *an appraisal is an estimate of value.* It is defined as an estimate because it is neither a statement of value nor a fixing of value. An appraisal is only one person's opinion based upon whatever skills, training, data, dedication, and objectivity that person has.

Since an appraisal is an estimate of value, value is an important concept that must be clearly understood. Value means that *worth, usefulness, or utility of an object to someone for some purpose.* The value of an object can vary, depending upon the purpose for which it is to be used or the person seeking to use it. There are many different types of values, and each is appropriate to a particular appraisal purpose or need. (The common types of value will be explained in Chapter 3.) Most often, questions concerning the value of an object involve estimating its most probable selling price. Accurately estimating what real estate should sell for is the focus of this book.

Informal Valuation

Have you ever estimated what price to pay for an object at a garage sale or auction? If you have, then you have made an appraisal. This type of informal appraisal is a common part of our lives. Every day we are bombarded with advertisements urging us to purchase bread, cars, razor blades, and other products. Whenever we buy any of these items, we usually perform an informal appraisal to judge if the prices are reasonable. We may compare one product to another or match the price of one item against that of a similar one. As we become more experienced in comparing items and prices, we develop an intuitive understanding of the value of an object. We use our intuition to appraise whether a particular price for a loaf of bread, a car, or a stereo is too high or low for the particular market.

Some people have developed their intuition, judgment, and expertise to such a degree that they can make very accurate and reliable informal appraisals of real estate. For example, brokers and salespeople with years of experience in a specialized market routinely use their intuition to make appraisals. Many can accurately estimate the selling price of a house after quickly walking through it. Obviously, the accuracy of these pricing opinions depends on the judgment of the agent, as well as his or her exposure to homes in that area.

Formal Valuation

Real estate practitioners and consumers sometimes need to estimate the value of objects that they have had little experience buying or selling. Without recent experience, their intuitive judgment about prices may be unreliable. One example involving a real estate consumer is that of an employee transferring to a new town. The employee has just sold his or her old residence at the prices prevailing in the old hometown and must buy another at the prices prevailing in the new town.

When intuition is inadequate, there are only three alternatives: (1) to guess, (2) to go to someone with informed judgment, or (3) to deliberately develop the information needed to make good price estimates. The last of these three choices has led to formal appraisal, or appraisal by a system of logic.

A *formal appraisal is an estimate of value that is reached by the collection and analysis of data.* Since the conclusion is based upon the analysis of factual material, a client or disinterested party can easily review the appraisal and understand how the conclusion was reached. This contrasts with the informal appraisal, where the conclusion is reached by using intuition, past experience, and general knowledge. An intuitive conclusion cannot easily be reviewed by a third party. To better understand the difference between formal and informal appraisals, see Figure 1.1.

In practice, formal and informal appraisals share some common ground. Although formal appraisals are based primarily upon supporting data, in practice they must also rely to a degree upon the appraiser's judgment and intuition. On the other hand, informal appraisals are based upon intuition but may include some data that supports the value estimate. Appraisals by professional appraisers are for the most part formal; those by experienced salespeople are for the most part intuitive and informal.

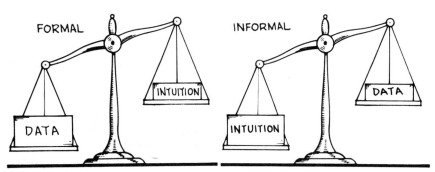

FIGURE 1.1
Formal and Informal Appraisals

The Appraisal Report

The manner in which a formal appraisal is communicated is called the appraisal report. Reports may be either oral or written, but they are usually written. The length of the written report can vary from one to many pages. However, the length of the report has nothing to do with the quality of the appraisal or the complexity of the appraisal assignment. A complex appraisal might be presented in a very short report, or vice versa. Appraisal reports will be discussed in more detail in the following chapters.

SECTION 1.2
HOW APPRAISAL
SKILLS ARE USED

Who Needs Appraisals?

Formal and informal appraisals serve two important functions in our society. The first function is to meet the public need for accurate value estimates. Some people do not have the skills, the time, or the knowledge to make good estimates on their own. Instead, they turn to others for assistance. Most informal appraisals made by salespeople, as well as many formal ones made by appraisers, are performed solely for this reason.

The second social function that appraisals perform is to provide an unbiased and disinterested estimate of value. Some questions of value are so important that this lack of bias is an absolute necessity. Appraisals in such situations must be formal, capable of being reviewed, and presented in written form. Like the notes of the certified court reporter or the signature of the notary public, the formal appraisal made by an unbiased appraiser serves an important role.

Occasions Requiring Appraisals

Throughout our society we can see numerous occasions when formal or informal appraisals are necessary. Such occasions can be divided into two major categories: market transactions and legal transactions. Each category requires the use of appraisal skills to develop some type of price or value estimate.

Market Transactions
Every sale of real estate involves at least two informal appraisals, the buyer's and the seller's. The pricing opinion of an involved salesperson could be a third. Most real estate transactions also require at least one formal appraisal, which is usually required by the lender. Separate formal appraisals may also be obtained by the buyer or seller. Where there are multiple buyers or sellers, as for some investment properties, each of the parties could conceivably have a separate formal appraisal performed. Thus, in a given market transaction, many formal appraisal reports may be prepared.

Formal appraisals are required in a number of other market circumstances. For example, an appraisal is sometimes needed to estimate the proper rent level at the time a new lease is negotiated. Also, an appraisal is often needed to estimate the values of property being exchanged. Or one may be needed to estimate proper insurance coverage, based upon the kind of coverage in the insurance contract. Another example is the need to appraise whether the cost of proposed remodeling is in line with the probable increase in the property's value. Finally, a formal appraisal may be necessary to estimate which of several possible uses of a vacant land parcel would prove to be the highest and best use, that is, the most profitable use.

Legal Transactions

Formal written appraisals are often required in connection with various legal disputes. One such circumstance occurs when an agency of the government uses its power of eminent domain (the right to acquire private property for a public purpose). Here the appraiser is called upon to estimate what the just compensation or payment should be under the law.

A second group of appraisals for legal purposes is required in connection with various forms of taxation. In the case of property taxes, the local property tax appraiser must estimate a value to be used as the basis for the tax. In turn, the taxpayer may have the property appraised to see if the agency's valuation is reasonable or whether it should be appealed. Appraisals are also necessary to establish a basis for inheritance, estate, or gift taxes. Appraisals may be required to support an income tax claim for a casualty loss. An appraisal may be needed to allocate the purchase price of property between the land and the improvements in order to set up income tax depreciation. On occasion, appraisals are needed to establish historical values so that capital gains can be calculated. As the various categories of taxation have become more complicated, formal appraisals have come into greater demand.

A third group of legal appraisals is needed for lawsuits between people. For example, there is an increasing need to appraise the property of a divorcing couple in order that the property can be divided by the court. Lawsuits between building owners and tenants involving questions of property value or monthly rental may also require appraisals. Additionally, most lawsuits over damages to real estate require an appraisal of the property as well as its loss in value. Damages may be either physical or economic.

Another occasion for appraisals arises when loans are in default, since many lenders want to know the market value of any real estate security while commencing the foreclosure process. Bankruptcy actions may also call for appraisals. If real estate is offered as security for bail bonds, appraisals might be required. Appraisals for legal purposes are among the most challenging of formal appraisals.

Many of the occasions that require appraisals are listed in Example 1.1. Most of these occasions will involve at least one formal appraisal.

Example 1.1
Uses of Appraisals
1. Market Transactions

(a)	Buyer	**(h)**	Option to purchase
(b)	Seller	**(i)**	Insurance
(c)	Sales agent	**(j)**	Feasibility study
(d)	Lender	**(k)**	Highest and best use study
(e)	Trade		
(f)	Landlord	**(l)**	Modernization or remodeling study
(g)	Tenant		

2. Legal Transactions

(a)	Eminent domain—condemnor	**(i)**	Capital gains tax basis
(b)	Eminent domain—condemnee	**(j)**	Property settlement upon divorce
(c)	Property tax	**(k)**	Damage lawsuits
(d)	Property tax appeal	**(l)**	Loan foreclosure decisions
(e)	Estate or inheritance tax	**(m)**	Company liquidation or merger
(f)	Gift tax	**(n)**	Security for bail bonds
(g)	Income tax—casualty loss	**(o)**	Partnership dissolution
(h)	Income tax–depreciation basis allocation		

SECTION 1.3
DEVELOPING APPRAISAL SKILLS

We believe that appraisal skills are important to everyone who is, or wants to be, involved with real estate. These skills are particularly important to salespeople, since they must be familiar with current price levels. By using appraisal skills, salespeople can effectively improve the accuracy of their pricing estimates and avoid many problems. For example, suppose that a sales agent accepts a new listing in an unfamiliar area. If the agent does not use appraisal skills to establish a reasonable price, he or she might accept the listing at too high a price. This could result in no sale, an unhappy client, and a waste of otherwise productive time. Accepting a listing at too low a price can also have undesirable effects.

Appraisal skills are also important for people working in other real estate areas. For example, investors can use appraisal skills to estimate the right price at which to buy or sell property. Lenders use appraisal skills every day to assure that a loan has adequate security.

A second important reason for studying appraisal is to acquire basic knowledge and learn the terminology that will help you in any future real estate course. Real estate finance, real estate investment analysis, and advanced appraisal courses all rely on the information and ideas presented in this book. Third, studying this book can also help you to pass the real estate broker's license test; most licensing exams include a section on real estate appraisal. Also, an appraiser must hold a real estate license to appraise in Texas.

Finally, a fourth reason for studying appraisal is to improve your understanding of the way appraisers work and converse. This will help you communicate with appraisers, evaluate their work intelligently, and improve your understanding of appraisal reports. Learning how to communicate better your own procedure for valuing property to your clients is another important benefit.

How Will the Format of the Book Help You?

The format of this book has been developed to assist you in learning easily and quickly. Since appraising is a process that follows a series of steps, we have provided a diagram of this process to aid you in understanding it. This diagram appears on the opening pages of Chapters 3 to 16, and the step covered in each chapter is highlighted. A full explanation of the appraisal process and the diagram can be found in Chapter 3.

Each chapter (except Chapters 1, 2, 17, and 18) begins with the appraisal process diagram. Next, a brief introduction previews the chapter and points out key learning objectives. The chapter ends with a summary so that you can again review what you have read and reinforce your understanding. The chapter summary is followed by a list of important terms to help you develop an appraisal vocabulary and remember which terms are most important. Review questions at the end of each chapter also reinforce key ideas.

Of course, the learning objectives, chapter summary, and review questions will help you most if you put them to work. So take the time to read each chapter carefully and thoughtfully. When you finish, if you can answer the questions without looking back, you are doing fine. If you *do* need to look back, don't feel upset; looking up the answers will aid your learning considerably. Remember, you only get back from a book what you put into it. Appraisal skills can contribute measurably to your success, so your effort *will* be rewarded.

The Chapters Ahead

This book outlines the entire formal appraisal process and explains the various skills that it comprises. Chapters 2 and 3 introduce the vocabulary you must be familiar with before the actual appraisal starts and include definitions of terms that you must understand. An overview of the entire process is also provided.

Chapters 4 and 5 outline the major forces that influence value and point out how these forces can be interpreted. Chapters 6 and 7 detail the tasks of the actual property inspection. Chapters 8 to 15 show you the analytical techniques that are considered when valuing the property. Chapter 16 outlines the structure of the appraisal report, detailing information that needs to be included and why. Chapter 17 introduces a number of advanced appraisal topics that will help you understand basic appraisal skills. Thus, the book includes some complex material that is typically presented in advanced appraisal courses. Chapter 18 turns your attention to appraising as a profession. It details the educational requirements and standards necessary to become an appraiser; it also lists many of the numerous appraisal organizations throughout the United States and their activities. The chapter closes with a brief description of professional appraisal work.

SUMMARY

In this chapter, we found that an appraisal is simply an estimate of value. Value generally means the worth or usefulness of something to someone for some purpose. Although there are many types of value, the purpose of most appraisals is to estimate the price at which something should sell.

Estimating the selling price of things is a process that everyone performs at one time or another. People do this by relying on their prior experiences with selling or buying an item. Such a value estimate is an informal or intuitive appraisal. When people have accumulated a lot of recent experience buying or selling a commodity, their intuitive appraisals may be very good. However, it is difficult for someone else to judge whether an intuitive appraisal is accurate or not.

Many people do not have the experience or judgment needed to make good, intuitive real estate appraisals. They can nevertheless learn to gather information systematically and analyze it logically, skills that yield as good an understanding of value as intuition can. These skills make up the formal appraisal. Formal appraisals have the advantage of presenting data and analyses that can easily be reviewed. This allows a client or reviewer to consider objectively whether the appraisal estimate seems reasonable. However, the appraisal report does not need to contain all the information and calculations that were developed during a formal appraisal.

Appraisals are a vital part of real estate. Every real estate transaction requires at least an informal appraisal by the buyer and one by the seller. One or more formal appraisals may also be needed, especially to meet the lender's requirements. In addition, the legal framework of our society requires many appraisals, including appraisals for eminent domain, for different taxation purposes, and for use as evidence in civil lawsuits involving real property.

The subject of real estate appraisal is important to all involved in real estate. Whether you are a real estate consumer or real estate professional, having appraisal skills will make your real estate decisions better, more profitable, and less prone to errors. Another reason for studying real estate appraisal is that this material can assist you in taking future real estate courses or real estate license tests. Studying appraisal also enables you to communicate better with appraisers. By learning their language and techniques, you will be able to view their work intelligently. A knowledge of appraisal skills also helps you to clearly communicate to others the way in which your own value decisions are reached.

IMPORTANT TERMS AND CONCEPTS

Appraisal (formal and informal)	Legal transactions
Appraisal process	Market transactions
Appraisal report	Usefulness
Independent appraisal	Value
Intuitive appraisal	Worth

REVIEWING YOUR UNDERSTANDING

1. The general term, value, means:
   (a) The function of an object
   (b) The average use and function of an object to all people

    (c) The worth, usefulness, or utility of an object to someone for some purpose

    (d) The highest price in terms of money that a property will bring with reasonable market exposure, neither buyer nor seller being under compulsion to act

2. An appraisal is:
   - **(a)** A fixing of value
   - **(b)** An estimate of value
   - **(c)** A statement of value
   - **(d)** A value determination

3. The two types of real estate appraisals are:
   - **(a)** Formal and informal
   - **(b)** Informal and intuitive
   - **(c)** Structural and formal
   - **(d)** None of the above

4. Appraisals are performed by:
   - **(a)** Many
   - **(b)** Few
   - **(c)** All

5. Informal appraisals rely *mostly* on:
   - **(a)** Judgment, intuition, and experience
   - **(b)** Facts, figures, and experience
   - **(c)** Analysis, review, and documentation
   - **(d)** Analysis, data, and correlation

6. Formal appraisals rely on:
   - **(a)** Experience, judgment, and speculation
   - **(b)** Intuition, data, and highest and best use
   - **(c)** Data, analysis, and judgment
   - **(d)** Experience, judgment, and data

7. The two important social functions appraisals serve are:
   - **(a)** To meet the public need for good value estimates and to provide an unbiased and objective opinion of value
   - **(b)** To moderate value estimates and provide an unbiased opinion
   - **(c)** To provide information about price trends and to provide a fixed value
   - **(d)** To provide an objective estimate of value and an estimate of property structural condition

8. Some common types of legal transactions that require appraisals are:
   - **(a)** Income tax casualty loss, estate or inheritance tax, and property settlement upon divorce
   - **(b)** Damage lawsuits, loan foreclosures, and security for bail bonds
   - **(c)** Company liquidation or merger, capital gains tax basis, and loan foreclosures
   - **(d)** None of the above
   - **(e)** All of the above

9. Some of the important reasons for studying appraisal are:
   - **(a)** To improve your value estimation skills
   - **(b)** To help you pass the real estate brokers' license examination
   - **(c)** To help you understand other real estate courses
   - **(d)** To improve your ability to communicate with appraisers
   - **(e)** All of the above

10. The form in which a formal appraisal is presented is called:
    (a) A presentation of value
    (b) An appraisal log
    (c) An appraisal report
    (d) A value certification

CHAPTER TWO

WHAT IS REAL ESTATE?

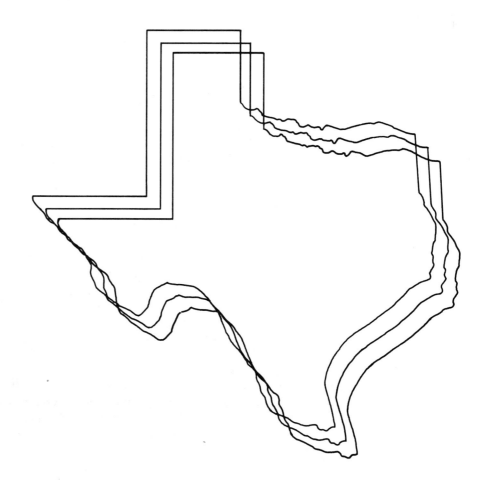

PREVIEW

In Chapter 1 we described what an appraisal is and how it is used in our society. We pointed out that having a knowledge of appraisal is important to people working in *all* areas of real estate. Before going on to the actual appraisal process, it is necessary to define real estate and real property carefully. In this chapter we define these terms, focusing on their physical and legal characteristics. We also explain how individual parcels of real estate are identified legally.

When you have completed this chapter, you should be able to:

1. Define real estate, real property, and personal property. Give examples and explain why you must know how these terms differ.

2. Define and give examples of the bundle of rights.

3. Explain and provide examples of the three broad categories of restrictions on the use of real property.

4. Define the four governmental restrictions on the private ownership of all property.

5. List and provide examples of the major types of legal descriptions.

SECTION 2.1
PHYSICAL AND LEGAL
CHARACTERISTICS
OF REAL ESTATE

What is real estate? Understanding this term is very important. People involved with real estate transactions can see, walk on, or go through the physical property in which they are interested. However, the property, itself, is *not* what they always get! Instead, they get documents that only convey specified and limited rights to the physical property.

Real Estate,
Real Property,
and Personal Property

In order to understand the meaning of real estate, we must first define property. Property consists of rights that have value. For example, the right to occupy a house is a right that is valuable. When these rights concern physical objects, such as a house or a car, the rights to these objects are called tangible property. If there are no physical objects but just valuable rights or obligations, these rights are called intangible property. A company's trademark constitutes one example of intangible property; a patent is another.

Another classification of property divides all property into either real property or personal property. Real property refers to the land and everything permanently fastened to the land. Personal property consists of movable property; but more accurately, it refers to all property that is *not* real property.

Originally, the term real property referred only to rights that one gained by owning land. In many states, real property by statute now includes the physical object (that is, the land itself), as well as the rights that go with it. In other states, the physical object is still described by the old technical term real estate. Today, real estate and real property are usually used interchangeably, which is how they will be used in this book.

The Components of Real Property

The term real property refers to more than just the land. Actually, real property comprises four components, as shown in the following list.

1. The land.
2. Objects permanently affixed to the land.
3. That which is appurtenant to, or legally accompanies, the land.
4. That which is immovable by law.

Examples of real property are given in Figure 2.1.

The Land

The land includes the surface, the soil and rocks beneath, and the space above. In the past, these rights extended "for an indefinite distance upward as well as downward." Now, however, ownership of the space over the land—the airspace—has been limited to that which the landowner can reasonably use and enjoy. Similarly, the ownership of liquids and gases (oil, gas, water, stream) below the surface has also been limited in several ways. Since these liquids and gases move naturally through the ground, they do not belong to a particular parcel of land, even if located under it, until they are physically "seized" by the landowner (for example, by being pumped out). The ways in which rights to underground liquids and gases are determined are especially complex and are not covered in this book. Generally, however, in real estate, the term land is easy to define.

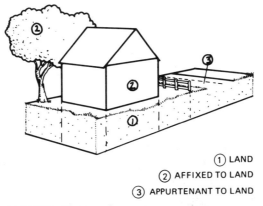

① LAND
② AFFIXED TO LAND
③ APPURTENANT TO LAND

FIGURE 2.1
Examples of Real Property. (Adaptation of illustration provided by the California Department of Real Estate

Permanently Affixed Objects

When an object is permanently fastened to the land, it is legally considered to be a part of the land and thus a part of the real estate. Clearly, objects such as trees, bridges, or buildings are permanently attached to the land and are easily identified as real property. Objects such as doors, which are permanently attached to a permanent building, are also real estate. However, when objects are not clearly attached to the land in a permanent way, their classification as either real or personal property can be difficult. A garden statue is an example. To make things even more complicated, objects that were once considered personal property can become permanently affixed objects. When this happens, the object is called a fixture, and becomes part of the real estate. The courts have developed a series of tests to determine whether items of personal property have become fixtures. These are listed below. In addition, state legislatures have adopted rules for deciding if an object is to be classified as a fixture or as personal property in different circumstances.

Appurtenant Rights

The third component of real property consists of appurtenant rights, or appurtenances. An appurtenance is a right that belongs to the owners of one property. It gives them the right to use another property (which they do not own), in a specific way that benefits their property. One category of appurtenance consists of the right to have the continued benefit of natural features (such as water courses or drainage channels), which extend beyond the property. Another category consists of an appurtenant easement that may be established by an agreement between the property owner and the easement owner-user, or by other legal means. The most common easement is for an access right-of-way across another owner's land. Other easements may protect a view or protect exposure to sunlight. A third category of appurtenance is the occasional situation in which ownership of a mutual, or community, water or telephone company is appurtenant to the land. In this instance, the shares of stock are tied to the land and can only be sold with the land. They cannot be sold separately as normal stock shares can.

That Which Is Immovable by Law

Many laws list this as a fourth component of real property. This component is similar to the category of objects affixed to the land, but it does not require permanent physical attachment. This fourth component functions as a catchall. Any objects that do not fit into the first three categories and are not clearly movable (i.e., are not clearly personal property) fall in this catchall category. The classification of these objects as being real or personal is up to the courts in many cases when it is not normally addressed in the sales contract and subsequent closing documents.

Property: Is It Real or Personal?

Real estate cannot be moved. It is permanently fixed in its location. Personal property, on the other hand, is movable. Fixtures are personal property items that have become attached to the real estate and converted into real estate.

The Law of Fixtures

The courts have established five tests to determine whether an object is a fixture or personal property. These five tests are weighed collectively.

1. The intention of the person incorporating the personal property into the land. For example, clear evidence that a dining room chandelier installed by a tenant in his or her present residence had previously been installed in, and removed from, the tenant's prior residence might be convincing proof of the tenant's intention to remove it from the current residence at the end of the lease.

2. How permanently the property is attached to the land and building. A built-in stove is considered real property; a free-standing stove can be judged as personal property. The courts sometimes refer to this test as the degree of annexation.

3. The extent to which the property is uniquely adapted to use with the land. A loose throw rug, if cut to fit an odd-shaped room, might well become a fixture. However, a rectangular throw rug, even if tacked down, probably would not be considered a fixture. Adaptation to use is commonly tested by the object's function. For example, a chalkboard attached to the wall of a classroom serves as a functional part of the building and thus should be classified as a fixture; however, the same chalkboard in a home might not be.

4. The existence of any agreement between the parties involved that defines ownership of the property and whether it is to be considered as real estate. Many leases contain such provisions.

5. The relationship between the person putting in the personal property and any other person with a claim to the real estate. For example, in a dispute, the courts might classify an object differently, depending on whether the dispute is between an owner and tenant or owner and lender.

Why should you be concerned with fixture definitions? You need to be able to determine which objects are to be included in the appraisal as real estate and which are to be excluded. It will often be necessary to find out what items the present occupants expect to take as their personal property when they vacate. These items can be individually evaluated by the five tests (given above) to determine if the personal property has become a fixture. In some cases, the appraisal may also include personal property left with the real property (for example, the refrigerator). Usually, we can simply specify which questionable items have been included in the evaluation. In some circumstances we may want to compare lists obtained from opposing parties, such as the owner and the tenant.

A variety of problems can crop up when you are trying to decide whether a particular object is real or personal property. Here are a few examples:

Wall-to-wall carpets: resolution depends upon intentions, who installed the carpets, whether they were cut to fit, how they are fastened down, and especially whether there is a finished floor or just subflooring under the carpet.

Venetian blinds: resolution depends upon intentions, who installed them, whether they were cut to fit, and whether there are also shades or drapes over the windows.

Chandeliers: resolution depends upon intentions and who installed them. Valuable antiques generally are considered personal property.

Garden decorations (driftwood, statuary, stone lanterns, etc.): resolution depends upon intentions, how they are fastened down, and whether the objects were modified for use in the specific location. These are often held to be personal property.

Curtain rods, switch plates, and so on: these items are generally held to be real property but could be personalty in a particular circumstance, depending upon the parties and their agreement or intentions.

Real Property Rights

As noted earlier, the term real estate originally referred to the object itself: the land and what was attached to it. As time went by, a second term, real property, was added to refer solely to the ownership rights to the object. This new term was added to express a new concept, that of dividing the rights to the property without breaking up the physical property itself.

Today, we recognize that the rights to the ownership of land actually consist of many different rights. Included in these are the right to occupy the property, the right to sell it, the right to exclude others from it, the right to borrow against it, and the right to convey ownership by inheritance.

In addition, many of these rights may also be broken up, to cover various time periods. For example, a lease gives the right of possession but only for a specified time period. All of the ownership rights have been compared to a large bundle of sticks with each stick representing a different portion of the rights of ownership. From this idea came the phrase bundle of rights. This concept has been carried further; now, when the rights are divided, people speak of "breaking up the bundle of sticks" among more than one owner. (See Figure 2.2.) You may, for example, give or sell the right to possess real estate to another person (or people). Such a person would then have the right to live on or use the property during the time that he or she possessed that "stick" from the bundle. For instance, a tenant under a lease has this right of possession.

(a) (b)

FIGURE 2.2
(a) Dividing the Property. (b) Dividing the Rights

You could also keep the right of possession but surrender the right to will the property away. In this event, the rights that you have left are called a life estate: the right to live on the property or control its occupancy during your lifetime only. You have agreed to surrender the property to another (called the remainderman) upon your death but without involving an inheritance or will.

When the owner has not restricted or transferred any of his or her ownership rights, the owner's rights are called a fee simple title to the property. When the owner leases or rents the property, the owner's remaining rights are called the leased fee interest in the property. The rights that are conveyed to the tenant are called the leasehold estate.

Examples of restrictions on the total rights of ownership to the property include:

1. Leases to tenants.
2. Life estates.
3. Easements appurtenant to other properties.
4. Financing obligations.

This concept of real property as a collection of rights is important to real estate evaluation. If the owner retains all the property rights, the owner's rights are worth more than if he or she retains only a portion of these rights. It is vital, then, to *determine what property ownership rights are to be valued in the appraisal and what rights are to be excluded.*

SECTION 2.2
USE RESTRICTIONS

Meaning and Importance of Use Restrictions

When people want to buy real estate, it is not only the object that they want. More precisely, they want the benefits of owning the real estate. These benefits may come either from using the property now or from some anticipated future use. In either case, the purchase is motivated by the expectation of future benefits. Upon what is this expectation based? The uses of a property are not determined just by an owner's whims. Instead, the possible uses are dictated by three broad types of restrictions. These restrictions are very important and must be carefully reviewed. They affect the value of the property. If they change, the value may change as well. Careful evaluations must take into account all significant use restrictions on the property. (See Figure 2.3.)

Categories of Use Restrictions

Government Restrictions
The government restricts the right to use real property in four ways. The authority to make these restrictions exists because all private ownership of real estate originates from a grant of title given by the sovereign body—the person or organization that is the central or principal authority of a country. In the United States, the sovereign body is "we, the people," collectively acting through our government. The laws of our country limit the

FIGURE 2.3
Types of Restrictions

ownership rights belonging to private owners of property. Four specific rights are retained by the sovereign. Thus every aspect of one's right to use a property is limited by these four restrictions. (As a way to remember these four powers, think of the name PETE, which has the first letter of each power: police, eminent domain, taxation, and escheat.)

Police Power   The sovereign body has the right to regulate property as necessary to promote the safety, health, morals, and general welfare of the public. The police power forms the basis of the controls that directly restrict the use of all property.

Eminent Domain   The sovereign body may take the property back at any time if it is in the public interest to do so (such as for roads, schools, etc.). When this is done, the sovereign body must pay the owner a "just compensation."

Taxation   The sovereign body may impose any level of taxes needed to raise funds, so long as the taxes are fairly imposed.

Escheat   The sovereign body will take back the title to the property if the owner dies or disappears and leaves no relatives or heirs.

Under its police power, the government can pass zoning ordinances, which state where various land uses can be located, and regulate the height and size of buildings, the extent of yards, decks, parking, and other features, and the appearance, exterior materials, and architectural detailing of buildings. Such ordinances can also specify the maximum noise levels allowed from users of buildings, along with the hours that stores can operate, the amount of light, vibration, or odor permissible, and the type and size of signs. They also determine whether buildings may have uses involving many visitors.

Under the police power, the government can also pass building, housing, electrical, and plumbing codes. These codes define in great detail minimum room sizes and heights, restrictions on the materials used, and floor-plan layout restrictions. The types of heat may be defined, as well as allowable systems for plumbing, waste, and electricity. These ordinances extend to regulating types and sizes of windows and doors, as well as types of finish. Minimum maintenance standards are often set by these codes, usually with penalties for violations. In short, almost no detail of a building is exempt from some form of control, regulation, or prohibition.

Numerous types of use restrictions are based upon the police power of government. The student of real estate should be aware of these restrictions because each of them may influence use and thereby influence value.

Air and water pollution—solid waste disposal.

Building, housing, and electrical codes.

Coastal preservation zones.

Condominium conversion ordinances.

Flood zones.

Historical preservation acts.

Master plans.

Park dedications.

Pipeline regulations.

Rent control.

Scenic corridors.

Seismic safety study areas.

Sign abatement ordinances.

Strip mining rehabilitation acts.

Subdivision requirements.

Underground utility requirements.

Wild river protection acts.

Zoning ordinances.

Private Restrictions

The government is not alone in restricting the use of land. When people sell real estate, they sometimes impose conditions that restrict the future owners or users. For example, at one time, many properties were sold with a clause prohibiting the sale of alcoholic beverages on the property. More recently, most condominiums and planned unit developments with common areas utilize recorded CC&Rs (conditions, covenants, and restrictions) to regulate their use, operation, and control. Usually, the existence of CC&Rs, or other private deed restrictions connected with the property, is revealed in a preliminary title report or title search. It is often advisable to inquire about the possible effects of such restrictions and, if necessary, review the actual documents.

Restrictions on the use of property can also be imposed by private easements and contracts. For example, the owners could grant an easement for an electric power transmission line, which could restrict building any structures under the power lines. An easement for a buried gas pipeline could bar any structures over the pipeline. A view easement granted to a neighbor could limit the height of any building to one story and perhaps require a flat roof. A lease could restrict the use of the property to a specific purpose (a high-priced retail shoe store, for example). A mortgage note could also contain provisions limiting the uses of the property. In other words, nearly every contract that a real property owner signs involving the property can impose limits on its use.

Market Restrictions

In an economic sense, neither the government nor the property owner really determines the ultimate use of land. Instead, the eventual use of land depends upon the restrictions imposed by the market, which operates within the limits set by the government and by private restrictions.

How does the market restrict the use of land? Each proposed land use must appear to be financially satisfactory or investors will not choose that use. Proposed uses of land must earn enough money, or create enough benefits at that location, to justify the cost of the land and buildings. Thus, the market encourages uses of land that are economically feasible, that is, those uses that are able to pay at least all the costs of using the site and any necessary improvements. If a use is economically feasible but forbidden by zoning and/or deed restrictions, there is an economic incentive for someone to have the restrictions removed. Otherwise, nothing will be done with the land until some use that is allowable becomes economically feasible.

The Results

It is the combination of the three types of restrictions (government, private, and market) that determines how land will be used. The government limits uses by zoning; the private owners limit uses through deed restrictions, and the marketplace dictates what uses are economically feasible at a particular location. The real estate appraiser must be aware of these restrictions and their impact on current use, as well as their possible impact on future uses of land and buildings. Knowing how real estate can be used will result in better evaluations.

SECTION 2.3
LEGAL DESCRIPTIONS
OF REAL ESTATE

When real estate is sold, leased, or borrowed against, legal documents must spell out the transaction. In each case, the property involved will be identified in these documents by its legal description.

Most people do not realize the importance of legal descriptions. For example, an error might cause a prospective buyer to look at a different property than the one covered by the legal description. What they may buy is the legally described property. What they wanted was the property they looked at. In other words, what you see may not always be what you get.

Most of the time, minor errors in legal descriptions can easily be corrected. On occasion, however, an error has resulted in confusion and lawsuits. In one instance, a contractor built an office building on the wrong lot! Everyone in the real estate industry should know how to read the various types of legal descriptions and compare them with the physical property observed. This avoids questions such as: Who owns the lot next door? Who owns the common driveway between the houses? Who owns that overgrown area at the rear of the lot?

Three Basic Types of Legal Description

Nationally there are three basic types of legal description: (1) the recorded lot, block, and tract description, also known as a subdivision map, (2) the metes and bounds description, and (3) the government survey description, only a portion of which is used in Texas. You may also find specific legal descriptions that use combinations of these types.

Recorded Lot, Block, and Tract

The most common type of legal description of urban land parcels is based on subdivision maps. When a developer buys acreage and subdivides it into lots and streets, the local government, in the process of giving its approval, requires that a map of the division be drawn by a surveyor. The surveyor first checks the legal description used in prior transfers of this parcel, and the parcels around it, to be sure that they do not have conflicting boundaries. Then the surveyor stakes out all of the boundary lines, using existing government survey markers established in the area as starting points, as well as all the markers that can be located from previous surveys of the property. Upon establishing that the legal descriptions and physical markers all agree, the surveyor enters all this information and the new property division lines on a map drawing. Figure 2.4 is an example of a subdivision map (plat).

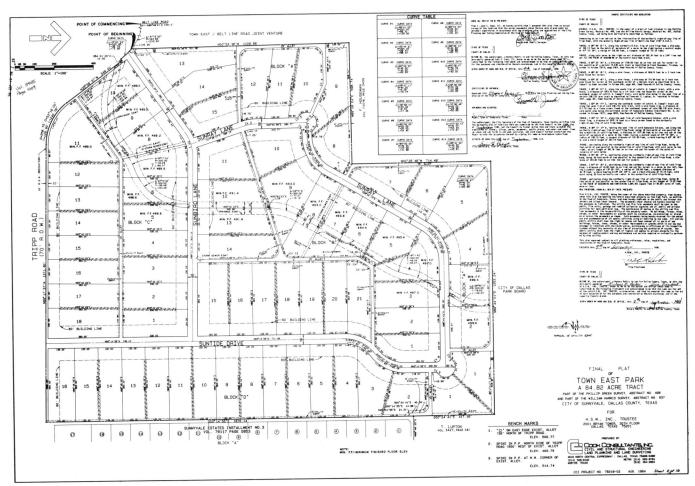

FIGURE   2.4
An Example of a Subdivision Map. (Courtesy of Cook Consultants, Inc., Dallas, Texas)

The subdivision map divides the property into lots and, for larger subdivisions, into blocks of lots. Each block and each lot is labeled on the map with a number. The map itself is identified with the name or number of the subdivision and is recorded in the public recorder's map records. The map records are indexed by the book and page.

With such a map on file, a written legal description of a lot need only contain the lot number, the block number if any, the subdivision name or number, and the map record volume and page number. With this legal description, another surveyor, years later, can look up the map and, by a field survey, again stake out the same boundaries of the described lot. The legal descriptions of subdivision maps (also called tract maps) are among the shortest and easiest to understand. A sample might read:

> Lot 12, Block 4 of Nottingham Forest, Section 7, a subdivision in the William Hardin Survey, Abstract No. 24, Houston, Harris County, Texas, Map recorded in Volume 138, Page 1 of the Map Records of Harris County, Texas.

Metes and Bounds

The earliest legal descriptions of property were by metes and bounds. Many legal descriptions today are also of this type, particularly descriptions for large and irregular parcels. A metes and bounds description simply gives the distance and direction of each boundary line of the property. It starts at a point of beginning and goes around the perimeter of the property, back to the point of beginning. Early metes and bounds descriptions often started at a well-known natural feature, such as a large oak tree by the Jones farm, and went from tree to rock to boulder to tree. Figure 2.5 contains the actual wording from such a deed. As the trees died of old age and the rocks were bulldozed away, such descriptions became unusable. Today, more durable legal descriptions usually start at governmental survey monuments or other known points and proceed by very accurate direction bearings and distances around the property and back to the point of beginning. *Any* parcel, even a lot in a recorded subdivision, could be described by a metes and bounds description. Here is one for a subdivision lot:

> Beginning at a point on the southerly line of Henry Street, 100 feet east of the southeast corner of Henry Street and 35th Avenue; running then due south 100 feet; then due east 75 feet; then due north and parallel to the first course 100 feet to the southern line of Henry Street; then due west along the southern line of Henry Street, 75 feet to the point of beginning.

Modern metes and bounds legal descriptions can describe lines that do not run exactly north, east, south, or west ("a line north 1 degree, 46 minutes, 30 seconds west 209.71 feet"). Such descriptions can also define lines that curve ("then along the arc of a curve to the right, of radius 203.3 feet, for a distance of 37.63 feet"). From this combination, a parcel of almost any shape can be described. However, metes and bounds descrip-

> # An Old-Fashioned Metes-And-Bounds Legal Description
>
> .....Running South with McMillions line 19 Poles to an Ash at a branch, Thence West with said line 54 Poles to a Blackgum, Thence North with said line 13 Poles to a Spanish Oak Sapling, Thence North 85 East 37 Poles to an apple tree, Thence North 80 East 17 Poles to an apple tree, Thence South 30 East 3 Poles to a stake, Thence South 2° West 4 Poles to the beginning.....

FIGURE 2.5
From a Deed Recorded in the Book of Deeds, Book C-1, Page 462, on the 6th Day of March, 1907, with the Office of the Registrar of Deeds, in Ashe County, North Carolina

tions can be pages in length. They are sometimes difficult to understand. Typing errors are an occasional problem as well. Despite these disadvantages, metes and bounds descriptions are necessary for some parcels and are a valuable cross-check for others.

Today, appraisers often calculate the area of a parcel by feeding the metes and bounds description into a desk-top microcomputer. The computer can also be used to simulate a survey around the perimeter or boundary of the property to see if the description ends at exactly the point of beginning. If it does not, there may be an error in the description. In order to have an unquestionable description, some legal documents will include both the parcel or tract map description and the metes and bounds description. Figure 2.6 shows an example of an irregular parcel map.

Government Survey
A third method of legal description in Texas is based on sections of land which contain 640 acres in a square, one mile on each side. The 640-acre section is a part of the Rectangular Survey System (also called the government survey system), which was established by the United States Congress in 1785 to describe rural land. All continental states except Texas and certain eastern states have been surveyed under this system by the federal government (see Figure 2.7). The system is based on principal meridians

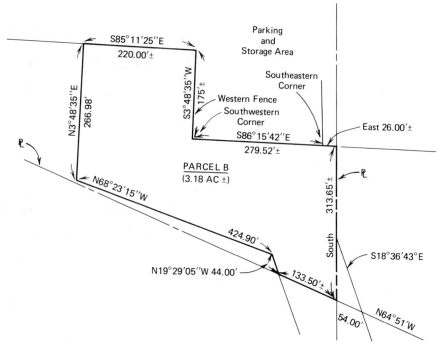

FIGURE 2.6
An Example of an Irregular Parcel Map

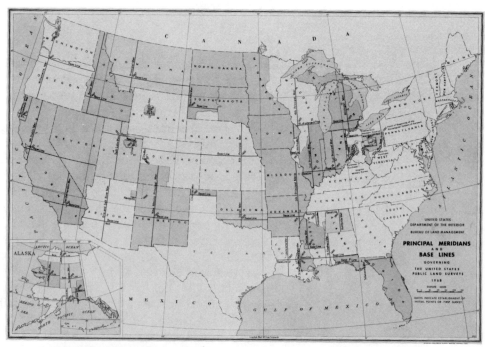

FIGURE 2.7
Principal Meridians of the Government Rectangular Survey System. (Courtesy of U.S. Department of the Interior, Bureau of Land Management)

(longitudes) and base lines (latitudes), from which townships (squares six miles on each side) are described. Each township consists of 36 sections (see Figure 2.8). Figure 2.9 illustrates how townships are located with reference to the intersection of principal and base lines.

Although not a part of the government survey system, the Republic of Texas and the State of Texas have made land grants to individuals and organizations (such as railroads and the builder of the state capitol) that were surveyed into sections on a metes and bounds basis. As a certain section was later broken up into smaller parcels, the legal description often consisted of reference to a specified part of the section, such as "160 acres consisting of the North East quarter" of the section. Later, the new owner might sell the western half of the 160 acres, and the legal description could include the words "80 acres, consisting of the W 1/2 of the North East quarter" of the section. If this new buyer later sold the lower 20 acres of the tract, the legal description could include the words "20 acres, consisting of the South half of the South West quarter of the North East Quarter" of the section. Figure 2.10 illustrates parcels of land described on the basis of a given section of land.

As precise and predictable as the government survey may look, there are complications. The first complication is that the survey grid is square, but the earth is round. Consequently, parallel sets of range and base lines must be tapered to match the shape of the earth. This taper causes the

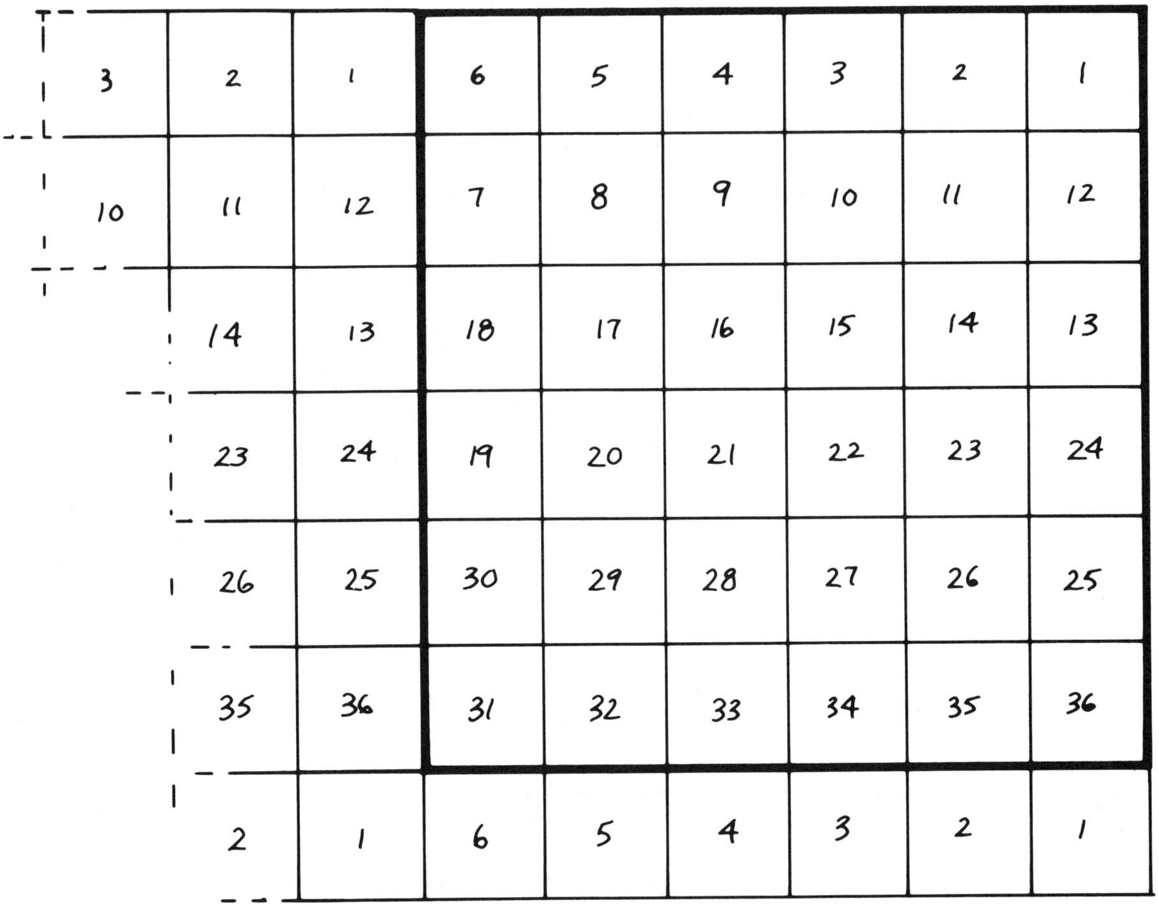

FIGURE 2.8
Map of a Township

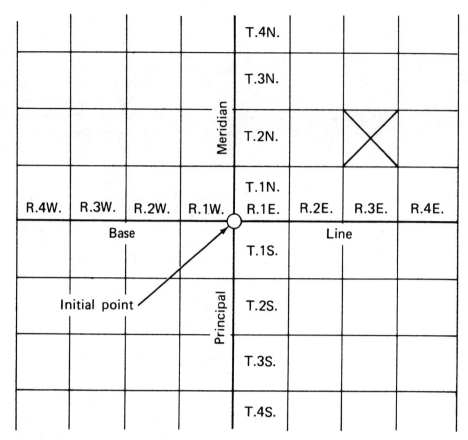

FIGURE 2.9
Map of Township Lines

north 6-mile boundary of each township to be about 50 feet shorter than the south boundary. Thus each township north of the reference point shrinks in width by 50 feet, and each to the south grows by 50 feet. To compensate for this, correction lines, both north-south and east-west, are run every 24 miles from the reference point. The result is that the actual dimensions and acreage area of a particular section can vary considerably from the "standard" one-mile-square section. A second complication is that a few early surveys contained actual errors, so that a given section might be quite different in size from what it was supposed to be.

Because of the importance of identifying the property being studied, real estate professionals must be able to read and understand the legal descriptions of property. Otherwise, neither they nor their clients will know for sure what property they are considering.

SUMMARY

In this chapter we explained how to determine what real property is. When making an appraisal, it is not enough just to look at a property and appraise what you see. Rather, you must first establish what legal rights exist

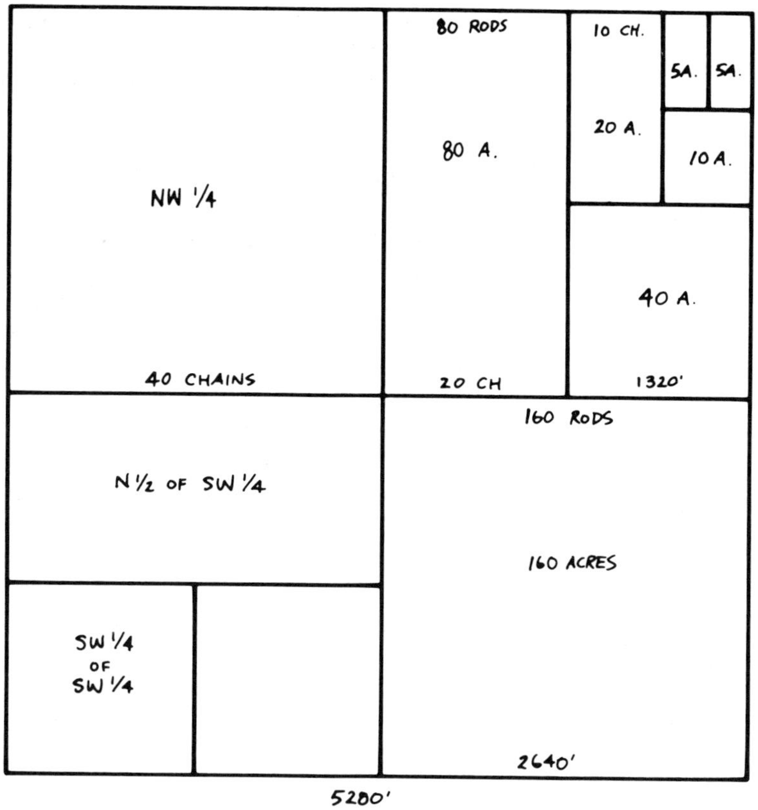

FIGURE 2.10
Map of a Section

for the property and then identify which rights are to be included in the appraisal.

Real estate is defined as the physical object, whereas real property refers to the rights gained by owning the object. Personal property includes all objects on the property that are not real estate. Real property is made up of four elements: the land, the objects permanently affixed to the land, the rights appurtenant to the land, and that which is immovable by law.

When personal property has been permanently affixed to the land, it changes into a category of real property called a fixture. To determine whether a particular object is a fixture depends upon legislative statute and five different court-applied tests. These are: (1) the intention of the person installing the object, (2) the permanence of the installation, (3) the modification of the object to fit or work uniquely with the real estate, (4) any agreement of the parties, and (5) the type of relationship (one created by a lease or mortgage, etc.) between the parties interested in owning the object. Numerous problems concerning fixtures and personal property can arise in an appraisal unless appraisers are careful to distinguish one from the other and define what is being appraised.

Next the chapter noted that real property refers to the many rights associated with real estate. The fact that this bundle of rights may be broken up, with different parties holding different parts of the bundle, or different rights, is very important. Partial rights to a property, such as those established by leases and mortgages, are very common. Thus, there are many occasions when you may have to examine or appraise portions of the bundle of rights.

We went on to point out that the value of land depends upon what it can be used for. This is restricted by three types of limitations: government, private, and market. The government limitations consist of four restrictions: police power, eminent domain, taxation, and escheat. Most governmental restrictions on land use, such as zoning and building codes, are based upon the police power. Private restrictions, often in the form of deed restrictions, are encountered less often than government restrictions are, but on occasion they are significant to the appraiser. Market restrictions have a powerful influence on value, since only economically feasible uses—ones that have a strong enough market demand—can be financially successful.

Finally, we noted that the buyer does not really buy the physical object, but rather specified rights to the property that are legally described in the purchase documents. The legal description of the property is needed to identify, with certainty, what real estate to appraise, so that it is important to understand this description. The three common description types (subdivision maps (plats), metes and bounds descriptions, and government surveys) were explained and illustrated. With an understanding of legal descriptions, you can review a particular legal description, have its accuracy checked, or use it to calculate land areas or dimensions.

IMPORTANT TERMS AND CONCEPTS

Appurtenance	escheat
Bundle of rights	taxation
Fixture	Real estate
Intangible property	Real property
Legal descriptions	Rectangular survey system
Market restrictions	Rights
Metes and bounds	Sovereign
Personal property	Subdivision Map (plat)
Police power	Tangible property
Power of eminent domain	

REVIEWING YOUR UNDERSTANDING

1. What are the two categories of tangible property?
   (a) Real property and personal property
   (b) Intangible property and real property
   (c) Real estate and intangible property

2. The four categories of real property are:
   (a) The land, the space above it, the space below it, and objects permanently fixed to the land
   (b) The land, objects permanently affixed to the land, appurtenant rights, and that which is immovable by law
   (c) Permanently affixed objects, tangible rights, the land, and appurtenant rights

3. List and define the five tests for a fixture.

4. The three types of use restrictions are:
   - **(a)** Government, market, and taxation
   - **(b)** Market, government, and private
   - **(c)** Private, appurtenances, and market

5. The sovereign holds four specific rights relative to private real estate:
   - **(a)** Appurtenances, eminent domain, police power, and escheat
   - **(b)** Police power, taxation, ordinances, and bundle of rights
   - **(c)** Taxation, escheat, police power, and eminent domain

6. Give six examples of government regulations based upon police power.

7. The three common types of legal descriptions are:
   - **(a)** Metes and bounds, recorded lot block and tract, and government survey
   - **(b)** Government survey, private survey, and county survey
   - **(c)** Metes and bounds, acreage blocks, and government survey

8. What is the shape, size, and area of a standard section?

9. What is the shape, size, and area of a township?

10. How many sections are in a township?
    - **(a)** 48   **(b)** 36   **(c)** 360

CHAPTER
THREE

THE FORMAL
APPRAISAL
PROCESS

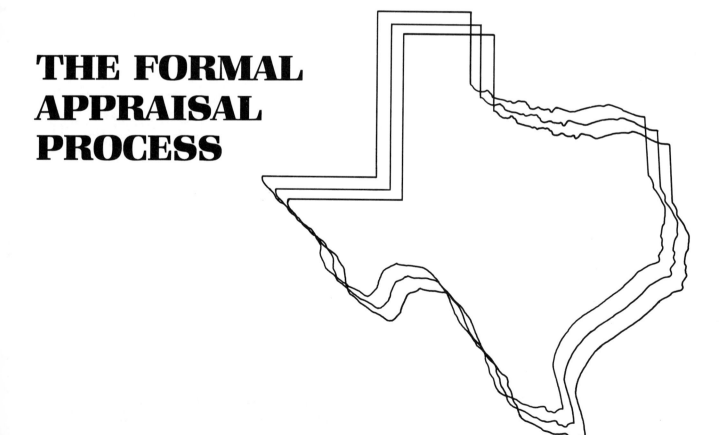

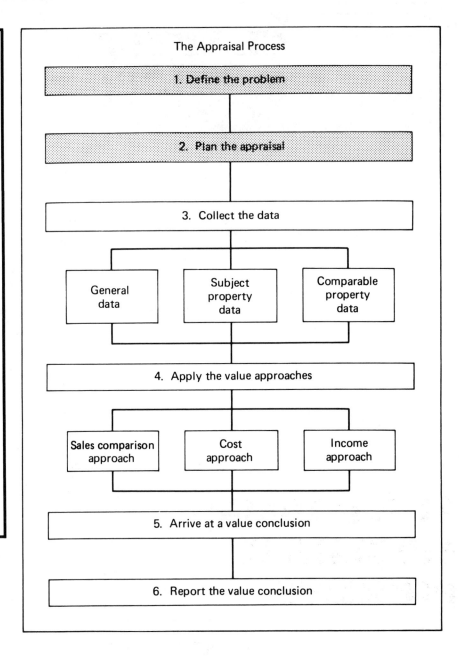

The Appraisal Process

1. Define the problem

2. Plan the appraisal

3. Collect the data

General data | Subject property data | Comparable property data

4. Apply the value approaches

Sales comparison approach | Cost approach | Income approach

5. Arrive at a value conclusion

6. Report the value conclusion

SECTION 3.1
THE APPRAISAL PROCESS

The appraisal process is the orderly procedure that appraisers use to help solve a valuation problem. Over a period of time, well-defined ground rules for this procedure have been established by professional appraisers.

The appraisal process consists of:

1. Clearly defining the appraisal problem.
2. Formulating an efficient appraisal plan.
3. Collecting and analyzing the pertinent data.
4. Applying the appropriate value approaches.
5. Arriving at a conclusion of value.
6. Reporting the conclusion of value.

These six steps in the appraisal process are shown in the flowchart at the beginning of this chapter and are further developed in the following discussion.

Defining the Appraisal Problem

The beginning of any formal appraisal requires a clear and concise statement of what the appraisal is to accomplish. By clearly defining the questions to be answered in the appraisal, the appraiser can then seek the exact information the client requires. In order to define the appraisal problem, five specific elements must be examined.

1. Identification of the property.
2. Property rights to be appraised.
3. The date of value.
4. The purpose of the appraisal.
5. The intended use of the appraisal report.

Identification of the Property

The property to be appraised must be precisely located and identified. Although a complete legal description is preferred, a less formal street address identity, such as that used in a sales listing contract, is often acceptable. For example, the property identification may read, "The property under appraisal is that which is known as 1714 Mountain View Road, El Paso, Texas. It consists of a 50 × 100 foot parcel of land improved with a single-family residence and garage." Note that the property identification must leave no doubt as to what land and improvements are included in the appraisal.

Property Rights to Be Appraised

The typical assignment is to appraise the value of all the rights of absolute ownership (commonly called fee simple or fee simple absolute). However, appraisals involving less than all the ownership rights are not uncommon. For example, appraisals may seek to estimate the value of the subsurface mineral rights of a property. Or the appraisal could cover only the landlord's interest, the leased fee, or other partial interests in real estate. Therefore, a clear statement of the property rights to be appraised is a necessary part of defining the appraisal problem.

The Date of Value

Defining the appraisal problem also requires a statement pinpointing the date as of which the value estimate applies. A specific date is important because real estate values are constantly changing. An appraisal conclusion will be valid *only* as of a particular point in time. For this reason, the date of value should ideally be agreed upon in advance between the appraiser and the client. When a current value is sought, the date of the appraiser's last field inspection is often selected as the date of the value estimate.

Sometimes, appraisals are needed to estimate value as of a past or historical date. For example, appraisals for inheritance tax, divorce, condemnation, and other legal purposes often must estimate value as of a different date than the date the appraisal is performed. When an historical appraisal is made, the report must clearly specify the historical date so as not to confuse the reader into thinking that the stated value is the current market value.

The Purpose of the Appraisal

Usually, the purpose of an appraisal is to estimate what is known as market value, which is the type of value most often sought in the sale and financing of a home. However, appraisals can be made for many different purposes. For instance, an appraiser might be asked to estimate the replacement cost of a property or maybe its liquidation value. Other appraisals may seek to estimate the insurable value, "going-concern" value, assessed value, loan value, or rental value of a property. Whatever the assignment, the type of value stated as the purpose of the appraisal must be given a precise and formal definition. Market value has its own special definition, which will be discussed in Section 3.2 of this chapter.

The Intended Use of the Appraisal Report

Buyers and sellers, banks and institutions, and public agencies all use appraisals for their own purposes, whether for sale, lending, property taxation, or public acquisition. Since each of these users has different requirements as to the form of the appraisal and the information required, the appraiser must clearly understand the intended function or use of the appraisal report. Knowing the intended use of the appraisal report will also enable the appraiser to calculate the approximate amount of time it will take to complete the report. An appraisal for inheritance tax purposes might be written in the form of a letter report in perhaps an hour or two, whereas a condemnation appraisal would require a detailed narrative report that might take several days to complete. The length of the appraisal report is often determined by the intended use of the report.

Formulating the Appraisal Plan

The second step in the appraisal process is to develop an appraisal plan. A well-organized plan increases efficiency by scheduling the various tasks in the sequence in which they are to be done and the time required for each. A good plan can also help reduce the chance of oversight or errors when collecting necessary information. The appraisal plan may take the form of a simple checklist of tasks to be performed or it may become an elaborate work schedule, designed to organize and expedite a complex assignment.

Whatever the format, a workable appraisal plan should include the following steps:

1. *Preliminary inspection of the property*   Often termed the preliminary survey, this preview of the subject property and its neighborhood helps the appraiser to size up the assignment. The preliminary survey will help the appraiser refine any tentative plans he or she may already have made for getting the job done.

   In some cases, a preliminary inspection may be unnecessary if the appraiser is thoroughly familiar with the neighborhood and the type of property under appraisal.

2. *List of needed data*   All general and specific data needs should be itemized during the planning phase. Neighborhood and community particulars, as well as all factual data required for the subject and comparable properties, belong on this itemized list. If special reports, such as engineering or geological surveys, are needed, these should also be noted.

3. *Outline and work schedule*   An appraisal outline should be used to plan the sequence of points to be covered in the appraisal report. The outline is essentially a flowchart of the order in which the work is to be done. Although not always necessary, a time schedule of all the work required to complete the appraisal is also a helpful tool.

Collecting and Analyzing the Data

As we learned in Chapter 1, a formal appraisal is not a wild estimate of value; rather, an appraisal should be an estimate of value based upon, and supported by, information and facts gathered in the real estate market. These market-derived facts are commonly called market data, and they form the backbone of all formal appraisals. Collecting and analyzing data form the third step in the appraisal process.

Most market value appraisals require:

1. *General data on the region, city, and neighborhood*   These include data on population, employment, income, and price levels, as well as data on the availability of financing and on current construction costs.

2. *Specific data on the subject property*   These include detailed legal and physical data on the land and the existing buildings.

3. *Specific data on comparable properties*   These include detailed legal and physical data on comparable land and buildings, as well as detailed information on the terms and sales prices of the comparable properties considered.

How Much Information is Needed?

The amount and kind of data required for any appraisal depends in part on what is known as a highest and best use analysis. Essentially, this is a study of how well suited the property is to its physical, legal, and economic environment. To illustrate, an appraiser might conclude that a single-family house on a commercial lot is not the most beneficial use of the land. A

FIGURE 3.1
Highest and best use?

well-prepared highest and best use study naturally requires that certain preliminary data on the region, city, and neighborhood be gathered at this point. Once the highest and best use has been established, the collection of more detailed property data can begin. Figure 3.1 points out a humorous aspect of a highest and best use analysis.

The amount and kind of data required in an appraisal also depends upon the type of property being appraised, the purpose of the appraisal, and the type of appraisal report required. Let us examine these points.

The type of property and the purpose of the appraisal may suggest the most appropriate value approaches, hence the kind of data needed. A single-family home being appraised for a loan would usually emphasize the cost and sales comparison approaches. Thus cost and sales data will certainly be part of the specific information required in the appraisal. Later on, we shall return to the issue of when to use each valuation approach.

The type of appraisal report and its intended use may govern the degree of detail needed when data are collected. The data needed in a longer form appraisal may be more detailed than those required in a short letter report. Also appraisals made for legal purposes generally require more supporting detail than those made for purchase and sale. *Comparable properties are the key*. Regardless of the type of property or the type of report, most appraisals require sales information on comparable properties fitting the general description of the property being appraised. For instance, if several recently built three-bedroom homes of approximately 1,800 square feet, in the same area, have recently sold for prices ranging from $150,000 to $200,000, then a newly constructed three-bedroom property might be valued by comparing it with the sold properties. Specific data on the size, quality, age, and general amenities of the comparable homes could suggest a reasonable value for the subject property. However, it would be logical and prudent to consider additional data before settling on a conclusion of value. What if the sold properties had better financing than currently available? What if market conditions have changed since the recent sales, as a result of serious unemployment emerging in the community? What if the new house being appraised recently cost the owner $230,000 to develop,

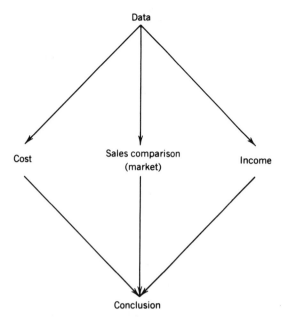

FIGURE 3.2
Three Appraisal Approaches to Valuing Real Estate

including land and building? Should this cost govern the estimate of value? Each question suggests a need for additional data. Of course, complex assignments, such as the appraisal of income or commercial properties, call for considerably more market data than single-family home appraisals.

Techniques for locating and analyzing both general and specific data required for appraisals will be fully discussed in subsequent chapters.

Using the Value Approaches

The fourth step in the appraisal process is to group the collected market data for further analysis, using one or more of the three approaches to value (see Figure 3.2). The sales comparison approach uses data on current sales of comparable properties. The prices people are willing to pay are usually a good indication of the value of any commodity. The cost approach relies on the appraiser's estimate of the amount required to buy vacant land and to construct the desired buildings and structures on it. Any loss in value from age or other causes is subtracted. Last, the income approach analyzes the income-producing capability of rental investment property to indicate its market value.

The approach or approaches to value that appear to be the most pertinent should be applied at this point in the appraisal process. As the appraisal assignment requires, one, two, or all three approaches to value can be tested. An outline of the three value approaches is included in Section 3.3.

Arriving at a Conclusion of Value

After two or more approaches have been used by the appraiser to estimate value, it is time for the fifth step in the appraisal process—reviewing the estimates produced by the approaches to arrive at a final conclusion. This procedure is referred to as the reconciliation (or correlation) process. Three primary considerations are involved in this reconciliation:

1. The appropriateness of each approach, in view of the purpose of the appraisal.

2. The adequacy and reliability of the data, and the validity of any assumptions made in its analysis.

3. The range of indicated values and the position of each value within that range.

If the purpose of the appraisal is to estimate market value, the sales comparison or market approach is often the most persuasive, because it is the most direct approach and the one with which most people have experience. It is generally the preferred method in single-family residential appraisals, as we shall explain. Where there are unique property characteristics or insufficient sales data, the cost and/or income approach may be emphasized, depending on the type of property under appraisal. For example, the income approach is often preferred in the appraisal of commercial properties.

Appraisers often rely on the placement (high, low, or middle) and range (amount of spread) of the values indicated by each approach to help suggest the weight or importance to be assigned to each indicated value. In other words, each approach is used as a check upon the others.

Although the appraisal process is designed to be as objective and factual as possible, the appraiser still must use personal judgment to reach a conclusion of value. The final value is dependent upon factual market information *and* the judgment and experience of the appraiser. The value conclusion should never be based on a simple averaging of the three value estimates.

Reporting the Conclusion of Value

The sixth and last step in the appraisal process is reporting the appraisal conclusion. On occasion, only an oral report is required, but most often the client wants some form of written report. There are three types of reports: the letter report, the form (or short form) report, and the narrative report. The type of appraisal report to be used depends upon the amount of background information and detail required by the client or user, and the format that best suits his or her purpose. A brief description of these reports follows. An expanded discussion will be presented in Chapter 16.

The Letter Report
The letter report is one to five pages long, setting forth the conditions of the appraisal assignment, a summary of the nature and scope of the appraiser's investigation, and an opinion of value. The letter form is used most often when the client is already familiar with the property and detailed explanations are unnecessary.

The Form Report
As the name implies, the form report uses a printed sheet to organize and standardize appraisal report content. A checklist is often used for describing and rating property characteristics. Institutions and government agencies that handle large quantities of appraisals use forms designed to suit their special needs. Separate forms are usually available for all the major property classifications, that is, single-family residential, multifamily residential, commercial, industrial, and so on. This is the most common type of report used for real estate loan appraisals.

The Narrative Report

The narrative appraisal is the longest and most formal of the appraisal reports. It is a step-by-step summary of the facts used by the appraiser to arrive at a value. The report also contains a detailed discussion of the methods used to interpret these facts. Narrative appraisal reports are preferred when the client needs to review each step taken by the appraiser.

Narrative reports are often required for appraisals to be used in court (as in eminent domain cases). Such reports are also common in the appraisal of major investment properties.

SECTION 3.2 MARKET VALUE

Most formal appraisals are made for the purpose of estimating market value, as opposed to other types of value, such as loan value or tax value. It is important to understand *how* market value differs from other types of value and *why* the term market value is used in appraisals. In this section we shall discuss the various meanings and types of value, the basic economic ways of measuring value and, finally, the market value concept itself.

Defining Value

Value is a word that has many different meanings but is generally defined as the dollar worth of something. However, the dollar value of a parcel of real estate may be different to a buyer or seller than to a lender, an insurance adjuster, or an accountant. This difference exists because value can be very subjective. For example, the real estate buyer and seller could be measuring value only by their personal desires and needs rather than against the price of similar listings or sales they have encountered. On the other hand, the lender's concept of property value is its most likely selling price in case of foreclosure. The insurance adjuster's idea of value, depending upon the policy, might relate strictly to the cost of replacing the improvements in case of fire or other disaster. The accountant may think of value in terms of the original acquisition cost, the cost basis, or so-called book value of the property.

In these examples, each interested party has a different concept of value, one that is limited in purpose and in definition. There are literally dozens of value types and concepts, each carrying its own identifying name. Here are some of the value labels you might encounter:

Assessed value	Lease value
Book value	Liquidation value
Capitalized value	Listing value
Cash value	Loan value
Depreciated value	Market value
Economic value	Nuisance value
Exchange value	Potential value
Face value	Rental value
Fair value	Salvage value
Going-concern value	Use value
Inheritance tax value	Value in foreclosure
Insurance value	

FIGURE 3.3
Market Value = Value in Exchange

Contrasting Value in
Use and Value in Exchange

Economic theory suggests that all the above value concepts fit into one of two basic categories. These categories are known as value in use and value in exchange. Value in use refers to the value of an item or object to a particular user. For example, a single-family home located next to a bakery might have a higher value to the family operating the bakery than to the public in general. Its higher value is a value unique to that user. This is often described as a subjective value concept.

Value in exchange describes the value of a thing to people in general. This can be termed objective value. Value in exchange can only be estimated for items or properties that are commonly bought and sold in the market, that is, "exchanged" for money or its equivalent. (See Figure 3.3.)

Almost 2,400 years ago, Aristotle said:

All things which are exchanged must be comparable to one another. Money measures and compares; it states whether and by how much the value of one thing exceeds another.

The vast majority of real estate holdings are indeed bought and sold on the open market at prices that are measured and compared by that market. Under the right conditions, we refer to this kind of price as market value.

Defining Market Value

Market value is broadly understood to mean "what property should normally sell for, assuming a willing buyer and a willing seller." However, the courts and others have defined it in a way that implies some important additional criteria. As most often used in appraisal practice, market value means:

. . . the most probable price in terms of money which a property should bring in a competitive and open market under all conditions requisite to a fair sale, the buyer and seller each acting prudently, knowledgeably, and assuming the price is not affected by undue stimulus.*

* B. N. Boyce, *Real Estate Appraisal Terminology,* rev. ed., Ballinger Publishing Co., Cambridge, Mass., 1981.

In other words, market value is a price arrived at in the market under certain prescribed conditions, regarding (1) the terms of sale, (2) market exposure, and (3) informed parties, not under duress.

Terms of the Sale

There is a saying in real estate that the price depends upon the terms: how much cash down and how much per month. Two identical houses will probably sell at different prices if each deal involves markedly different financing. This teaches us that price differences do not necessarily indicate value differences. If prices of comparables are to be taken as indicative of value, financing terms must be considered in an appraisal.

Market Exposure

Market exposure means making the potential buyers of a property aware that the property is available for sale. Some form of advertising is usually necessary to meet this condition. Figure 3.4 represents one possible form. Prices resulting from sales lacking adequate open market exposure do not typify the market and therefore do not represent market value. Family transfers and business expansion sales are usually not "open" or "arm's-length" transactions. Not only are they not advertised, but family sales are often available only to a select few family members. Lack of market exposure also invalidates many forced sales that result from job transfer, threat of foreclosure, or family breakup. What is adequate market exposure? There is no set standard; however, it is generally assumed that unique properties require a greater market exposure because they are of interest to a narrower market. For example, a rambling five-bedroom home may take two or three times as long to sell as a standard three-bedroom home in the same neighborhood.

FIGURE 3.4
An Example of Market Exposure. (Photograph Courtesy of ERA® Mid-Town Realtors®, Inc., Greenville, Texas)

Informed Parties

For a parcel of real estate to command a price matching its utility and value, the property's uses and purposes must be known to the potential buyers and sellers. Even in a normal market, buyers and sellers sometimes lack adequate information about the property. However, sellers are often more familiar with specific features of the sale property than the prospective buyer. The sellers may know about certain property defects or neighborhood nuisances not fully understood by the buyer. Without expert advice from real estate brokers, salespeople, and appraisers, parties on both sides of a given transaction may have a mistaken view of value, and the price agreed upon may not represent market value.

The concept of market value is important in appraisals because it clearly distinguishes between price and value. Price reflects not only the terms and conditions of sale, but the unique and sometimes subjective motives of buyers and sellers. Most appraisal purposes are best served by relating value to a more precise standard than price alone. Thus market value refers to the value of real estate to people in general, its value in terms of money, and its value between informed and knowledgeable people who are buying and selling on the open market. In summary, then, market value can be referred to as the most likely sales price, when the conditions referred to above have been met.

SECTION 3.3
THE CLASSICAL
APPROACHES TO VALUE

As indicated in Section 3.1, the appraisal process requires the application of one or more of the three classical approaches to value. The sales comparison, cost, and income approaches are considered as classical in the appraisal field because they incorporate time-tested techniques for valuing real estate. In early appraisal theory, all three approaches were required in every formal appraisal. Today, they are usually required only if they relate to the value problem at hand. Each approach has its own importance. The three approaches are briefly outlined below and will be covered in greater detail in later chapters.

The Sales Comparison Approach

The sales comparison approach, also known as the direct market comparison approach, is the most direct of the three approaches and usually the most reliable. Simply stated, the sales comparison approach compares the property being appraised to similar properties that have recently sold in the open market. From the prices paid, the appraiser estimates a probable selling price or value for the subject property by making a careful analysis of differences in sale conditions and property characteristics. An example using the sales comparison approach follows.

Example 3.1
Using the Sales Comparison Approach

Assume that the subject property is a medium-quality, 20-year-old, three-bedroom home, which has a two-car garage. The square footage of the home is 1,800 square feet. The appraiser locates three similar homes that have sold in the neighborhood at fair market prices. All have similar square footage and number of rooms.

Comparables

Data	Comparable A	Comparable B	Comparable C
Price paid	$140,000	$134,500	$120,000
Location	Better than subject property	Equal to subject property	Equal to subject property
Lot size	Equal to subject property	Larger than subject property	Smaller than subject property
Overall condition	Better than subject property	Equal to subject property	Worse than subject property

Dollar Adjustment Factors Indicated by the Marketplace

Location difference   = $5,000
Lot size difference   = $4,500
Overall condition difference   = $3,000

Adjustments

Data	Comparable A	Comparable B	Comparable C
Price paid	$140,000	$134,500	$120,000
Location	− 5,000	0	0
Lot size	0	− 4,500	+ 4,500
Overall condition	− 3,000	0	+ 3,000
Price comparables would have sold for if they were like the subject home	$132,000	$130,000	$127,500

Conclusion

Subject property's indicated value is $130,000.

In application, the sales comparison approach involves the following steps.

1. Investigating the sale of comparable properties, ascertaining motives of buyers and sellers, and determining conditions of the sale as to date, price, terms, and market exposure.

2. Analyzing and comparing the sales with the subject property and considering the time of sale, location, and other factors affecting market value.

3. Judging how the observed differences affect prices paid for the properties under study. These differences are normally treated as "adjustments" to the prices paid.

4. Arriving at a conclusion of value for the subject property based on the most comparable sales.

Comparing the sales of comparable properties with the subject property involves first listing desirable features that are found in the comparable properties but are not present in the subject property. Their estimated dollar values must be *subtracted* from the respective selling price of the comparables. Next, features found in the subject property that are not found in the comparable properties must be noted. The estimated dollar value of these features must be *added* to the prices of the comparables to "improve" their comparability. In deciding how much to adjust for differences in the properties being compared, appraisers often rely on techniques "borrowed" from the cost (or even income) approach. For example, a new house with a fireplace might be appraised at $2,000 more than a comparable sale lacking this feature if that amount represents the current market value of a fireplace. Sales comparison approach techniques will be more fully discussed in Chapters 8 and 9.

The Cost Approach

The cost approach is based on the principle that property is worth what it would cost in money to duplicate. (See Figure 3.5.) Adjustments to cost are made to allow for any loss in value due to age, condition, and other factors reducing market appeal. Thus the cost approach involves adding the depreciated replacement cost of the improvements to the value of the land as estimated from a market or economic study. Because of this addition step, the cost approach is also known as the summation approach.

Applying the cost approach requires that the appraiser:

1. Estimate the value of the land as if vacant and available for use.
2. Estimate the total cost of building the existing structure, figured at today's construction prices.
3. Estimate the appropriate amount to allow for accrued depreciation, that is, the loss in value of the subject building as compared to a new structure.
4. Subtract the estimated depreciation from the cost of the hypothetical new structure, giving a depreciated cost estimate.

FIGURE 3.5
Value Is Related to the Cost of Development. (Photograph Courtesy of Doug Frost)

5. Add the value of the land to the depreciated cost of the new structure. The result is the indicated property value by the cost approach.

Example 3.2 illustrates how to use the cost approach.

Example 3.2
Using the Cost Approach

Given
    Cost new
        Home: $50 per sq ft
        Garage: $15 per sq ft

    Depreciation
    Recent comparable sales prices
    decline about 1% for each year
    of age. Present age is 20 years

    Land Value
    $40,000, based on
    recent comparable sales

Solution
Replacement cost

Building:	Width in feet	60	
	Times: Depth in feet	× 40	
	Equals: Area in sq ft	2,400	
	Times: Cost per sq ft	× $50	
	Equals: Cost of home		$120,000
Garage:	Width in feet	20	
	Times: Depth in feet	× 20	
	Equals: Area in sq ft	400	
	Times: Cost per sq ft	× $15	
	Equals: Cost of garage		+$6,000
	Total improvement replacement cost		$126,000
Less:	Depreciation: Age in years	20	
	Times: Annual depreciation	× 1%	
	Equals: Total percent depreciation	20%	
	Times: Total cost new	×$126,000	
	Equals: Depreciation amount		−25,200
			$100,800
Plus:	Land value		+40,000
Equals:	Indicated value by the cost approach		$140,800

Since the cost approach requires an estimate of depreciation or loss in value, it is unreliable where buildings show major losses in value because of old age or substantial obsolescence. Realistic amounts of value loss from these causes are very difficult to estimate. The cost approach is normally given more weight in the appraisal of new buildings, as well as in service-type or special-use properties (such as churches and schools), which are not frequently bought or sold.

The Income Approach

The income approach (or capitalized income approach) is used to appraise commercial, industrial, and residential-income properties according to their ability to produce net income. Where the cost and sales comparison approaches are being emphasized in an appraisal, the income approach is often used to test the results. A building such as the one in Figure 3.6 is a typical income-producing property.

Basically, the income approach involves estimating what the market will pay for the property's expected income. Six steps are involved:

1. Obtain annual rent schedules for the subject property and compare them with the competition to arrive at a projection of reasonable gross rents for the subject.

2. Estimate annual vacancy and collection losses.

3. Subtract these from the gross income to arrive at the effective gross income.

4. Estimate the annual expenses and subtract them from the effective gross income to arrive at the net income. Net income is sometimes called net operating income.

5. Analyze comparable investments in order to arrive at a capitalization method and rate.

6. Capitalize the projected net income into an estimate of value.

There are a number of capitalization methods in common usage, each designed to handle a specific type of appraisal problem. In the case of

FIGURE 3.6
Example of an Income-Producing Property. (Photograph Courtesy of Doug Frost)

single-family homes, the gross rent multiplier method is often used instead of income capitalization. Both income capitalization and the gross rent multiplier method will be defined and discussed in Chapters 13 and 14. Example 3.3 illustrates how to use income capitalization.

Example 3.3
Using the Income Approach
A 20-unit apartment building has market rents of $500 per unit per month, or $120,000 per year. The estimated factor for vacancies and collection losses is 5% of the $120,000 potential income or $6,000. Annual operating expenses are:

Property taxes	$ 8,000
Insurance	$ 5,000
Management	$ 5,000
Repairs and miscellaneous	+ 5,000
Total	$23,000

The capitalization rate selected by the appraiser is 10%.

Solution

Gross annual income		$120,000
Less:	Vacancies and collection loss	− 6,000
Equals:	Effective gross income	$114,000
Less:	Annual expenses	− 23,000
Equals:	Net operating income	$ 91,000
Divided by:	Capitalization rate	÷ 0.10
Equals:	Indicated value by the income approach	$910,000

SUMMARY

A formal appraisal is usually a written estimate of value that results from following an orderly and well-established procedure known as the appraisal process. This involves (1) defining the appraisal problem, (2) planning the appraisal, (3) collecting and analyzing the data, (4) applying the appropriate value approaches, (5) arriving at a value conclusion, and (6) reporting the conclusion of value.

An estimate of market value is the object of most appraisals. Market value differs from other types of value primarily in that it attempts to measure value in exchange rather than value in use. Value in exchange means value to people in general rather than to a specific user.

The formal definition of market value attempts to remove any element of subjectivity (or personal bias) from the value question by requiring that the price paid be (1) in terms of money, (2) upon adequate market exposure, and (3) between knowledgeable parties not under duress.

Three classical approaches are used for valuing real estate: sales comparison, cost, and income. The sales comparison approach is often the most reliable because it is the most direct. It involves comparing the property under appraisal with similar properties that have recently been sold. The cost approach estimates the value of a property by adding its land value to the estimated cost of existing structures, less depreciation. The cost approach tends to be more relevant to the appraisal of newer properties and of single-purpose properties. It is based on the principle that property is worth what it would cost in money to duplicate. The income approach compares the income-producing capability of the property with that of properties that have been sold. The net income projected for the subject property is then translated into an indication of value by a process known as capitalization. The income approach is used to appraise property that generates income. For single-family homes, an alternate gross rent multiplier method can be used.

IMPORTANT TERMS AND CONCEPTS

Appraisal process
Comparison, market
Cost approach
Highest and best use
Income approach
Market exposure
Market price

Market value
Reproduction cost
Sales comparison approach
Value in exchange
Value in use
Worth

REVIEWING YOUR UNDERSTANDING

1. A formal appraisal is:

    (a) A written estimate of value as of a given date
    (b) A package of data to support a definite value
    (c) A definition of the appraisal problem
    (d) None of the above

2. The form and the substantiating data in an appraisal report vary according to:

    (a) The whim of the appraiser
    (b) The purpose and intended use of the appraisal report
    (c) The legal restrictions placed on the property appraised
    (d) The type of value being sought

3. To reach a value conclusion, the sales comparison approach uses:

    (a) The replacement cost of improvements, added to a comparable vacant land value
    (b) Data on current sales of comparable properties
    (c) The income-producing capability of the property
    (d) None of the above

4. The appraiser's conclusion of value should be based on:

    (a) An averaging of the three value conclusions indicated by the three approaches to value
    (b) A weighing of the importance of the value indicated by each of the three approaches to value
    (c) An averaging of the three closest comparable sales
    (d) None of the above

5. A formal appraisal report must include:
   - **(a)** The date of the value estimate
   - **(b)** The signature of the appraiser
   - **(c)** The identification of the property appraised
   - **(d)** All of the above

6. An objective kind of value that can be estimated for items and properties bought and sold in the market is called:
   - **(a)** Value in use
   - **(b)** Value in exchange
   - **(c)** Economic value
   - **(d)** Potential value

7. Market value in appraisal is most commonly identified with:
   - **(a)** Value in use
   - **(b)** Value in exchange
   - **(c)** Assessed value
   - **(d)** Listing value

8. The definition of market value in appraisal practice does not include:
   - **(a)** Highest or most probable price
   - **(b)** Exposure on the market
   - **(c)** Informed parties
   - **(d)** Topography

9. The cost approach is normally given more weight in the appraisal of:
   - **(a)** Old and substantially obsolete buildings
   - **(b)** Single-family tract houses over 10 years old
   - **(c)** New buildings and special-use buildings
   - **(d)** Commercial and industrial properties

10. Which of the approaches to value would involve an investigation into the rent schedules of the subject property and the comparables?
    - **(a)** The cost approach
    - **(b)** The sales comparison approach
    - **(c)** The income approach
    - **(d)** All of the above

CHAPTER
FOUR

FOCUS ON
NEIGHBORHOOD
AND COMMUNITY

PREVIEW

In the previous chapters we explained the necessity of correctly identifying the property and the legal rights that are to be appraised. In Chapter 4 we turn to the gathering of data for the appraisal. The first phase of the data program is to examine carefully the neighborhood and the community around the property and to note the community and neighborhood influences that have the most important effect on the property's value.

When you have completed this chapter, you should be able to:

1. Describe the neighborhood concept and how neighborhood boundaries are defined.

2. Explain how you can use information from a neighborhood study in the appraisal process.

3. Explain the economics of community origins and growth.

4. Name four different physical patterns of community land use.

5. Define a perfect market and explain why real estate markets are not perfect.

6. Discuss the real estate market actions that you should study and why.

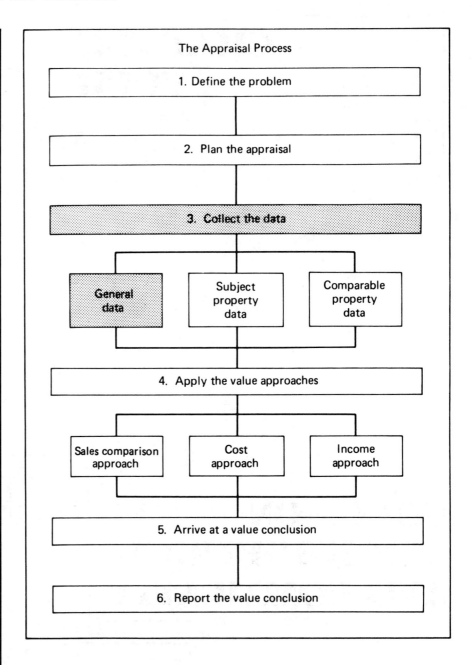

The Appraisal Process

1. Define the problem

2. Plan the appraisal

3. Collect the data

General data — Subject property data — Comparable property data

4. Apply the value approaches

Sales comparison approach — Cost approach — Income approach

5. Arrive at a value conclusion

6. Report the value conclusion

SECTION 4.1
THE NEIGHBORHOOD

No other aspect of appraising is as difficult to define as neighborhood analysis. As a result, its meaning and usage have often been misinterpreted. Each person, community group, and organization has certain ideas as to what a neighborhood is and how it affects property values.

People concerned about allegations of discrimination in housing have questioned how and why appraisers use neighborhood information. In fairness to all, it is essential for those in real estate to understand the concept of the neighborhood as it is used in appraisals and be able to analyze objectively the neighborhood around a subject property. In this section we shall explain the concept of the neighborhood and show how to use neighborhood information.

The Neighborhood Concept

The term neighborhood has been defined as follows:

*A neighborhood is a cluster of properties [most of which are] of relatively similar land use and value.**

A portion of a larger community . . . in which there is a homogeneous grouping of inhabitants, buildings, or business enterprises.†

More broadly, a neighborhood is an area whose occupants and users share some common ties or characteristics. Thus, some form of shared identity creates a neighborhood and binds it together. From this larger definition, we can see that one neighborhood may be residential, another commercial, another industrial, and so on.

What is the meaning of the term shared identity? Simply stated, shared identity can be defined economically, by the land uses; physically, by the buildings; or sociologically, by the occupants. It refers to whatever shared characteristics create a positive common bond. There can be many types of positive bonds. In an office neighborhood, for example, the bonds might include the sharing of a common work pool, similar surroundings, and accessibility to nearby services. Sometimes the nature of the bond is difficult to see. For example, in a very diverse residential-commercial neighborhood, the most powerful bond could be the desire to live in such a diverse and varied environment. The Montrose area in Houston has been considered such a neighborhood.

Boundaries of the Neighborhood

Neighborhood boundaries are influenced by a wide variety of factors, usually economic, physical, or legal in character. Economically, such boundaries are determined by where the benefits of the location seem to change. Evidence of such a boundary can be seen in the changes in the types of buildings, or land uses, or changes in the shared characteristics of the occupants. Physical features often define the boundaries of a neighborhood. Examples include rivers, lakes, and mountains, as well as highways, railroads, and other man-made features. City, school district, and zoning boundaries are also commonly noted by appraisers as establishing neighborhood boundaries.

The boundaries of a neighborhood are not always obvious. Property features often change gradually, as one moves from one neighborhood to

---

* D. J. McKenzie and R. M. Betts, *The Essentials of Real Estate Economics*, 2nd ed., John Wiley & Sons, New York, 1980.

† B. N. Boyce, *Real Estate Appraisal Terminology*, rev. ed., Ballinger Publishing Co., Cambridge, Mass., 1981.

the next. When this is the case, neighborhood boundaries are difficult to establish. Sometimes, however, the neighborhood boundary can be very precise. For example, the boundaries of commercial neighborhoods are often precisely defined by zoning laws and by where the commercial buildings are located. Also, industrial neighborhoods most often have boundaries that are precisely defined by zoning.

Adjacent neighborhoods may have similar characteristics. When adjacent neighborhoods lack noticeable physical boundaries and have important features in common, it is possible to combine them for study purposes and treat them as a larger neighborhood. On the other hand, almost every neighborhood can also be divided up into smaller neighborhoods by emphasizing minor differences in the bonds that define the neighborhood as a whole. So we can call the one the larger neighborhood and the other the immediate neighborhood.

In summary, neighborhood boundaries may be set by either physical features, legal boundaries, or by differences in the characteristics of occupants, buildings, or uses.

Rating Neighborhood Quality

Since every neighborhood offers different advantages to its inhabitants, neighborhoods are said to differ in quality. Although it is a very complex idea, the quality of a neighborhood can best be judged in terms of the needs and standards of its occupants. For example, the desirable features of an industrial district will be different from those of a residential district. The major factors to consider when rating any neighborhood can be grouped as physical, economic, social, or political in nature.

Physical Factors
The physical factors that affect neighborhood desirability include both natural neighborhood features and those created by people. Natural features that affect neighborhood desirability range from trees, lakes, and soil stability, to temperatures, rainfall, topography, and winds. Some residential neighborhoods have unfavorable weather (for example, high humidity in Houston or high dusty winds in Abernathy) that negatively influence home values in that neighborhood. Flood zones, soil condition, slides, and earthquake fault zones may also have negative effects on particular areas or properties. Desirable views, on the other hand, can affect values favorably, as can the presence of other sought-after natural amenities.

Many important physical amenities have been created by people. These include the appearance, accessibility, desirability, and convenience of the surrounding area, especially with regard to:

1. The transportation system: roads and public transit.
2. The school system.
3. Recreational facilities: parks, community centers, and arenas and theaters.
4. Shopping facilities.
5. Religious centers.
6. The utility system: water, electricity, gas, telephone, sewage, and garbage.

7. Compatibility between adjacent land uses (e.g., heavy manufacturing and residential).
8. Maintenance of buildings, yards, and landscaping.

Economic Factors

The first important economic factor is whether the income level of the neighborhood occupants is sufficient to maintain existing structures. This strongly relates to the stability of employment in the occupations that generate incomes for the neighborhood's occupants. In residential neighborhoods, for instance, you might study housing costs as a percentage of household income. In commercial neighborhoods you might study store sales volume per square feet of building floor area. Generally, the greater the economic strength, the greater the neighborhood's desirability.

Social Factors

Neighborhood desirability is influenced by the many social characteristics of the occupants. This is because people often seek to be in a neighborhood whose occupants have interests similar to theirs. For example, people with young children often want to live in a residential neighborhood where there are children of the same age as their children. Significant social factors include the education, occupations, ages, and family makeup of neighborhood occupants. The rate at which occupants move—the turnover rate—also affects how a neighborhood is viewed.

Neighborhood desirability is also dependent upon the effort and money that neighborhood occupants put into building maintenance and modernization. Community support for the existing legal and political order is also a factor, since neighborhood attitudes can influence political decisions, such as the amount of city services provided, tax rates, and the quality of the schools. Another neighborhood attitude that the appraiser might study is how the occupants rate the desirability of the neighborhood relative to other neighborhoods.

Political Factors

The level of taxes, assessment fairness, city services provided, public education, and protective zoning or planning all have an effect upon neighborhood desirability. Governmental positions on air and water pollution, job safety, social programs, and noise or odor controls can also be noted. Many political factors are the ultimate result of social attitudes, either in the neighborhood the appraiser is studying or in the city as a whole.

Neighborhoods and Change

Every neighborhood, regardless of land use, goes through a series of changes over the years. These changes usually follow a pattern. The first phase occurs when the vacant land is subdivided, streets and utilities are installed, and the first buildings are constructed. Over time, most of the available land is built upon. This first phase in the cycle of a neighborhood is called the development *phase*.

The second phase gradually begins as development slows down. It is called the mature or stable *phase*. The most significant feature of this phase is the relative stability of the existing buildings and occupants. This phase usually lasts for an extended period of time.

During the stable years, building maintenance and renovation generally keep up with the normal deterioration from weather and usage. In time, however, neighborhood occupants may postpone needed repairs; then the third phase, decline or decay, begins. Regardless of the type of building or use, the effects of age continually attack the stability apparent in the second phase. The elements, insects, pollution, and use of the buildings all cause wear and tear to the interior and exterior of structures. Over time, there is competition from newer neighborhoods and from new building designs, decorative finishes, or building layouts, which make the older neighborhood less desirable. The degree of neighborhood decline varies, as does the length of time until the beginning of the fourth phase.

The fourth phase of neighborhood change is called the renaissance: the transition to a new sequence of life for the neighborhood. Neighborhood renaissance can occur slowly or rapidly and may have either private or government sponsorship or a mixture of the two. This renaissance phase will involve either of the following events:

1. Demolition or relocation of the existing buildings and development of the land with new buildings, often for different uses.
2. Major renovation of the existing buildings to correct maintenance problems and obsolete features. The buildings may continue in the same uses or be converted to new uses.

The four phases of neighborhood change shown in Figure 4.1a to 4.1d form a cycle that occurs in almost every type of neighborhood. In older, more stable cities, there is evidence to suggest that this neighborhood cycle has been repeated several times and involves renovating the same buildings and continuing similar uses of the buildings.

Evidence of Neighborhood Change

As a neighborhood passes through each of the four phases of the neighborhood cycle, there are clear signs of transition. The transition from the growth phase to the stable phase, for example, is identified by a reduction in available vacant land and a decline in the construction of new buildings.

The transition from the stable phase to the declining phase is identified by marked changes in existing buildings. One common change is a decrease in the amount of building maintenance with noticeable deterioration resulting. Often, there will be a change in the density of use, with more people occupying the same space. In commercial or industrial property this increase in density often means that there will be smaller firms occupying a given building than in earlier years.

The transition to neighborhood renaissance is usually marked by the renovation of individual structures. Improved maintenance and increased remodeling are first noted at scattered locations and then gradually become more common.

The neighborhood renaissance phase may also involve demolition of old buildings and the construction of new ones. The transition into this phase is often marked first by changes in the uses of existing buildings. As the new, higher-priced uses begin to prosper, deteriorated buildings will be demolished and replaced. Substantial physical deterioration must be

FIGURE 4.1
The four phases of neighborhood change. (*a*) Development. (*b*) Stable. (*c*)
Decline. (*d*) Renaissance. (Photographs Courtesy of Doug Frost)

present if this phase is to be carried out by private capital because well-maintained structures are usually too valuable to be demolished.

Neighborhoods as Barometers of Change

Why should you learn about the neighborhood cycle or about neighborhood changes? The value of a property is influenced by the neighborhood around it. So, we study neighborhood changes in order to understand how and why a property's value is changing. Often, too, some other location in a neighborhood will show changes before similar changes actually reach the property being appraised.

The immediate neighborhood has the most impact on the subject property. For most land uses, this immediate area will include the properties in the same block, on both sides of the street, plus those "across the back fence" and even those on the cross streets. Figure 4.2 shows the neighborhood locations that are likely to have the greatest impact on the property

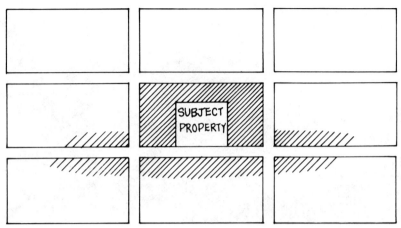

FIGURE 4.2
The Immediate Neighborhood—One Version

being appraised. Neighborhood locations that are farther away have a gradually diminishing impact upon the value of a particular property.

Every neighborhood is *always* changing, no matter how stable it may seem. Normal wear and tear from age, the elements, and neglect continually act to reduce a declining neighborhood's condition, desirability, and value. As the occupants work to delay or halt such decay, they can often reverse the decline, improving the desirability and value of the neighborhood. All the positive and negative forces present in the neighborhood eventually lead either to the renovation of the existing structures or to their demolition.

These changes in the neighborhood affect every property but usually at differing times. Noticeable change usually starts at the edge of a neighborhood, where land uses conflict with, or are different from, those of the adjoining neighborhood. Depending on the community reaction, the good or bad change may disappear or may spread to the rest of the neighborhood. For this reason, appraisers look beyond the immediate area of the subject property to the fringes of the neighborhood. They want to see what kinds of changes are occurring and how the neighborhood is meeting these changes. See Figure 4.3 for an example.

In summary, appraisers study neighborhoods and their changes in order to see physical evidence of what forces are affecting the neighborhood. These same forces are at work on the property being appraised but can often best be seen through their effect on other properties in the neighborhood. As we shall see, the appraiser uses this understanding of neighborhood change throughout the appraisal process.

**Using Information
About Neighborhoods**

Why do appraisers need information? One reason is the need to include an objective picture of the neighborhood in the description section of the appraisal report or file. A second and key reason is to define the geographic area that will be the center of the market-data search area. Whether one looks for land sales, improved-property sales, leases, costs, depreciation, or income capitalization rates, the neighborhood around the property is the starting point in the search.

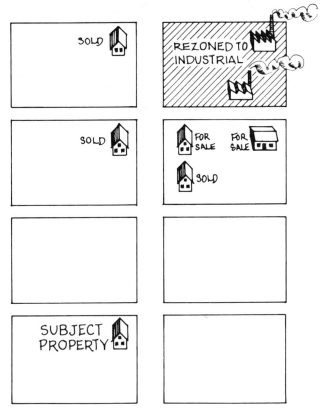

FIGURE 4.3
One Reason for Studying the Neighborhood

A third reason for studying neighborhoods is that it will assist you in defining the highest and best use of the property. (There are many possible uses of a property, varying in their legal and economic feasibility.) Recent history and trends in uses in a neighborhood tell the appraiser much about the feasibility of various uses, as well as the legal, social, and political problems that may block the success of a particular use. The term "highest and best use" will be more fully developed in later chapters.

The fourth reason for studying neighborhoods is to find out whether, and by how much, to adjust market data for differences. Comparable sales might have occurred too many months ago to be useful, or might represent smaller or older structures than the subject property, or might be too far away. As a result, market data must often be adjusted to reflect the differences. The amount of such adjustment must be based upon the importance of those differences in the particular market area or neighborhood. In home sales, for example, the price of a property lacking a basement should be adjusted if the subject property has a basement. This adjustment must be based on the importance of a basement in that market. In an industrial neighborhood, the absence of an office area in a warehouse must be considered in light of warehouse office usage in that neighborhood. In considering the sale of a large house, the appraiser must keep in mind the general range of house sizes in the neighborhood, as well as trends in family sizes and incomes.

In addition, neighborhood properties are rarely identical from one end of the neighborhood to the other. You must understand how the various locations within the neighborhood differ in order to correctly use and adjust market information that comes from different places within the neighborhood.

A significant problem arises when adequate information cannot be found within the neighborhood. When you lack sales of properties similar to the subject, you may need to use sales or information from other neighborhoods, communities, or even other states. Then you must try to understand each neighborhood in order to adjust for the difference in location.

The Neighborhood Controversy

In the past, appraisers have been accused of using neighborhood analysis to collect information that is entirely irrelevant to the appraisal or is intended to prejudice. Some have even suggested that neighborhood analysis should be eliminated from the appraisal process. The controversy arises, it seems, from appraisers' failure to define clearly how certain neighborhood information is to be used. When its purpose is not clear, some information may be challenged as irrelevant or no longer important. Reporting the race, creed, or national origin of occupants is an example of information irrelevant to nearly all appraisal assignments.

The study of neighborhoods is at the heart of appraisal and the estimation of market value. It is the study of the neighborhood that helps the appraiser discover what property characteristics are important to buyers and sellers and suggests the relative importance of such characteristics at any particular time.

SECTION 4.2 UNDERSTANDING COMMUNITIES AND HOW THEY GROW

All neighborhoods exist in relation to the social, economic, and political environment of a community. Understanding the origin, location, and layout of cities helps us understand the land uses within the community and the patterns of land use that tend to form. The factors that contribute to economic growth are especially important. As communities grow, they change in layout, and these changes affect value.

Community Origins and Growth

Each community is located where it is for specific social, political, physical, or economic reasons. The town's original location strongly influences its early physical layout. In turn, the early layout strongly influences how the town changes as it grows. For this reason, it is sometimes helpful for you to be aware of the origins of a town.

Townsite Selection Factors

Historically, town locations were often selected because food and water were accessible and the site could easily be defended against common enemies. Some townsites were chosen for religious purposes. In America most townsites were selected because of their commercial benefits. Often, the choice of a site was determined by the topography of the land, the availability of raw resources, and the transportation systems in use at the time.

Topography has always been one of the most important factors in the selection of a townsite because it usually determined where the existing transportation routes would be. In turn, these influence the accessibility of the land for habitation. Topography has particularly determined the location of towns whose major function was to provide services along transportation routes.

The availability of raw resources has long been a major factor in choosing the location for a townsite. Resources that had a *low* value for their bulk, such as copper ore, usually had to be processed near the mine, creating an industry. This processing industry often grew into a townsite. Resources that had a *high* value per ton, or per unit of size, could be shipped without processing. Thus some processing towns did not need to be as close to the mine. The total number of mines in an area also determined where processing was to take place, so the townsite remained just a mine town or grew into a larger village.

Finally, the choice of location, especially for water transport towns, depended upon the form of transportation in use at the time of the town's founding. If shallow-draft paddlewheel schooners were in use, a shallow, sheltered dock was sufficient for the site. When oceangoing steamers came into use, deep-water docks became necessary. Wind shelters were also critical for protection from storm waves. These examples show how the requirements for success as a townsite constantly change.

Types of Towns

In America, towns and cities usually fit into one of three types, depending upon the major functions they serve. The central town is one that performs a variety of services for a surrounding area. The area is first developed, usually for farming, with widely scattered residences. The need for a place to buy supplies and locate churches and schools soon leads to the formation of a town. The town grows in population as a result of the expansion and profitability of farming. Figure 4.4 shows a map of three central towns and their respective trade areas.

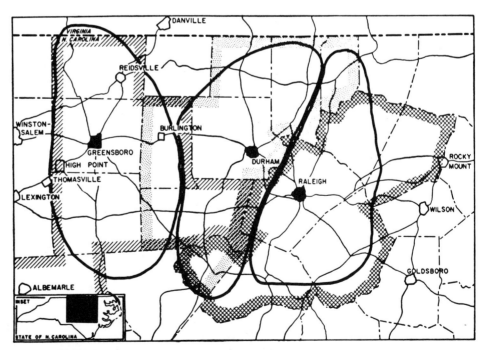

FIGURE 4.4
Three Central Towns in North Carolina and Their Trade Areas. (Copyright 1957 by the Board of Trustees of the University of Illinois Press. Reprinted by permission of the University of Illinois Press)

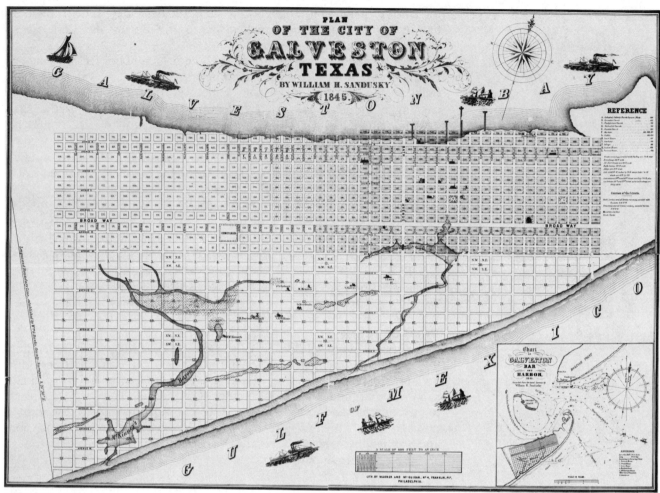

FIGURE   4.5
Galveston, Pre-1850. (Courtesy of the Rosenberg Library, Galveston, Texas)

The transportation service town, as noted earlier, provides services along a transportation route. Usually, these towns are situated at points called nodes. These are points where transport routes split or shift, or where a change in the type of transportation occurs. Typical nodes include ports, major rail intersections, highway intersections, navigable river forks, and mountain passes. Figure 4.5 shows Galveston when it was a port town. Transport service towns may also develop at a place where transportation systems must be maintained. Some railroad water stops in the western United States have become cities, including Texarkana and Denison.

Special-function towns are those that concentrate on one special service or purpose, such as a mining town, a government seat, or a retirement community. Other examples include resort towns and university towns. Figure 4.6 displays some examples of special-function towns.

Changes in City Function

As a town grows, it can change from one functional type to another. Pittsburgh, Pennsylvania, was founded at Fort Pitt beside a major river fork as a point of control over the commercial transportation in the area (then entirely by riverboats). It was first a transport service town. Because of the mining of nearby coal and iron ore deposits, Pittsburgh later became

FIGURE 4.6
Special-Function Towns. (*a*) University Town (Courtesy of Larry Murphy, University of Texas News and Information Service). (*b*) Mining Town. (Courtesy of Earl Dotter/Magnum). (*c*) Retirement Community, Sun City, Arizona (Courtesy of Georg Gerster/Rapho-Photo Researchers). (*d*) Government Town. (Courtesy of Smith Gilley, State Representative)

(c)

(d)

FIGURE 4.6
(continued)

FIGURE 4.7
Local and Export Production

a resource-oriented iron mill town. The nearby iron and coal are now exhausted, but the workers' skills and the huge mills allow Pittsburgh to continue as a special-purpose, resource-oriented manufacturing town.

Economic Growth

Once a town comes into being, its continued existence depends upon economic success. No town or community today is self-sufficient. The cars, radios, food, and other commodities we use come from other towns and we must pay for them. It follows that the many costs of imported goods and services must be earned by sales of the town's own products and services to other towns. Each town must perform some economic function: make products, mine a resource, or perform a service. Usually, a portion of the product or service will be for sale or for use in the town. This is called local production. More important, however, is the surplus production that is sold to other towns is called export production. An example of local versus export production is shown in Figure 4.7. The latter economic activity forms the economic base of the town. The growth of towns, then, depends upon the richness of the town's basic resources (oil and gas deposits, ore bodies, timber stands, and tillable fields) and the skills, creativity, and productivity of its workers.

Each community tends to develop a specialty, usually related to the town's origin. This specialty can be a product or a skill. When we compare one town with another, or one region with another, we can see differences in the products that are made in each town and in how the population is employed. These differences *reveal* the special products or skills that provide the economic base for the town or region. We use this knowledge of the economic-base activities to study the possibility of population growth or decline, the relative stability of employment, or the future of particular neighborhoods economically tied to the area's exports.

Physical Patterns of the Community

As towns grow, the different land uses in the community form patterns. As we noted in our discussion of neighborhoods, each use often concen-

"Say, were those houses there last night?"

FIGURE 4.8
Growing Communities. (Henry R. Martin, from *The Rotarian*, April 1978.)

trates at one location because the various users choose the most advantageous location for each use. The various neighborhoods, each with their characteristic uses, make up the land-use pattern of the community. It should be remembered that the pattern may change over the years in response to changing social and economic influences.

Major Factors in Land Use
A number of factors influence the land-use patterns and the location of new buildings in a community. Four factors are especially important. Each, however, is to some extent connected to the other.

1. **Topography**   The shape and slope of the land and its natural features, such as rivers, swamps, and lakes. Topography usually determines transportation routes and good building sites.

2. **The town's origin**   Where the town started and why. Both the functional origin and the point of origin of a community are determined by topography, transportation, and natural resources. In turn, the town's origin is a major factor in the subsequent development of the townsite.

3. **Transportation systems**   How people and goods move around. Early transportation systems, such as walking, pack animals, and carts allowed random movement in any direction, which contributed to the circular shape of towns. But as transportation systems

became more sophisticated, the shape of towns changed. Of all four factors, transportation is the most important in creating change in the pattern of land use, as you will see in our discussion of current trends in the following pages.

4. **Major existing uses** The presence of major buildings or concentrations of buildings continues to attract people, even when the original reason for selecting the location of these buildings no longer exists.

Typical Patterns

The most common land-use pattern is the cluster of commercial uses at the intersection of major transport routes (again, the node concept). In small villages the crossroads' commercial buildings become the downtown area. In towns larger than a small village, the number of land uses in the downtown area increases to the extent that the area around the crossroads becomes divided into different zones of uses. Although the prime commercial uses remain at the main intersection, the pressures of the town's growth eventually drive residences to the outskirts of town. High rents and values in the prime commercial area tend to cause offices, government buildings, schools, and other buildings with unprofitable commercial uses to move away from the main intersection and gradually fill in the intermediate area of the town. As this process continues, the town pattern begins to look like a series of rings around the downtown area. The prime commercial zone forms the inner ring, followed by a ring of office, government, and wholesale buildings. This ring, in recent years, has included a growing number of apartment buildings. The next ring contains older houses with some conversions to offices or boardinghouses, and some new structures moving out from the second ring. The fourth ring consists of single-family residences, with the newer homes on the outer circumference. Figure 4.9 shows this pattern of concentric rings.

As concentric rings form around the downtown section of many cities, various factors often cause the rings to become segmented. Depending upon the existing uses and the topography of the ring, each segment will

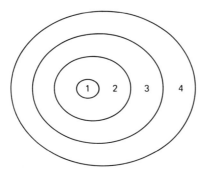

FIGURE 4.9
Typical Patterns of Land Use: Concentric Rings. (From Dennis J. McKenzie and Richard M. Betts. *The Essentials of Real Estate Economics*, 2nd ed., New York: John Wiley & Sons, Inc., 1980, p. 85)

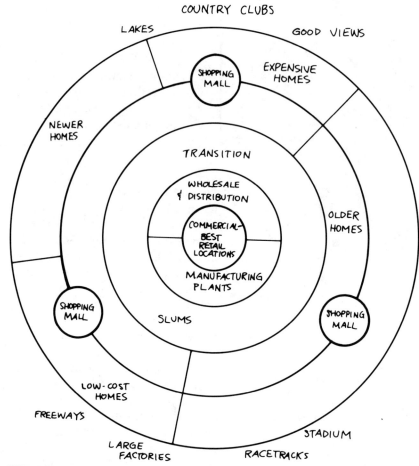

FIGURE 4.10
Segmented Rings

have some different use from the other segments in the ring. Often, service, retail, wholesale, and manufacturing uses will concentrate in segments on one side of the downtown, with offices and higher-priced commercial stores on the other. Particular segments on the outer rings will be favored for high-priced new homes. Another segment might be favored because of good views, favorable surroundings, or proximity to older luxury homes. Mid-priced new homes will usually be located on the remaining segments of the outer ring. Usually, the high-priced commercial ring segment will line up with the high-priced home segment, as Figure 4.10 demonstrates.

The concept of perfect concentric rings is somewhat oversimplified, but it still serves as a good analytical tool. Land-use patterns can be so dominated by topography that the ring may become oval-shaped in the case of a city on a peninsula or half-moon-shaped in the case of a port city that borders a bay, a lake, or a river. Economic use patterns are also altered by personal motives. People sometimes hold on to their old family homes despite economic pressures to sell or convert to commercial uses. In general, however, the pattern of land uses shows a strong concentric-ring relationship, which is especially noticeable in small cities.

Current Trends

The early transport systems were replaced by streetcars, traveling fixed linear routes. This change caused urban land-use patterns to change grad-

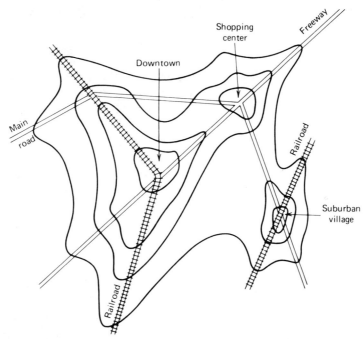

FIGURE 4.11
The Modern Star-Shaped City. (From Dennis J. McKenzie and Richard M. Betts, *The Essentials of Real Estate Economics*, 2nd ed., New York: John Wiley & Sons, Inc., 1980, p. 94)

ually from concentric to linear, as city growth began to follow the fixed-rail lines. Although automobile transportation at first encouraged a return to the earlier patterns of random movement and circular cities, arterial roads and highways soon took the place of the familiar fixed-rail routes, and cities developed an even more linear pattern.

As the arterial roads and freeways of large cities intersect, each major road intersection forms a node, and a commercial cluster often develops. In turn, small concentric rings often form about the cluster.

To summarize, in modern cities locations for new developments are chosen more by proximity to transportation lines than by the distance from the downtown area. Thus the concentric circles that we discussed earlier are altered in larger cities that have freeways, expressways, arterials, streetcars, subways, and so on. Now, commercial uses often form linear strips instead of rings. Each major intersection develops its own minor ring. Service industries and warehouses often adjoin the linear strip or occupy districts far removed from the old warehouse district. So, we can understand why the pattern of uses in most of the larger modern cities does not look like a series of concentric rings, but rather like an irregular spider web or a tangled pattern of yarn. The outline of the city itself, instead of being circular, is likely to look more like a star with a number of points. Figure 4.11 is an example.

Using Information About Communities

As the appraiser looks at the community and region surrounding the property being appraised, the scope and amount of information may appear to be staggering. Countless data about political, social, economic, and physical aspects of the community might be collected. In order to select the most relevant information, the appraiser must have a clear concept of how this information is to be used.

The appraiser uses regional and community information for several reasons. The first is that some community forces and trends affect the trends in the neighborhood. For example, if the town is growing, residential neighborhoods close to downtown could be under pressure to become locations for stores or offices. Understanding these community trends helps you to interpret what is happening in the neighborhood.

Second, some community trends can affect all the real estate markets in the community. For example, prices of all types of property in all neighborhoods in a town may decline if a dominant employer shuts down, or prices may increase if a large factory opens up. Understanding this second type of community trend helps you decide which sales occurred in comparable market conditions as of your date of value. For instance, in the case of an unexpected factory closing, sales prices for homes sold prior to the factory closing may differ from prices after the closing.

In summary, understanding community origin and patterns of growth helps the appraiser to analyze the economic and political factors affecting the subject property and its neighborhood. Some of these factors will affect the entire community. Other influences may affect properties and values over a smaller area. Notice that as the area you study gets smaller, the focus on the community gradually changes to a neighborhood study, as discussed earlier in this chapter.

SECTION 4.3
UNDERSTANDING MARKETS

Since appraisals usually involve estimating market value, appraisers must understand real estate markets. Knowing the condition of the market will help you in different ways. It will help you when selecting the market data to use in the appraisal. Sometimes, the market data selected may have defects. Frequently, such defects are caused by market imperfections. An appraiser with a solid grasp of what is going on in the market can often detect these imperfections and thereby reduce the possibility of error.

What Is a Market?

Most of us have some impression of what a market is. We have seen an auction, a farmer's market, or pictures of the trading floor of the stock market. These are general examples of a market: a place where buyers and sellers meet to exchange goods or services. The concept of a market also has an exact technical definition, based upon seven criteria.

The Perfect Market
From the study of markets has come the concept of the perfectly competitive market, or perfect market. It is a standard against which all other types of markets are compared. The perfect market is defined as one that meets *each* of the following criteria:

1. There are numerous buyers and sellers.
2. All parties are knowledgeable.
3. All parties are free to trade or not trade.
4. All products are similar and interchangeable.
5. All products can be transported to better markets.

6. Items are small, inexpensive, and frequently purchased.

7. The government plays a very minor role in pricing.

Markets such as the stock market come close to being perfect markets. In such markets, prices move continuously up and down, and neither seller nor buyer can control the price movement.

Imperfect Markets

Many markets cannot meet the seven tests of a perfect market. These are referred to as imperfect markets. For example, in some imperfect markets, such as uncut diamonds, there are very few sellers. These sellers tend to fix prices, and there is little price fluctuation. A limited number of sellers is one type of problem that causes imperfect markets.

Another common feature of imperfect markets is inadequate knowledge on the part of buyers and/or sellers, either about the product itself or, more often, about true conditions in the market. The lack of adequate knowledge means that buyers or sellers are not able to make good decisions so that when added information is finally obtained, price or location decisions turn out to have been wrong. When more information about a product becomes available, prices change. Some people get information ahead of the general market and use this information to their advantage and profit. When this occurs, the profits are made at the expense of those who lack full information.

Real Estate Markets

We can see from reviewing the definition of a perfect market that real estate markets are *not* perfect markets. In fact, real estate markets are often used by economists as examples of imperfect markets—the other extreme—because real estate markets do not meet *any* of the seven requirements for a perfect market.

At any one time in real estate markets, there are relatively few buyers and sellers of one type, price range, and location of real property. Neither buyer nor seller is very knowledgeable because the product, real estate, is complex and not as commonly bought and sold as other commodities. Both seller and buyer are often anxious to complete a deal in order to get housing or buy another property. Available properties are not very similar or interchangeable. Practically speaking, they cannot be transported to a better market, should the local market be poor. The properties are not small or inexpensive and are not frequently purchased by most market participants. Surveys of buyer characteristics reveal that few people have made more than a half-dozen real estate purchases. Finally, real estate pricing is strongly influenced by government actions. The FHA financing and income tax benefits, for example, tend to help buyers; at the same time, property-use controls such as zoning and building permits, tend to restrict sellers.

Because of the imperfection of the real estate market, prices for real estate do not rise or fall rapidly as do stock prices, for example. Thus, in the real estate market, individual sales can occur well above or below the prices that would occur with a more perfect market. A unique price can result when there is a poorly informed buyer or seller, or when there is some unique characteristic of the property from the point of view of the typical buyer. To illustrate the latter, there are very few buyers willing to pay a proportionately high price for a large house (3,500 square feet, say) with only one bedroom. To the right buyer, a relatively high price could be reasonable. To most buyers, however, the price would have to be considerably lower to be attractive.

Since real properties are so complex, there are many factors that can influence prices. These factors vary in importance, depending on the place, time, or property type. Consequently, real estate markets are more varied and unique than, say, bond markets.

In the real estate market, each subcategory of property is somewhat distinct from the others. Homes in Michigan may not sell at the same price as identical homes in Texas. Even within Texas, prices in Houston will have limited connection to prices in Ennis, about 200 miles away.

Interpreting Market Activity

Why does the appraiser study markets? Fundamentally, it is to find out what is happening in the marketplace. The information gathered will then be interpreted using the appraiser's understanding of economic forces. The appraiser uses this understanding of market forces in the appraisal process to help decide what kinds of market data to collect and what adjustment to make. For example, study could help in deciding whether to adjust land or building sales for differences in time.

Price Levels

The most obvious aspect of market activity to be examined is the level of prices. By comparing prices with current costs for new construction and lot prices, we can see how the market reduces the value of older homes. We can see how this value loss varies with the type of building, location, or market. Studying this market information helps us interpret market data.

We can also compare prices for other reasons. For example, within a neighborhood, we could compare and see the effects of age, size, an added half-bath, a swimming pool, or a view on sales prices. On the other hand, by comparing prices paid for similar properties in different locations, we can learn how the market views the desirability of these locations.

Price Movements

The appraiser can learn even more by studying price movements rather than just price levels. In studying price movements, we see which way prices are changing, how fast, and whether there are differences between various markets. The direction and speed of price movement tell us how strong or weak the particular market is. We can also compare the strength of the market with our knowledge of the community's economy. This sharpens our understanding of what economic forces may be causing prices to change.

For example, we might find that a city has two high-priced, residential neighborhoods, but one has declining prices, while the other has stable or increasing prices. As a result, market data from these two markets will have to be interpreted differently. Upon further study, we may be able to develop an idea of why the difference is occurring. Perhaps the declining neighborhood previously catered to wealthy central-city commuters who are now residing farther out. Perhaps the other neighborhood attracted local professionals, who have not been as quick to move to distant suburbs.

We might also want to compare the direction and speed of current price changes with past price changes or with price movement in other price ranges and in other types of real estate. Is the rate of price change speeding up, slowing down, or staying the same? Answers to such questions may shed additional light upon the appraisal problem at hand.

How do price changes compare with construction cost changes? If the price changes are greater, then we can see that either builder profits or land prices may be going up. If they are less, then land prices and builder profits may be under pressure.

This study of the direction and speed of price movements will demonstrate again and again a need to compare real estate trends to trends in the general economy. Are real estate prices going up faster than general prices? Than new construction costs? What about lot prices? Raw land prices? As we develop an understanding of the cost approach, we shall see that a change in the price of the completed house *must* involve changes in the prices of the elements that go into making up the house. Figure 4.12 shows the relationship between the cost of living and real estate rentals.

Levels of Activity

The appraiser should also study how active the market is. In real estate markets we noted earlier that prices do not always respond smoothly to

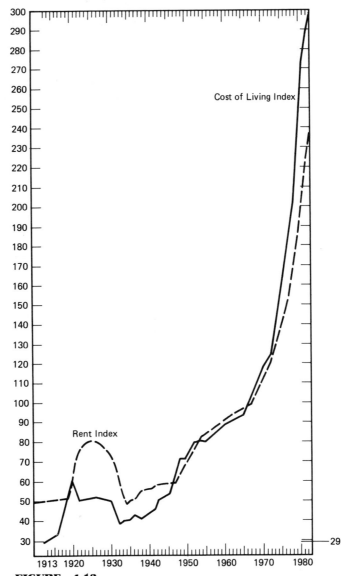

FIGURE 4.12

Comparing Rent Inflation with the Cost of Living. (*Source: Statistical Abstract of the United States, 1985*)

minor shifts in seller supply or buyer demand. Prices may move smoothly upward, as the general real estate price increases of 1976 to 1978 demonstrate. However, when real estate prices are under pressure to move downward, a more irregular pattern is typical.

When downward pressures develop, what usually happens first is that buyers refuse to buy at the old prices. In a more perfect market, prices would slowly start to fall. In real estate markets, however, what often happens is that sellers try to wait this period out, hoping for an offer every day. Many eventually withdraw their property from the market rather than sell for less. As a result the volume of sales falls off dramatically.

When this happens, the first clue to where the market is heading is the declining number of sales rather than a decline in prices. In time, either buyers will return to the market at old price levels or else the more anxious sellers will cut prices and entice a buyer into purchasing. If buyer resistance continues, then sellers may go through a wave of repeated cuts in the list price without getting a sale. When the sales finally do occur, they often will be a step lower than prior sales. Therefore, we might want to compare the current volume of sales with the volume in the past for that type of property. Is the volume up or down and by how much? How does the sales volume compare to the number of listings? Has this relationship changed?

The patterns of listing activity can also help us decide what is happening in a market. How long is it taking to sell property? Are many listings expiring unsold? Have there been many asking price reductions for the current listings? Have owners of current listings received any offers? How low were the offers relative to the listing price?

Finally, we are interested in the buyer activity just as much as the listings. What is happening to the number of lookers? How many people are showing up for open houses compared to earlier times? Are people coming back for a second look?

There are several unusual patterns of activity levels of buyers or sellers that you might find. One pattern consists of increasing numbers of lookers, sometimes also with declines in the numbers of listings, or with listings being withdrawn by the sellers. These signs can indicate a market condition in which an upward price jump could be forthcoming. This would be a different pattern of activity than for a stable market or one with gradual price changes.

The third pattern is the troubled market: one in which prices are about to drop. As we have observed earlier, when a real estate market turns downward, prices usually do not turn smoothly downward. Instead, list prices will be maintained at the old levels while buyer activity declines, often substantially. When sales finally occur, they often will be at lower prices.

In the absence of recent sales, then, the appraiser may not want to just use earlier sales. What may be needed is a careful study of recent listing activity and the reasons behind the absence of recent sales. Activity levels are perhaps the most sensitive measure of the state of real estate markets.

SUMMARY

In the first section of the chapter, we discussed the concept of the neighborhood and its importance to appraisers. It was shown that although the neighborhood can be defined in a number of ways, it is, in general, an area whose occupants or users share some common ties or characteristics. Economically, neighborhood boundaries are set by where the characteristics and benefits of a location change. Its quality depends on how the neighborhood serves the land uses and how the occupants maintain the neighborhood.

Neighborhoods go through a series of changes over the years, starting with the development of the initial buildings, then a phase of stability, which is followed by a third phase of decline. The fourth phase, called the renaissance, is the transition to a new life sequence, either by rehabilitation or by demolition.

Appraisers study the neighborhood because it leads to an understanding of the forces affecting the values of the subject properties. The locations immediately around the property being appraised are the most important to study because they will have the most direct impact on the subject property. Locations at the periphery of the neighborhood are also important to study because changes in a neighborhood tend to start at one edge and move inward.

The neighborhood study is used to define the center of the market-data search area. It helps estimate the highest and best use of the property, and establish what types of adjustments to the market data will be necessary.

This chapter then discussed the study of community trends. The influence that the town's origin has over its future growth was the first topic. Origins of American communities were usually commercially motivated. Growth of the town depended on its commercial success in developing some resource, product, or skill to trade to other communities for goods that the local town could not produce.

As towns grow in size, predictable patterns emerge for the various land uses. The major influences affecting these patterns are the town's origin, its topography, the transportation systems in use, and the attraction of existing major buildings. The simplest pattern is the cluster of commercial uses at the main intersection. As towns become bigger, the cluster becomes a series of rings around the major downtown intersection, and the rings of similar uses then break up into different segments. Depending upon transportation systems, the circles can be distorted by linear strip-commercial zones, making larger cities more star-shaped.

This study of the community enables the appraiser to better understand trends in the community that are affecting property and its value. The third section of the chapter focused on markets, beginning with a definition of the elements of a perfect market, followed by a description of the flaws that produce imperfect markets. Real estate markets were shown to be almost classic examples of imperfect markets.

The appraiser studies real estate markets for information to help interpret current market data. Price levels, for example, are compared to estimate the price difference between properties of different sizes, ages, and so on. Price movements tell even more about the market. We can compare prices at different times, for different areas or types of property, or against changing prices in other parts of the economy. In some cases levels of sales activity can be the most significant factor if there are no recent sales. All this information helps the appraiser to understand and adjust the many types of market data that will be used in the appraisal.

IMPORTANT TERMS AND CONCEPTS

Central town	Economic base
Decline phase	Imperfect market
Development phase	Land-use patterns

Neighborhood
Neighborhood cycle
Perfect market
Price levels
Price trend
Renaissance phase

Sales volume
Special-function town
Stable phase
Topography
Town origin
Transportation-service town

REVIEWING YOUR UNDERSTANDING

1. A neighborhood can be defined as:
   (a) A group of properties with similar land uses
   (b) An area in which the occupants and users share some ties or characteristics
   (c) An area of a city that contains similar land uses within a defined location or boundary
   (d) Both (b) and (c)
   (e) Both (a) and (b)

2. Shared identity can mean:
   (a) Some characteristic of a neighborhood that is common to most of the inhabitants, land uses, or buildings
   (b) Some common characteristic of the occupants
   (c) A common community pattern or trend
   (d) Both (a) and (b)
   (e) Both (b) and (c)

3. The boundaries of a neighborhood might be determined by:
   (a) An economic change in use
   (b) Physical features such as lakes, rivers, or highways
   (c) Zoning or city limits
   (d) Two of the above
   (e) All of the above

4. The four stages of the neighborhood cycle are:
   (a) Development, stability, decline, and renaissance
   (b) Development, stability, demolition, and renaissance
   (c) Demolition, decline, renaissance, and stability
   (d) Renaissance, stability, decline, and demolition

5. The three types of commercial townsites are:
   (a) The central town, the location town, and the transportation town
   (b) The central town, the transportation service town, and the special-function town
   (c) The special-function town, the central town, and the crossroads town
   (d) The shopping town, the central town, and the resource town

6. The four interrelated factors that heavily influence the shape of a community and the patterns of land use are:
   (a) Town origins, zoning, transportation, and major existing uses
   (b) The topography, town origins, transportation system, and major existing uses

    (c) Town origins, topography, transportation, and commercial success

    (d) Economic growth, zoning, topography, and transportation

7. A perfect market occurs when:

    (a) There are numerous buyers and sellers who are knowledgeable and are free to trade or not trade

    (b) All products are similar and interchangeable and can be transported to better markets

    (c) The items are small, inexpensive, and frequently purchased, and the government plays no role in pricing

    (d) Two of the above

    (e) All of the above

8. Real estate markets are imperfect because:

    (a) Real estate markets can be easily exchanged

    (b) They meet none of the criteria of a perfect market

    (c) They meet some of the criteria of a perfect market

    (d) Most real estate sales are resales of used property

9. The three indicators you can use to study and interpret market activity are:

    (a) Price levels, price movements, and price changes

    (b) Price levels, price movements, and level of activity

    (c) Price levels, price changes, and price trends

    (d) Market volume, price-earnings ratios, and yield rates

10. The main reason(s) for studying neighborhoods are:

    (a) To write an objective account of the neighborhood for appraisal reports

    (b) To define the geographic area that will be the center of market data

    (c) To assist in finding the highest and best use

    (d) All of the above

    (e) Two of the above

CHAPTER
FIVE

REAL ESTATE
ECONOMICS AND
VALUE

PREVIEW

Real estate is a basic and fundamental form of wealth. All material possessions of people can be traced to their beginnings in the land. To understand how real estate is produced, adapted, distributed, and utilized is to understand the economics of real estate and to gain insight into its value.

The value of real estate is created and modified by the many physical, economic, social, and governmental forces that act upon it. In this chapter we describe these basic forces, discuss economic trends affecting real estate, and outline the economic principles that govern appraisals.

When you have completed this chapter, you should be able to:

1. List the four basic elements of value.
2. List and give examples of the broad forces that affect value.
3. Define real estate cycles.
4. Name the major supply and demand factors that are involved in economic trends affecting real estate.
5. Describe the federal government's role in the economy.
6. Explain how the principles of value relate to the marketability and productivity of real estate.

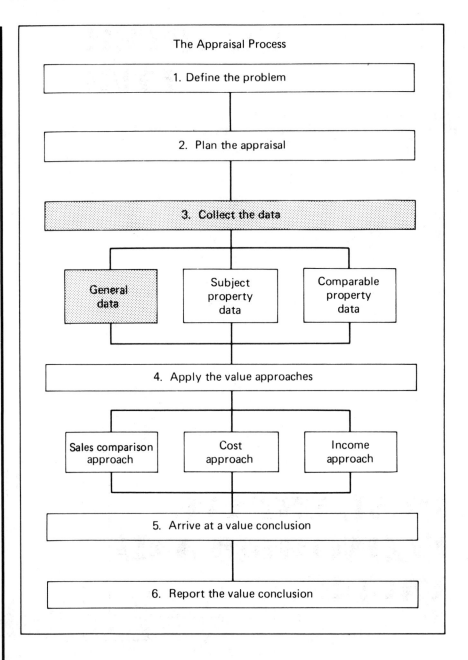

SECTION 5.1
THE BASIC VALUE INFLUENCES

Real estate has no intrinsic value. That means it has no value in and of itself. Instead, the monetary value of real estate is derived from the rights and benefits that come from its ownership, possession, and use. As we learned in Chapter 2 of this book, such rights are referred to as real property rights. When real property rights are bought and sold in the market, the value of such rights is measured by the prices that are paid for them.

For any object to have market value, certain essential elements must be present. A review of these elements is necessary if we are to understand the basic forces that influence the value of real estate.

FOUR ESSENTIAL ELEMENTS OF VALUE

In the context of the market, there are only four basic elements of value. These elements are sometimes referred to as prerequisites.

---

1. **Utility**   Usefulness; ability to arouse a desire for possession.
2. **Scarcity**   In relatively short supply; not in abundance.
3. **Demand**   Desire to plus the ability to buy; effective purchasing power.
4. **Transferability**   Capability of change in ownership or use; marketable title.

All these elements must be present before an object can have value in the marketplace. An object must be useful, and at the same time scarce, for there to be any measurable benefits from owning it. For example, desert sand and ocean water are useful for certain purposes; but because they lack scarcity, they have little value. Modern new houses and office buildings are extremely useful objects for human activity, but a serious oversupply of such buildings would without question reduce their market price. Why? Because oversupply adds up to the opposite of scarcity.

Where does demand fit in? For an item to have value, there must be people ready, willing, and able to buy it at some price. Utility and scarcity cannot create a market unless there is demand and the purchasing power to implement it. And, if an object does not have transferability, the demand is ineffective. For example, and parcel of real estate that lacks marketable title can have no value in the market because rights to its use cannot be transferred. In summary, utility, scarcity, demand, and transferability interact in combination to create the condition we refer to as market value. This is demonstrated in Figure 5.1.

Broad Forces Influencing Value

As we have seen, real estate have value because it meets the four tests listed above. Four broad forces increase or decrease that value; they are physical, social, economic, and political in nature. (See Figure 5.2.) In their many combinations and forms these forces involve all aspects of human behavior. When understood at the national, regional, community, and neighborhood levels, they help to explain why the nature and value of real estate are constantly changing.

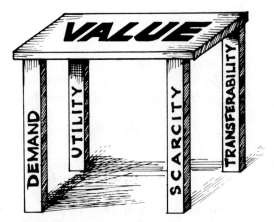

FIGURE 5.1
Basic Elements of Market Value

Physical Forces

Because they are most visible, physical forces (or factors) affecting value are perhaps the easiest to understand. Some are natural and others are man-made. Examples include:

1.   **Natural resources**   The land itself, its topography, soil, access, and location; climate, air, and mineral resources (including water); plant and animal life; and scenic beauty and ecological balance.

2.   **Developed resources**   The size and shape of land parcels; structures for human occupancy, commerce, and industry; public utilities, environmental control, and health and safety facilities; street and road improvements, highways, airports, waterways, and harbors; public transportation, communication and recreation systems; and facilities for education and cultural pursuits.

Social Forces

The social forces affecting value include all the characteristics and customs of the people that make up the community. Here is a partial list:

1.   Family sizes and age-group distribution in the neighborhoods and communities. Figure 5.3 shows one major recent change.

2.   Neighborhood stability and attitudes about property.

3.   Population growth, decline, and shifts at the community, regional, and national levels.

4.   Life-styles and living standards, often combined with other forces.

5.   Attitudes about law enforcement, the role of government, and individual responsibility.

6.   Attitudes about development, growth, and ecology.

7.   Attitudes toward public education.

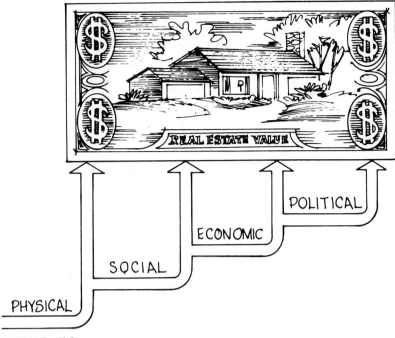

FIGURE   5.2
Forces Affecting Value

Economic Forces

Our earlier discussion of the essential elements of market value mentioned the interaction between utility, scarcity, and demand. These elements are, to a large extent, the products of our constantly changing economic climate. Thus, the major economic forces affecting real estate include:

1.   Income level of neighborhood and community residents.
2.   Employment opportunities and trends.

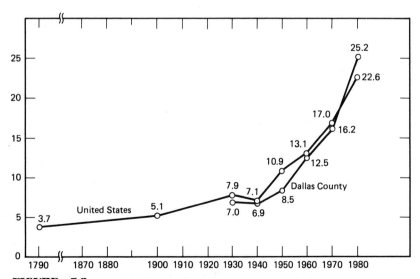

FIGURE   5.3

Percentage of One-Person Households: United States, 1790–1980; Dallas County, 1930–1980. (*Source: U.S. Census Reports*)

3. Level of wages.
4. Availability of money and credit, and interest rate levels.
5. Price levels and property tax burdens.
6. Personal savings levels and investment returns.
7. General business activity.
8. Supply and demand in housing.
9. Production of goods and services.

Real estate appraisers and analysts use statistics from many of these areas to help identify economic trends.

Political Forces

In Chapter 2 you learned about the authority of the government to restrict the use of property, to impose taxes for government expenditures, and to regulate property for the safety and welfare of the general public. Besides the limitations and burdens placed upon property by police power and taxation, there are many government programs that stimulate private enterprise and help create a healthy business climate. High employment, general economic stability, and business opportunity are partially the result of government involvement in our economy.

Various government actions, which can be classified as political forces, have a far-reaching effect on the value of real estate.

A partial list of political forces affecting value includes:

1. Zoning and land-use regulations.
2. Building safety regulations.
3. Environmental protection laws.
4. Police, fire, and health protection services.
5. Crime prevention, education, and recreation services.
6. Public works activity: power, water, transportation, and flood control.
7. Fiscal policy and taxation.
8. Monetary policy and controls.
9. Government-sponsored urban redevelopment and housing finance programs.
10. Regulation of industry and business.

In summary, the four great forces that maintain, modify, or destroy real estate value are known as physical, social, economic, and political forces. As you can see, these forces overlap; many factors appear under more than one category. For example, availability of money is listed under economic forces. Note that this same factor is heavily influenced by what is called monetary policy and controls, under the category of political forces. Even though the factors overlap and the forces interplay, carefully itemizing all relevant factors within each force can help the appraiser understand the conditions affecting each property to be appraised.

SECTION 5.2
HOW ECONOMIC TRENDS AFFECT REAL ESTATE

It is difficult to overstate the importance of real estate in the national economy. First, it represents two-thirds of the net worth of the country. Second, it is an essential part of the production process, since money or rent is universally paid for its use. Third, real estate is a major employer. Real estate development, construction, finance, management, and brokerage provide employment for a large segment of the population, accounting for billions of dollars of national income.

It is obvious that real estate does not exist in a vacuum. National and international events constantly change the social, economic, and political climate in which real estate functions. Economic trends are an important part of this climate.

Economic Trends and the Business Cycle

An economic trend is a pattern of related changes in some aspect of the economy. The most important national economic trends are those that affect the supply of, and demand for, goods and services. Examples include the balance of foreign trade, commodity price levels, and change in the annual gross national product.

National trends in the economy often help explain trends we can observe at local levels. Understanding economic trends at the regional, community, and neighborhood levels helps the appraiser interpret the market, cost, and income data that is pertinent to a particular appraisal. The local trends important to real estate include such factors as plant production, employment, construction activity, deed recordings, and the general volume of business. Changes in employment, income, price levels, and production have the greatest effect on real estate activity. Real estate price trends, such as that shown in Table 5.1, are the result of these local economic trends.

TABLE 5.1
Houston Average Annual Price of Homes Sold Through Reporting Multiple Listing Services

	Average Price of Houses Sold	Percent Change
1974	$36,262	——
1975	44,615	23.04
1976	48,476	8.65
1977	52,737	8.79
1978	59,455	12.74
1979	62,762	5.56
1980	76,615	22.07
1981	87,638	14.39
1982	97,840	11.64
1983	105,495	7.82

Source: Housing Sales in Texas, 1973–1983. Texas Real Estate Research Center, College Station, Texas, July 1984.

Some economic changes repeat in a seasonal pattern. Whether at the national, regional, or local levels, these usually are caused either by weather or social customs. For example, construction activity declines during the winter in many parts of the country. Travel and recreational activities typically increase during the summer. Retail sales volume often experiences a surge during the "Back-to-School" and Christmas seasons.

Information relating to economic trends is available from many banks, savings and loans, and trade associations. Government agencies such as the Federal Home Loan Bank, the Department of Commerce, and the Bureau of the Census are also major sources. Private research organizations often make data available to the appraiser upon request.

Cycles

Many important changes are cyclical in nature. The well-known business cycles are made up of expansions and contractions of general business activity that repeat on an average of every four years or so. Business cycles involve a series of stages. Prosperity increases to a point of stability, then declines; and a recession of the general economy follows. Finally, a recovery leads to growing prosperity, starting the cycle again. The length of the cycle is the time between one peak and the next.

The real estate cycle refers to the repeating changes noticeable in many areas of real estate, including the number of new subdivision lots, amount of new construction, and volume of sales. Some economists have contended that there are long real estate cycles lasting about 18 years. Recently, however, recurrent changes in real estate seem to involve a shorter cycle of three or four years in duration. For example, the recession associated with the 1982 "credit crunch" seemed to resolve itself rather quickly. Our understanding of the real estate cycle, especially the long cycle, is incomplete. However, the short cycle seems to relate directly to the cost and availability of money, as suggested previously.

Real Estate Supply Factors

In order to understand the supply of real estate, we must study both existing and new facilities. Usually, we must consider residential property separately from commercial and agricultural property. Some of the more important factors in this supply are listed and briefly discussed here.

Housing Supply

There are approximately 85 million housing units in the national supply. As Figure 5.4 shows, this existing supply continually changes, because of: (1) decreases caused by disasters, abandonment, demolition, and conversion to other uses and (2) increases resulting from new construction, conversion from other uses, and remodeling. To allow for new formations and building demolitions, the new construction of dwelling units should be approximately 3% of the existing inventory. In the late 1970s and early 1980s, the annual net additions have been below this amount.

Protecting the supply of existing housing is a matter of national concern. Hundreds of neglected and abandoned inner-city homes have been brought back into use in recent years by neighborhood revitalization pro-

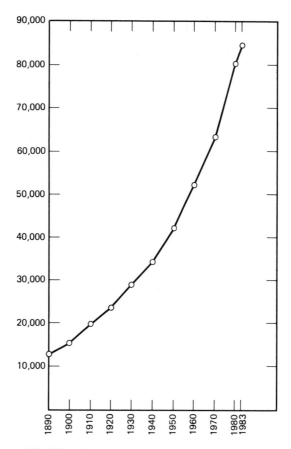

FIGURE 5.4
Real Estate Supply Factors: Housing Supply. Data for 1970, 1980, and 1983.
**(*Source*: U.S. Department of Commerce, *General Housing Characteristics:*
Annual Housing Survey 1970, 1980, 1983)**

grams, sometimes subsidized by state or local and federal funds. Examples include Dallas' Munger Place and San Antonio's Prince William district.

New Construction Activity

New construction spending in the United States is a good measure of conditions in this industry and the changing supply of real estate. In 1983 total new construction spending amounted to $262 billion, an increase of 13% from the previous year. Adjusting for inflation, the increase amounts to about 10%. Incidentally, the value of new construction in 1983 represented about 8.1% of the value of all goods and services produced in the nation.

Historically, the cost of construction has followed general price levels, increasing during inflation and declining somewhat during recessions. Added costs for labor and materials used in energy-efficient heating, cooling, and insulating systems are adding to the upward trend. Construction costs increased over 140% between 1971 and 1984. Higher costs tend to discourage development.

The Supply of Vacant Land

Political and social changes have greatly influenced the availability and cost of vacant land for real estate development. For example, environmental protection and subdivision reform laws, starting with the Federal Clean Air Acts of the early 1970s had the effect of decreasing the supply of buildable land and increasing the price. So did "open-space" and scenic easement agreements, where landowners agreed to restrict land to agricultural use in exchange for preferential property tax treatment (in Texas and a number of other states). "No-growth" or limited-growth local planning, coupled with time-consuming public approval procedures, has also increased the cost and reduced the supply of subdivided lots in many areas.

Real Estate Demand Factors

Earlier in this chapter we described demand as one of the essential elements of value. The two dominant factors that affect the real estate market are population and purchasing power. Although these two factors are obviously related, we shall try to look at them one at a time.

Population

All other things being equal, the demand for housing and the other forms of real estate increases in direct relationship to our population growth. Since there is a limited supply of land on earth, an increase in demand for real estate usually results in higher land prices. Thus, population increases usually mean higher real estate values.

Our interest in population change is not limited to the numerical increase or decrease that may occur at a particular location. In projecting housing needs, we study the composition and makeup of households. Thus, such population characteristics as birthrates, age, sex, occupation, and family income are important. The study of such characteristics, known as demography, makes it possible to estimate the rate of formation of new families and the probable changes in household composition. From this information we can predict specific demands for various types of housing, in terms of size, desired features, and price range. Figure 5.5 is an example of a study of changes in the number of persons per household.

Americans are often on the move—back and forth from city, suburb, and country and from region to region. The resulting migratory shifts continually affect the growth or decline of population in many communities. Population studies must therefore consider migration patterns as well as the national population growth factors already mentioned.

Purchasing Power

Population increases mean higher real estate demand only to the degree that the population has purchasing power. One measure of purchasing power is the size of the national labor force. The Bureau of Labor Statistics (BLS) makes long-range predictions in this area. These are based on birthrates, mortality rates, and worker-participation rates, all of which can be estimated from the national census information and other statistical data. According to BLS estimates, the labor force was expected to grow in the 1980s at an average yearly rate of between 1.8 and 2.0%, slowing from the

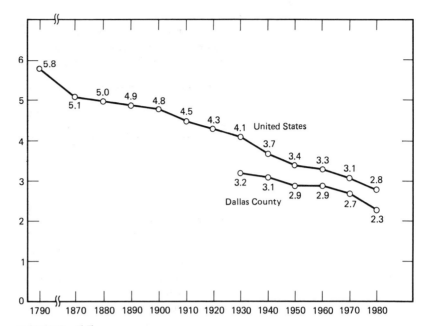

FIGURE 5.5
**Persons per Household: United States, 1790–1980; Dallas County, 1930–
1980. (*Source: U.S. Census Reports*)**

higher rate of the early 1970s, when unusually large numbers of both
young people and women were entering the work force.

Another important influence on purchasing power is the annual change
in the value of the gross national product (GNP). A gauge of the strength of
our economy, the GNP measures the value of all goods and services produced in the country. After allowances for inflation, the annual variations
in the GNP have ranged from a 2% decline to a 9% increase in the years
since World War II. Economists estimate that the average annual growth
rate of the GNP is approximately 5%, figured in constant dollars (i.e.,
adjusted for inflation). We are also interested in the amount of GNP per
person, that is, per capita. Table 5.2 shows how GNP per capita varies from
country to country, and also within the United States.

Statistics on employment, wage levels, and family income relate even
more directly to the purchasing power of the American consumer. These
figures allow economists to estimate the amount of money the average
family has available to spend after paying taxes. This is often called "disposable income," or "per-capita spendable income." Since the major share
of it is spent on living necessities, including housing, disposable income is
significant to the potential demand for real estate. Other statistical figures
used to study purchasing power include consumer-price-level indexes,
land-use and city-growth figures, and industrial-expansion rates.
Many economists pay close attention to the relative rates of increase
between inflation and disposable income. When disposable income
increases faster than inflation, the real estate demand tends to be
strong.

Purchasing power is also dependent on the availability of money for
mortgage financing, usually arranged by savings and loan associations,
banks, or insurance companies. The supply of money is largely dependent

TABLE 5.2
Approximate Per Capita Gross Domestic Product (GDP)[a]: Texas and the Dallas area Versus Leading Nations

Rank		GDP Per Capita (1979)
1	Qatar	$29,900.00
2	United Arab Emirates	24,360.00
3	Kuwait	18,390.00
4	*Texas*	*16,170.00*
5	Switzerland	15,750.00
6	*Dallas (11-county area)*	*14,011.00*
7	Denmark	13,700.00
8	West Germany	12,500.00
9	Sweden	12,390.00
10	Luxembourg	12,300.00
11	Netherlands	11,710.00
12	Belgium	11,370.00
13	Norway	11,360.00
14	Brunei	10,640.00
15	Iceland	10,600.00
16	France	10,010.00
17	United States	9,644.00
18	Saudi Arabia	9,500.00
19	Canada	9,350.00
20	Austria	9,150.00
21	United Kingdom	8,760.00
22	Japan	8,700.00
23	Australia	8,360.00
24	Bermuda	8,280.00
25	Faeroe Islands	8,280.00
26	Libya	6,960.00
27	Finland	6,530.00
28	Italy	5,700.00
29	East Germany	5,310.00
30	U.S.S.R.	5,210.00
31	Czechoslovakia	5,020.00
32	Bahrain	4,660.00
33	Israel	4,640.00
34	French Polynesia	4,550.00
34	New Zealand	4,220.00
36	New Caledonia	4,000.00
37	Martinique	3,950.00

[a] GDP was used rather than GNP since Texas and Dallas were included in the list. It is the same concept as GNP when referring to states, i.e., GDP = GNP for nations.
Source: Texas Fact Book 1984, Bureau of Business Research, University of Texas at Austin; *The World Fact Book,* U.S. Government Printing Agency and the Central Intelligence Agency, Washington, D.C., 1981).

upon the annual amount of personal savings and the general prosperity of the nation. As we shall see, the supply of money is also greatly affected by the monetary policy of the Federal Reserve System and the fiscal policy of government.

Federal Government Activity

Since real estate is our greatest national resource, the government makes use of programs involving real estate to pursue many of its social and economic goals. The areas of federal government activity that most directly affect privately owned real estate include housing and urban development, environmental protection and energy, monetary policy, and fiscal policy. We shall discuss these programs individually.

Housing and Urban Development Programs

Through the Department of Housing and Urban Development (HUD), the United States Government encourages low-rent housing and urban renewal projects. By stimulating new construction, the government helps create jobs, trying to attack social and economic problems simultaneously. Figure 5.6 is an example of a HUD program.

Other agencies fall within the HUD sphere of influence, including the Federal National Mortgage Association (FNMA), the Federal Housing Administration (FHA), and the Urban Renewal Administration.

Energy and the Environment

The government vested authority in the Environmental Protection Agency (EPA) to enforce federal pollution standards. The government also attempts to control the quality of air, water, and coastal-zone ecology by the requirement of environmental impact studies for major, proposed real estate developments and uses. State and local regulatory agencies sometimes carry out federal mandates in this area through their own elaborate regulatory activities. The Department of Energy was formed by Congress in 1977 to develop and carry out an overall plan to encourage efficient use of existing energy sources and development of new sources. One of the more

FIGURE 5.6
An Example of a Government Housing Program. (Photograph courtesy of Doug Frost)

direct effects of the program has been felt in the housing industry, where solar energy systems, electronic pilot lights, and minimum insulation standards were promoted. Income tax credits and preferential loan incentives have been adopted in order to increase the demand for energy-efficient homes.

Governmental Banking and Monetary Policy

The Federal Reserve System was established in 1913, as a semi-independent government agency. The function of the Federal Reserve Bank ("The Fed") is to regulate banking and the flow of money and credit. Today, the Federal Reserve System's goals are to stabilize the economy and control inflation, recession, and unemployment. The actions that the Federal Reserve Bank takes are called monetary policy actions.

An economic theory called the monetary theory holds that the supply of money in circulation influences the level of the economy—too much money leads to rapid expansion and resulting inflation; too little money causes contraction and recession or depression. The Federal Reserve Bank seeks to control the supply of money by buying and selling government securities, changing the discount rate (the interest rate the Federal Reserve Bank charges member banks for loans), and changing the amount of cash reserves that the Federal Reserve Bank requires member banks to hold. Because the Federal Reserve Bank controls the supply of money, this affects the supply of money for financing real estate and changes the cost of money—the interest rate. Changes in interest rates, in turn, change the market price of real estate. High rates tend to depress prices; low rates tend to increase them. The Federal Reserve Bank's Board of Governors and its Open Market Committee are constantly fine-tuning the money supply as they try to maintain a stable economy.

In a somewhat similar way the Federal Home Loan Bank Board regulates the availability of funds at its member savings and loan associations. Real estate financing is dependent on both sources.

Fiscal Policy

Our government also uses its taxation and spending powers to moderate recession, inflation, and unemployment, and to further the aims of various social reform programs. In 1984 the total federal government expenditures were estimated at $842 billion. In times of recession, increased government spending and reduced taxation act to stimulate the economy and increase the demand for land, labor, and capital. During periods of inflation, reduced government expenditures and increases in taxes will tend to reduce demand, thus reducing the pressure on prices and cooling inflation.

Real estate and business have long been favored areas for government programs designed to stimulate the economy. Home ownership is encouraged by allowing the mortgage interest and property taxes to be deducted for income tax purposes. Real estate and business investments benefit from the various income tax advantages, including interest and depreciation deductions for real estate holdings and investment tax credits on certain capital expenditures of private businesses.

The fiscal policy of government works parallel to its monetary policy. For example, the government provides money for real estate loans (through Federal Reserve money supply actions) beside insuring FHA loans and guaranteeing Veterans' Administration (VA) loans. As the state of the economy dictates, our federal government modifies its fiscal policy in well-publicized tax-reform acts that have become a familiar part of our economic system. Since the government budget has generally operated at a deficit in recent years, fiscal policy has had inflationary effects which monetary policy has not been able to counteract, although in recent years it has helped to moderate the rate of inflation.

In summary, it might be said that our economic environment is increasingly the result of governmental laws, regulations, controls, and policies intended to benefit the general public and to promote social equality. Although economists may disagree on the effects, and therefore the desirability, of such extensive government involvement, it appears that government laws and regulations will continue to shape and reshape our real estate economy.

SECTION 5.3
THE ECONOMIC
PRINCIPLES OF VALUATION

The economic principles of valuation are based on time-tested theories about real estate as both a form of, and a source of, wealth. As a form of wealth, real estate competes in the market with other goods and services. As a source of wealth, real estate combines with other economic forces and agents to produce income and other amenities for its users. Economic principles define and predict basic market patterns in both the consumption and development of real estate.

The principles of value covered in this section are the foundation for all appraisal methods and procedures. The principles apply collectively; none is independent. However, those that relate to real estate marketability help us understand the procedures and methods of the sales comparison and cost approaches. Those principles that relate to real estate productivity assist us primarily in understanding the various techniques of the income approach to value. Again, be aware that the principles often interrelate, as do the three value approaches. (See Chapter 3).

Principles of Real Estate Marketability

Real estate marketability is based on the following principles:

1. Principle of substitution.
2. Principle of conformity.
3. Principle of progression and regression.
4. Principle of change.
5. Principle of supply and demand.
6. Principle of competition.

Principle of Substitution
When a property can be easily replaced by another, the value of such property tends to be set by the cost of acquiring an equally desirable substitute property. A house listed at $180,000 will tend to sell for only $170,000 if there are others with the same amenities available for $170,000 in that

neighborhood. On the other hand, this same house might be worth only $165,000 if a similar one could be constructed nearby for that figure (including house and lot) with no unusual delay. Because it is a comparing tool for market price, cost, or income, the principle of substitution is basic to each of the three approaches to value.

Principle of Conformity

In many markets, maximum value results when properties in a neighborhood are relatively similar in size, style, quality, use, and type. This depends primarily on market attitudes but is particularly true in a relatively stable area of average homes. The rule of conformity predicts that a five-bedroom home in a neighborhood of three-bedroom homes, for example, would probably be an overimprovement. This means that its value would be less than if it were in a neighborhood of five-bedroom homes.

For high-valued homes or other types of properties, or in a high-demand market, much less importance is placed upon the conformity of physical features. In some markets, a greater amount of conformity is demanded than in others.

Principles of Progression and Regression

Lower-valued properties generally benefit (increase in value) from close proximity to many properties of higher value. This illustrates the principle of progression. Conversely, higher-valued properties tend to suffer (decrease in value) when placed in close proximity with lower-valued properties, following the principle of regression. The principles of progression and regression, which are related to the principle of conformity, assist us mainly in the analysis of sales in the market approach.

Principle of Change

Change is eternal. Changes in physical, social, economic, or political conditions constantly modify real estate use and value patterns. As suggested in Chapter 4, economists have a theory that neighborhoods, cities, and nations experience change in four stages, not surprisingly described as development, stability, decline (or old age), and renaissance or rebirth.

The appraiser must view real estate and its environment as always in transition. Since important change might be sudden or gradual, current market conditions cannot always be measured by assuming that past trends will continue unchanged. All things change, even the *rate* of change!

Principle of Supply and Demand

Prices and rent levels increase when demand is greater than supply and tend to decrease when supply exceeds demand. In real estate a strong demand for housing, for example, if coupled with effective purchasing power, can logically lead to a short supply and higher prices. When builders and developers increase production to meet demand, the new supply tends to force prices back to "normal." If severe competition among builders occurs during the shortage, oversupply often results, leading to weakened prices. In time, attractively low prices serve to bolster demand until the new supply has been absorbed. Theoretically, when supply and demand are in balance, market prices reflect the cost of production plus a reasonable profit. As we saw earlier in this chapter, a large number of factors affect the supply and demand of real estate.

Principle of Competition

Market demand generates profits and profits generate competition. When there is a strong demand for any form of real estate (as in houses, apartments, commercial or industrial facilities), developers and builders compete for the available profits by constructing new units for sale or rent. Competition usually holds down profits and keeps them stabilized. However, if excess profits are available, ruinous competition sometimes leads to oversupply and the collapse of prices.

Principles of Real Estate Productivity

The following principles govern the interaction between real estate productivity (benefits) and real estate value:

1. Agents of production.
2. Principles of surplus productivity, balance, and contribution.
3. Principle of increasing and decreasing returns.
4. Principle of highest and best use and consistent use.
5. Principle of anticipation.

Agents of Production

The benefits produced by real estate come in many forms. These may be intangible amenities, as in the case of certain benefits of home ownership, or they may be tangible, as in the case of dollar return on real estate investments. In economic terms all such benefits are labeled as real estate production. Such production always depends upon the use of labor, coordination, capital, and land. These are known as the four agents or factors of production. The balance between these factors critically affects the ability of any property to serve the purpose for which it was intended. To understand the potential value of real estate, we must define the four agents of production and understand their economic priorities. (See Figure 5.7.)

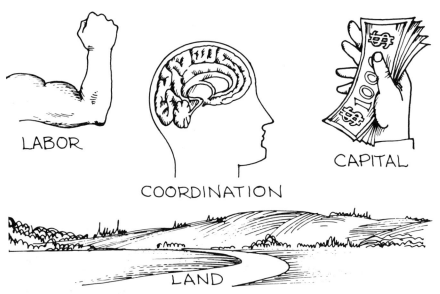

LABOR

COORDINATION

CAPITAL

LAND

FIGURE 5.7
The Agents of Production

Labor includes the cost of all operating expenses and all wages except management. It has the first claim on all money generated by production. Coordination, or management, includes charges for management and entrepreneurial effort. Such services have the second claim on returns of the enterprise. Capital includes all construction and equipment costs. Capital charges include return on, and repayment of, such investment monies. Capital charges have the third priority on production returns. Land includes the land, minerals, and air space. Economically, it has the last claim upon production revenues. This is why returns to the land are sometimes referred to as residual, that is, the residue remaining after all other claims have been satisfied. The concept of economic agents of production underlies many of the principles that follow.

Principles of Surplus Productivity, Balance, and Contribution

The net income or other benefits that remain after the cost of labor, coordination, and capital have been satisfied, has been described as residual returns to land. These same returns are often referred to as the surplus of productivity. Since the value of land depends upon its own earning power, the dollar amount of this surplus income becomes a basis for land value.

According to the principle of balance, a proper balance in the agents of production is required if the maximum value is to result from the costs invested. Consistent with the principle of conformity, an overly expensive home built upon a low-valued lot in a low-income neighborhood could probably *not* be sold for the full amount invested. A less expensive home is more likely to sell for its full cost and would represent a better investment. In a similar way the value of any individual agent of production depends not on its cost but on how much it contributes to the value of the whole. This is the principle of contribution. A swimming pool that adds $10,000 to the value of a home would be said to have a value of $10,000 even if it recently cost $15,000 to build.

The principle of surplus productivity forms the basis for the principle of increasing and decreasing returns and the principle of highest and best use.

Principle of Increasing and Decreasing Returns

It is possible to increase the value and potential income of real estate by adding appropriate improvements. However, there is a theoretical point of balance. Beyond that point additional expenditures will not result in proportional added value or income. This general rule is important in understanding the economics of development and investment for profit. If a builder can make a 20% profit by developing a small tract of large houses, such a project would be preferred to a larger tract of small houses where only a 15% profit might be made. Even if the larger subdivision promised a greater dollar profit, the higher percentage profit would generally be favored. In actual practice the investment decision would probably be based on a careful market study and also on the number of other investments available to the builder. The classic illustration of decreasing returns is in farming, where added increments of fertilizer do not result in equal additions to crop yield. After a point no matter how much fertilizer is added, no added production can be obtained.

Applied to existing properties, the principle of increasing and decreasing returns helps property owners make decisions about adding improvements or remodeling. If the market value of a home can be predicted to increase in proportion to the cost of a bedroom and bath addition, for example, the needed changes can be economically justified.

Principle of Highest and Best Use and Consistent Use

The highest and best use of a property means the most profitable or beneficial use that is likely. Such a use represents the theoretical balance between land and building investment that results in the greatest present value for the land, considering the economic life of the improvements or structures. The principle of highest and best use is helpful in determining land value and in making land-development feasibility studies.

In appraisal the highest and best use usually must be estimated both for the land as if it were vacant and also for the property as improved. Whether the two uses are different or the same will have a major impact upon all three value approaches, both as to the data selected and the methods of analysis.

As a corollary to the principle of highest and best use, the principle of consistent use requires that land and improvements be appraised on the basis of the same use. As a matter of economic consistency, it might be improper, for example, to add the "value" of a single-family structure to the value of the lot as if vacant, if this lot has an obvious highest and best use as an apartment site.

Principle of Anticipation

Property has value according to its expected or anticipated use, as measured by the benefits that should result from such use. A buyer with full knowledge of the uses and purposes to which a property may be put is concerned with future use, and not just previous use. The price he or she is willing to pay, then, is said to be equal to the present worth of such future benefits. Some of the benefits may be in the form of intangible amenities—as in the case of home ownership and use—or they may be in the form of tangible benefits such as rental income or capital gain. The principle of anticipation underlies the income approach to value.

SUMMARY

Although real estate is a basic and fundamental form of wealth, it has no intrinsic value. Its market value is a measure of the rights that owners control. Such rights are valued at prices set in the market, but in order to enter the market, the rights must have the four elements of utility, scarcity, demand, and transferability.

Four broad forces maintain, modify, or destroy real estate value. These important forces are physical, social, economic, and political in nature. In their many combinations and forms, these broad forces account for the dynamic nature of real estate value.

National and international events constantly change the social, economic, and political climate of our country. An understanding of real estate and its position in the national economy can help us understand the effect of these events.

We know that real estate is affected by changing business conditions such as employment, income and price levels, production volumes, and building construction costs. Thus, it is possible to analyze and better understand real estate by observing key supply and demand factors in the general economy. Economic trends tend to be cyclical in nature.

We have seen that the federal government is closely involved in vital areas affecting real estate. These include finance, housing, and urban development, as well as environmental protection and energy.

In this chapter, we also discussed in detail the economic principles that form the basis of most of the methods and procedures we use in appraisal. To summarize here, the principles that relate primarily to the marketability of real estate include the following concepts.

Substitution   The value of any replaceable property tends to equal its cost of replacement. As a comparing tool for market price, cost, or income, this principle underlies all three approaches to value.

Conformity   A reasonable degree of conformity is required for maximum value to result. A serious lack of market conformity in size, style, quality, or use type can be detrimental to value, particularly in single-family residential properties.

Progression and Regression   When a property does not conform in size or quality, its value tends to seek the level of the surrounding properties.

Change   Real estate values are constantly changed by the many social, economic, and political changes that occur in our society.

Supply and Demand   Real estate values tend to increase when effective demand exceeds supply, and tend to decrease when supply is greater than demand.

Competition   Market demand creates profits, which then generate competition. In turn, competition decreases profits because new supply tends to overshoot demand.

The valuation principles that relate mainly to the productivity of real estate primarily help the appraiser understand the income approach. We summarize them here:

Agents of Production   All real estate production depends upon the use of labor, coordination, capital, and land.

Surplus Productivity, Balance, and Contribution   Income that is available to land, after the other economic agents have been paid for, is known as the surplus of productivity. A proper balance of the agents maximizes the income available to land. The value of any agent is determined by its contribution to the whole.

Increasing and Decreasing Returns   Income and other benefits available from real estate may be increased by adding capital improvements only up to the point of balance in the agents of production. Beyond that point, the increase in value tends to be less than the cost increase.

Highest and Best Use, Consistent Use   The most profitable likely use of a property is its highest and best use. If the existing use does not qualify in this respect, consistency requires that the appraiser recognize this fact in the method used to value the existing structures.

Anticipation   Value is the present worth of future benefits, whether they be in the form of income or intangible amenities. The principle of anticipation is fundamental to the income approach to value.

Theory is no substitute for practical experience. But neither can any appraiser expect his or her intuitive knowledge always to suggest or recall just the right approach or procedure to follow in every valuation problem. When properly applied, the economic principles can suggest ways to solve problems encountered by the real estate appraiser.

IMPORTANT TERMS AND CONCEPTS

Agents of production
Amenity
Cycle, business, and real estate
Demography
Economic forces
Gross national product (GNP)
Physical forces
Political forces
Principle of:
  anticipation
  balance
  change
  competition
  conformity

consistent use
contribution
highest and best use
increasing and decreasing returns
progression and regression
substitution
supply and demand
surplus productivity
Purchasing power
Scarcity
Social forces
Transferability
Utility

REVIEWING YOUR UNDERSTANDING

1. One of the essential elements of value is:
   - **(a)** Highest and best use
   - **(b)** Transferability
   - **(c)** Location
   - **(d)** Environmental control

2. Which of the following is ineffective without purchasing power?
   - **(a)** Utility
   - **(b)** Supply
   - **(c)** Demand
   - **(d)** Level of wages

3. The broad forces affecting value do not include:
   - **(a)** Physical
   - **(b)** Price trend
   - **(c)** Political
   - **(d)** Social

4. Political forces affecting value may include:
   - **(a)** Life-style and living standards
   - **(b)** Topography
   - **(c)** Education and recreation services
   - **(d)** None of the above

5. The real estate supply factors include:
   - **(a)** Housing supply
   - **(b)** New construction activity
   - **(c)** Both of the above
   - **(d)** None of the above

6. Environmental protection and subdivision reform laws affecting the availability and cost of vacant land include:
   - **(a)** The Federal Clean Air Acts of the early 1970s
   - **(b)** Open-space and scenic easement agreements

      (c) Zoning changes to reduce the density of use

      (d) All of the above

7. Areas of government activity that directly affect privately owned real estate include:

      (a) Housing and urban development

      (b) Environmental protection laws

      (c) Monetary and fiscal policy

      (d) All of the above

8. Our government's fiscal policy helps control inflation by:

      (a) Regulating the flow of money and credit

      (b) Encouraging low-rent housing and urban development

      (c) Reducing taxes

      (d) All of the above

9. The four agents of production do not include:

      (a) Land

      (b) Waste

      (c) Coordination

      (d) Labor

      (e) Capital

10. The principle that would prevent an appraiser from appraising a lot for its commercial potential, and the improvement thereon for residential value, is the:

      (a) Principle of increasing and decreasing returns

      (b) Principle of consistent use

      (c) Principle of highest and best use

      (d) Principle of anticipation

CHAPTER SIX

PROPERTY INSPECTION AND ANALYSIS: THE SITE

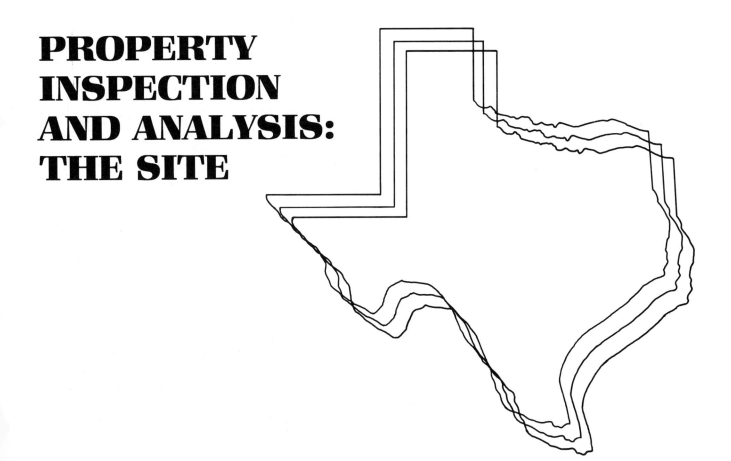

PREVIEW

This chapter takes you through the actual site inspection, by describing how each step is performed, and why. It explains how to inspect the property, what information to gather, and how to use this information. Several examples illustrate the reasons for site analysis, including the most important, the estimation of highest and best use. Finally, this chapter shows how to calculate the area of lots and buildings, a skill that is essential in both site and building analysis.

When you have completed this chapter, you should be able to:

1. List three reasons for making site inspections.
2. Prepare for the site inspection.
3. List the three main categories of site information.
4. Calculate the area of a square, rectangle, triangle, trapezoid, and circle.

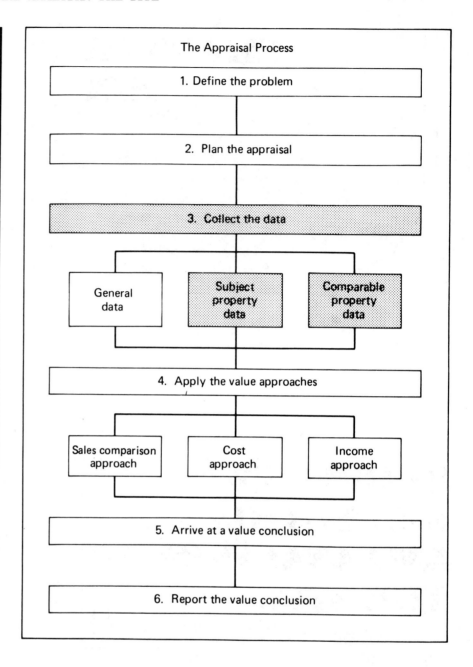

The Appraisal Process

1. Define the problem

2. Plan the appraisal

3. Collect the data

General data | Subject property data | Comparable property data

4. Apply the value approaches

Sales comparison approach | Cost approach | Income approach

5. Arrive at a value conclusion

6. Report the value conclusion

SECTION 6.1
PREPARING TO INSPECT THE SITE

Before performing the site inspection, you should ask yourself two questions: "Why am I inspecting the site?" and "What information do I need to gather?" Answering these questions in advance allows you to plan your site inspection and do a faster and better job. You should also try to ascertain whether there may be any special site problems so that you can study them during the actual inspection.

**Reasons for
Inspecting and Analyzing the Site**

Overall, there are three reasons for inspecting and analyzing the site.

1. To estimate the highest and best use.
2. To identify key features.
3. To identify possible problems.

Highest and Best Use

The most important reason for inspecting and analyzing a site is to collect information that you will need in order to estimate the highest and best use of the site, which means:

*That reasonable and probable use that will support the highest present value . . . as of the effective date of the appraisal.**

The highest and best use definition includes three criteria:

1. The use must be physically practical.
2. There must be a reasonable probability that the use is legally acceptable.
3. The use must generate a higher present land value than any other use, based upon the demand for these uses.

The first criterion in determining the highest and best use is to consider only uses that are physically practical. For example, uses that require a larger site than the subject property or are lacking needed utilities should be eliminated.

Second, consider only those uses of the land that are allowed under current zoning laws (or other similar constraints) and those uses for which there is a likelihood of getting the necessary legal approvals. Such approvals might include rezoning, a use permit or variance, an Environmental Impact Report, and so on.

Third, alternative uses must be economically analyzed to determine which can prove out the highest land value. Hence, you must consider the site as if vacant, even if it is presently improved with a new building.

Why does the appraiser estimate the highest and best use for the site? The answer is that a property may have different values for different potential uses. For example, the selling price of a 50 × 100 foot lot zoned for a triplex is usually higher than for a similar lot zoned for a single house. Whether improved or vacant, land can have different prices for different uses.

In estimating highest and best use, only uses that are likely to be in demand and profitable at that location should be considered. In this case, "profitable" refers to the ability of the use to return enough benefits to justify the capital invested in the land and buildings.

* B. N. Boyce, *Real Estate Appraisal Terminology*, rev. ed., Ballinger Publishing Co., Cambridge, Mass., 1981.

Estimating the highest and best use is a step that must precede the collection of data. In the cost approach, for example, the appraiser must estimate highest and best use before researching comparable land sales. Otherwise, there is no way to select the comparables. Also, this same highest and best use must be considered when estimating building cost depreciation so that the building value will be calculated on the same use basis as the land.

Existing improvements may or may not represent the highest and best use of the land. Hence, formal appraisals must also consider the highest and best utilization of the property as it is presently improved.

Identify Key Features

The appraiser should identify and note the significant characteristics of the property under appraisal. Although there are many factors to be considered in the site analysis, they may be summarized in a few questions:

1. *Quantity*   What size is the land parcel?
2. *Quality*   What is its quality? How good is the location?
3. *Features*   Does it have unique features or special appeal?
4. *Condition*   How well is the site protected and maintained?

The appraiser uses the significant characteristics to select comparable sales and establish the major distinctions between these sales and the property being appraised.

Identify Possible Problems

Another reason for inspecting and analyzing the site is to help identify possible problems. The appraiser is not trained to be an expert in every problem that may exist; however, it is helpful to be aware of the most common site problems and to recognize clues to their existence. Any unresolved issues can then be referred to qualified experts for their analysis.

Site problems could be of a legal nature, such as a nonconforming use, an easement by unrecorded agreement, or an unauthorized encroachment upon the land. Problems could also be physical ones, as suggested in Figure 6.1, such as flood risks, poor soils, proximity to highly flammable brush-covered areas, or excessive noise and dust caused by nearby industry or construction. Real estate is subject to many problems of this type. The responsibility of the appraiser is to estimate market value. If the market considers these problems and adjusts prices because of them, then the appraiser must do likewise. Estimating the effect of a land problem upon property value may require expensive study for which the client is unwilling to pay. In such cases, the appraiser should note in the report that the reliability of the appraisal is reduced.

What Data and Tools Are Needed?

It is wise to gather certain basic information about the site before the actual inspection. Having information in advance can make the fieldwork more efficient and can prevent accidentally overlooking any part of the property during the inspection.

Data

The size and shape of the parcel should be known; therefore, the appraiser should have a map or drawing of the site. Size and shape are likely to affect

"Gentlemen, I have some bad news about your proposed site."

FIGURE 6.1
Identify Possible Problems. (Bill Shelly, from *Shopping Center World*, May 1, 1980)

the usefulness of the parcel. For example, a triangular shape may or may not be a disadvantage to a particular parcel. It could depend upon the way the building is facing, what size building the zoning will allow, and even what use is involved.

Information on such legal characteristics as zoning and easements can also be acquired in advance. With such knowledge, a more intelligent site inspection is possible. Certain data on the neighborhood and city should also be known in advance. Appraisers often like to get an overall picture of the site and its surroundings by driving through nearby shopping areas, major transportation routes, areas of possible conflicting land uses, and so on. In some instances, appraisers will drive for several blocks in each direction around the site, in order to clarify their understanding of the neighborhood's characteristics.

Information on the availability of utilities is also useful prior to inspection. The absence of any municipal water supply in an area suggests a reliance upon private wells. Observing the location of existing wells will give you an idea of the chances of drilling a successful well on the subject property. Similarly, the absence of city sewer lines may mean that a sewer line extension is needed or that a septic tank and drainfield must be installed. The appraiser usually *cannot* tell with certainty whether septic tanks will be permitted (most health departments require a percolation test performed by a civil engineer). However, a check of public records as to soil type, the topography of the land, the minimum-size parcel required, and the proximity of neighboring structures and wells can suggest the likelihood of such approval.

Appraisers may also collect certain market data prior to making a field inspection. This data could include land sales, improved property sales, or market rent comparables. Collecting this information in advance allows

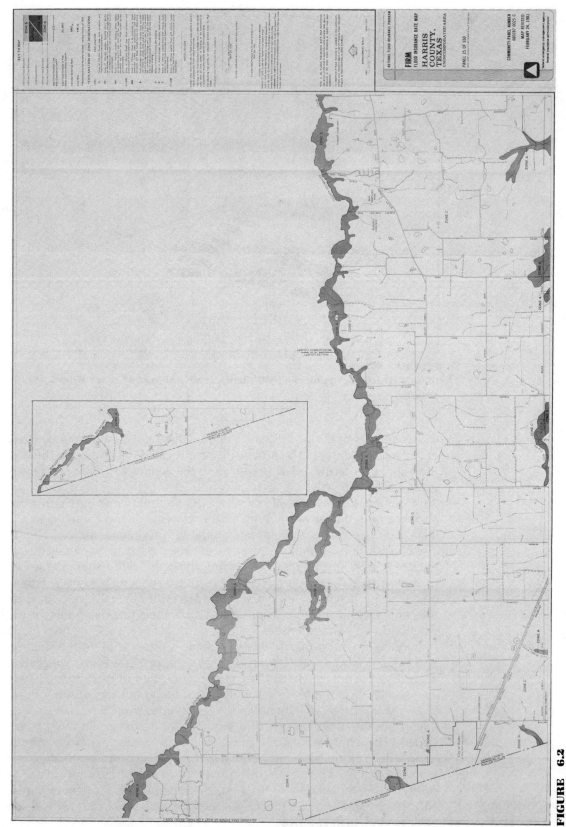

FIGURE 6.2
Flood Insurance Rate Map for Harris County. (Courtesy U.S. Dept. of Housing and Urban Development)

106

comparables to be inspected on the same field trip as the inspection of the property being appraised. However, collecting the comparables in advance is only possible when the appraiser has a fairly good idea of the type of comparables that will be needed. In some cases, information from the client can provide advance clues.

Data Sources

The data necessary for site inspection comes from a number of sources. For example, zoning information is usually acquired from city or county planning offices. Information on flood-prone areas is found in the 100-year flood maps produced for the National Flood Insurance Program and is available from county engineering departments. Figure 6.2 shows one such map. Geologic and topographic maps are produced by the national and state topographic and geologic agencies. The best place to inspect these maps is at city and county engineering departments. Site data may also be obtained from various other sources that are covered in Chapter 8.

Tools and Equipment

Since various tools and equipment are used during the inspection, it is a good idea to have this equipment ready in advance. Some appraisers use a standard checklist to ensure that they collect all needed information during the inspection. Appraisers use either their own checklists or the actual form on which the appraisal is presented, such as the FHLMC form "70" (also known as the FNMA or Fannie Mae 1004). A copy of the site description portion of the FHLMC 70 is shown in Figure 6.3. These forms will be discussed later.

Here is a list of tools commonly used during the site inspection:

1. A checklist or form and a clipboard.

2. A notepad and sheets of graph paper for making sketches of the property.

3. A measurement device such as a cloth or steel tape (usually 50 or 100 feet long), or a measuring roller, as shown in Figure 6.4. An additional 10-foot steel tape comes in handy.

4. An ice pick in a sheath is a common tool in many field kits. It may be used to anchor the end of the tape or to test for possible wood rot.

5. A camera to take photographs of the property either for the report itself or to keep on file.

6. A road map of the area to help you locate the site under appraisal.

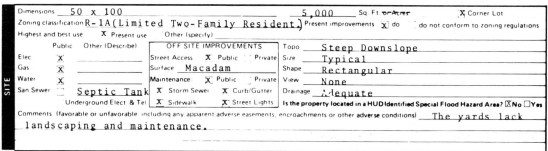

FIGURE 6.3

Site Description Section of the FHLMC Form "70"/FNMA Form 1004

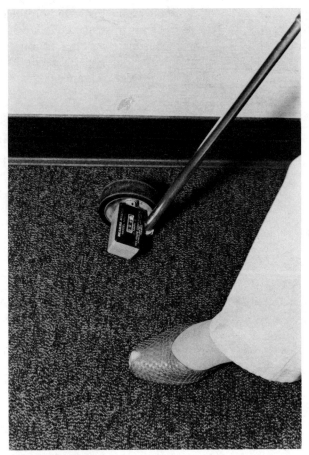

FIGURE 6.4
Measuring Roller. (Photograph Courtesy of Doug Frost)

An official county map and a map book can be especially helpful. Other kinds of maps may provide essential data about the land itself. United States Geological Survey topographical maps are helpful in rural areas. These show land contours and other important geographic features, such as creeks. On the other hand, geologic maps show 100-year flood plain contour and other significant land features that might affect the property being appraised. Flood maps are necessary to identify areas with the highest risk of flooding. Many real estate lenders require flood insurance for properties subject to a high risk of flooding.

SECTION 6.2
MAJOR CATEGORIES OF SITE INFORMATION

An appraiser identifies and records many different aspects of a site and its environs. These aspects fall into three main categories, shown in Figure 6.5.

Important Physical Characteristics

The physical features most important to the site's overall utility should be carefully noted in the site inspection. There are five main topics to be studied, as noted.

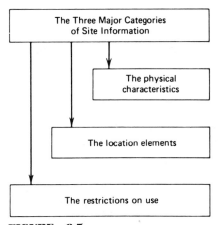

FIGURE 6.5
Information for a Site

1. Size and shape
2. Topography, soil, and drainage.
3. Form of holding.
4. Lot type and orientation
5. On-site and off-site improvements.

Size and Shape

Aside from location, the most important detail of the site is its overall size. The size, or area, of the lot is usually expressed in terms of square feet or acres, although older measurements are sometimes used. With the conversion to the metric system, appraisers may someday measure in square meters. Often, site area has been calculated and noted on the local assessor's maps or can be calculated from dimensions of the property as shown by the maps.

In some cases, the gross area of a site is not as important as its useful or net area. Depending upon topography, shape, zoning, soil type, and so on, some lots may have a useful area considerably smaller than the gross area. Indeed, the useful area could change with different uses. This difference could be great enough to influence the estimate of highest and best use.

Shape is a particularly important characteristic of the site. Shape generally refers to the relationship between the parcel's width and depth. Some lots are too narrow for ideal use, and others are too shallow. Shape can also refer to the configuration of the lot. Property with an ideal shape on a map may be found upon inspection to have features (such as a swamp or a cliff) that alter the shape of the usable area of the parcel, making it less useful (see Figure 6.6).

FIGURE 6.6
Be Sure to Check the Useful Shape of the Lot

The length of the property's "frontage" should also be recorded. Frontage is the boundary line or lot side that faces, or is adjacent to, a street or highway. The frontage length sometimes affects the economic usefulness of a site.

The depth of the parcel is significant. The projected use of a parcel determines its appropriate dimensions. A deep lot, that is, one that extends far back from the street, may be efficient for one type of use and not for another. When the rear portion of a lot obviously has less value than the front portion, the lot has what is known as "excess depth."

The usefulness of the excess depth will not only vary from use to use, but also from time to time, and community to community. This makes it difficult to evaluate the value of deeper parcels properly. Over the years, studies of how lot value varies with depth have been made. These studies resulted in depth tables. Usually, they have considered only one time period, one land use, or one town. Although depth tables may provide a means to adjust for depth differences, they are generally limited by their lack of connection to the particular market under study. One well-known depth table suggests that for the standard depth lot in a particular location, 40% of the value lies in the first one-quarter of the depth, 30% of the value is in the second one-quarter of the depth (making 70% of value in the first one-half of the depth), 20% for the third one-quarter, and 10% for the last, or back, one-quarter of the depth. If the standard depth in one community is 200 feet, and the going market prices for lots in this location is $25,000, a lot that is 50 feet deep would be considered to be worth 40% × $25,000 or $10,000. A lot that is 100 feet deep, or one-half the standard depth, would be considered 40% + 30%, or 70% × $25,000 or $17,500. Of course, zoning ordinance requirements for minimum lot size, or minimum front yards, can invalidate the results of such an analysis.

It is important to remember that published depth tables report the average values found in a particular market studied. There is no guarantee that these values apply to another market or type of property. Further, the values could have changed over the years since the study was made. Thus published depth tables are generally unreliable. Market sales, if available, are preferred.

As mentioned earlier, the size of a parcel may influence how the property will be developed. One location may have two different uses that are equally feasible but require different-sized parcels. In this case, a premium could be gained by combining two parcels to form a larger site (known as an assemblage or plottage) or by subdividing a larger site into parts. Any value enhancement or premium depends upon whether or not the larger or smaller site is in greater demand relative to the existing supply. When parcels are combined to generate increased value, the bonus obtained from this is called plottage value. Although lot assemblage does not always create plottage value, the appraiser should generally look at the size and usefulness of the subject parcel to evaluate the chances of combining this parcel with neighboring ones into an assemblage that does produce plottage value. If land subdivision seems in order, the feasibility and cost of such a process should also be investigated. For every land use, there is an optimum land size and configuration; when such lots are not available, they can sometimes be created by subdividing larger parcels or assembling smaller parcels.

Topography, Soil, and Drainage

After examining the size and shape of the parcel, the appraiser should look at the topography, soil, and drainage of the site. Topography (or contour) refers to the surface of the parcel and its particular features. These features may include hills, valleys, creeks, ravines, cliffs, and slopes. Although land with irregular topography is generally more costly to build upon, certain features can be assets or liabilities, depending upon the use and size of the parcel and the location of roads and utilities. For instance, slopes may command a premium when developed to take advantage of a good view of the surrounding area. However, if there are problems with providing utilities or gaining access for building materials during construction, slopes can cause substantial value penalties. The pros and cons of any land feature must be carefully evaluated and compared. While looking at the topography of the parcel, the appraiser should also look at the surroundings. What might be an impressive view may be obstructed by a roof or tree on a neighbor's property. Usually, the highest knoll in the area has the greatest value as a homesite because lower knolls may have others looking down on them. Do surrounding parcels pose threats of landslides or rock falls? This too can seriously affect the value of the subject property.

Soil is another important aspect of the land utility and value. A steep slope in rock is more stable than a steep slope in sand. Clays that expand when wet may make construction impossible without expensive excavations. Soils may be of such poor composition that pilings may be necessary or soil may be too moist for septic tanks to work. Public maps may indicate that the site is situated in a soil liquefaction area. Certain geologic factors may preclude *any* building on the site.

A topic closely related to topography and geology is water drainage. The natural topography creates its own drainage through natural systems of rainwater runoff and creeks. People modify the natural drainage and also construct drainage systems such as underground drain tile, culverts, and lined ditches. When surveying the site, the appraiser must decide how present and future drainage systems will affect the planned use of the site. The appraiser may find that the property is located in a mapped floodplain or flood zone, or that excessive soil erosion is being caused by uncontrolled drainage runoff. These and other factors can greatly influence the value of the site.

Form of Holding

Important site characteristics also involve the form of real estate holding, the type of lot, its orientation and physical access. The form of holding refers to the legal form of the parcel. The most common legal entity is the conventional detached lot, where the site is the entire lot. Its frontage will be on either a street or a permanent access easement.

The second type of legal entity involves a subdivided lot on which the improvements sit, plus an undivided interest in appurtenant common areas. These common areas could include recreational facilities, parking areas, driveways, walks, lawns, open space, and so on. This second type of legal entity is known by a number of names. Perhaps the most common of these is the planned unit development (PUD), named after the zoning category under which it is often developed. The term town house is also sometimes applied, named after the town-house building design style frequently used (see Figure 6.7). In some jurisdictions, this second type of legal entity is referred to as a condominium. More commonly, the term condo is used. The third type of legal entity involves the ownership of a defined block of airspace in a building, plus an undivided interest in the common areas. Such ownership is called a condominium or an airspace condominium (Figure 6.8). The difference between the planned unit development (PUD) type and the condominium is that the dwelling in a PUD is

FIGURE 6.7
Town House. (Photograph Courtesy of Doug Frost)

FIGURE 6.8
Airspace Condominiums. (Photograph Courtesy of Doug Frost)

built on a separate, wholly owned lot; in a condominium, the dwelling is one of a number of units that share one piece of ground. Both the PUD and condominium typically include an undivided interest in common areas. Of course, condominium ownership includes an undivided interest in the structural support and the building systems such as the pipes and drains necessary for the unit to function.

Since both PUDs and condominiums have common areas that are part of the total site, the appraiser's site inspection must review both the unit site *and* the common areas.

THE DE MINIMUS PUD   Lenders have created two categories of PUDs. The first is labeled a De Minimus PUD. It is defined as a PUD in which the unit owner (1) owns the fee title to the unit's lot, (2) maintains the unit interior *and* exterior, and (3) was primarily motivated to purchase the dwelling unit rather than the benefits of the recreation facilities or other amenities. The first of these three criteria is determined by the project's manner of subdivision and the second by its recorded conditions, covenants, and restrictions (CC&Rs). The third is a matter of judgment, depending primarily on how extensive are the commonly owned facilities. Usually, the developer submits the project to FNMA for approval as a De Minimus PUD. Approval allows lenders to process loans in the same manner as for detached homes so that each loan can be funded and closed separately.

The second category of PUD does not have a name. However, loans for PUDs that do *not* meet the De Minimus criteria usually must be processed as airspace condominium loans. This means that the loan package must include an appraisal of the entire development.

Lot Type and Orientation

Another physical characteristic to consider is the type of lot and its orientation to other lots and streets that surround it. The major types of lots are shown in Figure 6.9. The most common type of lot is the interior lot. This is a lot that fronts on only one street. Another common type is the corner lot, which has frontage (and usually access) on two intersecting streets. In the past, corner lots often sold at a premium over interior lots because people with home offices, such as doctors and lawyers, needed a separate side entrance for the office. Today, residential corner lots often command a premium because of the easy access to the rear yard. Such access is very desirable in communities that prohibit the parking of mobile homes or trailers on streets or in the front driveways of houses. When residential lots have wide frontages, the corner premium may disappear. Side yards on such lots are sometimes wide enough to allow easy parking for recreational vehicles. However, commercial corner lots nearly always sell for a premium price because of the increased frontage or showcase space. In summary, corner premiums today depend upon the use of the lot, its location, and its size.

A less common type of lot is the key lot. This is a lot that has several other lots backing onto its side yard. A key lot is often considered a less valuable lot than other types because of a loss of privacy.

A cul-de-sac lot is one that is located at the end of a dead-end street. Because most cul-de-sacs are now made with a curved turnaround, the lots taper and have very little street frontage. Although this may make guest

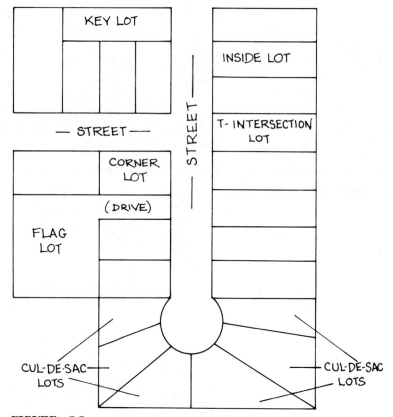

FIGURE 6.9
Common Types of Lots. (Courtesy of the California Department of Real Estate)

parking difficult, the disadvantage is usually counterbalanced by large backyards, extra privacy, and reduced street traffic. Cul-de-sac lots are usually considered especially desirable for family housing because of the large rear play area and the relatively greater traffic safety from reduced auto traffic.

Another type of lot is the flag lot. This is a rear lot, behind other houses or lots, with a long narrow access. The lot and access route resemble a flag and flagpole. Flag lots usually have excellent privacy but may be inconvenient for visitors since street numbers are hard to find. In snow country the long driveway is a drawback. The flag lot is also less desirable than other lots for people who enjoy having their attractive house viewed by the public.

Still another type of lot is the T-intersection lot, which is a lot at the end of a T intersection. In some cases, T-intersection lots suffer from the danger of speeding cars failing to turn the corner. However, T-intersection lots do not usually sell for a lower price and may even sell for a premium because the site can be seen from a long distance down the intersecting streets. This is particularly true of commercial parcels.

Just as important as the orientation of the lot to surrounding streets and other lots is its orientation to sun, prevailing winds, views, and surrounding land features. For example, a lot with desirable views of land or sea will command a higher selling price. Generally, water views are worth more than land views.

Views and exposure may depend upon whether a lot slopes uphill or downhill from the street access. Upslope lots are generally more expensive to build on than downslope lots and therefore may sell for less if there are no compensating factors.

Orientation to the sun is becoming more important as we consider the utilization of solar energy. For maximum solar efficiency, houses should have the glassed areas facing south and the windowless areas facing north. If the best views are to the north, only careful design will produce an energy-efficient house that also benefits from the good view.

The appraiser should check to see if the orientation advantages of the house can be considered permanent. New construction on the lot across the street or the growth of vegetation may destroy advantages of view or sun exposure. Protection may be provided by a view easement across the adjacent properties, by tract restrictions that require tree topping, by city ordinances, or simply by the natural topography of the land.

In order for any site to be utilized, it must have convenient access. Access depends upon the type of lot as well as the street and traffic patterns. Lots accessible only by circuitous travel routes will normally sell for less than competing lots located on more direct routes. Access routes in hilly, older neighborhoods can be so winding and narrow as to block fire trucks or other emergency vehicles. This can have a substantial impact on values.

Physical access is affected by the topography of the area. Banks, ravines, slopes, and creeks may all restrict access or make a potential access route an expensive proposition. Figure 6.10 notes this problem. It may also be necessary to obtain easements in order to allow physical access to a land-locked parcel (one with no road frontage or access). Remember that easement access can involve road construction and maintenance costs as well as the cost of buying the easement itself.

FIGURE 6.10
A Question of Access

On-Site and Off-Site Improvements

Improvements to the site represent another important part of the physical characteristics of a site. On-site improvements may consist of earth leveling: grading, filling in, compaction, or excavation. The property may be landscaped with trees, lawns, and shrubs and may also have a sprinkler or drainage system. In addition, there may be retaining walls or fences, walks, paths, or patios. Because some of these features may eventually be appraised as improvements instead of as land, they must be inspected and noted in the same manner as the main building improvements (to be discussed in the next chapter).

Adjacent off-site improvements include the width and paving of streets, the presence or absence of curbs, gutters, sidewalks, alleys, street lighting, and parking facilities. Some appraisal books include utilities as part of the off-site improvements. Here utilities are considered as part of the characteristics of that location.

Analysis of Site Location Elements

There is a humorous saying that there are three important factors in the value of property: location, location, and location! Analyzing the location of a property can be done in three easy steps, as shown in Figure 6.11. The first is to compare the site to the properties around it. The second is to note the availability of utilities to service the site. The third is to look at the transportation systems or facilities that link this location to the greater metropolitan area.

Comparison with Neighborhood Properties

When comparing the site to neighborhood properties, it is necessary to determine whether there are nearby properties with conflicting uses. Are neighboring properties being used in such a way that they will interfere with the usefulness of the subject property? Use conflicts result from unwanted noise, odors, or other negative characteristics such as those described in Chapter 4. Next, note the property's amount of privacy. Privacy can be measured by what other people hear or see of you and by what you hear or see of them. However, the standards of the local market will judge its value. In some markets, privacy is more highly valued than in others.

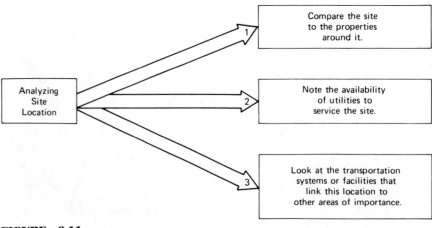

FIGURE 6.11
Site Location Analysis

Consider the impact of the neighboring properties on the value of the subject property. How are they maintained (judging by the standards of the neighborhood)? Is there evidence of renovation or remodeling? Does the immediate area have a history of high, average, or low crime rates, or of family or civic disturbances? Obviously, you must also consider whether the past record may be changing.

In the analysis of the site, it is also important to see how the site conforms to the average site characteristics in the neighborhood. Whatever the size, shape, and topography of the property being appraised, it must be put into the scale of those characteristics in that neighborhood. A one-acre site, for example, poses a special appraisal problem when surrounded by quarter-acre sites.

Utilities

The availability of utilities is the second element to consider in rating location. Cost, restrictions on service, reliability, and the sources of each utility are all pertinent considerations. This review should focus not only on water supply, trash collection, and electricity service, but also on telephone, cable TV, natural gas, or propane service. Provisions for either septic tank systems or public sewers, as well as storm runoff systems, should be carefully noted.

Since the services provided by utility companies are available over wide areas, the appraiser may not need to research utility company information for each and every appraisal assignment. It is worth noting, however, that many assignments will lie at boundaries where the availability or cost of utility services changes dramatically. The appraisal of existing properties, where services are already provided, will differ from vacant properties. The future cost of providing necessary services usually has a major impact on the value of a vacant site.

Transportation

The third element of site location is transportation and transportation access. In modern living, any site has value only if it can be connected to other sites where we live, work, shop, and play. Generally, the poorer the transportation and accessibility, the lower the value of the property. When reviewing transportation, the appraiser should be sure to consider both public and private systems. With public transportation, check to see how close the property is to public transportation systems and loading points: How well does this system connect to the main travel points? Find out the cost of the system, the frequency of schedules, and the travel time between the property and the places to which users of this property might travel.

The appraiser's concern for transportation services will differ depending upon the type of property under appraisal. With a residential site, for example, you should check the availability, cost, and convenience of the public transportation system for commuting and shopping. When appraising a commercial location, on the other hand, the concern is for midday shopping travel, easy access to working people, and access to those transferring between different transportation routes or lines.

In the review of private transportation, there are other things to consider. How close is the subject property to highways or arterial streets? How convenient is it to get on and off the freeway or throughway from this property? Is it convenient from both directions? Consider the probable time and patterns of travel of the users of this property. These should vary,

depending upon the peak traffic hours and the destination of the commuters.

Private and Public Restrictions

Nothing can be more important than understanding the public and private
restrictions on the use of property. As detailed in Chapter 2, such restrictions have a significant impact on value because they help to determine the
highest and best use. Thus the appraiser's analysis of the site must include
an investigation of private restrictions, public restrictions, and property tax
information. All of these factors may be important in comparing properties
or in determining the feasibility of different uses.

Private Restrictions

Private restrictions take many forms, ranging from simple deed restrictions
to complex agreements between groups of owners. The most simple deed
restriction might specify the minimum size of structures. For example, in a
residential subdivision, houses may be required to have at least 2,000
square feet of living area. Some older deed restrictions prohibited the sale
of alcoholic beverages. There are deed restrictions that forbid commercial
use of the property and some that restrict the property *solely* to commercial
or industrial uses.

The most complex private restrictions include those typical of planned
unit developments or condominiums. These are known as association
agreements. Here each property is part of a larger group of parcels and
is bound by the conditions, covenants, and restrictions that apply to all
properties within that association. Such agreements may mandate paint
colors; degree of maintenance; type of landscaping; type of shades, awnings, and drapes; and so on. These restrictions should be reviewed by the
appraiser and discussed with the association if a judgment is to be made as
to their effect on the value of the property.

Another type of possible restriction is an easement. This could be a
utility easement for underground gas or water lines, power lines, power
poles, telephone lines or poles, or telephone pole anchors. There could be
drainage easements that allow water to flow from a nearby property onto
the property being appraised, flood easements allowing the federal government to flood portions of the property from time to time, or aviation
easements (allowing aircraft to fly low over the parcel while using a nearby
airport). Clearly, such easements have some impact upon the use of the
property and its value.

Leases are another example of private restrictions. Depending upon the
length of the lease, the rent to be paid, and other terms, the impact on
property use and value can be significant. Appraisals made of a property
that is subject to an existing lease must consider *all* landlord and tenant
covenants that affect the benefits received by the owner. This topic will be
discussed further in Chapter 17.

Public Restrictions

There are many categories of public restrictions and the importance of
these restrictions is increasing. Zoning regulations are the most common
form. Common zoning regulations cover permitted uses, the density or
intensity of use, setback or yard requirements, height restrictions, and
parking requirements. Regulations for obtaining variances from these restrictions will differ from ordinance to ordinance. Zoning regulations will

also vary in how they handle a nonconforming use. This term refers to a use that is not allowed under the current zoning but was on this site before the ordinance was adopted. The appraiser must understand these ordinances and their provisions and be alert to their possible effect on the property. In residential income properties, for example, the parking requirements can combine with the coverage requirements and the shape of the parcel in such a way that an odd-shaped parcel might be uneconomic to build upon. Therefore, the parcel can end up containing fewer apartment dwelling units or providing smaller amounts of recreation space than would otherwise be possible. Public restrictions today also include community master plans and regional plans, both of which are growing in size and scope. Increasingly, these plans control the content of zoning ordinances.

Another category of public restriction is the building and safety regulations, including the housing code, the building code, the plumbing code, electrical code, and so on. Because these codes differ from jurisdiction to jurisdiction, there can be circumstances where a particular type of construction will be economically feasible in one town and not in an adjacent town. The appraiser should recognize this restriction. Similarly, such things as the soils, proximity to flood plains, and local geology can cause differences in the feasibility of different types of construction.

Another type of public limit on the use of property arises when the rights of access to a property are restricted. A common example is when access rights alongside a freeway are purchased and extinguished. Adjacent lands must then rely upon other access routes. Another example involves restrictions upon the location of driveways, which may limit the use and value of the property, particularly for commercial land. Gas stations and drive-in restaurants are prime examples of properties needing driveway access that may be unavailable because of such reasons as the proximity of throughway ramps.

In this era of environmental protection and concern for the health and safety of citizens, many new types of governmental restrictions are important in the analysis of vacant land. These include moratoriums on the granting of new sewer or water hookup permits until problems with the quality or capacity of sewer or water treatment plants can be resolved. In some slow-growth areas, there is an increasing tendency to ration building permits in ways that make a valuable piece of property lose its usability until building permits become available. As mentioned earlier, federal flood zones can severely affect the ability to use property. In other cases, however, several feet of relatively inexpensive fill may flood-proof the property and restore the land's usefulness. Clearly, restrictions such as these cannot be ignored. People dealing with real estate must try to keep abreast of them.

Property Tax

In concluding this discussion of private and public restrictions on the use of property, we turn to the subject of the property tax. The property tax can absorb some of the annual income of a property and reduce the profitability of its use or uses. This can shift the economic feasibility of particular uses and influence the highest and best use. Thus property tax functions as a governmental restriction (or interference) on the use of land through its effects on the economics of use. This makes it important for the appraiser, while doing a site analysis, to research the impact of property taxes. Because current property tax laws have become more complex, the property tax charged to a particular property can vary widely depending upon, for example, whether the use is one that is exempt from taxation or is subject to a preferential taxation (such as agriculture in many areas). Because of the effect that such special tax formulas can have on income and value, it is vital that the appraiser consider them in making an analysis of the property.

Taxes collected by special assessment districts are a unique type of property tax. Here the tax is charged in relation to a reported benefit gained by individual properties. This gain may be the result of the establishment of street lighting or development of sewer mains, water supply systems, treatment plants, and any necessary landfill. If two properties are otherwise equal but one has a large annual special tax assessment to pay for sewer and water and the other does not, we would expect the one with the assessment to sell for less. The appraiser must look for this possibility.

As this section suggests, there are a large number of factors that can influence the value of a site. The appraiser seeks to be aware of them all, in order to consider which ones appear to be especially significant to the value of the particular parcel of land being appraised.

SECTION 6.3
COMPUTING AREA AND VOLUME

The ability to do basic arithmetic is one of the necessary skills of an appraiser. This section demonstrates how to make simple calculations that assist the appraiser in estimating lot and house areas, room sizes, and surface area of walls, as well as measurements of volume. Area and volume measurements are often important in the sales comparison approach and also in the cost and income approaches to value.

Definition of Terms

Area

The area is the space or the size of a flat surface, which is a function of multiplying its length and width. Area refers only to a surface or plane, with no more than two dimensions of measurement. In real estate, circumstances calling for the calculation of area include finding the area of a lot or parcel of land, typically measured in square feet or acres of land area. In larger land parcels, area may be described in sections (as described in Chapter 2) or even in square miles. Area is also calculated to find the floor space in a building or the surface area of the roof cover (which, on a sloping roof, will be greater than the floor area of the building the roof covers). In some cases, you may need to know the kitchen counter area; the areas of individual rooms, garages, and finished versus unfinished basements; the sleeping porch area; and the average area per apartment unit.

Volume

The volume relates to size in three dimensions, that is, to the measurement of the content of a three-dimensional space. The most common example in real estate appraisal is the calculation of the airspace within a building, its cubic volume, which is sometimes used in estimating construction costs. One can see, for example, that in calculating the cost of a silo or a grain storage elevator, the cubic volume would be a helpful measure for cost calculations.

Computing the Area

The calculation of area requires (1) that only one system of measurement be used (all in feet or all in yards, for example), and (2) that the proper formula be used for the shape or figure whose area is to be calculated. The importance of scale is that if one dimension is given in feet and another is given in yards, the two cannot be directly multiplied to give an answer either in square feet or square yards. Consequently, the measurement in yards must be translated into feet, or the measurement in feet must be translated into yards, before the area can be calculated. For example, 3 yards, 1 foot would be changed to either 10 feet or 3.33 yards. Below are the formulas for calculating some of the more common figures or shapes that an appraiser might need. These include the square, the rectangle, the triangle, the trapezoid, and the circle. The formula for other types of figures will not be used as often. If needed, they can be located in a geometry text or mathematical reference book.

The Square

A square is defined as a closed figure with four equal sides and four right angles. A right angle is one-fourth of a full circle. The formula for the area of a square is as follows:

$$\text{area of a square} = \text{length}^2 \ (\text{or length} \times \text{length})$$

The concept of multiplying a number times itself is called the square of the number. Thus we could say that the area of a square equals the length squared. Let us calculate the area of a lot that is square in shape, with four equal sides, and four right angles, having a street frontage of 100 feet and a depth of 100 feet. By using the given formula, the area can be found to be 100×100, or 10,000 square feet.

The Rectangle

A rectangle is defined as a closed four-sided figure with four right angles, with its opposite sides equal and parallel. The formula for the area of a rectangle is

$$\text{rectangle area} = \text{width} \times \text{length}$$

Thus the area of a lot with a street frontage of 75 feet and a depth of 100 feet would be 75×100, or 7,500 square feet. Notice that a square is a special type of rectangle, and its area is the same using either formula.

The Triangle

A triangle is defined as any closed figure with three sides. We could create a triangle by first drawing a square and then connecting the two opposite corners with a diagonal line. This allows us to see that the two triangles created must have the same total area as the area of the square. The formula for the area of a triangle is as follows:

$$\text{triangle area} = \text{height} \times \text{base} \times \tfrac{1}{2}$$

In calculating the area of a triangle, be sure to determine the base and the height. By convention, the base is taken as the lower or bottom line of the triangle; however, any of the three sides can be used as the base if it makes calculation easier. Height is defined as the length of the line that is perpendicular to (at right angles to) the base line, and connecting the base

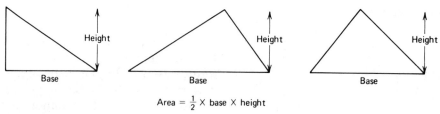

Area = $\frac{1}{2}$ × base × height

FIGURE 6.12
Examples of Triangles

line with the opposite point of the triangle. See the examples shown in Figure 6.12.

Appraisers encounter a variety of situations in which the formula for the area of a triangle is used. The most common use is in calculating the area of a lot that is wider at the rear than at the front (or vice versa). Such lots are common at the end of cul-de-sac streets. The area of such lots can be calculated by dividing the lot into a series of rectangles and triangles. The area of each rectangle or triangle is calculated. If necessary, missing dimensions can be scaled on a map. The areas of the several rectangles and triangles are then totaled to give the area of the total parcel. This method is not as accurate as the calculations performed by surveyors or by computer surveyor programs, but it is adequate for most appraisal purposes if more accurate calculations are not available.

The Trapezoid
The trapezoid is defined as a closed, four-sided figure with two parallel sides. The two other sides are usually not parallel. From what you have already studied, a little doodling will show you that it is possible to calculate the area of a trapezoid by breaking the figure up into a rectangle and a triangle, calculating the area of each, and adding the two areas together. However, it is quicker to use the formula for the area of a trapezoid because it takes fewer calculations. The formula for the area of a trapezoid is

$$\text{trapezoid area} = \frac{(\text{side 1} + \text{side 2}) \times \text{height}}{2}$$

In this formula, the two sides mentioned are the two parallel sides. The height is the perpendicular distance between them, just as in a triangle (see Figure 6.13). In a common real estate example, you might need to calculate the area of a lot that had a street frontage of 100 feet. Both side lines go back at right angles to the street, with one side line being 110 feet deep and the other side line being 130 feet deep. The rear line, as you can see from the drawing of the lot in Figure 6.14, slants at a diagonal to the street, making the lot deeper in one corner. This lot is in the shape of a trapezoid. The

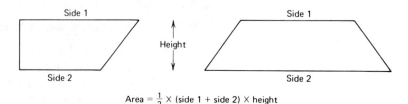

Area = $\frac{1}{2}$ × (side 1 + side 2) × height

FIGURE 6.13
The Area of a Trapezoid

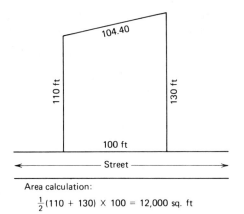

Area calculation:

$\frac{1}{2}$(110 + 130) × 100 = 12,000 sq. ft

FIGURE 6.14
Example of a Trapezoid-Shaped Lot

height (the perpendicular distance between the sides) is the 100-foot frontage on the street. The area would be $\frac{1}{2}$ (110 + 130) × 100 = 12,000 square feet. Since lots are often trapezoidal, this formula is one that appraisers often use.

The Circle

The circle is defined as a curved line that forms a closed figure, which has a center of equal distance from all points on the curved line. A line joining two points on the circle and passing through the center is called the diameter. A line joining the center point to one point on the curve is called the radius of the circle and is, of course, one-half of the length of the diameter. The distance around the circle is called the circumference. The formula for the area of a circle is

$$\text{circle area} = \text{pi} \times \text{radius}^2 \text{ (or pi} \times \text{radius} \times \text{radius)}$$

This calculation involves a new feature: the constant "pi," also expressed as π. A constant is something that has the same numerical value at all times. The value of pi is 3.1416+. Whatever the area of a circle, whether large or small, pi is always the same, 3.1416. It should be remembered here that a number squared means the number multiplied by itself. A circle is shown in Figure 6.15.

Thus, if the appraiser is seeking to calculate the area of a house built as a geodesic dome and finds that the distance across the house from one outside wall to the opposite outside wall is 100 feet, then the area of the structure would be 50 × 50 × 3.1416 = 7,854 square feet—a substantial floor space! The formula for the area of a circle is useful not only under rare circumstances when you are appraising a geodesic dome, but also for homes that have half-circle bay windows. In this case, the area of the bay window would be one-half of the area of the circle. Similarly, there can be round swimming pools, round buildings, round gazebos, and even half-circle sections of lots where the appraiser can use the formula for the area of a circle.

Using Area Formulas

However irregular or unusual the shape of the object that you have, the same procedure is used to calculate its area. The first step is to prepare a scale diagram of the shape of the object. This might be taken from existing

The Circle

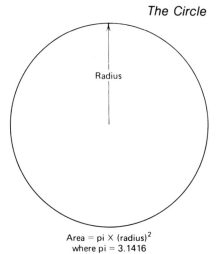

Area = pi × (radius)^2
where pi = 3.1416

FIGURE 6.15
Area of a Circle

drawings or maps or might require measuring the object itself. The second step is to analyze the figure that is before you and decide how it can be broken down into a series of regular geometric shapes such as rectangles, triangles, trapezoids, half-circles, and so on. The third step is to determine the dimensions of each of the subdivided shapes. This may require scaling the known distances on the map and using this calculation to estimate the length of unknown distances or lines. In some cases it is also possible, using formulas in geometry books, to calculate some unknown distances from others that are known. The fourth step is to compute the area of each of the geometric shapes that were developed. The final step is to total the areas of each of the shapes. A practical example of this process is shown in Example 6.1.

Example 6.1
Using Area Formulas

Steps

1. Prepare a scale diagram.
2. Decide how to break it down.
3. Determine the dimensions.
4. Compute the area of each shape.
5. Total the areas of each shape.

    (a) $20 \times 55 =$ 1,100
    (b) $3.1416 \times (10 \times 10) \times \frac{1}{2} =$ 157   (rounded)
    (c) $15 \times 25 \times \frac{1}{2} =$ 188   (rounded)
    (d) $25 \times 60 =$ 1,500
                            2,945 sq ft

Computing Volume

Volume is calculated by multiplying the three dimensions of an object. All three must be the same scale; that is, they must all be measured in feet, all in yards, or all in inches. The formula for calculating volume is as follows:

$$\text{volume} = \text{area} \times \text{average height}$$

The use of this formula requires that the area be calculated first. Once the area is calculated, it is multiplied by the average height. In a building with flat ceilings or a flat roof, the average height would not be hard to determine. With pitched or sloping ceilings, however, the average height (the average of the lowest and highest height) must be calculated. In multiple-story buildings, the average height is calculated using the distance from the floor level to the next floor level up. Here is an example of the use of volume calculations in real estate appraisal: you are appraising a single-family residence with a living area of 2,340 square feet. The ceiling height is 10 feet, including the ceiling joist and roof structure. You are using a cost manual that reports building costs only in the cost per cubic foot, and for your building, the cost per cubic foot is $7.00. You calculate the cubic volume of the structure to be $2,340 \times 10 = 23,400$ cubic feet, and multiply it by $7.00 to estimate its replacement cost new at $163,800. The use of cubic costs is less common now than it once was.

SUMMARY

The actual site inspection is one of the most important parts of the entire appraisal process. Therefore, the inspection should be planned well in advance.

The three major reasons for inspecting the property follow.

> 1. To estimate the highest and best use of the site. The highest and best use generally means the legal and feasible use that will support the highest land value. The use must be physically possible and legally acceptable. The value of a property will vary depending upon its uses, so that it is important to know how to estimate the highest and best use.
>
> 2. To identify the key site features. Note any significant characteristics of the property, such as the size, quality, features, and condition.
>
> 3. To identify possible problems. Although you may not be an expert in all the areas in which a problem can exist, there are potential legal and physical problems to watch for.

It is desirable to have certain kinds of information before the actual site inspection begins. Data on the size and shape of the parcel, its legal characteristics, and the availability of utilities generally should be known beforehand. Information on comparable properties may also be useful. With this information, the site and comparables can be inspected on the same field trip.

The tools and equipment necessary to perform the inspection were then outlined. Many appraisers use a checklist during the actual inspection to make certain that they gather all of the necessary information.

A great variety of information about the site and its surroundings can be noted during the inspection. This information is divided into three categories:

1. The physical characteristics of the site.
2. The locational features of the site.
3. Public and private restrictions on the use of the site.

During the inspection the appraiser should first investigate the physical characteristics of the site, which include the size, shape, and frontage of the site, and the depth. The topography, soil, and drainage of the site are also important. Land with irregular topography may be more costly to build upon but may contain advantageous features, such as a sweeping view. Is the soil of good quality? Will it support the uses being considered for this site? The type of water drainage systems, man-made or natural, should also be inspected.

Physical characteristics also include the type of lot, its orientation, and its physical access. There are many types of lots, ranging from the conventional detached lot to the planned unit development (PUD) to the condominium. The conventional detached lot is a site that is the entire lot. The

PUD site involves ownership of a subdivided lot upon which the owner's unit is built, plus an undivided interest in the common areas. A condominium unit includes the fee ownership of a block of airspace (within which the unit sits), plus an undivided ownership in the common areas and the building's supporting walls.

There are a variety of lot types that you should be familiar with. These include the key lot, the cul-de-sac lot, and the flag lot. It is also important to note the lot's orientation to views and to the sun and other climatic factors. In recent years, utilization of the sun's energy has become more important.

The property must also be reasonably accessible. Properties situated in areas less accessible to large emergency vehicles, such as fire trucks, could face a reduction in value.

The improvements made to the site or surrounding areas should also be examined. Such improvements include landscaping, grading, excavation, and the width and paving of streets and sidewalks.

The second category of information to note during the site inspection is the location of the site. Analyzing the location involves three steps:

1. Compare the site to the properties around it.
2. Note the availability of utilities.
3. Examine the transportation systems that connect the site to nearby shopping and jobs.

The third category of information to consider during the site inspection is the private and public restrictions. A variety of private restrictions can affect the property's use. These range from simple deed restrictions to complex agreements between owners (as in PUDs). Public restrictions are becoming more complicated and influential in our sophisticated society. Examples include zoning regulations, building and safety code regulations, and health and environmental protection restrictions.

A final form of restriction is the property tax. Property taxes take away some of the annual income of a property, reducing the profitability of a use or uses. It is a good idea to research the impact of such taxes on the site.

Related to the property tax are taxes collected from special assessments. Such taxes are used to pay for a particular public improvement such as street paving. Special assessments are generally based upon the benefit the project will provide the properties abutting the improvement.

Since public and private restrictions have a direct influence on the use and value of real estate, it is important that they be carefully considered during the site inspection and analysis.

In Section 6.3 we discussed the importance of having some basic arithmetic skills. These mathematical skills are required throughout the appraisal process, as in measuring the area of lots, building floor areas, or building volumes.

Some buildings and lots have very irregular shapes so that calculating their areas may seem impossible. However, complex shapes can usually be broken into simple ones: squares, rectangles, triangles, trapezoids, and circles. The area of each of these shapes is easily calculated using the proper formula.

The volume, or cubic area, of a building can also be easily calculated by a formula. Such a volume calculation is sometimes used in the cost approach.

IMPORTANT TERMS AND CONCEPTS

Access
Area
Assemblage
Condominium
Corner lot
Cul-de-sac lot
Depth
Frontage
Interior lot
Location
Lot orientation

Lot shape
Planned unit development (PUD)
Plottage
Private restrictions
Public restrictions
Site features
Site improvements
Topography
Transportation
Utilities
Volume

REVIEWING YOUR UNDERSTANDING

1. Before performing the site inspection you should:
   (a) Gather basic information about the site
   (b) Be sure you know the reasons for the site inspection
   (c) Have a map or drawing of the site
   (d) All of the above

2. The first important reason for inspecting and analyzing the site is to:
   (a) Estimate the highest and best use
   (b) Note any unusual characteristics
   (c) Find comparable sales
   (d) None of the above

3. Why is it important to identify possible site problems?
   (a) To identify the highest and best use
   (b) To isolate serious problems which can then be referred to experts for analysis
   (c) To identify how to correct the problem
   (d) To estimate the cost to repair the problem

4. The three criteria that best define the highest and best use are:
   (a) The use must be physically possible, legally acceptable, and generate a higher present land value than any other use
   (b) The use must be legally acceptable, politically possible, and socially advantageous
   (c) The use must be physically possible, comparable to other uses in the neighborhood, and legally acceptable
   (d) The use must be comparable to other uses, physically possible, and generate a higher present land value than other uses

5. The data needed before the site is inspected comes from:
   (a) The district appraisal office
   (b) City and county planning offices
   (c) A number of sources
   (d) None of the above

6. The three major categories of information about a site are:
   (a) The physical characteristics of the site, the topography, and the highest and best use

(b) The physical characteristics of the site, the site location elements, and the legal and private restrictions

(c) The physical characteristics, the legal restrictions, and the private and public restrictions

(d) The shape, the topography, and the drainage

7. A key lot is:

(a) A lot that is shaped like a key

(b) A lot that is located at the end of a dead end street

(c) A lot that has several other lots backing onto its side yard

(d) None of the above

8. What is plottage value?

(a) The value of land between the subject property and another property

(b) The bonus that may sometimes be obtained from combining parcels

(c) The price of land per plot

(d) The depth divided by the frontage

9. The three steps for analyzing the location of a property are:

(a) Compare the property to others in the town, investigate the availability of utilities, and check the ease of access

(b) Compare the site to other properties in the neighborhood, note the availability of utilities to the property, and investigate the availability of transportation

(c) Note the availability of transportation, note the availability of utilities to the property, and note the availability of goods to the neighborhood

(d) Note the availability of transportation, note the orientation of the lot, and check the availability of utilities

10. The formula for the area of a trapezoid is:

(a) $\dfrac{(\text{side } 1 + \text{side } 2) \times \text{height}}{2}$

(b) $\dfrac{(\text{side } 1 + \text{side } 3) \times \text{height}}{3}$

(c) $(\text{side } 1 + \text{side } 2) \times \text{height}$

(d) $\dfrac{(\text{side } 1 + \text{side } 2) \times \text{height}}{4}$

CHAPTER
SEVEN

PROPERTY
INSPECTION AND
ANALYSIS: THE
IMPROVEMENTS

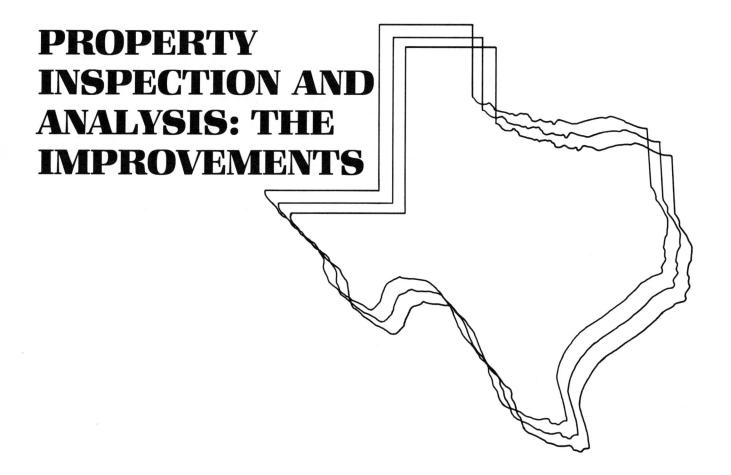

PREVIEW
In the last chapter we discussed the inspection and analysis of the site and its surroundings. Now we will cover the inspection and analysis of the improvements. As used in appraisal terminology, improvements include everything attached to the vacant lot, that is, the building, swimming pool, shed, patio, fence, and whatever other structures are to be found.

When you have completed this chapter, you should be able to:

1. Describe what tools are required to make a field inspection of the improvements.

2. Describe the data emphasized in each of the three approaches to value.

3. Name the major items of a structure that the appraiser seeks to describe and rate.

4. Name and describe the four main classifications of building construction.

5. Explain what is meant by functional utility.

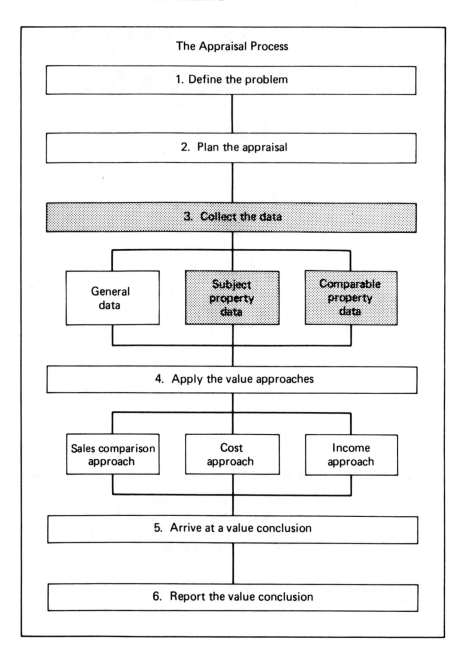

The Appraisal Process

1. Define the problem

2. Plan the appraisal

3. Collect the data

General data | Subject property data | Comparable property data

4. Apply the value approaches

Sales comparison approach | Cost approach | Income approach

5. Arrive at a value conclusion

6. Report the value conclusion

SECTION 7.1
PLANNING THE
BUILDING INSPECTION

Any appraisal will go more smoothly if you prepare for the building inspection. This means assembling the necessary tools to perform the inspection and planning what data to collect.

Equipment

The building inspection requires a few special tools in addition to the clipboard and pencil, measuring tape or roller, ice pick or nail, and camera

[X] Existing [ ] Proposed [ ] Under Constr.	No. Units 1	Type (det, duplex, semi/det, etc.)	Design (rambler, split level, etc.)			Exterior Walls				
Yrs. Age: Actual 60 Effective 39 to 44	No. Stories 1	Detached S. F. R.	Cottage			Stucco				

IMPROVEMENTS

Roof Material	Gutters & Downspouts [ ] None	Window (Type): Dbl. hung wood frm	Insulation [X] None [ ] Floor
Composition	Wood and G. I.	[ ] Storm Sash [X] Screens [ ] Combination	[ ] Ceiling [ ] Roof [ ] Walls

[ ] Manufactured Housing	Ø % Basement	[ ] Floor Drain	Finished Ceiling
Foundation Walls		[ ] Outside Entrance	Finished Walls
Concrete		[ ] Sump Pump	Finished Walls
		[ ] Concrete Floor ___ % Finished	Finished Floor
[ ] Slab on Grade [X] Crawl Space		Evidence of: [ ] Dampness [ ] Termites [ ] Settlement	

Comments The only apparent updating of the subject is the electrical service and outlets. This appears to have been done at least 15 years ago.

ROOM LIST

Room List	Foyer	Living	Dining	Kitchen	Den	Family Rm.	Rec. Rm.	Bedrooms	No. Baths	Laundry	Other
Basement											
1st Level		1	Nook	1				2	1		Service porch
2nd Level											

Finished area above grade contains a total of 4 rooms 2 bedrooms 1 baths. Gross Living Area 730 sq. ft. Bsmt Area Ø sq. ft.

INTERIOR FINISH & EQUIPMENT

Kitchen Equipment: [ ] Refrigerator [ ] Range/Oven [ ] Disposal [ ] Dishwasher [ ] Fan/Hood [ ] Compactor [ ] Washer [ ] Dryer [ ] ___

HEAT: Type Wall Fuel Gas Cond Average AIR COND: [ ] Central [ ] Other [X] Adequate [ ] Inadequate

				PROPERTY RATING	Good	Avg	Fair	Poor
Floors	[X] Hardwood	[ ] Carpet Over ___ [ ] ___		Quality of Construction (Materials & Finish)	[ ]	[X]	[ ]	[ ]
Walls	[ ] Drywall	[X] Plaster		Condition of Improvements	[ ]	[ ]	[X]	[ ]
Trim/Finish	[ ] Good	[X] Average [ ] Fair [ ] Poor		Room sizes and layout	[ ]	[X]	[ ]	[ ]
Bath Floor	[X] Ceramic			Closets and Storage	[ ]	[X]	[ ]	[ ]
Bath Wainscot	[X] Ceramic			Insulation—adequacy	[ ]	[X]	[ ]	[ ]

Special Features (including energy efficient items) Built-in hutch in the dining nook.

	Good	Avg	Fair	Poor
Plumbing—adequacy and condition	[ ]	[X]	[ ]	[ ]
Electrical—adequacy and condition	[ ]	[X]	[ ]	[ ]
Kitchen Cabinets—adequacy and condition	[ ]	[ ]	[X]	[ ]
Compatibility to Neighborhood	[ ]	[X]	[ ]	[ ]
Overall Livability	[ ]	[ ]	[X]	[ ]
Appeal and Marketability	[ ]	[ ]	[X]	[ ]

ATTIC: [X] Yes [ ] No [ ] Stairway [ ] Drop-stair [ ] Scuttle [ ] Floored [ ] Heated

Finished (Describe) Crawl space

CAR STORAGE: [X] Garage [ ] Built-in [ ] Attached [X] Detached [ ] Car Port

No. Cars 1 [X] Adequate [ ] Inadequate Condition Average

Yrs Est Remaining Economic Life 16 to 21 .Explain if less than Loan Term

FIREPLACES, PATIOS, POOL, FENCES, etc. (describe) Fences of stone and wire, brick patio, & a stone fireplace. 10x14.5' detached room with the floor partially rotted out.

COMMENTS (including functional or physical inadequacies, repairs needed, modernization, etc.) The subject shows a general lack of maintenance, which appears to have lasted over a period of time. The house has several broken windows, rusted-out downspouts, the floors and some walls need refinishing and the window panes need to be repaired.

FIGURE 7.1
Property Description Section of the FHLMC Form "70"/FNMA Form 1004

that you have already assembled for the inspection of the site. The most important of these is a checklist or appraisal form for recording your data in an organized manner. Appropriate checklists include the standard FNMA appraisal forms (referred to later in this text) and also forms developed by many savings and loan associations, banks, and mortgage and insurance companies. The property description section of the FNMA appraisal form is shown in Figure 7.1. Methodical use of a standard checklist avoids having to return to the site for details overlooked at the first inspection.

To help in the building inspection, you may also want to carry a pocket flashlight for looking under houses and into dark corners. A marble is handy for testing surfaces to see if they are level. For difficult jobs, take along plot plans and blueprints if they are available. These plans can help you verify the location and dimensions of the improvements and spell out important structural and mechanical details.

What Information Should You Collect?

The information collected for an appraisal varies with the purpose of the appraisal and the intended use of the report. Also, some special data may be necessary to support the particular value approach being emphasized.

Consider the Appraisal Purpose

The purpose of most appraisals is to estimate market value. An inspection for this purpose usually requires a detailed and accurate description of the physical structures and a rating for market acceptability. Conformity to building codes, deed restrictions, and zoning regulations should also be reviewed. In this regard, any nonconformity should be carefully noted so that its influence on market value can be considered. Finally, the highest and best use of the property as improved should be analyzed.

Appraisals made for purposes other than market value may demand more specialized data. For example, appraisals made for the purpose of finding insurable value would probably emphasize such data as construction costs, rating of the structure's fire resistance, and the physical condition of the building.

Consider the Intended Use of the Report

The intended use of the appraisal report will also determine its form and content and, therefore, the data to be collected. When the appraisal report is to be used by the seller of a single-family dwelling to determine a realistic price, a brief set of comparable sales, with a short discussion as to comparability, may be all that is required to satisfy the client. However, if the appraisal is being made for loan purposes, the lender's requirements may be more demanding; the appraiser may need to collect more information on such factors as market acceptability, compatibility with surrounding land uses, and the marketable physical condition of the subject property.

Many lenders still apply old FHA standards to their appraisals.* The FHA standards of property acceptability were set forth in FHA's Minimum Property Standards. These were complex documents; however, appraisers should have a working knowledge of their content. Generally, the FHA requirements for one- and two-family dwellings included:

1. Safe, secure, healthful, and attractive living facilities.
2. Convenience of traffic circulation and ease of housekeeping.
3. Visual and auditory privacy.
4. Appropriate light and ventilation.
5. Fire and accident protection.
6. Economy of maintenance.
7. Adequate sanitation facilities.
8. Efficient use of space.

The FHA standards were quite detailed, covering specifics as to acceptable room sizes, door and window placement for cross ventilation, heating, plumbing, finish materials, storage access, and privacy. As you can see, physically measuring room sizes and noting window openings could take more time and effort than you might have allowed if you had planned only a quick measure of the outside dimensions. When an appraisal report is prepared for court proceedings, more specialized information and added documentation are also necessary.

What Value Approaches Are to Be Emphasized?

The information you gather during the visual inspection will be influenced by the value approach you expect to emphasize. Generally, the cost ap-

* The FHA discontinued the standards in December of 1985 because most cities and counties have building requirements that are more stringent as well as more relevant to local markets.

proach requires the most descriptive detail. Besides the appraiser's rating for age, condition, and utility of the improvements, the data collected must be adequate to allow you to calculate the building cost estimate. Cost estimates often rely on the use of published cost manuals. Here are some of the factors that cost manuals usually consider as determinants of cost.

1. Design or use type.	**4.** Size, shape, and height.
2. Construction classification.	**5.** Special equipment.
3. Rating of quality.	**6.** Yard or site improvements.

Some cost-estimating methods (such as the segregated method that is an option in the Marshall Valuation Service) utilize detailed measurements of individual building components. This might call for the dimensions of the floors, exterior walls, interior partitions, storefronts, roof structure and cover, and so on. The rating for age, condition, and utility will strongly affect the allowance for depreciation in the cost approach, so close attention to details of property maintenance and repair is also important.

The sales comparison approach requires improvement data that can be compared with the features of similar properties that have sold. Familiarity with the type of data to be compared is important to avoid a second inspection to fill in the gaps. Here is a list of the typical property characteristics to be noted in single-family home appraisals. Most of these items are included in the various computerized, residential sales lists used by appraisers:

Architectural style.	Total number of rooms.
Construction type.	Square feet of living area.
Type of exterior.	Basement area.
Type of roof.	Type of heating and cooling.
Number of stories.	Fireplace(s).
Floor plan.	Built-ins and storage.
Overall quality.	Adequacy of insulation.
Condition.	Garage or carport.
Year built.	Outside improvements (such as
Number of bedrooms.	pools and patios).
Number of bathrooms.	Kitchen equipment.

If the income approach is to be emphasized, the appraiser should be aware of the property characteristics that have the greatest effect upon the income potential and the probable expenses. For example:

1. Number and types of units.

2. The ratio of rentable areas to the total area.

3. Quality of the tenant space.

4. Recreation, parking, services, and other amenities.

5. Durability of the structure and materials.

6. Physical condition of the structure and equipment.

Now that we have assembled the necessary tools and made appropriate plans for the task, we are ready to begin the building inspection.

SECTION 7.2
PERFORMING THE
BUILDING INSPECTION

The purpose of the building inspection is to identify the condition, quality, features, and problems of the property being appraised. In this section, we shall describe the building inspection techniques most appraisers use.

When you have your equipment in order, your checklist in hand, and have made an appointment with the owner, manager, or tenant of your subject property, you are ready to begin the building inspection.

Recording and Rating Improvement Characteristics

As you start noting the physical features of a property, be prepared to follow the checklist or appraisal form you have selected for the job. Most checklists suggest a logical sequence of observations which, if followed, prevents the oversight of important data. It is desirable to use correct construction terminology in your descriptions. Structural components and finish materials will be discussed in the next section.

The exterior is often inspected first, starting with the foundation, then the exterior finish, and finally the roof. Be sure to note the type, style, materials used, and condition of each part of the exterior.

Next, the interior is inspected. The number and type of rooms and their arrangement are noted. The interior finish is rated as to type of materials and quality of workmanship.

Finally, the built-in kitchen equipment, as well as the heating, air-conditioning, and other systems are inspected and rated as to their type and adequacy. Be sure to note any special energy-efficient factors, such as solar heating and the type and thickness of insulation in the walls and ceilings.

Rating for Appeal and Marketability

As you walk through the building, you should be able to get some idea of the general marketability and appeal of the property. Be aware of the demands and tastes of the specific market in the neighborhood of the property. Do the features of this house fit in with others in the neighborhood? If you were attracted to this neighborhood, would you like this house?

It is generally agreed that the marketability and appeal of a single residential property depend upon:

1. The quality of construction, the materials used, and their finish.
2. The physical condition of the structure, finish, equipment, and floor coverings.
3. Room size, floor plan, and privacy.
4. Closets and other storage areas.
5. Adequacy and condition of plumbing and bath facilities.
6. Adequacy of electrical wiring.
7. Adequacy of heating equipment and any air conditioning.
8. The adequacy, condition, convenience, and quality of kitchen cabinets and equipment.

9. Landscaping and outdoor improvements.
10. General livability of the property.

Every person has an ideal home in his or her imagination. While inspecting a residence, the appraiser tries to "wear the shoes" of the typical buyer of the particular property in order to see the faults and advantages of a home. Qualities such as privacy, adequacy of storage space, and a pleasing exterior ("curb appeal") may increase the marketability of a home far more than extra equipment, whereas other factors, such as a pervading musty odor in the bathrooms and closets or poor room arrangement, may seriously detract from the appeal of an otherwise sound building.

Evaluating Construction Quality

Quality can be a very subjective word. However, in appraising, it is used to describe the basic structural integrity, materials, finishes, and special features of the building. The quantity and type of fixtures, cabinets, and built-in equipment are considered to be part of the quality rating, as is the level of overall workmanship.

Quality is also relative, that is, we can only judge it by comparison with a given standard. Most appraisers attempt to rate buildings according to typical specifications provided in published cost-estimating guides. Generally, these guides use the four ratings of (1) low cost, (2) average, (3) good, and (4) very good or excellent. These quality ratings will be discussed in detail in Section 7.3.

Evaluating Physical Condition

Although the physical condition of a building is often closely related to its age, each aspect is of concern to the appraiser. Has the house generally been kept in good repair or allowed to run down? When rating a building for condition, any deferred maintenance or structural defects found should always be examined and described.

Note the condition of paint, floor and wall coverings, kitchen countertops, shower walls, hardware, equipment, and fixtures. Describe any remodeling or renovation you may find, as well as any abnormal neglect or wear.

Are there any signs of water leakage or moisture inside the house? These may be caused by roof or plumbing leaks, inadequate seals or flashing at windows or doors, or improper ventilation. Look for discolored or peeling paint on the walls or ceilings. Notice recently patched spots, discolored or moldy seams, or a musty odor in bathrooms and kitchens. Any of these conditions may indicate problems.

Pay special attention to whether additions, major repairs, and remodeling conform to the building codes. Sometimes you will find garage conversions and even more ambitious structural work that has been done without a building permit. If you suspect such a condition, you should investigate and report your findings in the appraisal.

Every building inspection should include a check for any possible structural problems or foundation settling. Any such problem could reduce both the marketability and value of a property. Therefore, it is very important to note such telltale signs as large cracks or fresh patchwork in the foundation, walls, and ceilings. Structural cracks caused by a sagging foundation most often show up at the door and window openings, as demonstrated in Figure 7.2. Cabinets that have pulled away from the wall or that

FIGURE 7.2
Example of Structural Damage. (Photograph Courtesy of Doug Frost)

are not plumb (exactly vertical); doors that stick or have been trimmed out of square; floors that hump, dip, or are not level (see why you needed that marble?), all suggest either a settling of the foundation or a shifting of the structure. The most common causes are either poor soil compaction under the foundation or inferior construction of the improvements.

Part of the appraiser's job is to estimate the cost to cure any deferred maintenance or structural defects. Depending on his or her cost-estimating experience, the appraiser may need to consult contractors or engineers before making a cost-to-cure estimate or before completing the report. Sometimes the owners have already consulted such experts and have obtained a written estimate.

Effective Age

Some appraisal procedures require the assignment of an effective age to a building. Effective age is usually defined as the relative age of a structure considering its physical condition and marketability. Thus, a very old building that compares in these respects with similar buildings that are, say, 10 years old may be said to have an effective age of 10 years. In assigning effective age, appraisers usually consider historic age and degree of maintenance, as well as room additions and remodeling.

Often, the first step in an effective age analysis is to calculate the average age of a remodeled structure. For example, if a 30-year-old house was remodeled 10 years ago, and about 80% of the original structure remained unremodeled, then the average age, based solely on the physical elements, would be 26 years. Here is how that would be figured:

$$80\% \times 30 \text{ years} = 24 \text{ years}$$
$$20\% \times 10 \text{ years} = \underline{2 \text{ years}}$$
$$\text{average age} \qquad = 26 \text{ years}$$

In actual practice, remodeling may or may not extend the useful life of a structure. Thus effective age need not agree with average age. It is the market that really determines the effect of age upon value. In many communities, age can be a positive factor due to the special appeal of a well-preserved neighborhood, such as the Park Cities or Lakewood areas of Dallas.

Thus, the second step in estimating the effective age of the property is to judge the market reaction to the property's standard of maintenance, considering how recently such major areas of potential obsolescence as kitchens have been remodeled. Often, this analysis can be bolstered by examining the sales, to see if sales prices of remodeled property are noticeably higher.

Measuring Improvements and Preparing Drawings

Most appraisals call for information on the area (and sometimes the volume) of the buildings. Necessary dimensions are usually included on a diagram prepared by the appraiser. Sometimes you will need to include a floor plan of the rooms. Traditionally, building measurements are expressed in feet and inches (as opposed to metric measures).

For most detached residential structures, the total living area or floor area is measured on the exterior of the building and includes the exterior walls and finish. These measurements are usually rounded to the nearest foot, half-foot, or inch. However, condominium units are often measured using interior rather than exterior measurements, since the airspace is what is bought and sold. In commercial buildings, interior measurements of room size or rentable space are often required. These measurements are also taken between the finished wall surfaces.

It is easier to record your field measurements on a rough sketch as you work; graph paper of the proper scale helps. Later you can draw a final sketch when you have a better writing surface and your hands are cleaner (taking measurements can make them grimy). One-tenth or one-twentieth inch to the foot are the most commonly used scales, depending on the size of the building.

Have you ever wondered how to measure a building? It is really quite simple. Just start at one right-angle corner, usually the front left corner as you face the building. Using the hook on your tape or an ice pick stuck into a crack (or on the ground), attach your tape and measure across the front of the building to the other corner. Move your tape hook to the second corner and continue the same procedure along one side, then the back, and the other side, until you return to your starting corner. Be sure to pick up any special measurements you might need, such as patio dimensions, while you are there. Your plane geometry from high school will come in handy if you run across angles that are not right angles. Be sure the building outline is "in balance": horizontal measurements across the front must equal the horizontal measurements across the back; also the right and left side measurements must equal each other when totaled. Example 7.1 may help you see what is meant by balancing the building diagram.

When you have completed your diagram, you must compute the building areas. Divide the living area into "natural rectangles" by sketching light broken lines horizontally or vertically across the diagram. Compute each of the areas separately by multiplying the length by the width of each rectangle. Add these areas together for your total living area. Methods of computing areas of irregular building shapes may be found in Chapter 6.

Open porches, garages, carports, and other outside areas are figured separately, since they are not a part of the living area. Small entryways and bays are usually counted as part of the living area.

Example 7.1
Example of a Building Diagram

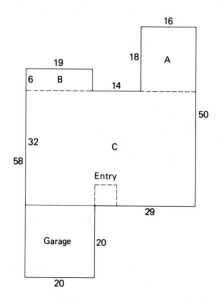

Area Calculations

Floor area:
A. $16 \times 18 = $ 288
B. $6 \times 19 = $ 114
C. $32 \times 49 = $ 1,568
                 1,970 sq ft

Garage:
$20 \times 20 = 400$ sq ft

Proof That Drawing "Balances"

Front (house and garage): $20 + 29$ = 49 ft
Rear: $19 + 14 + 16 = 49$ ft
   Front and rear are in balance

Left side: $58 + (18 - 6) = 70$ ft
Right side: $50 + 20$ = 70 ft
   Left and right sides are in balance

SECTION 7.3
UNDERSTANDING
CONSTRUCTION DETAILS

It is important for the appraiser to understand the basic principles of construction and be familiar with typical structural details. (Figure 7.3 shows examples of wood framing details.) This section will cover (1) the classification of basic construction, (2) the selection of building materials, (3) typical building specifications, and (4) the standards used for judging the quality of a building.

Construction Classification Systems

Historically, most systems for classifying types of construction were based on the structure's resistance to fire. For this reason, buildings are generally classified according to their particular type of basic frame, wall, and floor construction.

In standard building codes and construction cost manuals, basic construction types are classified by either an A, B, C, D or a 1, 2, 3, 4 designation system. Details of Class A, B, and C construction are shown in Figure 7.4; Class D details were given in Figure 7.3. The typical specifications for all four classes follow.

Class A buildings have fireproofed, structural steel frames and reinforced concrete or masonry floors and roofs. Major institutional buildings,

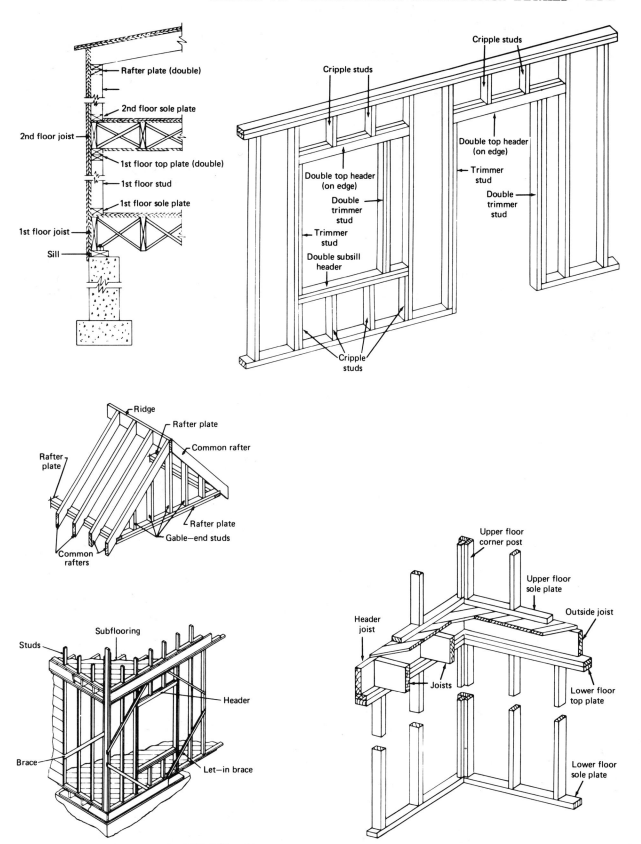

FIGURE 7.3
Structural Detail: Wood Framing. (From *Builder 3 & 2*, Bureau of Naval Personnel, 1965)

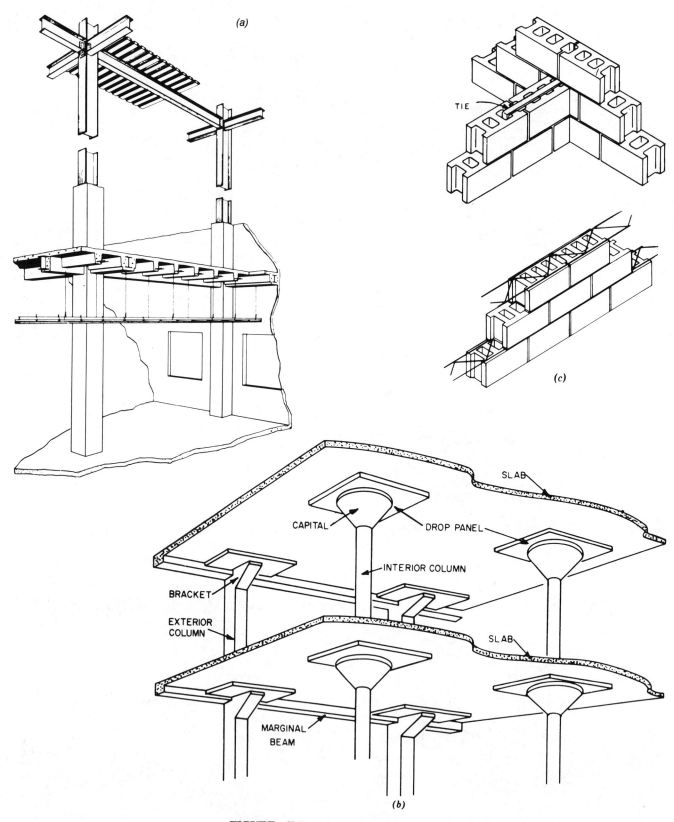

FIGURE 7.4
Construction Class Details. (*a*) Class A (Courtesy of Marshall & Stevens Publication Company). (*b*) Class B (From *Design Manual—Structural Engineering*, Department of the Navy, Naval Facilities Engineering Command, October, 1970). (*c*) Class C (From Builder 3 & 2, Bureau of Naval Personnel, 1965)

as well as high-rise office and hotel buildings, are usually Class A construction. Class A construction is the strongest for its weight but is the most expensive.

Class B buildings have reinforced concrete frames and reinforced concrete or masonry walls, floors, and roofs. The typical Class B building is a three- to five-story office building or a heavy industrial plant. Class B construction is second only to Class A in cost and fire resistance.

Class C buildings have masonry exterior walls, and wood or exposed steel floor and roof structures. Many one- and two-story commercial and industrial buildings fall into this category. Also, many residential buildings in colder climates belong in this classification.

Class D buildings have wood or light steel frames and roof structures. Most residential buildings in the West and South fall into the Class D construction classification. Basic construction features of Class D construction include concrete or concrete-block foundations; concrete-slab or raised wood floors; wood frame; stucco and/or wood siding exterior; drywall or plaster interior; and tar and gravel, composition-shingle, wood shingle, or shake roofing.

Choice of Materials

Traditionally, the materials used for structural and mechanical components, as well as the finish of buildings, are dependent upon the climate, availability, cost, style, durability, and building code requirements.

The climate can dictate the type of foundation, walls, insulation, roof pitch, and finish material. In the moderate climate of America's West and Southwest, stucco and wood structures prevail. Insulation is primarily needed against the summer heat. In colder climates, extensive insulation may be needed to provide better protection from the elements. Heating and air-conditioning systems should be designed to meet climatic conditions. In today's energy-conscious economy, such systems need to be energy-efficient; hence the trend toward solar heating and design features that minimize energy loss.

The selection of materials also depends upon their availability. Since the earliest times, mankind has used readily available materials for shelter. Adobe was used in the early Southwest because it was plentiful, easily made into building blocks, and suitable to the hot, dry climate. Brick is the most popular building material in Texas because it is more durable than wood and is relatively inexpensive as a result of extensive deposits of clay found throughout the state.

Cost is also a factor in the use of materials. Custom homes may still incorporate expensive marbles and rare woods, but the average builder must think twice about the comparative cost of the materials used. As wood is becoming more and more costly and scarce, some builders are beginning to experiment with plastic, steel, and fiberglass walls, prefabricated to meet the building specifications. We are already conditioned to the use of fiberglass tub enclosures and plastic counters in bathrooms. Plastics and polymers have also replaced expensive metals in rough plumbing and electrical building components in many areas of the country.

The style of the construction will often suggest that certain materials be used. Shingles and shake roofs are traditional on ranch-style and Cape Cod houses. Tile roofs and textured stucco are typical of Spanish- or Mediterranean-style houses.

The durability of materials must also be taken into consideration when deciding upon the materials to be used in a structure. Durability is partly dependent upon climate. Most exterior woods deteriorate in areas of high temperature or humidity. One exception to the rule is redwood. Although more expensive than many other types of wood, redwood is quite impervious to weather, does not require paint, and may in the long run be more economic for exterior siding. Durability also depends on usage. Interior finishes that are subject to heavy wear must meet a reasonable durability test. The modern vinyl floor coverings and plastic laminate counter tops that increasingly replace hardwood and ceramic tiles are not quite as resistant to wear. But they are less expensive.

Local building code requirements are also important in determining the materials to be used. The stress and load requirements for wood framing in construction eliminate many varieties of forest products. Douglas fir is most often preferred for its relative strength. Many codes do not allow any wiring except copper for the electrical circuits in a structure. Plastic pipes and sewers are not allowed in some areas. Each locality has its own fairly rigid building code.

Although they often contribute to high housing costs by restricting the types of materials to be used, for the most part, building codes offer the community protection from fire, health hazards, insect and rodent infestation, and unsafe buildings.

Typical Residential Specifications

As already noted, residential structures differ widely in materials and specifications. Examples of the range of choices are shown in Figure 7.5. Here are some typical features found today.

Foundations:
  Concrete or block piers.
  Perimeter foundation walls of reinforced concrete or concrete block.
  Reinforced concrete-slab foundation and floor.

Frames:
  Wood, steel, or masonry.
  Douglas fir, cypress, or hemlock preferred as framing lumber.

Trim and Sash:
  Trim: wood, brick, stone, or fiberglass simulation.
  Sash: wood, steel, or aluminum (double-hung, casement, or sliding), sliding glass doors to private areas such as backyards.

Roofing:
  Built-up composition, asbestos, or fiberglass felt, covered with hot-mopped asphalt and gravel.
  Shingles: asbestos, composition, wood, concrete, or clay tile.
  Shakes: split cedar.
  Other: Spanish or Mission tile, concrete tile, or slate.

Exterior:
  Stucco, wood, or aluminum shingles or siding, wood or plywood board and batten, brick or stone veneer.
  Types of wood: pine, Douglas fir, spruce, cypress, hemlock, cedar, or redwood.
  Masonry walls: brick, adobe, stone, concrete block, or precast concrete panels (usually reinforced for bearing walls).

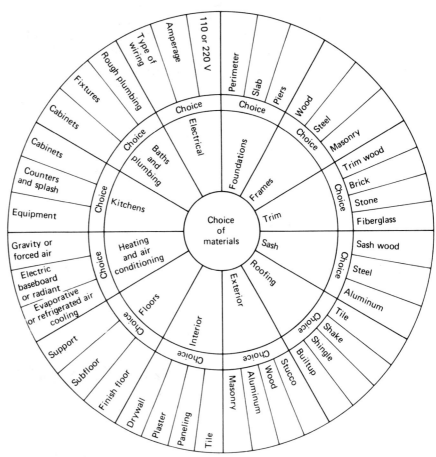

FIGURE 7.5
Choice of Materials

Interior:
   Wallboard, drywall (sheetrock), or lath and plaster; special finishes may include plywood, hardwood veneer, Douglas fir, redwood or hardwood plank (tongue and groove), ceramic tile, plastic, or marble.
   Unfinished or painted masonry walls, sometimes furred-out and finished as above.

Floors:
   Concrete slab.
   Raised subfloors of plywood, particle board, or lightweight concrete.
   Finished flooring of tongue and groove (or parquet) hardwood, asphalt tile, linoleum, sheet vinyl or vinyl tile, ceramic tile, terrazzo, or carpeting.

Heating and Air Conditioning:
   Gravity or forced-air circulation.
      Gas-fired floor, wall, or central furnace.
      Oil or wood-burning furnace.
      Solar heating system.
   Baseboard or radiant:
      Electric or hot water, using various fuels, including solar heat.
   Wood-burning fireplaces.

Air cooling:
   Individual through-wall unit or central ducted unit.
   Evaporative or refrigerated.

Kitchens:
   Cabinets: pine, particle board, plywood, hardwood, plastic laminate
      veneer, or baked enamel prefabricated steel.
   Counters and splash: ceramic tile, stainless steel, laminated wood, or
      plastic laminates.
   Equipment: sink, garbage disposal, vent-fan and hood over stove;
      built-in range and ovens, microwave oven, grill, barbeque, dish-
      washer, or trash compactor.

Baths and Plumbing:
   Rough plumbing: of polyvinyl chloride (PVC) or other plastic, galva-
      nized iron, or copper pipe; cast iron or PVC for sewer connections.
   Plumbing fixtures: vitreous china toilet; bathtub of porcelain enam-
      eled cast iron, steel, or fiberglass; enameled cast iron or molded
      plastic basin (sometimes integral with vanity counters).
   Enclosures, counters: plastic laminate, fiberglass, ceramic tile, cul-
      tured marble, quarry marble, and mirrored vanities.

FIGURE 7.6
Electrical Systems. (a) Old-Type Fuse Box. (b) Modern Circuit Breaker Box
(Photographs Courtesy of Doug Frost)

Electrical:
> Older systems: 110-volt system with fuse-box or circuit-breaker overload control, 70- to 100-ampere capacity (Figure 7.6*a*).
> Newer systems: 220-volt circuit-breaker system, 100- to 150-ampere capacity (Figure 7.6*b*).
> The most common type of wiring in single-family residences is BX or armored cable—a self-contained, heavily insulated flexible wiring, which resists deterioration from aging and vermin. Most commercial buildings are required to have rigid metal conduit—hollow pipe to protect the insulated wiring it houses. Another alternative permissible in some cases is flexible metal conduit.
> Outlets vary from one to five or more per room.

Building Quality

The published cost-estimating guides most often used by appraisers provide guidelines for rating the quality of most types of buildings. Typical standards for single-family residential structures are as follows:

1. *Low cost*   This refers to a minimum-quality or even substandard building, with limited equipment, plain exterior and interior, and minimum cost.

2. *Average cost*   This rating stands for a medium-quality standard. Acceptable to most standards, with no extras.

3. *Good*   To achieve this rating, the building must incorporate better than average architectural design, materials, and workmanship. A residence receiving this rating usually has at least two bathrooms, some form of central heat, and some built-in appliances.

4. *Very good to excellent*   These are the luxury homes. The custom design is combined with very good-quality workmanship and materials. Extra features typify structures rated in this category.

SECTION 7.4
FUNCTIONAL UTILITY AND
ARCHITECTURAL STYLES

It is often said that good architectural design is the use of appropriate materials in a proper scale and in harmony with the setting. Good architectural design and functional utility work together.

Defining Standards of Functional Utility

Functional utility consists of the combination of the usefulness and attractiveness of a property. Functional utility measures the livability of a house in terms of how well it is placed on the site, the general suitability of the floor plan, and the comfort and convenience provided by the equipment. A functional design yields the most benefits for a given cost. Some design features that contribute to functional utility in homes are contained in the previous FHA minimum property standards already discussed in Section 7.1.

In income-producing properties, functional utility is often measured by using economic standards. Design features that are in demand by tenants, and at the same time help maximize investment return, are the functional ideal. The open and bold styles found in the newest shopping centers, office and industrial complexes, and apartment projects are reflective of these goals.

Orientation and Floor Plan

Ideally, any residential structure should be oriented or placed upon the site to take advantage of the view, sun, weather, and natural topography. Such orientation should also provide adequate front, side, and backyards, as well as light air, privacy, and access to the street. Provisions for parking, storage, refuse areas, and recreational facilities also contribute to property acceptability.

Inside the residence, the floor plan is considered an important factor in determining functional utility. Easy access to each room, a good flow of traffic, separation of areas of different use, cross ventilation, wall space for the placement of furniture, and adequate storage space are sought. Efficient and pleasant layout of the kitchen, and a convenient access to yards and utility areas also affect the usefulness and marketability of a home, whether it is a conventional free-standing house or a condominium unit. See Figure 7.7 for typical differences in floor plans.

Architectural Styles

Historically, architectural styles sprang up in diverse geographical locations of the world. Now, the traditional styles are named after the location of their origin or by the historical period during which they were the most popular. The combinations and modifications of various styles lend spice and variety to our neighborhoods. Examples of some common styles are shown in Figure 7.8 and described here.

Contemporary styles, sometimes called modern, feature a low, flat roof, a low outline or profile, and a floor plan that is oriented to the outdoors. Often, these homes are designed with extensive glass areas.

The ranch style is closely related to the contemporary style but precedes it historically. The main elements are a low, rambling profile, with a gable roof, wide roof overhang, and lots of heavy wood trim. The ranch style also shows some relationship to the Spanish style of architecture through the use of brick or stone trim and design elements.

The Spanish style is popular in the southwestern states. It is characterized by its thick-appearing stucco walls (adobe or simulated), wood-beam trim, and red tile roof.

The Colonial style includes several types of early American architecture, including New England, Cape Cod, Dutch, Southern, and Georgian. These are recognized as square or rectangular, stately, and symmetrical buildings, with steep-gable roofs, shutters, and dormer windows. Each locality added individual variations that set them apart from their neighbors.

The English half-timber style looks like many houses in the English countryside. The key features are the half-timber walls with masonry or stucco between the timbers, steep-pitched roof, and casement windows.

Because it was so widely copied at the turn of the century, the Victorian style is still apparent in almost every city in America. It is typified by a roof with many gables and a wood exterior. The elaborate wood trim

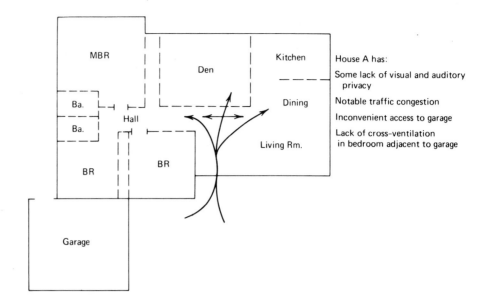

House A has:

Some lack of visual and auditory privacy

Notable traffic congestion

Inconvenient access to garage

Lack of cross-ventilation in bedroom adjacent to garage

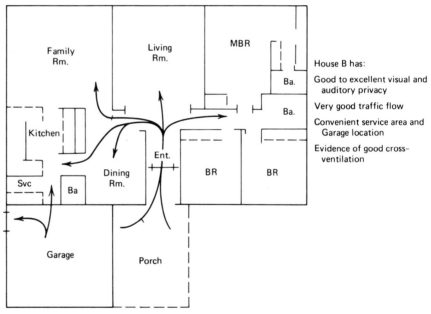

House B has:

Good to excellent visual and auditory privacy

Very good traffic flow

Convenient service area and Garage location

Evidence of good cross-ventilation

FIGURE 7.7
A Study in Floor Plans

designs around windows, roof eaves, rails, doorways, and ceilings have given this style the description of "gingerbread" architecture.

French Provincial, also known as French country, is usually a large house on a large land parcel. It is identified by its very high, steep-pitched hip roof, dormers, and overall formal, balanced appearance.

By no means are today's architectural styles pure. Most modern construction incorporates features of two or more traditional building designs. Nor is it always possible to judge the market acceptability of a particular style. The many different tastes in architecture suggest that a variety of styles is more important than purity of styles.

FIGURE 7.8
Some Examples of Architectural Styles. (*Source: Reference Book*, California Department of Real Estate, 1974)

SUMMARY

The inspection and analysis of real property improvements require preparation and planning. The appraiser should prepare to arrive at the field inspection with the equipment and tools needed for an efficient physical inspection of the building. The most important tool is the checklist, or appraisal form, for recording data. The amount and kind of data to be collected depend upon the purpose of the appraisal, the intended use of the report, and the value approach to be emphasized; therefore, the appraisal should be planned in advance. In this way the appraiser is alerted to note the relevant information at the time of the inspection.

The purpose of most appraisals will be to estimate market value. This requires a detailed and accurate description of the physical structures and a rating for market acceptability. Appraisals made to estimate some other type of value require more specialized data.

The intended use of the report will greatly affect the amount and kind of data required. The seller of a single-family dwelling might be satisfied simply with a set of comparable sales and a short discussion of comparability. A lender's appraisal report requirements may be much more detailed and demanding.

If the cost approach is to be emphasized, the data collected must support the building cost estimate and the rating for age, condition, and utility. If the sales comparison approach is to be stressed, the data required will include items such as the architectural style, number of rooms, and parking accommodations, which can be compared with features of similar properties that have sold. If the income approach is to be emphasized, the appraiser should record the features that most affect the income-potential and probable expenses.

Regardless of the approach to be emphasized, the building inspection should accurately describe and rate the physical features of the structure for marketability, quality of construction, and physical condition. Measuring and diagramming the subject property are usually required.

Last but not least, the inspection and analysis of improvements require a working knowledge of structural detail. Industry standards should be understood by the practicing appraiser.

Since market acceptability is the ultimate test of value, it is important that the appraiser have a basic knowledge of design principles in construction. Good architectural design incorporates not only the building style, but also those features that most effectively contribute to the utility of the building.

IMPORTANT TERMS AND CONCEPTS

Ranch style	English half-timber style
Class A, B, C, or D construction	French Provincial style
Colonial style	Functional utility
Construction classification	Living area
Contemporary style	Spanish style
Effective age	Victorian style

REVIEWING YOUR UNDERSTANDING

1. The most important tool you will need for recording your data during the building inspection is:

   (a) A plat map
   (b) A measuring tape
   (c) A checklist or appraisal form
   (d) A marble

2. The building inspection must be geared to:

   (a) The purpose of the appraisal
   (b) The use of the appraisal report
   (c) The value approach to be emphasized
   (d) All of the above

3. The FHA minimum property standards include:

   (a) Convenience of traffic circulation and ease of housekeeping
   (b) Adequate sanitation facilities

(c) Both parts (a) and (b)

(d) None of the above

4. Some of the factors usually considered as determinants of cost are:

(a) Design or use type

(b) Construction classification

(c) Rating of quality

(d) All of the above

5. The major items to describe and rate in a structure include:

(a) Foundation, exterior, and roof

(b) List of rooms

(c) Interior and built-in kitchen equipment

(d) All of the above

6. Rating a single-family residence for market appeal considers:

(a) The demands and tastes of the market in the neighborhood of the subject property

(b) The quality of construction, materials used, and their finish

(c) General livability and condition of the property

(d) All of the above

7. Effective age refers to:

(a) Original age

(b) Average age

(c) Relative age considering the physical condition and marketability of a structure

(d) All of the above

8. The total living area of a residential structure is measured by:

(a) Exterior measurement including walls and finish

(b) Interior measurements only

(c) House and garage area combined

(d) None of the above

9. Classification of basic construction refers to:

(a) Type of use

(b) Type of basic frame, wall, floor, and roof construction

(c) Quality of construction

(d) All of the above

10. The criteria used in the selection of building materials include:

(a) Climate

(b) Availability

(c) Durability

(d) All of the above

11. Good architectural design consists in part of:

(a) A unique floor plan

(b) Functional utility

(c) Using expensive materials

(d) All of the above

12. The architectural style that uses elaborate wood trim designs around windows, doorways, and roof eaves is:

(a) English

(b) Spanish

(c) Victorian

(d) French Provincial

CHAPTER
EIGHT

THE SALES
COMPARISON
APPROACH

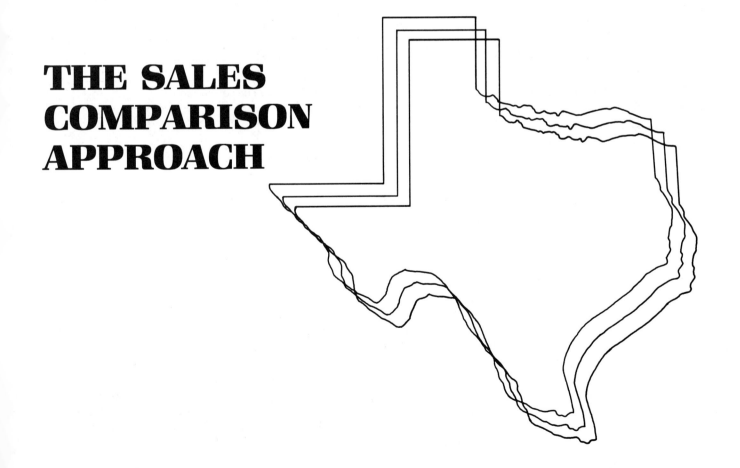

PREVIEW

One of the three approaches that appraisers use to estimate value is the sales comparison approach. This approach involves analyzing recently sold properties and comparing them to the property being appraised. Chapter 8 outlines the steps in the sales comparison approach and describes the important process of selecting comparable sales.

When you have finished this chapter, you should be able to:

1. List and explain the four steps in the sales comparison approach.

2. Explain the several important concepts behind the sales comparison approach.

3. Explain how to decide if a sale is comparable.

4. Discuss what information about a comparable sale should be collected.

5. Identify the major sources of market data.

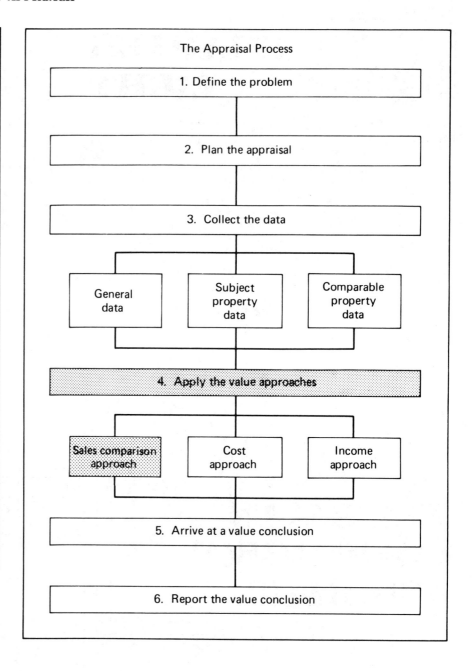

SECTION 8.1
INTRODUCING THE SALES
COMPARISON APPROACH

The sales comparison approach (also called the market approach) is a process that analyzes and compares sales to the property being appraised. This process is based on the principle of substitution. In order to understand and use the sales comparison approach and the principle of substitution, a thorough understanding of the neighborhood, city, and region, as well as a complete inspection of the property, is needed. You should review Chapters 4 through 7 if you have any questions concerning this material.

Outline of the Sales Comparison Approach

The sales comparison approach involves four steps, which are summarized in Figure 8.1. *The first step is to seek out recent sales of properties that are comparable to the subject property.* This requires understanding the meaning of the word *comparable*, identifying comparable properties, and collecting the necessary information about each property.

Once the necessary information about comparable sales has been obtained, *the second step is to analyze these sales* and compare them with the subject property. The purpose of analyzing the sales is to identify which features or characteristics are important in establishing prices. The process has two parts. The first is to identify the ways in which the sales differ from each other and from the subject property. Important differences could include the terms, conditions, or date of sales. Physical differences such as location, age, and/or size almost always exist. The second part of sales analysis is to compare the differences in the sale prices of the comparables with the differences in property features. We are trying to find out what causes the price of this type of property to vary. If the available sales are essentially identical to the subject property, the prices should be in a very narrow range. However, the sold properties will often be different in various ways, with a wider range of prices.

The third step in the sales comparison approach is to adjust for the differences between the sales and the subject property. The purpose of this step is to adjust the price of each comparable to reflect what the price would have been if that sale had been more nearly identical to the subject property. To carry out this step, you will select and use one or more of the adjustment techniques discussed in the next chapter.

FIGURE 8.1
Steps in the Sales Comparison Approach

After the sales have been located, analyzed, and adjusted, *the fourth step is to arrive at a value estimate as indicated by the adjusted sales.* This final step in the sales comparison approach is also covered in Chapter 9.

Key Concepts of the Sales Comparison Approach

Several concepts are needed to understand the sales comparison approach, its significance to appraisers, and its strengths and weaknesses. These concepts are described as the importance of substitution, the simplicity of market comparisons, the relationship to statistics, the relevance of adjustments, and the significance of market data. A discussion of each concept follows.

The Importance of Substitution

The principle of substitution (Chapter 5) is particularly important to the sales comparison approach. If well-informed buyers are interested in a particular property, they will generally pay no more than the cost of acquiring another property that is a satisfactory substitute. This process of substitution is commonly used by buyers and sellers: buyers compare a number of competitive listings and select the one they like best, considering the features and the list prices. Sellers, in turn, set these list prices by seeing what buyers have paid for similar property in recent transactions.

Simplicity

Generally, the sales comparison approach is simpler and more direct than the other two approaches, and it often requires fewer calculations. Consequently, there is less possibility of either an error in appraisal judgment or mathematics. Since the sales comparison approach is often the easiest approach to understand, it is usually the easiest to explain to clients. In summary, the simplicity and directness of this approach may produce a more reliable value conclusion than could be obtained by other approaches.

Statistical Connections

Another aspect of the sales comparison approach is its use of concepts from the field of statistics. For example, when we obtain information about recent sales transactions, these are usually only a portion of the total activity occurring in the market at that time. This involves the use of the statistical concept called sampling. Appraisers seek to find out, through sampling and market analysis, how buyers and sellers behave in a particular real estate market. This is a task similar to the work of statistical economists.

Bracketing is another concept that appraisers employ that is derived from statistics. Statisticians try to make predictions only *within* the range of the data they have studied. Gathering data that include both extremes of the subject being studied gives economists a more accurate understanding of the subject. (See Figure 8.2).

Appraisers apply the same concept of bracketing when selecting market data (such as comparable sales, rent comparables, or land sale comparables). If the comparable sales differ in any major way from the subject property, sales should be selected to reflect features both better and worse than the subject property's. For example, if comparable sales differ from the subject property in building size, comparable sales data for *both* larger and smaller buildings should be obtained. Differences such as age and

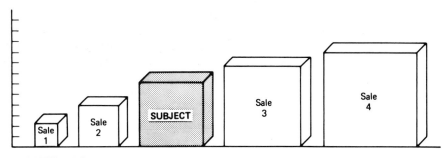

FIGURE   8.2
The Concept of Bracketing

location should be treated in the same way. By including some sales that are better than the subject property and some that are worse, you develop a better view of the range of market reactions.

Adjustments

As mentioned in Chapter 1, people with expertise in a market can estimate sales prices by intuition. Such appraisals, however, provide no specific analysis of relevant property differences. In contrast, the adjustment techniques contained in the sales comparison approach enable you to identify *specifically* property differences that are important in a given market or neighborhood. Sales comparison approach techniques can also indicate how much to adjust prices for any particular difference. Once an adjustment for a single factor is accurately estimated, you may be able to identify smaller adjustments that you might have missed before. Finally, using specific adjustments allows the appraisal to be objectively reviewed by the client. For these reasons, adjustment techniques are one of the most important contributions that formal appraising offers to the broker or salesperson.

Market Data as the Foundation

Market data are essential to *each* of the three value approaches. (See Figure 8.3.) For example, the sales comparison approach is used to estimate land value in the cost approach. Similarly, one of the best ways to estimate accrued depreciation in the cost approach is by the analysis of market sales. In the income approach, market rents are estimated by analyzing market

FIGURE   8.3

rental transactions. Vacancy and expense information for the income approach is often obtained from competitive buildings. Usually, income-approach capitalization rates are obtained by analyzing market sales, or from studies of other market information.

The relationships between the three approaches will become clearer to you as you read the following sections. For now, remember that when you estimate market value, by whichever approach, *the market is the support for that estimate.* If your opinion of value is to be based on objective analysis instead of subjective intuition, you must obtain and analyze some type of market data.

SECTION 8.2
COLLECTING
COMPARABLE SALES DATA

As we have already stated, the sales comparison approach depends upon comparing the subject property with current sales of similar properties. In this section, we discuss the first step in the sales comparison approach, which involves (1) selecting the comparable sales, and (2) locating the appropriate information about the sales.

Selecting the Comparable Sales

A sale must meet three criteria to be considered a valid comparable. First, the property must be a competitive property. Second, the sale must qualify as an open market transaction. Third, the sale must have occurred recently. Let us take a closer look at these three criteria, which are summarized in Figure 8.4.

The Competitive Property

To be a competitive property, a sale property must be a reasonable substitute or alternative for a potential purchaser looking at the subject property. A competitive property is located in an area that a buyer of the subject property would also consider. The comparable must be similar enough to the subject property in size, shape, and features to satisfy the requirements of the buyer. In general, a competitive property should appeal to the same

FIGURE 8.4
What Is a Comparable?

group of buyers. In economics this group of buyers is called a submarket. Thus you should consider to which submarket the subject property is likely to appeal.

In residential property, the different owner-occupancy submarkets are identified by such important characteristics as family size, age, and economic status. Each group of buyers will have its own housing needs. For example, families of different sizes would seek homes of different sizes. Thus a two-bedroom home would not usually qualify as an appropriate comparable for a four-bedroom home under appraisal. Such a home clearly would be sought by buyers in a different submarket in terms of family size. Note, too, that in owner-occupied residential property, family incomes of the buyers of the comparable properties should be similar to those of likely buyers of the subject property. For residential property purchased as an investment, on the other hand, the buyer submarket will be different because the buyer's motives are different.

In nonresidential property, the submarket may have other characteristics that are important. For example, among potential buyers of small neighborhood stores, one buyer submarket may consist entirely of local investors. Another buyer submarket may be people who intend to have their businesses occupy the stores. Since the two groups of buyers have different motives for purchasing the property, the factors that they consider important could vary.

Open Market Transactions

The second criterion for comparability is to determine whether a sale was an open market transaction. This test seeks to eliminate sales that are not "arms-length" market sales. For example, an income property that has sold directly to a tenant may or may not have been at the market price. In such a transaction, the sale price might represent either a bargain given by an uninformed seller or a premium offered by a tenant seeking to avoid the cost and uncertainty of relocation. Adequate exposure to a number of prospective buyers is essential to establish a market-determined price.

Further, when applying this test for an open market transaction, consider if the sale involved any unusual conditions. At times, personal property is included in the sale price or there is seller financing at favorable interest rates. Transfers between relatives may result in favorable prices. In short, you must consider whether there are unusual circumstances about any particular sale that could have distorted its price. In some cases, the appraiser may simply discard a sale where the sale price is not in line with that of the other sales. If the sale is important, however, a careful investigation and an interview with the parties involved in the transaction may be necessary.

Date of Sale

The third criterion for a comparable sale is that the date of sale must be relatively close to the date of value. The supply and demand, and thus the value, of real estate changes with time. These changes can be rapid, as with a sudden shift in interest rates, an oil embargo, or the announcement that a major factory is to be built in the area. If certain sales occur before such a change, and you are appraising a property after that time, such sales are unlikely to be comparable. Over a longer period of time, more subtle changes in market attitudes may not shift prices but may shift the importance of particular property features or locations. For example, an oil embargo could increase the values of properties close to public transportation routes. Consider any circumstances or events that might have had an effect on market attitudes. Be wary of using comparables that reflect earlier market attitudes toward particular features or locations.

The appraiser must also consider general market price trends. The sales prices of all properties are generally affected by the underlying inflation, *or* deflation, in the economy. However, real estate is affected by local influences much more than by national ones. Even during a period of inflation, prices will be going down for some locations and property types. Similarly, during a depression, prices might be going up in some locations and for some property types. Real estate price trends are somewhat unpredictable. They may change from month to month or may remain stable for months at a time, in the same manner as general economic price indexes.

How Comparable Must a Comparable Be?

Every property is unique in some way. As a result, the appraiser may not find enough recent market sales of completely comparable properties. The appraiser should *try* to collect sales that are as similar as possible in time of sale, location, and important characteristics. The appraiser should *not* use sales that do not meet the criteria for an open market transaction. However, it may be necessary to widen the other standards of comparability in order to obtain an adequate number of sales. For example, if the subject property is a house built in 1962, we would probably prefer to find comparable sales that were built between, say, 1955 and 1970. However, if we can only find one such sale, then we have to widen the range of acceptable ages to houses built between, say, 1950 and 1975 to obtain sufficient comparable sales data.

What Information Is Needed?

Once you have investigated the sales and decided which are comparable to the property being appraised, the next step is to collect the pertinent data. General information is needed about the sales transaction, the property's physical characteristics, its legal status, and its location.

The Sales Transaction Data

Several items of information about each sales transaction are needed. One is the date of sale; appraisers prefer the date that the sales price was agreed upon rather than the date that the sale was recorded. Why? Because the sales price is sometimes established by an option or other agreement by the parties well before the actual recording of the sale. The date of the "meeting of the minds" is the theoretical ideal for the date of sale. You also need to know the correct sales price and the terms of sale; by terms of sale we mean the financing arrangements that were made. You should know if the financing was by the seller or by a third party and whether it was at market interest rates. Where seller financing was at favorable rates, the advantage to the buyer may have been offset by a higher price. Ideally, you should know the actual interest rate, the payment schedule, amortization period, and due date. You should also know whether or not the mortgage had a due-on-sale acceleration clause, a variable interest rate clause, or any other special provisions. This information is needed to see if the sales price should be adjusted because of the financing. Unfortunately, complete information on sales terms is not always available.

Depending upon the type of appraisal and its intended use, additional sales transaction data may be needed. The property's legal description makes it possible to verify exactly what property was sold. Although required only in the more formal appraisals, obtaining the name of the seller (the grantor) and the buyer (the grantee) can also be useful. This helps to determine whether the sale was a family transfer. Sometimes, you may need to contact one or both parties to verify details of the transaction. Try to find out if there were any items of personalty, such as drapes, kitchen or laundry appliances, rugs, pianos, and lawn furniture, included in the sale price. In large transactions, such as apartments, some personalty is often included with the sale.

Finally, you must consider the buyer's and seller's motives. Was it a family transfer? Was it a sacrifice sale? Was it a tenant purchase? Was it bought by the adjacent property owner? As already indicated, answers to these questions may be required to establish that a sale is a valid comparable.

Physical Characteristics of the Sale

After you have collected information about the sales transaction, find out what the physical characteristics of the property are. Try to identify the characteristics that are important to the market being studied. These could include:

1. Land size, shape, topography, soil, and so on.
2. The size and nature of the structure or structures.
3. The age of the structures and the quality of their design and construction.
4. Any special features, such as kitchen built-ins, remodeled baths, patios, swimming pools, room additions, air conditioning, electronic filters, solar heating, insulation, and desirable views.
5. The condition of the structure and the quality of any modernization done.
6. Any problems with the property, ranging from small room sizes or poor floor plans to substantial deferred maintenance, inadequate wiring, roof leaks, landslides, and so on.

Legal Data About the Comparable Sale

In addition to these physical characteristics, the appraiser should be aware of certain legal characteristics of the comparable property. One example is the property's zoning: the uses that are permissible in that zoning category and the ways in which these uses compare with the subject property's zoning. Note the current property taxes and whether these taxes will be changed by resale. Any special assessment taxes should also be identified. Finally, are there any other public restrictions on the property? Or are there private restrictions such as deed restrictions, easements, or leases?

Location of the Sale

When investigating a comparable property, the appraiser should watch for any differences between the subject property's location and those of the comparable sales that are likely to be important to people in that market. These might include differences in access to public transportation, the cost

SUBJECT PROPERTY

SALE#1

SALE#2

SALE#3

FIGURE 8.5
Comparing Locations

of fares, and the ability to transfer to other routes. Are freeways easily accessible? How similar is the proximity to jobs, schools, cultural and recreational facilities, and local shopping? Check for detrimental influences such as noisy streets, incompatible land uses, and possible natural hazards. Properties around the sale must also be reviewed to see if their age, value, quality, condition, and use are substantially different from the properties around the subject. In short, compare the neighborhood around the sale and the neighborhood around the subject property (Figure 8.5) to see if there are differences that would significantly affect the attitude of prospective buyers.

Market Conditions
For each sale, you must consider what the state of the market was at the time of the sale. Were market conditions at the time of the sale different from those as of the date of valuation? As mentioned before, oil embargoes are an example of an unusual market condition; the high costs of conventional financing or lack of funds for FHA financing in particular areas are added examples of changes in market conditions that could affect prices.

Using Listings or Offers
The sale that has recently closed escrow and has been recorded is probably the most reliable comparable to use in the sales comparison approach. Sales that are still in escrow are nevertheless useful. Such prices do represent the current attitudes of market buyers and sellers. This will be true even if there is some contingency, such as approval of financing, that has delayed the closing of the sale.

   If no better evidence is available, listings of property currently for sale can sometimes be used to show the upper limit, or highest probable market value. It is important to select listings that are current and have characteristics similar to those of the subject property. Offers that have been refused are also helpful, since they can indicate the lower limit of the value range. It is wise to ask people who know about an offer, such as a broker or principal party, whether there were any unusual conditions and why the offer did not result in a sale. Perhaps only personality conflicts between the principal parties blocked a particular offer from becoming a sale.

How Many Sales?

There is no specific number of comparables that is right for every appraisal. The desirable number depends, in part, on how comparable the sales are. For example, if the sales are very similar, located nearby, and fairly recent, three sales are considered adequate for most residential appraisal assignments. But where the sales are less comparable or the appraiser has less confidence in the reliability of the information obtained about the sales, a large number of sales is usually desirable. Sometimes, too, a larger number of sales will be needed in order to provide market support for the adjustments required.

The desirable number of comparables is also influenced by the techniques used in the sales comparison approach. Some statistical techniques, for example, cannot be performed with 3 sales and might even require 30 or more comparables. The purpose or use of the appraisal report can also influence the number of comparables needed. An appraisal made for loan purposes usually requires fewer sales than an appraisal for court testimony.

Defining the Sales Search Area

How wide an area should you search for comparable sales? In general, the rule is that the more sales activity there is in an area, the more geographically restricted the appraiser's search can become. In an active market it is often possible to find an adequate number of comparable sales within several blocks of the subject property, particularly if the subject is located in a residential tract. On the other hand, in appraising a large, new custom home in the middle of a neighborhood of older, smaller homes, the appraiser would have to enlarge the comparable search area. Similarly, when few sales occur because of a market slowdown, the appraiser must widen the boundaries of his or her comparable search area in order to collect adequate sales.

For some types of property, such as larger industrial property, buyers are able to purchase satisfactory substitute properties at a considerable distance from the subject. In some markets, they will even buy property in another state. To define the search area for comparable sales in this kind of a market, the appraiser must use the definition of comparability to suggest where a buyer of this property would look for likely substitute properties.

Verification

Finally, you must consider whether the sales information you have collected is reliable. You may find that one sale has a price that appears way out of line with the other sales. It is wise to recheck the key information about that sale. There could be a mistake in your information concerning the price, terms, or physical and locational characteristics.

Basically, you have two ways to improve the reliability of the information you obtained. The first is to inspect the sales. In many appraisals, a field inspection of the comparable sales is routine. This customarily consists of viewing the exterior of the property. It helps to verify the data collected and to better evaluate the quality of the property, its condition, and its overall market appeal. Note that in making this survey, you must be careful to identify any work that appears to have been done on the property since the date of the sale. The sale price would have been based on the condition of the property at the time of the sale, and not at the time of your field inspection. Such factors as new exterior paint, new roof cover, or visible remodeling would suggest that you should check with a party to the transaction to verify the condition of the property at the time of sale.

In more complex or controversial assignments, the appraiser might need to view the interior of each comparable sale. This may be difficult, since the occupants often resent a stranger knocking at the door. However, a careful explanation of who you are, what is happening, and why an interior inspection is desired can often produce positive results.

The second way to improve data reliability is to cross-check the data already obtained by contacting another information source. When sales data are obtained from a data service, such as the Society of Real Estate Appraisers (SREA) Market Data Center or from public records, it may be desirable to verify the price and terms of the sale with a party to the transaction. This could be the real estate broker, a lawyer, the buyer, the seller, or the loan officer involved in the financing. There is no clear rule as to when this should be done. Generally, it depends upon the reliability of the source from which the sale was obtained, as well as the type of appraisal assignment involved. Thus, in preparing a residential loan appraisal in a stable market with ample, consistent sales, many appraisers would not verify the data with a party to the transaction. On the other hand, when appraising a unique property for some type of litigation (such as an eminent domain lawsuit), most appraisers find it wise to verify the price and terms with a party to the transaction.

Sources of Market Data

Becoming an efficient appraiser includes identifying the available sources of sales data for an area and knowing the advantages and drawbacks of each. Each source may be useful for different types of information. Obtaining information quickly is an important appraisal skill because it affects how much time is used to perform the appraisal.

Public Records

One major source of sales information is public records. Most public records (usually in county seats) include copies of all the deeds transferring ownership to real estate. These deeds are filed by document number on the date that they are recorded at the office. They are usually kept on microfilm and are referenced either by a document number, the microfilm reel and image numbers, or by book and page numbers. Each deed is indexed both by the name of the grantor (seller) and by the grantee (buyer). In all Texas counties, the office where the records are kept is called the county clerk's office. Figure 8.6 depicts a deed and the type of information available.

You can obtain other types of information from the deed. Some counties will not record a deed unless it contains a mailing address to which it is to be returned. Often the mailing address for the buyer or the buyer's attorney or broker is used. Most deeds also contain the new address to which the property tax bill should be mailed. This could be the buyer's address, the buyer's agent (if the property tax is being paid by another party), or the buyer's bank (if taxes are to be paid from an escrow account). Either or both of these addresses can lead you to someone who can verify information about the sale.

Most deeds also indicate which party requested that the deed be recorded. This is particularly common when deeds are recorded as part of a

Prepared by the State Bar of Texas for use by lawyers only. Reviewed
1-1-76. Revised to include grantee's address (art. 6626, RCS) 1-1-82.

WARRANTY DEED

THE STATE OF TEXAS

COUNTY OF DALLAS   } KNOW ALL MEN BY THESE PRESENTS:

That   Louise Bales, a feme sole,

of the County of Dallas   and State of   Texas   for and in

consideration of the sum of Ninety-three thousand two hundred ($93,200.00)

DOLLARS

and other valuable consideration to the undersigned paid by the grantee   herein named, the receipt of

which is hereby acknowledged,

have GRANTED, SOLD AND CONVEYED, and by these presents do GRANT, SELL AND CONVEY unto
James King Smith and wife, Mary Ellen Smith,

of the County of   Dallas   and State of   Texas   , all of

the following described real property in   Dallas   County, Texas, to-wit:

Lot 33, Block 1/7568, Castle Creek subdivision out of the J. O. Crutchfield survey,
abstract 247, according to a plat thereof recorded in book 34, of the Plat Records
of Dallas County, Texas

TO HAVE AND TO HOLD the above described premises, together with all and singular the rights and
appurtenances thereto in anywise belonging, unto the said grantee ,   their   heirs and assigns
forever; and   do hereby bind   her   heirs, executors and administrators to
WARRANT AND FOREVER DEFEND all and singular the said premises unto the said grantee ,
heirs and assigns, against every person whomsoever lawfully claiming or to claim the same or any part thereof.

EXECUTED   this   31st   day of   December   , A.D. 1985

Louise Bales

FIGURE 8.6
Recording Information

title or escrow company closing. Usually, the name of the title company is on the deed, as well as the escrow account number, and the code letters indicating which title company branch handled the transaction. Title companies will not divulge the details of a transaction but will often disclose the name of the broker(s). The broker, in turn, can provide information about the property.

When an institutional lender makes a new loan on the property as part of the sale transaction, the lender's loan number is sometimes typed on the deed. This loan number can prove helpful when discussing the property with the lender, or the lender's appraiser, facilitating location of the file.

Finally, you should note that the deed contains dates other than the date of recording. Often, the date next to the signatures indicates either the date that the document was signed or the date it was prepared. Another date will be on the notary public's affidavit of signatures. This will be the date the individual sellers had their signatures notarized.

If a new loan was placed on the property at the time of sale, the deed of trust securing that loan will be recorded as the document immediately following the deed. This deed of trust will give the lender's name and the amount of the loan. It will indicate whether it is a variable interest-rate loan and if a clause was included making the loan due in full when the property is resold. The loan number will sometimes be on the deed of trust, as will a mailing address for the borrower, a date of signature, and another notary's signature with the date and county of business. Much of this information may already be on the deed, but occasionally, differences will be found that will help the appraiser to identify and locate the various parties.

Additional documents may also be recorded, such as a chattel mortgage for any personal property and an assignment of rents if the property generates income. A second mortgage might have been placed by the broker to secure a note for the commission due. This would identify the broker's name and location. There may also be second mortgages from the seller or from third parties.

A second major public source of information for appraisers is the central appraisal district. Although the exact jurisdiction will differ from one location to another, assessment records are usually maintained by the central district in any area. The primary document to look for is the appraisal list or roll which lists all privately owned property and its tax bill mailing address and notes the property value that is appraised as of January 1 of the current year. Most jurisdictions have a standard series of maps, so that each parcel can be described by map reference number of chief appraiser's parcel number. This number also appears on the appraisal roll. Appraisal rolls will often show the date of the most recent transfer of ownership and the document number used by the county clerk's office for that transfer. The rolls also contain a use code (which identifies a category of use for the property, such as residential, commercial, industrial, vacant land) and may show the age and size of buildings. (See Figure 8.7.)

The appraisal maps include index maps for the entire county, area index maps, and maps showing each of the parcels in a block. These maps give the dimensions of the parcels and usually show major easements, as well as streets and railroads. Often, the area of larger parcels will be calculated and noted on the map.

There are also indexes for the appraisal roll. The roll itself usually lists property in parcel number order. One index will list property by address and a second index by the name of the owner.

PAGE _____ 1939

FORM B _____

ASSESSMENT OF PROPERTY IN ___HUNT___ COUNTY PAGE_____ 1939

OWNED AND RENDERED FOR TAXATION BY THE OWNERS OR AGENTS THEREOF YEAR _____ 1983

OWNER	ABSTRACT OR LOT NO.	TRACT OR BLOCK	ORIGINAL GRANTEE CITY OR TOWN	ACRES	VALUE	CODE	H.S. VALUE	PERSONAL PROPERTY VALUE	COUNTY TAX VALUE	STATE TAX VALUE	STATE TAX	COUNTY TAX	SCH TAX NO	SCHOOL TAX	HOSP TAX	LATE FILING	TOTAL TAX	RECEIPT NO.	DATE OF HALF PAYMENT	DATE OF TOTAL PAYMENT
00000333190 MOREHEAD MILES M 3211 ONEAL ST GREENVILLE TX 75401	0020 03211 43852720002041	2720 ONEAL	ORIG TOWN OF GR IV		1800 2704	H	20000		8840	8840		2629	41		561		3390	30926		
00000327910 MORELAND MATTIE 1612 MEMPHILL GREENVILLE TX 75401	001A 01612 43851640001441	1640 MEMPHILL	ORIG TOWN OF GR IV		640 8710	H	9350						41					30927		
00000310000 MORELAND HELEN P O BOX 159 COMMERCE TEXAS 75420	0051 LOT 5 A 43800060005131	0060	ORIG TOWN OF CO IV		2650 24620				27270	27270		8126	31		1732		1045	30928		
00000339960 MORELAND IRENE J 1804 GORDON GREENVILLE TX 75401	0010 01804 43853940001041	3940 GORDON	ORIG TOWN OF GR IV		510 7440	H	7950						41					30929		
00000482060 MORELAND RAY L 1103 MIDWAY DR RICHARDSON TX 75080	4550 54650300455056	0300	WHISKERS RETREA		440				440	440		141	56		28		169	30930		
00000482180 MORELAND RAY L 1103 MIDWAY DR RICHARDSON TX 75080	4680 54650300468056	0300	WHISKERS RETREA		450				450	450		144	56		29		173	30931		
00000152260 MORELAND WILLARD RT 1 CAMPBELL TX 75422	1082 ABST 1082 G W WRIGHT .50 A 10820710000017	0710	WRIGHT GEORGE W IV	50	1150 38120				39270	39270		12566	17		2494		1506	30932		
00000074980 MORENO GREGORIO BOX 9 CADDO MILLS TX 75005	0563 0563M50000000010 0563 0563M50000000010	M500 M500	JOHNSON J M NON-AGRIC VALUE 24,120 JOHNSON J M IV	321 200	3060 7090 1500 26920				38570	38570		12344	10 10		2450		1479	30933		
00000115990 MORENO GREGORIO BOX 9 CADDO MILLS TX 75005	0849 0849M14000000010	M140	PIPER NATHANIEL NON-AGRIC VALUE 28,500 IV	600	7800 1500				9300	9300		2476	10		591		3567	30934		
00000361310 MORENO JOSUE R 2904 WANDA WAY SEAGOVILLE TEXAS 75159	0090 44450010009056	0010	PANORAMA EST AD		1000				1000	1000		420	56		64		3843	30935		
00000028790 MORENO NOE 2317 CAMP DAVID DR MESQUITE TX 75149	0229 0229M42000000010	M420	DAVIS GEORGE W	400	9200				9200	9200		2944	10		584		3528	30936		
00000319700 MORGAN G WARREN P O BOX 1057 GREENVILLE TX 75401	0028 00000 43850040002041	0040	ORIG TOWN OF GR LTS S PT 2-3 IV		2060 2120				4180	4180		1336	41		265		1603	30937		
00000319720 MORGAN G WARREN PO BOX 1057 GREENVILLE TX 75401	0050 02612 43850040005041	0040	ORIG TOWN OF GR JORDAN IV		2040 34320				36360	36360		11635	41		2309		1394	30938		
00000003110 MORGAN BEN J MRS 2907 POPLAR GREENVILLE TX 75401	0024 00000 RT 5 EDWARD F ANDERSON 00240010000042	001A	ANDERSON EDWARD	1430	42890				42890	42890		13725	42		2724		1644	30939		
00000002640 MORGAN BENTON J MRS BOX 656 GREENVILLE TX 75401	0019 00000 RT 3 BAILEY ASHMORE 00190010000040	0010	ASHMORE BAILEY	440	34670				34670	34670		11094	40		2202		1329	30940		
00000003250 MORGAN BENTON MRS BOX 656 GREENVILLE TX 75401	0025 00000 RT 5 E F ANDERSON 00250020000040	0020	ANDERSON EDWARD	210	22050				22050	22050		7056	40		1400		845	30941		

TOTAL ACRES RENDERED	TOTAL VALUE ACREAGE PROP.	TOTAL HOMESTEAD	TOTAL VALUE CITY PROPERTY	TOTAL VALUE PERSONAL PROP.	TOTAL VALUE FOR COUNTY TAX	TOTAL VALUE FOR STATE TAX	STATE TAX				TOTAL TAX
177.90	195,950	STATE H.S. 115,840			274,490	274,490		COUNTY TAX 878.36	SCHOOL TAX	HOSP TAX 174.33	TOTAL TAX 1,052.69
		D.V.	D.V. USED		CO. 37300	SCHS	SCHA	SCHV			TRIPLICATE

WESTERN DATA SERVICES

FIGURE 8.7

A Sample Assessment Roll. (Courtesy of the Hunt County Appraisal District)

Multiple Listing Services

In many areas, there are multiple listing services (often called MLS). These are usually sponsored by a local board of realtors, or by local brokers. All of the property listings submitted by members are combined and made available to subscribers. These current listings are published in a weekly book and are available via computer in most locations. Usually, at the end of the book you will find an index of listings that have sold in the immediate past. A quarterly book is published summarizing all of the sales and expired listings that have occurred during that quarter. Many multiple listing services restrict use of the books solely to their members.

Data Services

In recent years, the number of organized, private sources of appraisal data has increased. One of the best known of these is the SREA Market Data Center, Inc., a nonprofit corporation sponsored by the Society of Real Estate Appraisers. The sales data are generated by cooperating lenders and appraisers and are made available to Data Center members, or franchise members, in several formats. For example, listings of single-family sales are available in many areas through a monthly sale book, and also by

SREA MARKET DATA CENTER INC. **SINGLE FAMILY RESIDENTIAL SALES DATA** COUNTY HARRIS

MAP CODE -- CITY -- CENSUS TRACT	PROPERTY ADDRESS	UNIT	$ SALE PRICE	TYPE	CASH DOWN	% 1ST MTG	SALE DATE MO/YR	SALE CLOSED	LOT SIZE OR AREA	FLOOD ZONE / SITE INF	WATER / SEWER	STYLE	STORIES	FLOOR PLAN	QUALITY / CONDITION	YEAR BUILT	ROOMS	BED RMS	$ SQ FT / OTHER ROOMS	BATHS FULL	BATHS HALF	SQ FT LIVING AREA	BASEMENT AREA SQ FT	BASEMENT BEDRMS	BASEMENT BATHS	BASEMENT 1/2 BATHS	BASEMENT % FINISH	A/C	PARKING	POOL	FIREPLACE	EQUIPMENT	REMODELED	OTHER IMP	HEATING	FUEL	TYPE CONSTR	EXT WALLS	TYPE ROOF	FLOORING	AMENITIES	LEASEHOLD	TYPE OWNER	TYPE IMP	
450 -E	10335 LONE BROOK DR		57,500	F		96%	2-85	N	63X116	N	PP	K	1		AA	84	6	3	41.55D	2		1,384	S					C	A2		1	RDG			A	E	F	L	C	C				S	C
	10324 SOMMERVILLE		49,900	F		94%	1-85	N	32X 79	N	PP	D	2	G	AA	78	6	3	37.98D	2	1	1,314	S					C	A2		1	RDG		F	A	E	F	L	C	C				S	
450 -K	9614 KEMPWOOD		59,000	F		96%	1-85	N	8,780	K	PP	K	1	G	GG	63	7	3	35.04FDY	2		1,684	S					C	A2		1	RDG		L	A	G	F	X	C	C	S			S	
450 -M	8667 SONNEVILLE DR		48,000	F		91%	1-85	N	60X 80	N	PP	K	1	A	AG	56	6	3	48.19D	1		996	S					C	A1			D		F	A	G	F	W	C	H				S	
450 -N	2110 LONGHORN		120,000	C	5%	95%	1-85	Y	10,000	N	PP	A	2	A	A	75	9	5	47.02DY	2	1	2,552	S					C	A2		1	RD		F	A	G	B	L	C	C				S	
450 -P	2534 PINE VILLAGE		75,000	F		96%	1-85	N	71X113	N	PP	K	1	A	AG	67	7	3	44.83F	2		1,673	S					C	B2			RDG		F	A	G	F	X	C	C				S	
450 -S	1607 MAUX DR		105,000	C			11-84	N		N	PP	K	1	A	AG	59	7	3	48.36DY	2		2,171	S						A2			RDG		FN	A	G	F	X	C	C				S	C
	* * *					11.12%	2.00		5.00																																				
	1811 NOCTURNE		102,000	F		82%	9-84	N	75X144	W	PP	K	1	G	GG	61	8	3	47.95RFDB	2		2,127	S					C	D2		1	RDG		FL	A	G	F	X	C	C				S	
450 -U	9338 WALTERSVILLE RD		62,000	B		65%	1-85	N	105X130	N	PP	K	1	A	AA	52	6	3	35.47	2		1,748	S					C	A2			RD			A	G	F	X	C	H				S	
	* * * FIX	1	360			11.12%	2.00		5.00																																				
450 -W	10151 WHITESIDE		100,000	C		86%	1-85	N	78X125	NW	PP	K	1	A	AA	67	8	3	48.19RD	2		2,075	S					C	D2	P	1	RGH		F	A	G	F	X	C	C				S	C
	* * * CONV		30			12.50%	4.00																																						
450 -Y	9003 LUPTON CT		139,000	C	5%	95%	2-85	N	85X150	N	PP	D	1	A	AG	65	9	4	65.17F	2		2,133	S					C	D2		1	RDG		Z	A	G	F	X	C	C				S	C
	* * * ARM	1	360			10.25%	3.50		3.50																																				
451 -G	5714 W 43		63,500	C			11-84	Y						A	AA	55	6	3	46.15	1	1	1,376						C	A2																U
	4301 COSTA RICA		69,500	V			3-85	N	9,288	NJ	PP	K	1	A	AG	55	6	3	56.83FD	1	1	1,223	S					C	A2			E		FS	A	G	F	X	C	V				S	
	5122 DELANGE		59,900	F		96%	12-84	N	60X115		PP	K	1	A	AA	55	5	3	52.92F	1		1,132	S					C	A3					F	A	G	F	X	C	H				S	C
451 -K	6618 UNDERHILL		47,000	F		96%	10-84	N	55X100	N	PP	K	1			50	4	2	54.27	1		866	S					L	A1					F	X	G	F	Z	C	C				S	
451 -L	3815 COSTA RICA		84,000	F		96%	10-84	N	60X109	N	PP	K	1	G	AG	61	8	3	41.48	2		2,025	S					C	A2		1	RDG		F	A	G	F	X	C	C				S	
	4926 HIALEAH		68,000	C		95%	3-85	N	7,000	N	PP	K	1	A	AA	55	7	3	41.90RD	2		1,623	S					C	C3			RDG		FN	A	G	F	X	C	C				S	C
	* * * FIXED	1	360			12.75%	5.00		7.00																																				
451 -R	4119 MARLBOROUGH		73,000	F		73%	1-85	N	7,756	NM	PP	D	1	G	GG	58	7	4	40.35RD	2		1,809	S					C	A2			RDG		PF	A	G	F	L	C	C				S	
451 -S	1901 COULCREST		52,000	F			2-85	Y						A	A	50	6	3	32.42	1		1,604						W	A1																U
	2107 RIDGECREST		55,000	V			1-85	Y						A	AA	50	6	3	40.95	1	1	1,343						C	A2																U
	2021NW SPENWICK DR	315	29,900	F		97%	1-85	N			PP	K	2	G	GG	83	3	1	36.20F	1	1	826	S					C	C1		1	RDG		L	A	E	F	X	C	C	SP		C	Z	
451 -W	8497 BURKHART		243,060	C			12-84	N	70X260	N	PP	L	2	G	GG	84	9	4	78.03DOY	3	1	3,115	S					C	C2		1	RDG		QP	A	E	F	X	C	C				S	
	8506 MERLIN		80,000	F		96%	12-84	N	70X120	N	PP	A	1	G	FF	60	7	3	46.46FD	2		1,722	S					W	A2			H		F	A	G	F	B	C	W				S	
	1702 MONARCH OAKS DR		67,000	C	5%	95%	1-85	Y	100X150	N	PP	K	1	A	A	70	6	3	42.30D	1		1,584	S					C	A2		1	DG		F	A	G	B	W	C	C				S	
452 -G	1042 RICHELIEU		122,000	C	20%	80%	3-85	N	9,112	N	PP	E	2	A	AA	70	8	4	45.57FDY	2	1	2,677	S					C	D3		1	RDG		PF	A	G	F	L	C	C				S	
	* * * CONV		360			12.75%	3.50		6.00																																				
452 -J	1625NW LAMONTE LN		53,800	F		98%	1-85	N	7,095		PP	K	1	G	AG	59	5	2	42.90F	1		1,254	S					W	A1				A	F	X	G	F	L	C	C				S	
452 -K	958 GARDENIA DR		62,000	F		95%	10-84	N	60X146		PP	K	1	A	AA	40	5	2	49.64F	1		1,249	S					L	A1			D	KA	GP	A	G	F	L	C	H				S	
	826 LAMONTE		68,000	C		95%	3-85	N	12,000	N	PP	K	1	A	AA	46	5	2	61.48RD	1		1,106	S					C	C1			RDH		FS	A	G	F	Z	C	H				S	C
	* * * BOND	1	360			11.12%			6.00																																				
452 -L	5307 BRINKMAN		80,000	F		96%	1-85	N	70X120	NW	PP	A	1	A	AA	69	9	3	45.58FDB	2		1,755	S					C	D2		1	RDG		N	A	G	F	X	C	C				S	
452 -N	1650 DUBARRY		49,000	V			3-85	Y	53X116	N	PP		1	G	AG	55	4	2	67.22	1		729	S					C	A1						A	G	F	L	C	C				S	
452 -S	2015 BROOKTREE		150,000	C	27%	73%	2-85	Y	80X120	N	PP	K	1	A	A	74	7	3	70.99FDY	2	1	2,113	S					C	D2	P	1	RDG		PF	A	G	B	W	C	C				S	
452 -U	1423 W 22 ST		54,396	A	71%	21%	3-84	Y	72X150	NW	PP	K	1	A	A	60	5	3	45.33	2		1,200	S					W	A1			H		PF	A	G		X	C	C				S	
	* * * LIEN2		$4400	12		10.00%																																							
452 -W	2706 HAVERHILL		83,000		5%		2-85	N	89X110	N	PP		1	A	AA	60	6	3	65.20R	1	1	1,273	S					C				RDG			P	G		X	C	C				S	F
	* * * CONV	1	360			11.12%			6.00																																				
452 -Z	1009 W 13 ST		54,600	A	7%	93%	3-85	Y	50X125	NW	PP	K	1	A	AA	35	5	2	64.39	1		848	C						G			DGC	CX	HD	A	G	F	L	C	C				S	
	* * * ASSUM	1	$613 360			12.00%																																							
	1017 RUTLAND		87,500	C	5%	95%	3-85	Y	67X132	NW	PP	K	1	G	GG		6	3	60.72D	1		1,441	C						G1			RF	C	GD	G	G	F	L	C	S				S	
453 -B	212 SOREN		45,000	F		84%	1-85	N	69X102		PP	K	1	G	GG	40	7	4	33.36FD	2		1,349	C					C	G2		1		CA		A	G	F	L	C	W				S	
453 -C	814 INNSDALE		44,000	V			3-85	N	67X133	N	PP	K	1	G	AA	61	5	3	39.01	1		1,128	S					W	A1					PL	W	G	F	X	C	W				S	
453 -E	511 E JANISCH		52,300	F		96%	1-85	N	65X115	Y	PP	K	1	G	GG	58	6	3	43.69	1		1,197	S					C	A1					F	A	G	F	X	C	H				S	
	226 WEATHERLY WY		60,000	V			2-85	N	70X105	N	PP	K	1	G	AG	73	7	3	30.29RD	2		1,981	S					C	D2		1	RDH			A	G	F	X	C	C				S	
453 -K	4221 ROGERS		35,000	C			2-85	N	50X100	N	PP	K	1	A	AA	45	5	2	38.04RD	1		920	C						D1						X	G	F	Z	C	C				S	C
	* * * CONV		360				5.00																																						
453 -M	923 CAPERTON		40,000	F		85%	11-84	N	60X195		PP	K	1	G	GG	45	6	2	28.65FDO	1		1,396	C					W	D2			H		L	F	G	F	P	C	H				S	
	1825 MCCLELLAND		37,500	F		98%	1-85	N	70X200	N	PP	K	1	A	AG	50	6	2	35.61	1		1,053	C						D1					PH	X	G	F	W	C	H				S	
453 -T	1403 WALTON ST		45,000	C	10%	90%	3-85	N	50X100	NJ	PP	K	1	A	AA	30	5	2	54.55DAO	1		825	C						A1					F	X	G	F	L	C	H				S	C
	* * * ADJUS	1	360			9.87%	6.00		6.00																																				
453 -U	909 CANADIAN		73,500	F		97%	2-85	N	60X110	N	PP	K	1	A	AA	44	6	3	43.83RD	1	1	1,677	C					C	D1			DG	A	Z	A	G	F	V	C	C				S	
453 -V	813 CANADIAN		51,900	C	6%	94%	3-85	N	50X106	N	PP	K	1	A	AA	45	6	3	37.58FDA	2		1,381	C					C	C2			DG		PF	A	G	F	Z	C	C				S	C
	* * * FIXED	1	360			12.10%	4.50		4.50																																				
453 -W	636 E 12 1/2		72,900	A		75%	2-85	N	62X125	N	PP	K	1	A	AA	50	6	3	52.71RFD	1		1,383	S					W	D2			RD		FD	A	G	F	Z	C	H				S	C
	* * * ASSUM	2				9.50%																																							
	745 E 16 ST		48,000	C			2-85	N	50X100	N	PP	K	1	A	AA	30	5	2	41.85FD	1		1,147	C					W	D2		1			F	X	G	F	L	C	H				S	C
	* * * FIXED		360			13.25%																																							

** THE ABOVE DATA BELIEVED TO BE RELIABLE BUT ACCURACY IS NOT GUARANTEED -- 15-- SOUTH TEXAS 4/85 450 -E / 453 -W

FIGURE 8.8
(Courtesy of SREA Market Data Center, Inc.)

computer terminal. A sample page is shown as Figure 8.8. Quarterly books of apartment sales are available in the same areas. Industrial and commercial property sale books have recently been added and are available in a nationwide quarterly book. The majority of the sales data is developed from loan appraisals. The SREA Data Center is also developing and publishing transfer information based on recorder's and assessor's information. Data Center coverage started in Southern California about 15 years ago and gradually spread across the United States. The coverage in each area varies depending on the cooperation of local lenders.

A number of other private firms provide some type of data service. Several of these are nationwide. For example, Real Estate Data, Inc., is a profit-making firm in Miami that originally provided only copies of county assessor's records. Today it provides monthly sales recording information in many areas of the country. A similar firm is Microfiche Publishers, Inc., which provides assessor's records on microfilm sheets called microfiche. There are a number of local sales services that exist in various areas. Some services specialize in monthly sales microfiche, which are available for many of the larger counties in Texas. Other services may specialize in one county, providing microfiche or deed copies as their basic data. In many areas there are local appraisal cooperative data centers. These can range from a large company to informal agreements between two appraisers to share sales data.

Finally, sales data information service can be provided by title insurance companies. Every title insurance company has an extensive collection of copies of the public records affecting real estate, including assessment records and sales transfer records. Appraisers can obtain copies of these documents from a title insurance company. In some cases, appraisers can make arrangements with the title company for title company personnel to research the sales in a particular location for a reasonable fee. This information is provided as part of the insurance company's plant service. Sometimes, if the research is quite limited, title companies provide the information without charge. Most appraisers find it essential to contact title companies from time to time.

Parties to the Transaction

In researching sales, you should consider the possibility of obtaining information from the parties to the transaction. These parties include not only the buyer and seller but their respective agents as well. Other parties that may also have relevant information include any brokers who had offers on the property at the same time or brokers who had prior listings that expired. Any lender involved with the sale can also be a source of information. Sometimes a particular broker's office, or a particular lender's branch, may originate the transaction or be a party to a large percentage of all the transactions in an area. If so, such an office would be an important resource.

Appraisal Office Data Files

Many appraisers find that the types of properties they appraise will change from time to time. Houses are the most common appraisal assignment; usually the information needed to complete the appraisal is plentiful and easy to find. However, there will be times throughout an appraiser's career when an unusual property will be assigned and the necessary data will not be accessible. With this in mind, many appraisers keep the market data that were researched for an unusual assignment. If a similar assignment comes up in the near future, the market data can be reused. Files of this type are also a useful source of information for other appraisers. One appraiser may have information on file that another appraiser cannot find without a major effort. In many areas appraisers will share their sales data with other appraisers, especially local ones. However, a clear policy concerning this type of cooperation does not exist. In areas where such cooperation is not customary, it is up to the individual appraiser to decide whether to cooperate with other appraisers.

Locating good comparable sales data efficiently is an art. You must be imaginative, resourceful and, above all, determined. Very often, the most important differences between a fair appraisal and a good one are the several added sales and the several added relevant facts about the sales properties. Like all arts, skill at appraisal improves with experience, so do not be dismayed if it seems difficult at first.

SUMMARY

The sales comparison approach is one of the three approaches used to estimate value. The main feature of the sales comparison approach is the process of analyzing and comparing sales to the subject property, based on the principle of substitution. The sales comparison approach consists of four steps.

---

1. Research sales.
2. Analyze sales.
3. Adjust sales for differences between the sales and the subject property.
4. Arrive at a value conclusion.

When employing the sales comparison approach, an appraiser should consider concepts that are fundamental to it. These concepts include the principle of substitution, the importance of simplicity, the application of statistics, the relevance of adjustments, and the foundation—market data. Each of these concepts is important in understanding how to use the sales comparison approach.

The first step of the sales comparison approach—researching comparable sales—consists of two parts: (1) selecting comparable sales, and (2) locating the appropriate sales information. When selecting comparable sales, three criteria must be met for a sale to be considered a comparable sale: the sale must be a competitive property, an open market transaction, and a recent sale. The ideal is to find comparable sales that meet all three criteria. If you cannot, try to find sales that were open market transactions and are as comparable and as recent as possible.

Once you have decided upon the sales you are going to use, the next step is collecting the necessary information about the sales transaction, the physical characteristics of the property, its legal status, and its location. It is also important to consider whether there were unusual market conditions at the time of sale.

The number of comparables needed varies with each appraisal situation. How comparable the sales are and which adjustment techniques are used will both affect the number of sales needed to support your conclusion.

The area of the sales search will vary as well, depending on the type of property being appraised and the amount of market activity.

After deciding on the sales data to be used, you must then decide whether your data are reliable. Inspecting the sales and cross-checking your data with another source are two good ways to assure reliability.

Since there are many sources of market data, the trick is knowing where to find the information you need as efficiently and easily as possible. There are a variety of places with which you should be familiar, ranging from public records at the appraisal district office to private firms that provide information on sales for a fee.

Public records include deeds, which contain such needed information as names of grantor and grantee, a legal description of the property, transfer tax information, a mailing address for the buyer, and dates of transactions. The appraisal district office contains the assessment roll, which lists privately owned property, its value for property tax purposes and its tax bill mailing address. Appraisal maps provide measurements of parcels and show major easements, streets, and railroads.

One private data source is the multiple listing service (MLS) sponsored by local boards of REALTORS®. Private data sources are becoming increasingly valuable, particularly the SREA Market Data Center, Inc., a nonprofit corporation of the Society of Real Estate Appraisers. Whenever possible, the appraiser also seeks out the parties to a transaction—the buyer, the seller, and their agents—to obtain information. If you learn to utilize all these sources, you will master the art of finding good comparable sales.

IMPORTANT TERMS AND CONCEPTS

Adjustments	Location
Bracketing	Sales comparison approach
Buyer's motives	Open market transaction
Comparable search area	Physical characteristics
Competitive property	Seller's motives
Data reliability	Verifying sales information

REVIEWING YOUR UNDERSTANDING

1. The sales comparison approach involves:
   - (a) Analyzing sales
   - (b) Comparing sales to a subject property
   - (c) Both (a) and (b)
   - (d) None of the above

2. The four steps in the sales comparison approach are:
   - (a)
     - (1) Researching comparable sales
     - (2) Analyzing sales
     - (3) Adjusting for differences between sales and the subject property
     - (4) Arriving at a value conclusion
   - (b)
     - (1) Researching comparable sales
     - (2) Analyzing the sales

        (3) Adjusting for differences between the sales

        (4) Arriving at a value conclusion

    (c) **(1)** Researching comparable sales

        (2) Adjusting for differences between sales and the subject property

        (3) Analyzing the sales

        (4) Arriving at a value conclusion

    (d) None of the above.

3. The sales comparison approach is simpler and more direct than the income or cost approaches because:

    (a) Fewer comparable properties are required so it is easier to outline the results to clients

    (b) There are fewer mathematical calculations, so there is less chance of mathematical errors

    (c) Both (a) and (b)

    (d) None of the above

4. Appraisers use bracketing in order to:

    (a) Apply the cost approach to large mansions

    (b) Estimate the upper and lower range of value

    (c) Estimate the adjustment for units of comparison

    (d) Study markets that are better and worse than the market for the subject

5. Market data is used:

    (a) In the sales comparison approach

    (b) In the income approach

    (c) In the cost approach

    (d) None of the above

    (e) All of the above

6. For a property to be considered comparable:

    (a) It must have sold within five years.

    (b) It must be a competitive property.

    (c) It must be an open market transaction.

    (d) Both (a) and (b)

    (e) Both (b) and (c)

7. In economics, a submarket is:

    (a) A group of buyers interested in the same type of property

    (b) A group of sales that occur at the same time

    (c) A group of similar properties in the same area

    (d) All of the above

    (e) Two of the above

8. To meet the definition of an open market transaction, a comparable property must always have been:

    (a) Listed for at least 30 days

    (b) Listed on a multiple listing service

    (c) Advertised in local newspapers

    (d) All of the above

    (e) None of the above

9. You need to know all the following information about a comparable property except:

    (a) The sales price

    (b) The date the sales price was decided

(c) The date legal work began on the transaction

(d) The loan interest rate and payment schedule

10. To improve the reliability of information about comparable sales, you may want to consider, as an additional step:

(a) Having a partner or assistant go over your work

(b) Applying the statistical technique called sampling

(c) Conducting an interior inspection of the comparable sales

(d) Checking your data through another source

(e) Both (c) and (d)

CHAPTER NINE

ANALYZING AND ADJUSTING COMPARABLE SALES

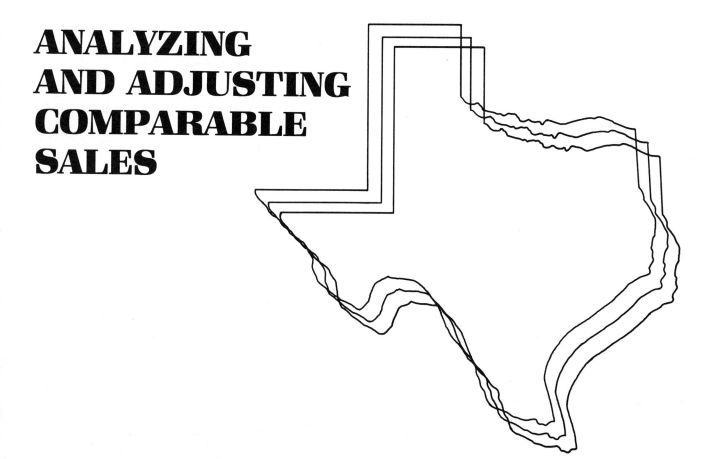

PREVIEW

Continuing our discussion of the sales comparison approach in this chapter, we will consider how and why sales are analyzed. We will also describe how to make adjustments for differences between the sales and the subject property. Finally, we will explain how to arrive at a value conclusion using the sales comparison approach.

When you have finished this chapter, you should be able to:

1. Define the three methods of calculating adjustments.

2. Show how adjustments are calculated.

3. Explain how a value conclusion is reached.

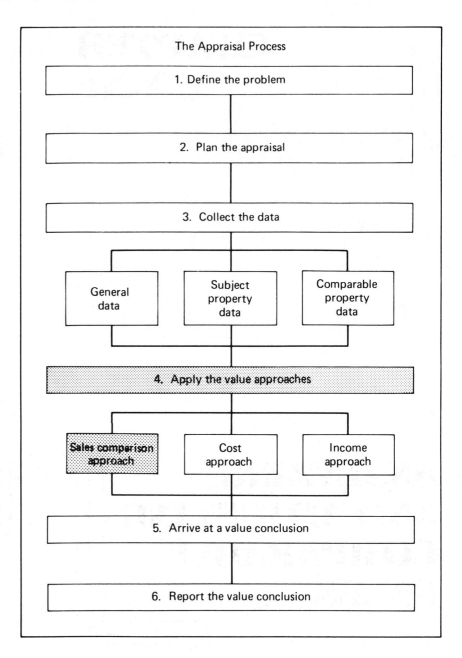

The Appraisal Process

1. Define the problem

2. Plan the appraisal

3. Collect the data

General data | Subject property data | Comparable property data

4. Apply the value approaches

Sales comparison approach | Cost approach | Income approach

5. Arrive at a value conclusion

6. Report the value conclusion

SECTION 9.1
ANALYZING
AND ADJUSTING SALES

In this section we discuss the comparison of sales, a key element in the sales comparison approach. If you can find property sales that are similar to the subject property, you can compare these sales in a number of ways. The comparison and analysis process leads to an accurate and objective estimation of value.

Elements of Comparison

Once sales have been found, all relevant data about them are gathered. These two steps were covered in Chapter 8. The next step is to identify and compare the *differences* between the sales and also between the sales and the subject property. In this step we want to identify the differences that cause variations in the prices of the sale properties. All the information about each sale is divided into four categories, known as the four elements of comparison.

1. Terms of sale.
2. Time of sale.
3. Location elements.
4. Physical elements.

Terms of Sale

The terms of the sale can influence the selling price. For instance, favorable financing often results in a selling price that is higher than typical. In this circumstance, an adjustment should be made to reflect the advantage. If unfavorable terms are found, they should be adjusted to show the disadvantage. The purpose of the adjustments is to convert the sale price to the equivalent of a cash sale.

Several situations that can call for financing adjustments are:

1. *Seller financing*   When loans are more favorable than terms of third party lenders.
2. *Assumed financing*   When the assumed loan has more favorable terms than those of a new conventional loan.
3. *Seller-paid points (as for FHA loans)*   When points reduce the seller's net receipts in the same way as when the seller sells at a lower price. Sellers usually increase the selling price to cover the amount paid for points.

Techniques for adjusting for terms of sale will be discussed later in this chapter.

Time of Sale

Since market price levels can change over time, the time of sale of each comparable should be studied. Dramatic changes in market conditions since an earlier sale date may invalidate a sale as a useful comparable.

Location Elements

The location factors covered in Chapter 8 are also important elements in the comparison process. Such differences as the condition and quality of nearby properties, the availability of utilities and transportation, and the effects of social, economic, and political forces must be studied in order to determine which sale differences require adjusting.

Physical Elements

The property and lot characteristics discussed in Chapter 8 are important elements of comparison. Such characteristics as the size, shape, and age of improvements; the degree of modernization; the improvement quality and condition; and any special features or problems should be considered.

Comparing Sales Directly

At the turn of the century, there were no real estate appraisers. Value estimates were made when local brokers and/or bankers rode in a buggy to the property. They would stop in front of the house, look it over, discuss its merits and demerits, and settle on a price estimate. This is the origin of the term curbstone appraisal. As appraising evolved, brokers and bankers began to debate the accuracy of a value conclusion by referring to the prices of sales with which they were familiar. In essence, they compared sales directly to the subject property. A knowledgeable broker, who is working in a territory that he or she has successfully "farmed" over a period of time, often does the same thing. Appraisers have a similar technique, called the direct comparison method.

Technique

There are several ways to make direct sales comparisons, but the most common and effective method involves the application of a series of steps. First, locate a few property sales that appear similar to the subject property and are close enough in time and terms of sales. Consider *all* the important similarities and differences among the various properties, such as age, size, condition, and quality.

Next, arrange the list of sales so that they are placed in the order of their relative value or desirability. This means that the property that is overall the most attractive to buyers should be put at the top of the list, followed by the next choice, and so on. The property considered to have the least market appeal will be last. The list could be in price order, that is, from the highest-priced sale on the top to the lowest-priced sale on the bottom. However, it is usually better to ignore prices at this stage and rank the sales by listing them in the order of their overall appeal.

Upon completing the list of properties, the appraiser compares the subject property to those on the list. Properties that are judged to be more desirable than the subject property could be identified as "Better," those less desirable as "Worse," and those that are uncertain with a question mark. You would expect to find that properties marked with a "B" are the higher-priced sales and those marked with a "W" are the lower-priced sales. The sales in between often are a mixture of Better, Worse, and question marks. It is within this middle zone that the value of the subject property is likely to lie. Example 9.1 shows such a list of sales.

Limitations

The direct comparison technique has severe limitations. For example, all of the sales *must* be relatively similar to the property being appraised. In addition, this technique relies heavily upon the appraiser's intuitive ability to judge which sale property is more attractive to buyers. Since such an ability generally results from experience, beginning appraisers may have trouble using this technique. (See Figure 9.1.)

The Process of Comparing and Adjusting Sales

Since it is rare for sales to be similar enough for simple, direct comparisons, appraisers have developed techniques to adjust sales. These techniques focus upon every feature of the sale that influences its value and differs from features of the subject property.

Example 9.1
Direct Comparison of Sales

Sale Address	Time Since Sale (months)	Price	Age	Building Sq Ft	Comparison to Subject
991 Arlington Ave.	5	$97,000	1925	2,093	W
195 Arlington Ave.	7	160,000	1924	2,427	W
820 Red Rock Ave.	4	180,000	1921	1,519	W
1295 Cougar Ave.	2	190,000	1940	1,776	W
230 Hilldale Ave.	1	192,500	1930	1,645	W
214 Leroy Ave.	5	235,000	1935	3,043	?
319 Hemlock St.	3	255,000	1925	3,300	B
2150 Euclid Ave.	2	255,000	1924	2,152	?
775 Hemlock St.	9	262,500	1936	3,400	B
200 Creston	5	318,000	1937	3,136	B

Note: W: worse; B: better; and ?: questionable.

The Two Steps

The process of adjusting sales that are notably different involves (1) the comparison or analysis of sales and (2) the adjusting of sales prices. The first step of comparison or analysis involves identifying the significant differences among the sales and then, in turn, the significant differences between the sales and the subject property. Some of the houses may be painted green and others brown. Does this difference matter in that market? Some of the houses may be built with slab-on-grade whereas others may have a raised floor. Will this affect prices? Some of the houses may be one story; others with similar footage may be split levels or two stories. Will there be a need for an adjustment? You must be aware of all the differences before you can decide which differences are significant.

Factors that are most important in affecting market price can, in part, be identified by your knowledge of the local market or by asking brokers and others who are knowledgeable about that market. However, you can usually best judge which differences are significant by examining the sales information. For example, can you find several sales that differ from each other in only one way, say two identical houses that sold six months apart? Is there a price difference? If so, then the time difference between the two sales is the likely reason.

The second step in the comparison and adjustment process is the actual sales adjustment. Once you know which property differences are signifi-

FIGURE 9.1
Appraisers' Intuition: Which Sale Property Is More Attractive to Buyers?

cant, you then estimate the dollar amount needed to adjust the sales price to make the comparable like the subject and thus account for the difference. There are several precautions to observe to obtain good results. First, the adjustments should be reasonable. In other words, the dollar amount of the adjustment must have a *reasonable relationship* to the feature being adjusted. For example, it would be unreasonable to use a $10,000 adjustment for an extra one-half bath if the costs of building a half-bath are considerably less than $10,000. Second, the adjustment amount must be consistently applied to each sale. For example, if there are three sales with similar half-baths, the same amount should be deducted from the sale price of each. Third, the adjustments should reduce the price spread between the sold properties. If the adjustments were accurate and the sales prices themselves resulted from a perfect market, then the prices after adjustment should be identical.

From this discussion, it should be clear that analysis and adjustment are two sides of the same coin. They are treated separately in order to emphasize the necessity of examining the causes of differences in sale prices. This is the analysis portion of the process. Without analysis, adjustment is simply a mechanical calculation. The practicing appraiser, however, often combines these two steps.

Rules for Making Adjustments

The process of adjusting comparable sales for differences cannot be executed in a haphazard manner. A reliable appraisal will only result from a careful analysis of significant differences and careful application of the following rules for making adjustments.

1. The sale property (and its price) must be adjusted to be more like the subject property, as shown in Figure 9.2. Adjust the sale toward the subject. For example, if the sale property has extra features, their value must be subtracted to make the sale like the subject. If the sale property is smaller than the subject, the value of the extra space must be

ADJUST **TO** THE SUBJECT: **ADD** GARAGE VALUE TO THE PRICE OF COMPARABLE

ADJUST **TO** THE SUBJECT: **DEDUCT** VALUE OF THE ROOM ABOVE GARAGE FROM PRICE OF COMPARABLE

FIGURE 9.2
The Adjustment Process

added to the sale price. If the sale was made several months ago in a rising market and the appraisal is at current value, then the sale price must be raised to account for the increase in prices. Always remember: You must adjust *to the subject*.

2. Use market adjustments. The appraiser's personal reaction to the differences is not what matters. It is the *market's* reaction that is important. You may like modern houses, but are they popular in this market? You might refuse to buy a house located 45 steps above the street, but will others?

3. Make adjustments in the proper sequence. Usually, this means that general adjustments come first and adjustments for specific features are made later. A logical sequence of adjustments is terms of sale, time and market condition, location, and physical features.

Types of Adjustments

The appraiser can choose from three types of adjustments. In practice, these methods are generally used in combination. The three types will be discussed briefly; details on how to calculate them are provided later in this chapter. (See Figure 9.3.)

The first type of adjustment is the lump-sum dollar adjustment. Here you select a specific dollar amount as the appropriate adjustment. This amount is added to, or subtracted from, the price of the comparable sale in order to have it more like the subject. For example, one comparable sale might have a swimming pool whereas the subject property has none. On investigation, the appraiser decides to use an $8,000 lump-sum adjustment. This amount would be subtracted from the price of this sale.

Sale price		$205,000
Less:	Adjustment for swimming pool	− 8,000
Equals:	Adjusted price	$197,000

The second type of adjustment is the percentage adjustment. Here the difference between the comparable sale and the subject is calculated as a

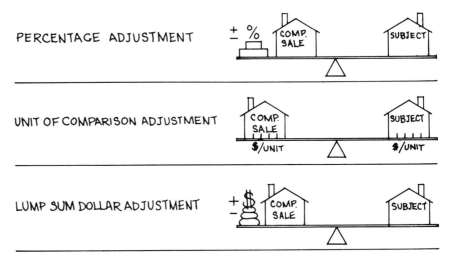

FIGURE 9.3
Types of Adjustments

percentage of the sale price. For example, a sale that is four months earlier than the data of valuation might be adjusted by 4% because of rising market prices in the intervening time. If the comparable sold for $155,000, then the adjustment would be 4% of $155,000 or $6,200.

Sale price		$155,000
Plus:	Time adjustment (4%)	+ 6,200
Equals:	Adjusted price	$161,200

More than one percentage adjustment might be applied to a particular comparable sale. For example, the sale may need a percentage adjustment for both time and neighborhood differences. Multiple percentage adjustments can be added, subtracted, or multiplied. The appraiser must decide whether an adding or multiplying percentage adjustment is proper for the data with which he or she is working. Thus, if a plus 4% time adjustment was called for, along with a plus 3% neighborhood adjustment, the total adjustment would be 7%. If values in both neighborhoods have gone up by 4% over this time period, then the 3% neighborhood adjustment logically applies to the new price levels. Hence the two factors may need to be multiplied. However, to be mathematically correct, a factor of 1 must be added first to each adjustment; thus the total adjustment becomes 1.04 times 1.03 equals 1.0712 or + 7.12%. When minus adjustments are multiplied, they are first subtracted from the factor 1. For example −5, +7 becomes 0.95 times 1.07, which equals 1.0165. This means a plus adjustment of 1.65%.

The third type of adjustment is the unit of comparison. Using the unit of comparison involves, first, selecting an appropriate unit such as the selling price per square foot of the building area and then converting the sales prices to prices per unit—in this case, the price per square foot. The unit of comparison is usually described as an analysis tool rather than an adjustment tool. However, it can adjust for size, for example, when the market-found price per square foot of the comparables is multiplied by the square-foot size of the subject. (More will be said about this later.)

Calculating a Unit of Comparison

Sale	Building Area	Price	Calculated Price per Sq Ft
1	1,877	$105,600	$56.26
2	2,120	110,000	51.89
3	1,795	102,000	56.82

Using a Sales Analysis Grid

It is often difficult to communicate the information in an appraisal report to the reader, especially when a series of sales are involved and a number of adjustments are made. To explain clearly what you have done, it is usually necessary to show your work in the form of a table. Most form appraisal reports have such a table, called a sales analysis grid or sales adjustment grid. Filling in this grid (Figure 9.4) is a regular part of appraisal practice. Using a grid usually limits analysis and adjustment techniques to those easily presented within a grid, and these might not be best in any one case. On the other hand, grids offer the advantage of providing a clear comparison of the sales—their differences and how they were adjusted.

ITEM	Subject Property	COMPARABLE NO. 1	
Address	2279-68th Ave.	1811 Church St.	
Proximity to Subj.		3 blocks	
Sales Price	$ 55,000	$65,000	
Price/Living area	$ 53,76 ⌀	$56,18 ⌀	
Data Source	Inspection	S.R.E.A.	
Date of Sale and Time Adjustment	DESCRIPTION 12/81	DESCRIPTION 9/81	+(−)$ Adjustment 500
Location	Average	Equal	
Site/View	Typical/none	Superior	(1,000)
Design and Appeal	Average	Equal	
Quality of Const.	Average	Equal	
Age	1932	1935	
Condition	Average	Superior	(5,000)
Living Area Room Count and Total	Total 5 | B-rms 2 | Baths 1	Total 6 | B-rms 3 | Baths 1	(2,000)
Gross Living Area	1023 Sq.Ft.	1157 Sq.Ft.	(1,000)
Basement & Bsmt. Finished Rooms	None	None	
Functional Utility	Average	Average	
Air Conditioning	Wall	None	500
Garage/Car Port,	1 car + shop	Open	3,000
Porches, Patio, Pools, etc.	Deck	Equal	
Special Energy Efficient Items	None	Unknown	
Other (e.g. fire-places, kitchen equip., remodeling)	Fireplace Floor furn.	Alum. windows Fireplace Wall furn.	(4,000) (500)
Sales or Financing Concessions	Conv.	Conv. 91%	
Net Adj. (Total)		☐ Plus; ☒ Minus	$ 9,500
Indicated Value of Subject			$ 55,500

(left vertical label: MARKET DATA ANALYSIS)

FIGURE 9.4
A Portion of the Sales Analysis Grid of the FHLMC Form 70/FNMA Form 1004

Selecting and Using Units of Comparison

The unit of comparison technique takes some major varying aspect of the sale properties and uses it to compare the sales. The price per room is one example. In order to calculate the price per room for each sale property, divide the sale price by the number of rooms. The sales are then compared, using the price per room as the measure. This approach eliminates the major price differences that were caused by the varying numbers of rooms. Once this major property variable is accounted for, you will find it easier to see other influences causing price differences.

There are three types of units of comparison: the total property, physical units, and economic units. Each type will be discussed, followed by an explanation of how to apply units of comparison. (See Figure 9.5).

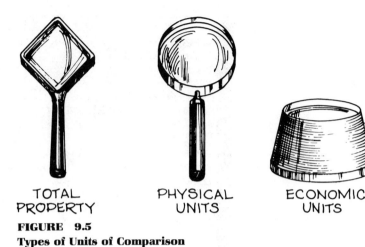

TOTAL PROPERTY   PHYSICAL UNITS   ECONOMIC UNITS

FIGURE 9.5
Types of Units of Comparison

Total Property

Here the total property is the unit of comparison. When the various sales are similar to the property being appraised, a total property comparison is helpful. Minor differences between the sales can be considered by ranking the sales in the direct comparison method described previously or by making lump-sum dollar adjustments to the sale price of the various sale properties. Techniques for determining the needed amount of adjustment are outlined in the next section.

Physical Units

A physical unit of comparison uses any physical characteristic of the sales that varies. Most often, the size of the property is used as a unit. Here the sale price of each property is divided by its size. The answer is the price per unit of size.

The most widely used physical unit of comparison is the price per square foot of land or building area. For vacant land, the price would be per square foot of land. For larger land parcels, the price per acre might be best. In some cases, instead of using the land area, you might use the frontage of the parcel. (The frontage is the linear distance of the lot, or building, that fronts on, or faces, the major street or traffic-way.) Commercial land is often described by its price per front foot. Commercial rentals are often based upon rent per front foot of land or building.

For improved properties, many different physical units can be used. For example, homes or apartments are sometimes compared by price per room or price per square foot. Apartments and motels are often compared by price per rental unit. Rooming houses or fraternities can be compared by price per bedroom, or price per bed. Convalescent hospitals are often compared by price per bed and marinas by price per berth, or price per foot of boat dock.

The most common unit of comparison in the appraisal of single-family homes is the selling price per square foot of living area. When there are only moderate differences in land and building size and the size data are available, the method is generally recognized as one of the best comparison techniques for single-family residential properties.

The use of a size-related unit of comparison has two main advantages. First, it eliminates the price variations that result from differences in size. This makes it easier to see other differences that were not previously apparent. The second advantage is that the calculation of value is easily done by selecting an appropriate unit value and multiplying it by the size measurement of the property being appraised.

Economic Units of Comparison

An economic unit of comparison is some economic feature or characteristic of the property that closely relates to its value. There are many examples of economic units of comparison. One of the most common is used in appraising vacant acreage. Instead of examining land sales in terms of price per acre or price per square foot of land, the land is studied in terms of its usefulness, or what can be done with it. For residential land, for example, this means calculating the price per buildable dwelling unit. In appraising land for commercial or office use, the zoning ordinance often sets restrictions (such as floor area–land area ratios, parking requirements, height restrictions, or coverage percentages) that limit the size of a new building.

If comparables are in different zoning categories, the allowable building size may vary even when the lot size does not. Here comparing land sales by price per square foot of land may not be useful. Instead try the following: First, examine the zoning ordinance to calculate the amount of floor space that can be developed, considering story-height limits, parking requirements, and so on. Second, take the total, calculated, potential building floor area and divide it into the price. This result is the price per buildable square foot of floor area. Using this unit of comparison can often automatically adjust for the differences we have cited. Example 9.2 shows how to calculate such a unit of comparison.

Example 9.2
Physical Versus Economic Units of Comparison

A.   Assume that there are four sales of land parcels, all zoned for office use. We first analyze by price per square foot of land area, a physical unit of comparison.

Sale	Price per Sq Ft of Land Area
1	$2.20
2	7.50
3	3.12
4	1.65

Conclusion
A wide range of value indications.

B.   The same four sales, adjusted for differences in the allowable building size, to give an economic unit of comparison. The price per square foot of land area is divided by the floor area ratio (FAR) permitted by the zoning. The answer is the land price per square foot of potential building area.

Sale	Price per Sq Ft of Land Area		Allowable Building/Land Ratio (FAR)		Land Price per Building Sq Ft
1	$2.20	÷	1.00	=	$2.20
2	7.50	÷	3.00	=	2.50
3	3.12	÷	1.50	=	2.08
4	1.65	÷	0.75	=	2.20

Conclusion
A narrow range of value indications.

What are some other economic units of comparison? The price per convalescent hospital bed has already been suggested as a physical unit of comparison, but it is also economic. When comparing gasoline stations, you could look at the sale price per 1,000 gallons pumped per year. Since the gallonage is commonly used to establish rent, it is often used to determine the sale price. With retail stores, there generally is a relationship between the rent that is paid and the sales volume the store generates. Consequently, rent as a percent of sales volume is an economic unit of comparison. This applies to restaurants as well. There is also a relationship between the rental income that a property generates and its sale price. This relationship is mathematically represented by gross income multipliers (GIM). Because of the importance of GIMs, they are discussed as a separate topic.

Economic units of comparison are not much harder to apply than physical units of comparison. For vacant parcels, some additional zoning analysis may be necessary. This additional work is worth the effort because economic units of comparison have a big advantage. For complex properties, economic units will give you a clearer understanding of the final price than simple physical comparison. In other words, if you adjust ten sales and use a physical unit of comparison, you can expect to find some remaining variation in the price per unit. If, instead, you calculate the economic unit that applies, you can expect to find *less* remaining variation in the price per unit. In other words, another cause of price variation is eliminated when you use economic units instead of physical units. You will then find it easier to see the factors causing the remaining price variation. Such factors as age, date of sale, and location are much easier to understand when the small differences they cause are not swamped by the larger differences associated with size.

Rent Multipliers
Rent multipliers are also economic units of comparison because they measure an economic characteristic of the property, its income. They are calculated by dividing the price by the rent or income. The answer is called a multiplier. A multiplier, when multiplied by the income of the property being appraised, will give an indication of its value. Multipliers can be calculated by using either the annual or the monthly income. Traditionally, monthly income has been used for single-family residences, but annual income is most commonly used for apartments or other income property. In the past, this type of unit comparison was called a gross rent multiplier (GRM). Increasingly, however, the term gross income multiplier (GIM) is being used. This change in language indicates that the multiplier should be based on *all* the income the property commands and not just its rental income. The added income could include laundry income, parking, furniture rentals, and so on.

Note that income multipliers use the property's income, whereas here we are discussing the market approach. Income multipliers have traditionally occupied a place somewhere between the income and sales comparison approaches. With single-family homes, multipliers are sometimes considered an acceptable income approach. However, with apartments and commercial property, income multipliers are usually considered as part of the sales comparison approach. The distinction is not important; the multiplier is a tool for the appraiser to use whenever it is suitable. Gross income multipliers will be studied further in Chapter 13.

Applying Units of Comparison

The first step in applying this technique of analysis and adjustment is to calculate the unit price. Each sale price must be converted to a price for the unit selected; this means the price per square foot, price per bedroom, or price per whatever unit is selected. Once the unit prices for the sales are calculated, these unit prices should be analyzed to identify the causes of any remaining price variation. Are the unit prices for recent sales higher than for older sales? Are the unit prices for the larger properties less than for the smaller properties? Are the unit prices for the older structures lower than for newer structures? The appraiser identifies these differences and adjusts for them. In making adjustments, remember how the unit size of the subject property compares with those of the sales. Again, the rule is *adjust to the subject.*

Consider how the sale properties vary. If all your sales are of 9-room homes, why bother to calculate the price per room? On the other hand, if your sales range from 4-room homes to 20-room homes, then different problems arise. Actually, if the sales have such an extremely wide range of sizes, unit of comparison prices must be handled more carefully. One reason is that the sales at each extreme may be so unusual that they lose their reliability. The second reason is that the price per unit of comparison generally declines as the number of units increase. Larger structures usually sell for a lower price per physical unit *or* economic unit. For example, the unit price may decline considerably between houses of 1,000 feet in size and 1,500 feet in size. However, houses of 2,000 feet in size, which are another 500 feet larger, might decline less in price per unit. In larger homes, the lot value is spread over more square feet of floor space; also, the increased space often consists of inexpensive bedroom space or enlarged living rooms. So we might find prices of $97.00 per square foot at 1,000 square feet, $90.00 per square foot at 1,500 square feet, and $88.00 per square foot at 2,000 square feet.

Graphing the Sales

Variable units of comparison can best be analyzed by graphing the sales. The procedure for preparing a sales graph is to first set up the vertical and horizontal scales on the graph paper. Usually, the vertical scale shows the selling price (or the price per unit) and the horizontal scale shows the property characteristic being studied, for example, the square-foot building area. Each sale is plotted on the graph paper by finding the point that matches both the selling price line and the line for the square-foot area. Next, a line is drawn to pass through (or line up with) as many of the sales points as possible. (Statistical techniques that fit a line to these points will be discussed later.) Then, study the sales above and below the line. What difference is causing them to be above and below the line? Finally, the appraiser can calculate where the subject property will lie on the line, indicating an estimate of its value.

Figure 9.6 shows a graph of price per square foot versus total square feet of living area. As is often true in the market, the sales prices per square foot decline as the houses get larger. Based on the graph, the indicated selling price per square foot of building for a house the size of the subject is $57.50.

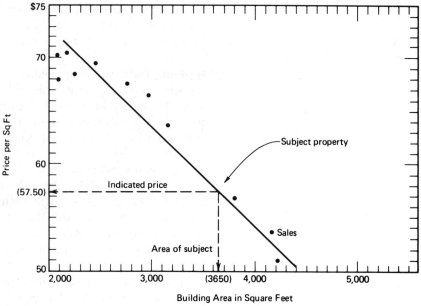

FIGURE 9.6
Graph Shows Price per Sq Ft vs. Building Area

The subject house contains 3,650 sq ft so that the indicated price is 3,650 × $57.50, or $209,875, rounded to $210,000.

In some cases, the appraiser might conclude that the subject property is likely to be above the line and in others below it, based on the characteristics of the property as compared with the sales.

Perhaps the date of sale or even the age of the buildings needs to be analyzed. Here, the appraiser could graph the price per square foot of living area versus the date of sale or versus the age of the properties. In fact, the appraiser with plenty of time could experiment with sales adjustments, graphing the sales after each adjustment to see what the effect was. For example, the appraiser could adjust the sales for time at 4, 5, and 6% per year and could, by looking at the three graphs, consider which adjustment appears to be a better match to the market.

At present, graphing has a limited use in appraisals because it may take a long time to plot. Wide use of computerized data services, however, may make graphs routinely available.

The appraiser must recognize that the price per unit of comparison can change in a complex manner. For example, if you are calculating the price per bed in a convalescent hospital, you must consider the licensing requirements of the state. The license law in several states requires a large increase in the nursing staff for a 100-bed building. This increase is expensive when compared to a 99-bed building. Thus the price per bed, instead of changing slowly as the number of beds gradually changes, shifts dramatically at sizes where the licensing staff requirements change.

Remember that a unit of comparison adjusts for only the one variable selected. The price per unit can still change widely, depending upon other differences such as location, quality, and so on. Methods of estimating the appropriate dollar or percent adjustments for such differences will be the next topic covered.

**How to Estimate Dollar
and Percent Adjustments**

The adjustment of the sales prices of comparison properties in a market value appraisal is perhaps the most demanding step in the sales comparison approach. Why? Because, ideally, the adjustments to be made should first and foremost be related to the market. The unit of comparison method described previously has this as its major strength. It relies upon "reading" the market reaction to some important physical or economic variables. Of the three additional adjustment methods available, two depend directly, and one indirectly, on market inputs.

Direct Market Method
One of the best methods of estimating adjustments is by the direct comparison of sales. The appraiser searches for sales that differ *only* in the single property characteristic being studied. The difference in price between two such properties (sometimes referred to as a matched pair) can indicate the appropriate dollar or percent adjustment for the feature under study.

Application of Method
This method is simple. First, find at least two sales that have no major differences except the type of difference that you want to examine, say a large age difference. Although these sales need not be completely comparable to the subject, they should be similar enough so that the difference being studied will have the same effect on both the sales and the subject property. Second, compare matched-pair sales prices to see how big the difference is. This can be expressed either in dollars or as a percentage of the sale price.

The third step is to adjust the sale prices of the comparables to make them more like the subject property, using the amount found by studying the market data. Example 9.3 demonstrates these three steps, with the ages of the buildings being the feature analyzed.

Example 9.3
Calculating an Adjustment for Age by the Direct Market Method

Sale	Age	Size	Rooms	Price	Price per Sq Ft
1	1960	2,242	7.5	$265,000	$118.20
2	1920	2,190	8.0	204,000	93.15

Price difference		$25.05
Difference in percent		21%
Divided by: Age difference		÷ 40 years
Equals: Percent adjustment per year of age		0.5%

It is also possible to use this method by finding sets of *rental* comparables. You identify the rental difference caused by the feature being studied. This rent difference is then multiplied by the GIM appropriate for that market. The result is the value difference associated with the feature being examined.

When should the direct market method be used? It is the most reliable method when the appraiser needs to adjust for one single major factor, such as terms of sale, date of sale, location, or physical factors. Adjustments for the date of the sale are made by comparing earlier sales and later sales. (Obviously, a resale of the same property might be the most direct evidence of how prices changed with time.)

Here is an example of how this method can be useful in adjusting for location. Assume your subject property is a three-bedroom home and that no three-bedroom homes have sold recently in the subject property's neighborhood, but many two-bedroom homes have. Look for another nearby neighborhood with sales of *both* two and three-bedroom homes. If you compare prices of two-bedroom homes in the subject property's neighborhood with the two-bedroom homes in the other neighborhood, the percentage difference can be your neighborhood adjustment. If, for example, your neighborhood sold for 9% more, now you can use the three-bedroom comparables from the other neighborhood and adjust their prices up by 9% for the neighborhood difference.

A broad range of physical differences between the subject property and the comparables can be adjusted by the direct market method. Physical differences, such as size, quality, age, or condition, or the presence or absence of a specific feature, such as a swimming pool, basement, or extra bedroom, can be measured. The method is also useful in adjusting for remodeled rooms, such as kitchens or bathrooms.

Matched pairs of sales are sometimes used in combination with other techniques. For example, you can first adjust your sales for specific differences, such as swimming pools; these adjusted sales might then be studied further by using some unit of comparison, such as the price per square foot of living area. However, recognize that as more adjustment methods are used, the probability of individual adjustment errors increases.

This direct market method is now being used with very large sets of sales. Such larger sets of sales can be processed easily by using computerized sales data services. For example, a reliable adjustment for time for one area might be obtained by calculating the average price per square foot of *all* the sales each month, as shown in Example 9.4.

Example 9.4
Analysis of Market Month-to-Month Price Changes

Month	Number of Sales	Average Price per Sq Ft	Increase (Percent)
January	1,117	$80.05	—
February	1,009	81.61	2.0
March	1,191	83.33	2.1
April	1,228	84.90	1.9
May	1,466	86.59	1.9
June	1,530	88.40	2.1
July	1,223	90.03	1.8
August	1,370	91.75	1.9
September	1,215	93.51	1.9

Source: An analysis prepared by Robert Foreman, MAI, SREA.

Depreciated Cost Method

The second method for estimating dollar or percent adjustments is called the depreciated cost method. The adjustment is calculated from an analysis of the depreciated replacement costs for the particular property feature. When costs and depreciation schedules are correctly related to the market, the depreciated cost method can be said to represent an indirect market method.

This technique involves the following steps: first, select the particular feature or difference between the properties that is to be adjusted. For instance, you might need to adjust for differences in the size of the buildings, the installation of special kitchen equipment, or the absence of a garage. The second step is to estimate the *additional* cost to include that feature when building a new house. (Techniques for estimating new building costs will be covered in Chapter 11.) The third step, after estimating the current construction costs, is to deduct an allowance (called depreciation) for the age and condition of the feature being studied. (Methods for calculating depreciation will also be covered later, in Chapter 12.) The final step is to adjust the sale price of the comparable sale by adding or subtracting the depreciated cost amount.

Remember that the purpose of figuring the cost difference is to modify or adjust the price of the comparable so that it will better represent the value of the subject. If the comparable has no garage, for example, and the subject does, then the depreciated cost of this feature would have to be added to the comparable's sale price. Example 9.5 shows how to prepare this adjustment.

Example 9.5
Adjustment by the Depreciated Cost Method

The Problem
The subject property is an eight-room home, new in 1956 with a double garage. Sale No. 4 is very similar except that it has no garage.

The Solution
Adjust the price of Sale No. 4 upward to reflect the lack of a garage.

The Adjustment Steps
1. Estimate the garage cost new. The area is 20 × 22 feet, or 440 sq ft. Current replacement cost, for this quality and feature from a local cost handbook, is $23.50/sq ft.

2. Estimate depreciation. The garage's actual age is 29 years, and its total economic life is estimated to be 75 years. Depreciation is believed to be straight line, or 29/75, or 39%.

3. Calculation:

Cost new:	440 × $23.50	$10,340
Less:	Depreciation: $10,340 × 0.39	− 4,033
Equals:	Adjustment amount	$6,307
	Rounded to	$6,300

The best use for this method is to adjust for physical property differences, particularly for a specific building feature, such as a swimming pool or covered porch.

The depreciated cost method is also useful when a property has some particular problem that must be corrected such as a leaking roof or termite damage. The total current cost of these repairs (without any deduction for depreciation) would be the price reduction demanded by a knowledgeable buyer.

The depreciated cost method of estimating adjustment amounts is a common tool of the practicing appraiser. Cost manuals are handy and easy to use; the logic of the adjustment process is easily explained. However, it is often difficult to prove the depreciation deduction. Although depreciated cost adjustments have less accuracy than they initially appear to have, they remain a common and useful tool in adjusting sales.

Adjusting for Sale Terms

As we discussed earlier in this chapter, it is possible for the sale price of a property to be affected by the type of financing involved. If any of the comparable sales used have unique financing, then adjustments must be made. The amount of the adjustment can be calculated from a direct market comparison with similar properties that have conventional financing. However, if such sales are not available, it might be necessary to use a mathematical analysis to calculate an adjustment.

One simple financing adjustment arises when the seller must pay substantial loan points or other loan charges. In conventional loan practice, the buyer pays the loan points, or fees, that are charged to set up the loan. However, in some types of loans (particularly FHA loans), the interest rate is fixed for a time period and cannot change as market interest rates change. Lenders compensate for this fixed interest rate by charging an extra loan fee, called points, which discount the loan and thus effectively adjust the fixed interest rate to the current market interest rate. Since loan points are often paid by the seller, the effective or net sale price received by the seller is reduced. To make the adjustment, you subtract the loan points paid by the seller from the stated selling price, as shown in Example 9.6.

Example 9.6
Adjusting for Points

	Sale 1	Sale 2	Sale 3
Sale price	$110,000	$95,000	$130,000
Loan amount	$103,000	$94,000	$110,000
Loan points (%)	6	7	5
Cost of points	$6,180	$6,580	$5,500
Adjusted price	$103,820	$88,420	$124,500

A more complicated situation arises when a property is sold with unusually favorable financing. This involves a loan that was more advantageous to the buyer than the conventional lender financing available at that time. A desirable loan can substantially increase the selling price of the property. Such loans may be either assumable third-party loans or new loans that are taken back by the seller at the time of sale. The favorable loan may have an interest rate that is lower than normal for the current market. Or the loan could involve a very low down payment (for example, with a seller take-back loan) or a long amortization period.

It is possible for unfavorable financing to depress the selling price. Sometimes an undesirable loan, with an above-market interest rate, either must be assumed by the buyer or a stiff prepayment penalty paid. In this case, the sale price could well be reduced below the "market value" level.

Calculating the amount of adjustment for favorable or unfavorable loans may be done by studying the discount at which mortgages are being sold in the current finance markets. It is also possible to analyze these mortgages using mathematical techniques similar to those used by lenders to calculate loan points. Since such techniques are a type of annuity capitalization normally covered in the advanced appraisal course, they will not be detailed here.

Unfortunately, it is difficult to estimate accurately adjustments for terms of sale. Judging what buyers and sellers consider as favorable loan terms in a particular market can be very subjective. Although the mathematical techniques referred to above may seem sophisticated and precise, few buyers or sellers understand or use them. As a result, the actual adjustments that occur in the market could differ from what the mathematical calculation suggests.

Statistics—Linear and Multiple Regression

An advanced method of calculating the amount of a sales adjustment uses a statistical technique called regression analysis. There are two techniques of regression analysis currently used in appraising. The first type is called simple linear regression. This technique adjusts for one difference or variable such as the date of sale or the age of the house. As the term linear implies, the technique assumes that the relationship between the price and variable is a straight line. If the variable is age, then each change in age that occurs shows the same change in price. Thus, if we graph the sales prices versus the ages, we would expect the sales to form a straight line. The linear regression calculation effectively averages the sales to find out what the average change in price is. Figure 9.7 is a graph of the various sale prices; the line represents the results of linear regression.

Although the linear regression technique involves a complex mathemat-

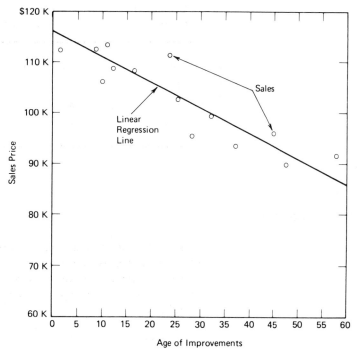

FIGURE 9.7
Using Linear Regression to Analyze Sales

ical formula, pocket calculators programmed for linear regression make it relatively simple to apply. If a single variable, like the date of sale, is being studied, the appraiser merely inputs the price of each sale along with its date (or the number of months since the sale). When all the sales are entered, the program computes the price trend. It is also possible to calculate whether such a trend accounts for most of the differences in price. For reliable results, linear regression usually requires larger groups of sales than the other sales adjustment methods previously discussed.

Multiple regression is the second type of regression analysis. The same process is carried out, but you can look at any number of variables. It is usually done with a computer. For accuracy, you need to have 20 to 30 sales and at least twice as many sales as the number of variables being studied. Some types of statistical flaws can reduce the reliability of the conclusions without the appraiser's being aware of them. However, multiple regression is used increasingly by district appraisers and lenders doing appraisal review work. This technique will probably be used more as appraisers become familiar with its application and understand its limitations better. A detailed analysis of this technique is part of advanced appraisal study.

In conclusion, then, Section 9.1 has covered the related topics of sales analysis and sales adjustment. The two combine to form the process of sales comparison, which is the heart of this approach. Sales analysis and adjustment can be performed as separate steps. However, as with direct sales comparisons, they are sometimes performed as one integrated step.

SECTION 9.2 ARRIVING AT AN INDICATED VALUE

The last step in the sales comparison approach is to arrive at a value conclusion. To do so, you need to follow these four steps:

---

1. Review the entire approach.
2. Review the sales.
3. Estimate a value range.
4. Select a final value.

Step One—Reviewing the Sales Comparison Approach

The first step in arriving at a value conclusion is to consider the limitations of the sales comparison approach and how these limitations apply to the particular circumstances of your appraisal. Taking time to review each step taken in the sales comparison approach provides an overall look at the entire process.

Comparability

The sales comparison approach is only reliable when used to appraise kinds of property that are commonly bought and sold. If there are no

FIGURE 9.8
The Rarer the Property, the Less Useful the Sales Comparison Approach.
(Photograph Courtesy of Doug Frost)

comparable sales, the comparison approach cannot be applied. Similarly, the more unique, specialized, or rare the property being appraised is, the less useful the sales comparison approach can be. (See Figure 9.8.)

Activity Levels
Even in common types of properties, the rates of sales (often called the turnover rates) will vary from time to time. During a period when no sales are occurring, the sales comparison approach may not be very reliable. Similarly, in appraising a type of property that is rarely sold, such as a major automobile assembly plant, the sales comparison approach is less reliable. Why? Because comparables are few and far between and may require large adjustments for time and location.

Adjustment Accuracy
Appraisers often say that no two properties are identical. Almost every comparable will need to be adjusted for some differences. The final appraisal is only as reliable as the adjustment. When the amount of the adjustment is not based on convincing market evidence, the sales comparison approach may not be reliable.

Statistical Limits

Statistical techniques that are used as part of the market comparison approach can have serious technical flaws. This is particularly true of linear and multiple regression. Complex mathematical calculations are needed to determine whether conclusions based on these methods can be relied upon in any given appraisal.

Lagging the Market

One problem with the sales comparison approach is that the appraiser generally must use sales that occurred prior to the date of the appraisal. If the market is changing, then all of the sales have a built-in lag. If values are going up, then the sale prices of available comparables should be lower than current values. If prices are going down, then the sale prices should be higher than the current values. The appraiser may be able to easily adjust for this time lag, provided that the rate of price change has remained constant through the present time. However, if the rate of change has varied since the last sale, then the adjustment will be more difficult. When you suspect that rate changes have occurred, try to solve this problem by looking only for very recent value evidence. Local brokers could be contacted for current listing prices, offers, refusals, recent sales, and so on. When such information is available, the time-lag problem may be resolved.

Motivation

The sales comparison approach assumes that the price is the result of vigorous arms-length bargaining by knowledgeable buyers and sellers. As you know, actual sales are not always reached in this way. So, try to understand the motives behind the sales. You should eliminate sales within a family, as well as sales in which there is evidence that suggests a panicky seller or buyer. It is difficult to find out whether a particular sale involves rational and aggressive bargaining over the price. When the appraiser has only a few sales or must rely heavily upon one or two, motivation becomes an even more important factor to consider. If a particular sale is critical to your analysis and it is defective, then the sales comparison approach is of doubtful use. Therefore, in this review process, you must consider the extent to which your analysis relies upon any one sale.

Step Two—Checking the Data

The next step in arriving at an indicated value through the sales comparison approach is to review the detailed data about the actual sales.

Sales Data

First, consider the reliability of the information. What was the source? How reliable is that source, based on previous experience? If certain data are questionable, would an error lead to too high or too low an answer? Can that error be cross-checked against other information? If a particular sale is critical to an appraisal, consider whether enough information about that sale has been collected. If not, cross-check the information with another source or make a second field inspection. The collection of additional information about one sale may sharpen your understanding of all the sales.

Reviewing the Adjustments

The appraiser must review how the sales were adjusted. What type of adjustment was made? Direct market comparisons are usually more reliable than those from statistics or from a cost approach. However, this reliability could depend upon the type of adjustment and the quality of data. At this point, consider the total amount by which each sale was adjusted. This gives the best single indication of how comparable a sale is. The less adjustment needed, the more comparable it is. The more comparable it is, the more weight that sale should be given in arriving at a final value conclusion. The more extreme sales are given less weight and may even be eliminated at this point.

Step Three—Estimating a Range of Values

The third step in arriving at an indicated value is to estimate the probable range of value from a low number to a high number. The upper limit of this range of value is the highest price that can reasonably be concluded, based

TABLE 9.1
Estimating Upper and Lower Limits of Value

Items	Estimated Adjustment	Probable Adjustment Range	Upper Limit Adjustment	Lower Limit Adjustment
Date of sale and time adjustment	$500	$300–600	$600	$300
Location	0			
Site/view	(1,000)	(800–1,300)	(800)	(1,300)
Design and appeal	0			
Quality of construction	0			
Age	0			
Condition	(5,000)	(4,700–5,500)	(4,700)	(5,500)
Living area room count	(2,000)	(1,500–2,300)	(1,500)	(2,300)
Total gross living area	(1,000)	(800–1,300)	(800)	(1,300)
Basement and basement finished rooms	0			
Functional utility	0			
Air conditioning	500	200–600	600	200
Garage/car port	3,000	2,600–3,200	3,200	2,600
Porches, patio, pools, etc.	0			
Other (e.g., fireplaces, kitchen	(4,000)	(3,700–4,300)	(3,700)	(4,300)
equipment, heating, remodeling)	(500)	(300–600)	(300)	(600)
Sales or financing concessions	0			
Total adjustment	(9,500)		(7,400)	(12,200)
Sale price	$65,000		$65,000	$65,000
Adjusted sale price	$55,500		$57,600	$52,800
			Upper limit of value	Lower limit of value

Source: FHLMC Form 70 grid.

on the sales and their adjustments. In arriving at this upper limit of value, you should analyze the adjustments and select the adjustment or amount that leans toward a higher value but still appears reasonable. Estimating the upper limit is a question of giving all the benefit of the doubt in one direction—toward a higher price.

Next, estimate the lower limit, that is, the lowest price that can reasonably be developed. Again, examine the sales and the adjustments and, this time, give the benefit of the doubt to adjustments that lower the price. When estimating the upper and lower limits of value, consider any uncertainty you have about the amounts of the adjustments. In practice, this process of estimating limits is usually done by intuition. The concept is displayed mathematically in Table 9-1 (page 195).

After you push the adjustments to their highest reasonable price indication and then push them the other way, to their lowest price, consider how wide the range is from the low price to the high price. The narrower the range, the more reliable the value conclusion. You should then consider which sales appear to be the most comparable and what the adjusted prices of these sales are. If the adjusted prices of the sales that you believe are more comparable cluster in a particular area within the range, then you should select the value conclusion from that area.

Step Four—Estimating a Value

Selecting an indicated value from the sales comparison approach is not a science. There is no mathematical formula for it; to a large degree, it requires judgment. There are, however, some sensible rules. First, give the greatest weight to the sale (or sales) that needs the least total adjustment (ignoring the plus and minus signs). This reduces the impact of any errors made during the adjustment process. See Example 9.7.

Example 9.7
Which Sale Needed the Least Adjustment?

Sale Number	1	2	3	4
Price	$73,500	$66,800	$78,000	$69,900
Adjustments:				
Time	+7%	+3%	+2%	+5%
Size	−4%	+5%	−4%	0
Location	−3%	+3%	−3%	0
Total	0	+11%	−5%	+5%
Adjusted price	$73,500	$74,148	$74,100	$73,395

Answer: Sale No. 4 needed the least adjustment.

The second rule is to favor the sales (or the method of adjusting them) that involve the fewest assumptions or the most reliable adjustments. Finally, do *not* average the sales prices or the adjusted sales prices. Averaging assumes that the difference in price from one sale to the next is the result of pure chance and that each sale should have equal weight in the conclusion. With real estate, neither is likely to be true. Instead it is more likely that the variation in the adjusted sales prices is caused by some problem that the appraiser has not yet found. Since such problems do not occur randomly, averaging will not eliminate the cause. The best action to take is to go back and reconsider why the adjusted sales still vary and try to find a logical explanation. If that is not fruitful, choose the most reliable sales. Using the most reliable sales will reduce the chance that the unknown problem will affect the value conclusion.

In summary, to arrive at an indicated value, make an overall review of the sales comparison approach. Reconsider the data used and verify that it was interpreted in the best manner. Then narrow the adjusted sales prices into a range within which you feel that the value must lie. Finally, within this range, select an appropriate single price based on a careful and thorough analysis of the entire process.

SUMMARY

The comparison of sales is one of the most important parts of the appraisal approach. Many techniques can be used. One is to make direct sales comparisons. However, direct comparisons are often difficult, so appraisers have developed other methods. These involve two steps: (1) comparison or analysis of sales, and (2) adjustment of sales prices.

In the comparison or analysis step, the sales are compared in order to identify differences in location, properties, prices, date of sale, or terms of sale. Next the differences are studied in order to establish which differences in location, property, time, or terms caused the variation in prices.

In the adjustment step, the prices of the sales are adjusted to account for any differences between the sales and the subject property. Each of the sales is adjusted to make it more like the subject. There are three types of adjustments that can be used independently or in combination: the lump-sum dollar adjustment, the percentage adjustment, and the unit of comparison. For the clearest explanation of an adjustment analysis, a special table called the sales analysis grid is included in most appraisal reports. However, the sales analysis grid is only suitable to present a few adjustment techniques.

The amounts of adjustments can be calculated in several ways. One, the direct market method, uses the direct analysis of sales to calculate adjustments. The depreciated cost method calculates adjustments using indirect market information: cost and depreciation. It is especially useful when property differences consist largely of physical improvements or when a property has a defect that needs correction. The kind of financing a property has may also affect its sale price; therefore, adjustments must sometimes be made for the type of financing. A sophisticated statistical technique called regression can be used to calculate the amount of a dollar or percentage adjustment. Appraisers use two types of regression: linear and multiple.

The final step in the sales comparison approach is arriving at a value conclusion. This is achieved by the following four steps:

---

1. *Review the entire approach*   Consider and try to account for the limitations of your method.
2. *Review the sales*   Determine the overall reliability of your sales data.
3. *Estimate a value range*   You should determine a lower and an upper limit of value.
4. *Select a final value*   You must ultimately select a single value after rechecking all the above steps.

IMPORTANT TERMS AND CONCEPTS

Adjusting sales
Adjustment amounts
  dollar
  percent
Analyzing sales
Gross rent multipliers
Price range
Property differences

Regression
  linear
  multiple
Terms of sale
Total property comparisons
Units of comparison
  economic
  physical

REVIEWING YOUR UNDERSTANDING

1. The steps in the direct sales comparison technique are:
   (a) Locating similar sales, rearranging the sales in order of desirability, and adding the cost differences of the sales together to obtain the subject property's value
   (b) Locating similar sales, rearranging the sales in order of desirability, and comparing the subject property to the comparable properties
   (c) Locating sales from other neighborhoods, adjusting for differences in price, and rearranging the sales in order of desirability

2. The process of adjusting sales involves two steps. These are:
   (a) Identifying the similarities between properties and adjusting the sales
   (b) Analyzing the comparables and adjusting for similarities
   (c) Identifying the significant differences between properties and adjusting the sales
   (d) Locating competitive properties and placing them in the order of their desirability

3. To use the lump-sum adjustment:
   (a) Calculate the percentage difference between the replacement cost new of a comparable and its present market value; then multiply this percentage times the replacement cost new of the subject property
   (b) Calculate the difference between the comparable sale and the subject property as a percentage of the sale price
   (c) Select a specific dollar amount as the appropriate adjustment
   (d) Locate the appropriate number in a lump-sum adjustment table

4. To use the percentage adjustment:
   (a) Calculate the difference between the comparable sale and the subject property as a percentage of the area
   (b) Calculate the percentage price difference between two comparable properties that are very similar except for the feature being studied
   (c) Select a specific dollar amount as the appropriate adjustment
   (d) Divide the price of the subject property by the percentage difference between the sale prices of the two best comparables

5. To use the unit of comparison adjustment:
   (a) Select an appropriate unit and convert the sales prices to prices per unit
   (b) Figure the sale price per square foot for the subject property and multiply it by the average size of the sales
   (c) None of the above
   (d) Both parts (a) and (b)

6. A physical unit of comparison generally refers to:
   (a) The largest physical characteristic of the subject property compared to the largest characteristic of the comparable properties
   (b) Any physical characteristic of the sales that varies
   (c) The gross rent multiplier
   (d) None of the above

7. An economic unit of comparison is:
   (a) An economic measure of the property and its value
   (b) The characteristic of the subject property that relates more to size than to utility
   (c) The price divided by the age

8. A rent multiplier is an economic unit of comparison because:
   (a) It measures the square feet of the rental property
   (b) It compares the present income to the property against the past income of the property as a percentage
   (c) It relates to the income of the property

9. Linear regression:
   (a) Adjusts for only one variable
   (b) Adjusts for a number of variables at the same time
   (c) Adjusts for two variables at the same time
   (d) Is used to calculate the replacement cost new for the subject property

10. In the last step of the sales comparison approach, you need to:
    (a) Review the entire approach
    (b) Review the sales
    (c) Estimate a value range and select a final value
    (d) None of the above
    (e) All of the above

CHAPTER TEN

VALUING
THE SITE

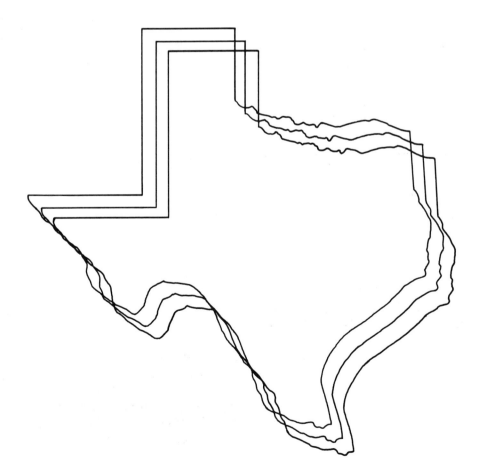

PREVIEW

In Chapter 6 we discussed the main factors affecting the value of land and the techniques used to physically inspect a site. In this chapter we shall outline the four methods used to appraise land and explain how they apply to undeveloped acreage, vacant lots, or sites improved with buildings. Since all land appraisal methods rely upon property comparison in some form, an understanding of the sales comparison approach techniques covered in Chapters 8 and 9 is essential.

When you have completed this chapter, you should be able to:

1. Name five different uses of site value appraisals.

2. List the four methods of appraising land.

3. Name five physical characteristics of a site that affect its value.

4. Name three legal and economic considerations in site value.

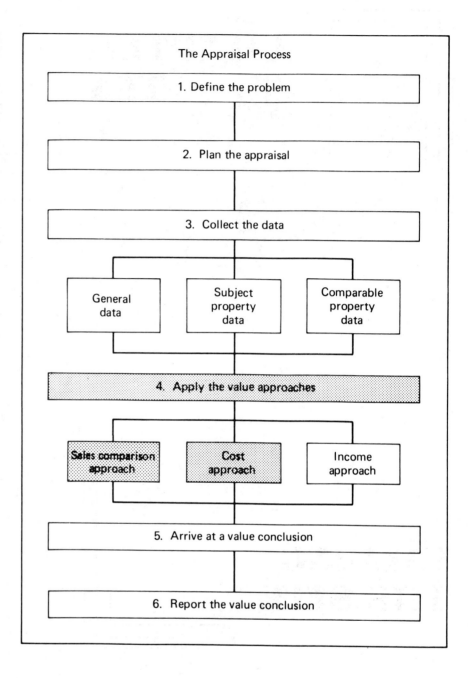

The Appraisal Process

1. Define the problem

2. Plan the appraisal

3. Collect the data

General data | Subject property data | Comparable property data

4. Apply the value approaches

Sales comparison approach | Cost approach | Income approach

5. Arrive at a value conclusion

6. Report the value conclusion

**SECTION 10.1
PURPOSE OF LAND OR
SITE VALUE ESTIMATES**

Land or site value estimates are useful not only in the appraisal of vacant or undeveloped land, but in other circumstances as well. The site is appraised as if it were vacant whenever a separation of land and building value is necessary for improved properties. Also, a separate site value may be needed in any of the three approaches to value. We shall explore each of these reasons here. In market value studies, we generally appraise land on the basis of its highest and best use.

Appraisals of Acreage or Vacant Land

The appraisal of vacant land usually requires more specialized experience than the appraisal of improved property. The reason for this is that a very limited percentage of real estate transactions involve vacant land. Bare acreage varies more in location, size, and shape than most improved properties. Thus buyers and sellers often require the services of an expert to interpret the physical, legal, and economic factors that determine land value.

Land is frequently leased instead of being sold outright. Whether the lease is for agricultural, commercial, or residential purposes, appraisals are often needed to estimate rental value or the equitable return on investment capital. Land leases can be for very long-term periods, so correctly estimating the initial rental amounts becomes quite important. Appraisers often base fair rent upon a current market value estimate.

Real estate developers, lenders, agricultural interests, government agencies, and courts of law rely upon land appraisals to make important decisions on the use and distribution of land. Developers and subdividers need to include the value of land as one of the costs of the finished product. Thus, many project feasibility studies incorporate vacant land appraisals. Banks and other lenders often furnish construction financing for real estate developments. Since such loans are often based on the value of the vacant land, formal appraisals are usually needed.

Many government acts, such as taxation, eminent domain, and redevelopment, may require estimates of land value and frequently require formal appraisals. Also, courts are concerned with questions of land value in connection with inheritance settlements, divorce cases, and other legal actions.

Allocation of Value for Tax Purposes

Certain tax laws require that the value of land and improvements be estimated separately for improved properties. First, ad valorem (according to value) property taxes are usually based on separately stated land and improvement values. Second, income tax laws generally allow an annual "write-off," or depreciation deduction, when buildings are held for investment purposes. Since such depreciation is allowed only on the value of the structures, an allocation of value or purchase price between land and buildings is required.

Site Value in the Three Value Approaches

Since land and buildings may be regarded as separate economic parts of the property, site value estimates are routinely needed in many improved property appraisals. Even when the defined purpose of an appraisal is to estimate the total market value of an improved property, the particular techniques used by an appraiser may require an estimate of the value of the land.

The cost approach (covered in Chapters 11 and 12) uses an estimate of the site value as a base figure to which the value of the improvements is added. This means that the site must be appraised first. Next, the value of the buildings is estimated as the cost new less depreciation. Note that for appraisal purposes, depreciation refers to the difference between the present value of the improvements and their replacement cost new.

In the income approach, certain capitalization procedures (to be discussed later) split the net income for the property between the two production agents, land and building. Hence a separate land value estimate can be required in the income approach, too.

Finally, some sales analysis techniques in the sales comparison approach subtract the land value from the sale price to see what the various buildings "sold for." In order to use this technique, the appraiser must estimate land value for each sale and also for the subject property. Example 10.1 summarizes various reasons for estimating land value separately from building value.

Example 10.1
Reasons for Estimating Land Value

1. One viewpoint

    (a) Sale price
    (b) Rental value
    (c) Feasibility studies
    (d) Loan security
    (e) Property tax
    (f) Eminent domain
    (g) Income tax basis allocation

2. Another viewpoint

    (a) Cost approach
    (b) Income approach—residual capitalization
    (c) Sales comparison approach

SECTION 10.2
FOUR METHODS
USED TO APPRAISE LAND

Among practicing appraisers, there are four recognized methods of appraising land. These are (1) the sales comparison method, (2) the allocation or abstraction method, (3) the development method, and (4) the land residual method. (See Figure 10.1.)

THE SALES COMPARISON METHOD

THE ALLOCATION METHOD

THE DEVELOPMENT METHOD

THE LAND RESIDUAL METHOD

FIGURE 10.1

As we discuss these land appraisal methods, it is important to keep in mind that land is almost always appraised for its highest and best use, which is not necessarily its current use. It would usually be incorrect, for example, to appraise a potential commercial site as residential just because its current use is residential. This is in violation of the principle of highest and best use, discussed in Chapter 5.

The Sales Comparison Method

The most reliable method of appraising land is the sales comparison method. In concept, it is little different from the sales comparison approach used to appraise improved properties (see Chapters 8 and 9). However, the sales comparison method of determining site value and the sales comparison approach have one important difference: the basis of comparison between parcels.

The Basis and Criteria of Comparison

Whether the land is actually vacant or improved, the method of site appraisal compares the subject property as if it were vacant. When this is understood, it follows that all sales comparisons should be recent sales of vacant land. (See Figure 10.2.)

How are comparables to be selected? Vacant land sales should be similar to the subject land in location, physical characteristics, and potential use. Location is important for the many reasons already discussed. Close proximity to the subject property contributes to the credibility of the sales since the same value-influencing factors are present. (See Figure 10.3.)

Physical features should also be similar. Comparing a steep hillside lot with a flat valley lot would probably require unreasonably large adjustments. Such adjustments might cover higher site preparation costs (for the hillside lot) and also the value difference associated with a view.

FIGURE 10.2
Vacant Land in Proximity to Developed Land. (Photograph Courtesy of Doug Frost.)

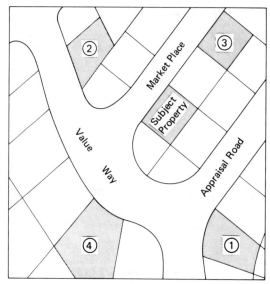

FIGURE 10.3
Four Recent Site Sales of Varying Comparability

In the sales comparison method of land appraisal, vacant land sales should be chosen for their similarity to the subject land in terms of potential use. The most likely use for a parcel is determined primarily by location, zoning (and/or permissible use), and market demand at the time of the appraisal. (See Chapter 6, Section 6.1, for a review of highest and best use.)

Applying the Sales Comparison Method

Since the sales comparison method is the most direct method of appraising land, it is preferred whenever sales of comparable vacant land are available. The method is suitable to appraise either vacant or improved sites, whether they are zoned for residential, commercial, industrial, agricultural, or recreational usage.

The application of the sales comparison method of site appraisal involves the same sales comparison approach procedures described in Chapter 8. (See Figure 10.4.) The appropriate steps are as follows:

1. Locate vacant land sales that are similar to the subject site in terms of potential use. Gather information as to sale conditions, terms of each sale, and the price paid.

2. Compare each sale with the subject property as to the date of sale, location factors, and physical characteristics.

3. Adjust the selling price of each comparable site to reflect any important differences between it and the subject site. Adjustments may be made in either dollar or percentage amounts.

4. Arrive at an indicated value for the subject site based on the most comparable of the sales analyzed.

Specific techniques of comparison and adjustment will be discussed later in this chapter.

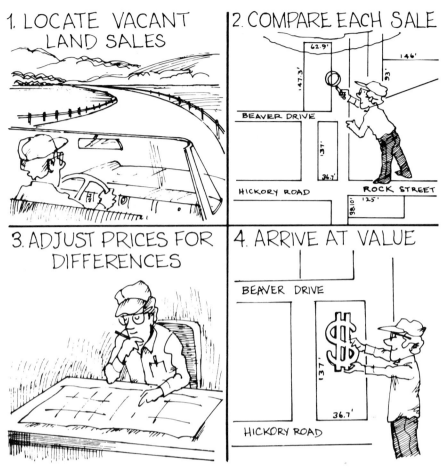

FIGURE 10.4
Appraisal of Land by the Sales Comparison Approach

The Allocation or Abstraction Method

When comparable sales of vacant sites are not available, the direct sales comparison method cannot be used. As one alternative, land value may be allocated or abstracted from sales of improved property. The allocation or abstraction method typically would be used in built-up areas, where little vacant land remains. This method can also be useful in the appraisal of portions of a shared land interest, such as those in condominiums, cooperatives, and planned developments.

Since the allocation method is less direct than the sales comparison method, it is usually much less accurate. Consequently, if vacant land sales are available, you should not rely upon the allocation method of land appraisals.

The first step in the allocation or abstraction method is to find sales of improved properties with site characteristics comparable to those of the subject property. Next, allocate a proportion of the sales price to the land and a proportion to the buildings. To do this, you might select the value relationship (percent or ratio) that you have found to be typical for similar properties in similar areas. For example, where your research shows that the site represents 20% of the total value, a $100,000 sale of an improved property indicates a site value of 20% of 100,000 or $20,000. Land and

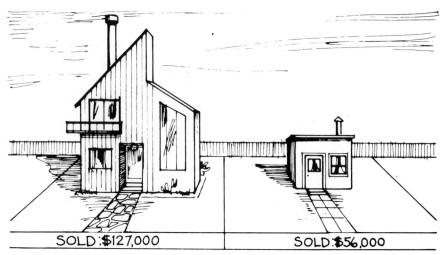

SOLD:$127,000   SOLD:$56,000

FIGURE 10.5
Each Lot Is Worth $50,000

building ratios are subject to constant change, so it is important that your research be recent. Ratios also vary among communities and types of property; therefore, you must be cautious in using them.

When there is no well-defined ratio of land value to building value among the sales, you may select an abstracted site value. You obtain this by estimating the cost of the building less depreciation (discussed in the next two chapters) and subtracting that figure from the total sales price. This would leave a value that is attributable to the land. (See Figure 10.5.) An example is as follows:

Sales price of the property		$165,000
Less: Depreciated cost of the improvements		− 125,000
Equals: Abstracted land value		$40,000

Instead of using either of these allocation methods, it is sometimes acceptable to use the land-to-building value ratio shown on the local assessment roll. If the roll shows a total value of $93,000, broken into a $21,000 land and $72,000 building value, the ratio is $21,000/$93,000, or 22.6% land. If the property actually sold for $100,000, a land value of $22,600 is suggested by the assessment ratio method ($100,000 × 22.6%).

The site value indicated by the allocation or abstraction method is considered to have a limited reliability. Since the ratio of land value to total property value is usually different for each location and type of property, an abstracted site value estimate may be useful only to verify some other value indication.

The Land Development Method

As its name implies, this method is used only to estimate the value of vacant acreage that is ready to be subdivided. It is generally used when there are no sales of comparable acreage or when a detailed analysis of the project is desired. The land development method shows how the raw land value relates economically to its anticipated market value as developed land. Thus, this method of estimating value requires that we study current

FIGURE 10.6
A Residential Subdivision Under Development. (Photograph Courtesy of Doug Frost.)

sales of subdivided lots and make a projection of land development costs for the property under appraisal. (See Figure 10.6.)

To estimate value by the land development method, let us assume a residential subdivision. First, estimate the number of lots to be developed, allowing for zoning, lot size requirements, and the land area needed for streets, parkways, and other open space. Next, estimate the typical current price that the lots could be sold for, based upon sale prices for comparable subdivision lots. Obtain a total dollar amount to be realized from the gross sales by totaling the estimated prices of the lots. Account for all direct and indirect costs of development, including engineering and government fees. Add costs for promotion, sales, and closing charges. Finally, you must allow for the developer's profit (to cover work effort, overhead costs, and return on capital), typically either as a percentage of gross sales or a percentage of the capital invested in the raw land. After deducting all these development costs and profits from the gross revenues, the remaining amounts constitute the value of the raw acreage. If the lots will take more than a year to sell, a further deduction may be necessary to adjust for the time that the developer's capital is tied up in the project. There are a number of different methods of performing subdivision analyses, varying in format and in complexity. Example 10.2 displays one method.

Example 10.2
Valuing Acreage Ready for Subdivision
Suppose that you were appraising a 12-acre parcel of land for development into 50 single-family residential lots. Similar lots nearby, ready to build on, are selling for $30,000 each. You project sales revenues and expenditures as follows. The example allows a developer's return of 30% on the raw land investment, which is both a return on the developer's capital and also payment for the developer's risk, entrepreneurial skills, and overhead costs.

Projected sales: 50 lots at $30,000		$1,500,000
Less: Development costs		
Direct expenses:		
Design and engineering	$10,000	
Clearing and grading	50,000	
Utilities and streets	+ 250,000	
Subtotal	$310,000	
Indirect expenses:		
Studies and reports	$5,000	
Legal costs and fees	50,000	
Construction financing costs	75,000	
Property taxes	25,000	
Sales and promotion	+ 75,000	
Subtotal	+ 230,000	
Total deductions from sales		−$540,000
Equals: Net proceeds		$960,000

These net proceeds represent the land purchase price plus the developer's profit of 30%, for a total that is 130% of the land value. Therefore:

$$\text{Indicated raw land value} = \frac{\$960,000}{1.30} = \$738,500 \text{ (rounded answer)}$$

The Land Residual Method

This method of estimating the value of the land is based on the principle of surplus productivity, discussed in Chapter 5. The land residual method calculates land value by measuring the amount of income (either actual or potential) that is left after deducting the amount of income that should be attributed to any buildings. Hence the method is one version of the income approach to value.

The land residual method is useful where there are no comparable land sales, and commercial, industrial, or residential income properties are being appraised. The techniques used in this method will be discussed in detail in Chapter 14.

SECTION 10.3
HOW TO USE SALES
COMPARISON TECHNIQUES

The comparison of properties is an essential part of all four methods of appraising land. While the same rules discussed in Chapters 8 and 9 apply to the techniques of site comparison, data and techniques that are unique to site appraisals will be emphasized in this section.

Types and Sources of Data

Although the specific types and sources of data needed for comparison of land sales may differ from those required in the appraisal of improved property, the quality and quantity of data to be gathered are essentially the same.

Criteria for Comparable Sales

For vacant land sales to be used as adequate comparables, they must be competitive with both the subject property and each other. They should be located in the same neighborhood as the subject property, or one like it, and be affected by similar social and economic influences. In fully built-up, older neighborhoods, vacant land sales are usually not available. Therefore, sales from a different location may be considered if the sites are similar in physical and legal characteristics and influenced by the same market factors. Similar prices for comparable improved properties may be convincing evidence of such comparability.

The comparable sales must be open market transactions; distress sales and sales where the buyer gains a unique benefit are not usually considered valid comparables. An example of such a special benefit would be a business buying an adjoining vacant property for much needed expansion. If the alternative to expansion is to relocate to larger premises, the business can often afford to pay a premium to get the adjoining lot.

To be useful, a sale should be recent. This is a relative term, measured from the value date of the appraisal. Depending on the market activity at the time and the type of property being appraised, a sale could be considered recent if it occurred as long ago as two or three years before the date of value. In an active or changing market, however, sales more than a few months old may be unacceptable.

What Data to Include

The data collected for each comparable sale should include detailed information about physical, legal, and locational factors. This information helps in determining the comparability of the subject property. Specific physical data usually include lot size, shape, frontage, slope, and topography. Specific legal data, such as zoning, taxes, special assessments, and public and private restrictions, should also be considered. Sales work sheets are often used, providing the appraiser with a convenient means of recording these and other necessary details such as street address, legal description, name of grantee (buyer), name of grantor (seller), date, price, and terms of sale. All of these items will be discussed in this chapter.

Sources of Data

Data on vacant land sales may be obtained from public records. For example, ownership records may be discovered by researching recorded deeds in the public recorder's office, or the records of the property tax assessor. Checking for demolition and new construction permits or subdivision map applications can also reveal parcels where a recent land sale may have occurred, as well as the likely parties to contact.

Buyers, sellers, brokers, land developers, realty board listings, title companies, and lenders are all good private sources of information on recent market activity involving vacant land. Even newspaper advertisements may help. Real estate professionals are usually willing to cooperate in providing data.

Market data "banks" accumulate information furnished by participating appraisers. Figure 10.7 is a sample of the land sales data available from the DRESCO, Inc. of Dallas. Such groups can be helpful sources of data although they may have only limited information on vacant land sales. Nevertheless, this can help supplement data from other sources.

```
¢ 1985 :    :PAGE   1                              T H E   R O D D Y   R E P O R T                                              Jun
```

SALE# MAP- SEC MAP- SCO	LOCATION	DESCRIPTION	SIZE	IMPROVEMENTS	GRANTOR/ GRANTEE	DATE/ VOLUME/ PAGE	AMOUNT OF D/T: PAYABLE TO	DEED RETURNED TO
0099 13B	E & W/S FM-2933 APPRX 4,300' S OF CR-341	A-227, A-335 & A-226 Sale Price Available	293.503 AC.	NONE ZONED AGRI FOR RESALE	TOM ALLEN JR EX: FOR EST OF BEN R HILL TO SHAUL C BARUCH	04/17/85 2133 46	EX: $862,898 GTR	GTE 13601 PRESTON RD STE 709 DALLAS TX 75240
0089 17B 459L	SE/S SH-121 APPRX 500' SW OF STACY RD (CR-153)	A-879 (ALLEN) Sq Ft Price Available	10.0 AC.	NONE FUTURE OFC BLDG SITE	RAY L GALARNEAU ETUX & ROBERT R: RANTZOW ETUX TO SHADDOCK & COOK INVESTMENTS (SHADDOCK & COOK LTD INC & SHADDOCK & COOK DEVELOPERS INC/ PETER H SHADDOCK PRES)	04/17/85 2132 437	EX: $742,050 GTR	GTE 17330 PRESTON RD STE 200-D DALLAS TX 75252
00¢2 23D 10B	W/S HOOPER RD 1,600' S OF FM-544	A-835 Acre Price Available	51.0336 AC.	NONE WILL SUB-DIVIDE & RESELL	VINCELEE ALESANDER TO K C SWAYZE	04/18/85 2112 678	EX: $287,000 GTR	GTE 204 N 2ND ST WYLIE TX 75098
0065 13A 361B	NEC E UNIVERSITY (US-380) & TENNESSEE ST (215 E UNIVERSITY)	A-248 (MCKINNEY) Sale Price Available	2.9214 AC.	20,010 SF SHOPPING CENTER INCOME PROPERTY	WILLIAM A MINYARD III D/B/A THREE EIGHTY PLACE ASSOC JV TO THREE EIGHTY PLACE ASSOC JV	04/22/85 2113 723	EX: $1,450,000 LANDMARK SAV BK FSB (HOT SPRINGS AR)	GTE C/O L FISCHMAN 13355 NOEL RD STE I 1600 DALLAS TX 75240
0098 06A	NWC FM-428 & CR-54 & SWC CR-54 & CR-8	A-168 Acre Price Available	330.67 AC.	NONE ZONED AGRI WILL RESELL IN 100 AC TRACTS	ROBERT S FOLSOM TR TO B L NELSON TR	04/23/85 2115 10	EX: $2,568,040 (WRAPAROUND) GTR (INCL OTHER PROPERTY)	GTE 7311 FERGUSON RD DALLAS TX 75228
0067 16A 456J	S/S HICKORY ST APPRX 3,800' W OF SH-289 (PRESTON RD)	A-591, A-618, A-1004 & A-5 Sq Ft Price Available	26.941 AC.	LAND VALUE ZONED MFM (20 AC) & LIGHT COMM (7 AC) FOR RESALE	ALLAN ZIDELL (12201 MERIT DR STE 670 DALLAS TX 75251) TO MICHAEL KLEPAK TR	04/23/85 2114 852	EX: $1,553,712 GTR	GTE 14180 N DALLAS PKWY STE 400 DALLAS TX 75240
0066 13A 261X	E/S SH-5 APPRX 200 N OF CHURCH ST	A-248 (MCKINNEY) Sale Price Available	2.0 AC.	NURSING HOME WILL RENOVATE INTO MINIUM SECURITY FACILITY (JAIL)	NATIONAL LIVING CENTERS INC (JAMES W RICE SEC) TO COLLIN COUNTY (HON WILLIAM J ROBERTS)	04/23/85 2114 702	$10 OVC	GTE COLLIN COUNTY COURTHOUSE MCKINNEY TX 75069
0070 22A 558Z	APPRX 1,500' W OF ALMA DR & APPRX 1,300' S OF CARPENTER RD	A-714 Acre Price Available	10.47 AC.	NONE ZONED PATIO HOMES PT FUTURE 14 LOT PATIO HOME DEV SITE (RUSSELL CREEK #3)	PLANO/CARPENTER ROAD JV (REAL EARTH JV/ROGER THORNHILL & PENTA DEVELOP- MENT GROUP/G RUSSELL HUTCHINS) TO CENTENNIAL HOMES	04/24/85 2115 886	$10 OVC	GTE 5720 LBJ FRWY STE 610 DALLAS TX 75240
0071 22A 558Z	APPRX 1,000' W OF ALMA DR & APPRX 1,300' S OF CARPENTER RD	A-714 Acre Price Available	17.82 AC.	NONE ZONED PATIO HOMES PT FUTURE 141 LOT PATIO HOME DEV SITE (RUSSELL CREEK #3)	REAL EARTH CORP (ROGER C THORNHILL PRES) TO CENTENNIAL HOMES INC	04/24/85 2115 889	$10 OVC	GTE 5720 LBJ FRWY STE 610 DALLAS TX 75240
0088 01B	NWC SPUR-483 & CR-58	A-140 Acre Price Available	56.793 AC.	NONE WILL SUB-DIVIDE INTO 2 AC TRACTS & RESELL FOR RESI DEV	BOBBY D APPLE & RICHARD L DONALDSON TO WILLIAM L CHAILLOT JR ETUX	04/29/85 2119 188	EX: $197,000 FIRST STATE BK (CELINA TX)	GTE RT 3 BOX 203 LEWISVILLE TX 75056
0085 06D	E/S SH-289 APPRX 2,600' N OF FM-1461	A-1030 Acre Price Available	24.0862 AC.	NONE ZONED AGRI PT FUTURE 40-50 TRACT RANCHETTE DEV SITE	JACK MOORE ETUX TO FOLSOM INVESTMENTS INC (ROBERT S FOLSOM PRES)	04/29/85 2119 125	EX: $308,303 GTR (INCL OTHER PROPERTY)	GTE 16475 N DALLAS PKWY STE 800 DALLAS TX 75248
0086 06D	E/S SH-289 APPRX 2,000' N OF FM-1461	A-1030 Acre Price Available	24.086 AC.	NONE ZONED AGRI PT FUTURE 40-50 TRACT RANCHETTE DEV SITE	JACK MOORE ETUX TO FOLSOM INVESTMENTS INC (ROBERT S FOLSOM PRES)	04/29/85 2119 139	EX: $308,300 GTR	GTE 16475 N DALLAS PKWY STE 800 DALLAS TX 75248
0084 06D	APPRX 2,500' E OF SH-289 & APPRX 3,200' N OF FM-1461	A-532 Acre Price	16.5743 AC.	NONE ZONED AGRI PT FUTURE 40-50 TRACT RANCHETTE	JACK MOORE ETUX TO FOLSOM	04/29/85 2119 122	$10 OVC	GTE 16475 N DALLAS PKWY STE ˚

FIGURE 10.7

Sales Transactions, Collin County, Texas: April 17, 1985 Through April 29, 1985. (Courtesy of DRESCO, Inc., Roddy Publications)

Verification of the Data

Any information you collect must be properly verified and interpreted to be of value. Ideally, the total price and terms of the sale should be verified with one or both principals to the transaction. This often helps to qualify the sale as an open market transaction. With land sales, it can be especially important to identify the terms of sale. Since institutional loans on vacant land are uncommon, more seller loans are used. When favorable interest rates or terms are provided, the selling price may be significantly increased to reflect the premium value of the loan.

When direct verification of data is not possible, seek out some of the public and private sources already mentioned. As we have already suggested, data from public records may not accurately indicate the full purchase price. For example, recorded deeds may reflect only loan amounts instead of total consideration.

Major Land Features Affecting Value

In the comparative process, it is essential that those features of the property that are important in the marketplace be thoroughly understood. Therefore, we shall review here the major factors affecting land value, previously discussed in Chapter 6. In this chapter the important site characteristics have been divided into physical, legal, and locational groupings. (See Figure 10.8.)

Physical Features

Here are some of the most basic physical features to consider:

1. Size can be measured in square feet, acres, or hectares (the metric land measure—1 hectare is about 2.5 acres), or simply by frontage. The size of a parcel is basic to utility and value. Although its relative importance depends upon both use and zoning requirements, size is often the best unit of comparison in the analysis of sales.

2. Shape refers to the general parcel configuration and its relative dimensions. An irregular or long and narrow shape, for example, may reduce the utility of a site.

3. Frontage refers to the width of the lot on the access street. Its importance is a function of the land use and specific zoning requirements. This measure affects access to the property. It also affects the exposure to public view, which is very important in some commercial properties.

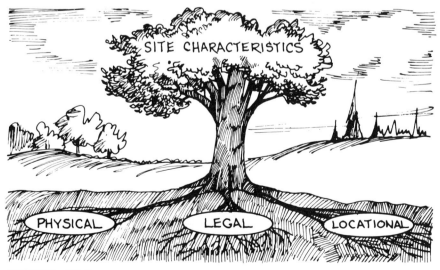

FIGURE 10.8

4. Width is important to the *effective* size of a lot. Most zoning ordinances not only regulate minimum lot width but also require side-yard setbacks. Hence, for relatively narrow lots, the side yards have the effect of reducing the net buildable area.

5. Depth of the site is also important. Street setback requirements of local zoning ordinances can considerably reduce the utility of a shallow lot; on the other hand, extra depth may not contribute proportionate to the value of a lot. In urban single-residential properties, deep lots may be worth little more than standard-depth lots for the street or neighborhood.

6. Plottage value refers to the added value generated when two or more smaller sites can be combined to provide greater utility. For example, two or more commercially zoned lots can sometimes be combined to form the site of a larger, more economically profitable project. However, the assembly of lots does not always result in a plottage value increment; such added value depends upon an economic need for the larger unit.

7. The type of lot may affect its relative appeal and marketability. Preference for different lot types, such as corner, inside, keyed, and flag lots, may vary from neighborhood to neighborhood.

8. Topography refers to the slope and surface features of the site. It can have a dramatic effect on access, drainage, and view; it can also help to determine how buildable a site is.

9. Other attributes to be considered include drainage, soil and subsoil features, climate, and view. Such off-site improvements as streets, alleys, sidewalks, and curbs also affect the value of the land itself and are therefore important comparative features.

These features are illustrated in Figure 10.9.

Legal and Locational Features
Although we are accustomed to thinking of a site as having only physical characteristics, legal and locational features also must be compared in appraisals.

First, we must consider the legal form of the land itself. Would it be possible to compare the airspace and common area interests of a condo-

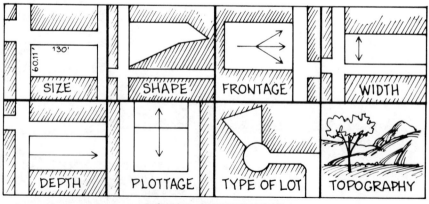

OTHER ATTRIBUTES:
* DRAINAGE * SOIL * CLIMATE * VIEW

FIGURE 10.9
Major Physical Features Affecting Land Value

minium site with a conventional detached lot? Probably not. As we learned in Chapter 6, the legal rights associated with condominiums and planned unit developments make them uniquely different from the site we most commonly associate with "conventional" housing. Compare like with like whenever possible.

Zoning and other land-use regulations are also critical legal elements to consider in site comparisons. As mentioned before, the highest and best use of land is limited to those uses that are legal under the current zoning (or any probable rezoning).

Consider the effect of zoning on the typical lot size, for example. As we learned in Chapter 6, zoning often regulates the number of square feet of land required for each living unit. In single-family residential neighborhoods, the minimum lot size may be as little as 4,000 square feet under one zoning designation, and as large as an acre or more under another. It follows that sales comparisons generally would be made with sales having the same zoning designation.

What effect do you suppose federal, state, and local environmental protection laws have on the appraisal of land already in use? Such laws can restrict the legal uses allowable for vacant land but do not usually restrict a use already in existence. When this happens, land that is already improved may not be readily comparable with vacant land selling under restricted-use laws. For example, land developed with apartment buildings prior to open-space laws that reduced allowable density might now represent privileged, nonconforming properties.

A number of other legal restrictions that limit land use were covered in Chapter 6 and need not all be repeated here. It is just necessary to remember that easements, right-of-way regulations, deed restrictions, and private encumbrances can make the affected parcels unique. Hence such restrictions must be investigated, for they may detract from the comparability of otherwise similar land.

Utilities and other municipal or public services available to the site are largely a function of the site's location. The level of property taxes and other economic factors also should be considered in making land value comparisons. Differences in the quality of schools, fire and police protection, refuse collection, street lighting, and the level of taxation are often so important that it becomes impractical to compare land in different political jurisdictions.

Analyzing the Sales Data

As in the sales comparison approach for improved properties, it is necessary to analyze and compare vacant land sales. We must consider the circumstances of the sale and also compare the properties involved. This process uses four elements of comparison.

Elements of Comparison
Sales should be compared and adjusted by using four elements of comparison: (1) terms of the sale, (2) time of sale, (3) location, and (4) physical characteristics.

It is frequently true that the terms determine the price. When vacant land is sold for other than cash, it is frequently financed by the seller. If the terms of the seller loan are more favorable than outside lenders offer, the buyer may agree to an inflated price. Low down payments, low interest rates, and subordination clauses are often encountered. (A subordination clause is an agreement by the seller-lender to subordinate this loan to a later development or construction loan.) It takes a considerable amount of expertise to adjust vacant land sale prices for the effects of unusual financing. Adjusting for terms of sale was discussed in Chapter 9.

The time of sale is most often the second element of a sale to be compared and adjusted. Changing market conditions may affect vacant land prices even more quickly and dramatically than prices of improved properties. Changes in zoning, parking requirements, and environmental impact laws are good examples of changing value influences.

Adjustments for location are perhaps the most critical and difficult of the adjustments to make in the appraisal of land. That is why close proximity to the subject property is important so that this adjustment can be minimized.

The physical characteristics of land were referred to earlier in this section. The characteristics of the subject and the comparables should be compared, with priority given to those differences that affect the potential use of the site. How much do size, shape, topography, and so on, affect the value of a site? These questions can only be answered by an analysis of the market's reaction to them. Several techniques help to interpret the market's reaction to these important physical differences. One of these is the direct market method discussed in Chapter 9. This technique makes use of matched pairs of sales. For example, if two lots with only one notable difference—say, standard versus excess depth—have recently sold at different prices, the adjustment for depth might be read from the sales. Or it might be possible to locate a depth table that conforms to the sales data and can serve as a guide. (The use of depth tables to suggest how lot value may vary with relative depth was discussed in Chapter 6.) When a large number of sales are available, linear and multiple regression techniques can assist in the analysis of two or more physical differences in the sale properties.

Units of Comparison for Land Appraisals

The appraiser normally compares sales by whatever criteria are most significant in the market. Using a unit of comparison helps you to do this. Appropriate units of comparison are often determined by the type of zoning and potential use. For example, residential lots are usually sold and compared by selling price per lot, square foot, or acre. In the case of lots zoned for multiple-residential or condominium projects, the selling price per dwelling unit to be developed is generally the important unit of comparison. Commercial or industrial land is usually sold and compared by the selling price per square foot, but larger parcels are sold per acre. High-valued commercial property is usually sold in terms of price per front foot, where foot traffic is heavy and merchandise display is important. (See Example 10.3.)

In the hypothetical sales sample shown, there seems to be less variability in the price per square foot than in the price per front foot. This implies

Example 10.3
Using Units of Comparison in Appraising Land

Sale	Size	Price	Price per Front Ft	Price per Sq Ft
A	50 × 100	$25,000	$500	$5.00
B	100 × 120	57,000	570	4.75
C	55 × 80	23,320	424	5.30
D	75 × 100	36,750	490	4.90

that the appropriate market unit is the price per square foot. In any given study, you may need to make several analyses in order to discover which is the most significant unit of comparison in that market.

The Adjustments

Land prices are analyzed and adjusted as part of the comparative process. By way of review, the analysis of sales data usually involves adjusting the comparable sales prices to make the comparables more like the subject property or as close to a substitute as possible in market appeal. These adjustments can be made by adding or subtracting the lump-sum amounts from the sales price of the comparable, by adding or subtracting percentages, or by accumulating percentages. You can review these adjustment methods in Chapter 9.

A sales adjustment grid, such as that shown in Example 10.4, is a convenient method of displaying the important sales differences and keeping track of all these adjustments.

Example 10.4
Land Sales Adjustment Grid (Showing Percentage Adjustments)

Sale	Price	Time	Location	Size	Total Percent	Indicated Value
1	$35,000	+2	0	−5	−3	$33,950
2	32,000	+4	−5	+5	+4	33,280
3	30,000	+5	+5	0	+10	33,000
4	28,000	+5	+10	+5	+20	33,600
5	36,000	+1	0	−5	−4	34,560

When you have been able to locate a large enough sales sample, sales that require very large adjustments are usually discarded. If valid comparable properties have been used and the adjustments are reasonable, the adjusted prices should now fall into a fairly narrow range.

In reconciling the adjusted sales prices to a value conclusion, it is a good rule to give the greatest weight to the sales requiring the least total adjustment. Both the plus and minus adjustments should be considered in this determination. Averages are rarely justified in appraising.

SUMMARY

Appraisals of vacant or undeveloped land are used for many purposes including sale and purchase, public actions, and land development. In improved properties, a separation of value between land and buildings is necessary for income and property tax purposes. A separate site value is also required in the cost approach and in several forms of the income approach to value.

The four primary methods used by appraisers for arriving at land values are:

1. The sales comparison method.
2. The allocation or abstraction method.
3. The land development method.
4. The land residual method.

The sales comparison method is the most reliable for appraising land because it is the most direct. The site is compared to sales of similar parcels of vacant land. The comparison is made as if it were vacant and available for its highest and best use. When no comparable sales of vacant land are available for comparison, the site may be appraised by the allocation, abstraction, development, or land residual methods.

The allocation and abstraction methods use sales of improved property and allocate a portion of the sales price to the land. They are useful in built-up areas where little vacant land remains.

The development method of land appraisal relates the value of raw land to its potential market value as developed land. It is used to appraise parcels likely to be subdivided in the near future.

The land residual method is a technique of the income approach and applies mainly to commercial and investment projects. It is an estimate of site value, based on the actual or potential income remaining after deducting the claims of labor, coordination, and capital.

Each of the four methods of appraising land relies upon property comparison in some form. The data needed for land sales comparisons are basically the same as for improved property. For land sales to be considered valid comparables, they must be competitive with the subject property and with each other. They must be qualified as open market transactions and should be recent.

For appraisers to compare market sales, it is essential that they understand what site characteristics are important. These characteristics are placed in three categories: physical, legal, and locational. Most important physical factors include location, size, shape, frontage, width, depth, plottage value, type of lot, topography, and utilities available. Legal and economic factors include the most likely profitable use, zoning, and other land-use regulations. The four major elements of comparison used in the analysis of sales data are terms of the sale, time of sale, location, and physical characteristics. Sales prices should be compared by what the market considers most important.

In the analysis of vacant land sales, the most common units of comparison are those that compare selling price per lot, per square foot, per acre, per front foot, or per unit developed. The sales prices are adjusted from the comparables toward the subject property, by adding or subtracting a lump sum or a percentage from the sales price of the comparable. If valid comparables have been used, the adjusted prices should fall into a fairly narrow range.

IMPORTANT TERMS AND CONCEPTS

Abstraction method
Access
Ad valorem tax
Allocation method
Depreciation basis

Development method
Land residual method
Sales comparison method
Potential use

REVIEWING YOUR UNDERSTANDING

1. Land or site value estimates are important in the appraisal of both vacant and improved property; thus, such appraisals assist in:

  (a) The sale and purchase of land
  (b) Land development
  (c) Ad valorem and certain income tax situations
  (d) Certain appraisal procedures
  (e) All of the above

2. The sales comparison method or direct sales comparison method of estimating site value:
   (a) Does not apply to acreage appraisals
   (b) Is the most reliable method available
   (c) Is considered inferior to other methods
   (d) Is used only when the subject property is a vacant lot

3. Land value may be abstracted from the sales of improved property. The method is most useful:
   (a) In built-up areas where little vacant land remains
   (b) As an alternative to the sales comparison method when comparable sales are not available
   (c) For acreage appraisals
   (d) Both parts (a) and (b) are correct

4. The land development method in appraisal is used only to estimate the value of vacant acreage that is ready to be subdivided. This method requires:
   (a) The study of current sales of subdivided lots
   (b) The projection of land development costs
   (c) Both parts (a) and (b) are true
   (d) Neither part (a) nor part (b) is correct

5. Many project feasibility studies incorporate vacant land appraisals. If a lot zoned for commercial use is being studied and there are no comparables available, which of the following methods would probably be most applicable?
   (a) The sales comparison method
   (b) The land development method
   (c) The land residual method
   (d) None of the above

6. The sales comparison method is suitable to appraise either vacant or improved sites zoned for:
   (a) Residential
   (b) Commercial
   (c) Industrial
   (d) Any of the above

7. For land sales to be adequate comparables, they must be:
   (a) Competitive with the subject and each other
   (b) Relatively recent
   (c) Open market transactions
   (d) All of the above

8. The unit of comparison for vacant land appraisals is ideally:
   (a) The square foot
   (b) The total lot
   (c) A combination of square foot and front foot units
   (d) The unit considered to be important by the market

9. Land prices are analyzed and adjusted as part of the comparative process. These adjustments could involve:

(a) Adding or subtracting lump-sum amounts
(b) Adding or subtracting percentages
(c) Accumulating percentages
(d) Any of the above

10. From the land sales adjustment grid shown in the following table, calculate the total adjustment and indicated value for each sale, and then choose a logical market value of the subject. (Give the most weight to the sale requiring the least adjustment, considering both plus and minus adjustments.)

Sale	Price	Time	Location	Size	Total	Indicated Value
1	$38,000	+3	−5	−5	_____	_____
2	$40,000	+5	−5	+5	_____	_____
3	$35,000	+2	+5	0	_____	_____
4	$45,000	+1	−10	−5	_____	_____

(a) $37,450
(b) $35,340
(c) $38,700
(d) $42,000

CHAPTER ELEVEN

ESTIMATING THE COST OF CONSTRUCTION

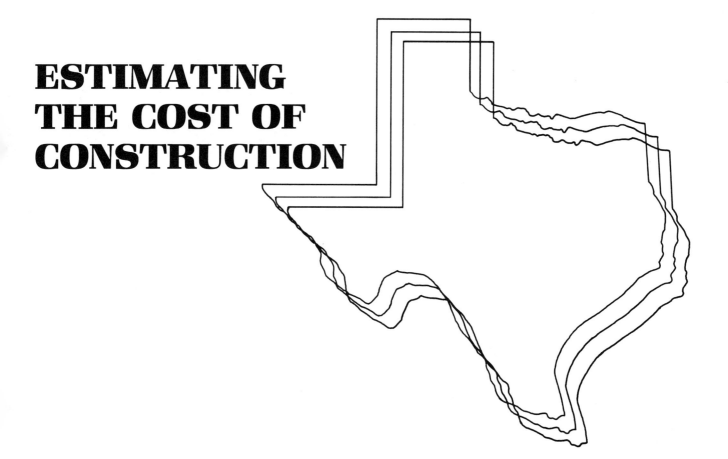

PREVIEW

The ability to estimate construction costs accurately is an important skill that is useful throughout the appraisal process. In this chapter we outline the techniques used to estimate costs and discuss the importance of each technique. In Section 11.1 we outline the cost approach and also explain the difference between reproduction cost and replacement cost. Examples of how these two different types of costs are used are included. In the next two sections we cover the four common methods of estimating costs and the direct and indirect elements that make up the total cost of a structure. In the final section the design factors that most directly affect the construction costs of buildings are identified. This section also shows you how to use the typical cost data publication.

When you have completed this chapter, you should be able to:

1. List the five basic steps in the cost approach.
2. Define the terms reproduction cost and replacement cost, and explain their use in appraisals.
3. Name four methods of estimating costs, and explain when each is used.
4. List the direct and indirect costs that make up a building's total costs.
5. Name the important physical design features that influence the construction costs of a building.

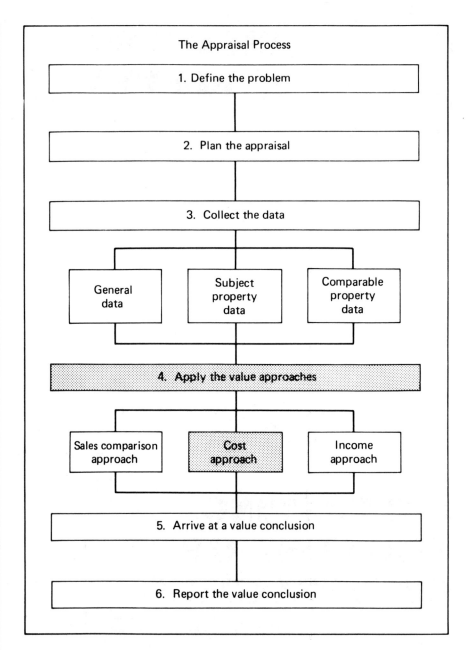

The Appraisal Process

1. Define the problem

2. Plan the appraisal

3. Collect the data

| General data | Subject property data | Comparable property data |

4. Apply the value approaches

| Sales comparison approach | Cost approach | Income approach |

5. Arrive at a value conclusion

6. Report the value conclusion

SECTION 11.1
USE OF COST
ESTIMATES IN APPRAISALS

The principle of substitution suggests that the value of an existing property can be measured by the cost of producing a similar new property as a substitute. The cost approach is based upon this principle. Estimating the construction cost is an essential part of the cost approach. Actually, cost estimates of one form or another are used in all three approaches to value. In the cost approach, the value of a property is estimated by adding the land value to the depreciated cost of the improvements. Cost estimates are also used in the sales comparison approach, where they help to adjust sales, a procedure described in Chapter 9. In the income approach, the cost of improvements is a consideration in capitalizing the income of new or proposed investment properties.

The cost estimates used in appraisals are described as generalized economic costs. This simply means that they should always reflect:

1. Current cost levels, not book costs or historic costs.
2. Typical costs to build a building, rather than the actual construction costs. These two costs could be the same, of course.
3. Costs that include all the charges to the consumer, not just the cost to the developer or builder. All-inclusive costs are sometimes referred to as turnkey costs, because all the occupant has to do is to turn the key.

Purpose and Outline
of the Cost Approach

In practice, appraisers use the cost approach for three main purposes:

1. To estimate the value of new (or nearly new) and economically sound developments. Here, possible depreciation errors will be the smallest.
2. To appraise institutional or special-use properties, such as a church or a government building, not commonly rented or bought and sold in the open market. In this case, the cost approach may be the *only* approach available.
3. To check the other value approaches. This option is available *whenever* improved properties are appraised. Using the cost approach can reduce the chance of making an undetected gross error in the other approaches used.

Steps in the Cost Approach
The cost approach involves five basic steps:

1. Estimating the value of land as if vacant and available for use. Generally, this is accomplished by market comparison.
2. Estimating the current cost to reproduce or replace the existing improvements.
3. Deciding on appropriate amounts for accrued depreciation (loss in value).

4. Deducting the accrued depreciation from the cost new of the improvements.

5. Adding the depreciated cost of the improvements to the estimated land value to arrive at the property value as indicated by the cost approach.

Since the estimation of accrued depreciation is an important and often complex procedure, all of Chapter 12 has been devoted to this subject. Land valuation was covered in Chapter 10.

Limitations on Using the Cost Approach

The cost approach has certain important limitations. First, some cost elements are difficult to define and estimate, as we shall explain later in this chapter. Second, measuring or estimating accrued depreciation can be difficult and quite subjective. For this reason, the cost approach should *not* be emphasized in the appraisal of unusual or older buildings unless no other method is available.

The Choice of Reproduction or Replacement Costs

Real estate appraisal is basically a process of comparison. The cost approach compares the utility of the structure with its economic cost in today's dollars. It may begin with either an estimate of the reproduction cost—the cost of creating a duplicate or identical building—or it may begin with an estimate of replacement cost—the cost of constructing a building that would have a similar utility to the subject improvement. Although these two terms are often used interchangeably in casual conversation between appraisers, there is an important technical difference that should be understood.

Using Reproduction Cost Estimates

Since reproduction cost is defined as the cost of a duplicate or approximate replica structure, every physical component must be included. If certain features, such as the intricate design of an out-of-style house, are no longer in demand, their cost is still estimated and included. The reproduction cost estimate is intended to capture the building exactly as it is. It must include the cost of every peculiarity and feature, whether or not they contribute as much to the property value as they do to the cost. With reproduction costs, all judgment of the relative marketability or utility of a particular feature is handled in the depreciation portion of the cost approach procedure, and not in the cost-new estimate. (See Figure 11.1.)

Using Replacement Cost Estimates

Replacement cost is defined as the cost to build a structure of similar utility. In this method you do *not* include every feature of the building in your estimate of current cost new. Instead, you examine the current utility or usefulness of the improvements and estimate the cost to build a structure that provides similar utility. For example, if the subject property had 9-foot ceiling heights, and you concluded that the market considered 8-foot ceilings to provide equal utility, your replacement cost estimate would be of a structure with 8-foot ceilings. Thus, a replacement cost estimate requires a judgment of building utility at the time of estimating cost new, instead of later in the depreciation analysis. Any building features that do not add to

FIGURE 11.1
The Choice: Reproduction or Replacement Cost. (Photograph Courtesy of Doug Frost)

the general attractiveness or marketability would not be included in the cost estimate. These features fall into two basic categories:

1. Components of the original building that are no longer being used by builders, due to changes in construction and technology. Examples include molded-plaster ceilings, carved fireplace mantels, floor furnaces, and hand water pumps.

2. Components that do not add to value because they are not currently in demand at the location. These components could be high-cost features in a low-priced neighborhood, as shown in Figure 11.2, or design features that are not consistent with the highest and best use.

Replacement Versus Reproduction

Although there is no clear-cut industry standard, replacement cost estimates are probably used more often than reproduction costs. From the appraiser's point of view, using replacement costs avoids making time-consuming estimates of the cost of old-fashioned materials found in older construction. Also, appraisers argue that using replacement costs provides a direct rating of the market demand for quality and design and that this makes the cost approach more realistic.

FIGURE 11.2
High-Cost Features in a Low-Priced Neighborhood

From the client's point of view, however, an appraisal based on reproduction cost is sometimes preferred. Such a cost requires the appraiser to identify and describe specifically the nonmarketable features of the building and to explain judgments concerning the amount of utility lost. Any value reductions due to such nonmarketable features are thus exposed as specific depreciation allowances instead of being hidden as they are in the replacement cost method. Because of these advantages, the standard FNMA Single Residential Appraisal Report Form (illustrated in Chapter 16) requires the use of reproduction cost estimates exclusively. However, if the building components being estimated are no longer available, then replacement cost estimates could be used.

In practice, the choice of cost method to be used depends substantially on the appraisal problem. The following examples should serve to illustrate common usage of both the reproduction and the replacement cost methods.

Example 11.1
Excess Quality for the Location
The subject is a custom-built 1960 residence located in a neighborhood of lower-quality homes. Market acceptance of the subject is judged to be less than its high quality should command.

Estimated reproduction cost	$68.00 per sq ft
Less: Loss in usefulness (excess quality)	−18.00 per sq ft
Equals: Reproduction cost less utility loss	$50.00 per sq ft
(*Note:* Loss in utility should be estimated by one of the methods outlined in Chapter 12.)	
Secondary method:	
Estimated replacement cost	$50.00 per sq ft

The reproduction cost method is preferred in this example. Reproduction costs make the actual quality of the house a part of the record and require the appraiser to show how the deduction for the excess quality was handled.

Example 11.2
Antiquated Materials
The subject building is a 1927 custom residence construction of hollow-tile walls and other antiquated components not readily available now. It is estimated that construction cost today would be $65.00 per square foot if we substitute modern construction materials and technology.

Estimated replacement cost	$65.00 per sq ft
Secondary method:	
Estimated reproduction cost	$80.00 per sq ft
Less: Estimated loss in utility	−15.00 per sq ft
Equals: Reproduction cost less utility loss	$65.00 per sq ft

The replacement cost method is preferred in this example because it saves on the amount of time and effort spent on locating and pricing scarce materials and unusual construction features.

When both excess quality and antiquated materials are found, an optional method used by appraisers combines the two methods shown. First, a modified replacement cost estimate is made, discounting only for the antiquated materials; then a separate allowance is made for the loss in utility due to excess quality.

SECTION 11.2
PRACTICAL
COST-ESTIMATING METHODS

Construction cost estimating is considered by many to be a specialized skill requiring a great deal of knowledge about building specifications and construction technology. For routine appraisals, however, reasonable results can be achieved by the appraiser who understands the four basic methods of estimating costs. Although most appraisers use only the first two methods listed, it is important to know the others, for they can be helpful in special situations.

1. The comparative square-foot method.
2. The unit-in-place method.
3. The index method.
4. The quantity survey method.

The Comparative Square-Foot Method

The comparative square-foot method is the most widely used method of estimating construction costs. It is also the most practical. Here, the appraiser applies the comparative square-foot method either by referring to published cost manuals or by citing typical costs discovered in the field. Since cost manuals represent the average cost level at any one time, they are generally preferred over the actual costs for any one specific project. The cost of a particular building is estimated by applying the average or typical square-foot costs of similar buildings. Differences in building specifications and components not included in base costs are adjusted by appropriate multipliers or adjustment amounts.

Example 11.3
Estimating Reproduction Cost

Assume that you are estimating the reproduction cost of an average quality dwelling with three bedrooms and two baths. It has 2,000 square feet and six perimeter corners. The general specifications of the most nearly similar house in your construction cost manual match those of the subject, except for the built-in kitchen appliances and air conditioning in the subject house. The adjustments for floor area and shape are obtained from the cost manual. Proceed as follows:

Base cost factor from manual	$60.00 per sq ft	
Area and shape multiplier	× 0.973	
Base cost factor, adjusted	$58.38	
Base cost: 2,000 sq ft × $58.38 =		$116,760
Plus: Refinements		
Built-in appliances	$2,400	
Air conditioning	+3,800	
Total additives		+ 6,200
Equals: Estimated total cost of house		122,960
Plus: Garage and yard improvements		+ 22,000
Equals: Total cost estimate		$144,960
Rounded		$145,000

The Unit-in-Place Method

The unit-in-place cost-estimating method calculates the separate cost of each component of the building. Typical components would include foundations, walls, floors, roof, ceiling, heating, and so on. The cost estimate for each component includes the cost of attaching or installing the component into the structure. The costs for the various components are added to reach a total cost estimate.

The unit-in-place cost-estimating method is most commonly used to modify or adjust the comparative square-foot method described earlier. Note that in the previous cost example, the basic square-foot cost was refined by using unit-in-place costs for the built-in appliances and air conditioning.

As a primary cost technique, the unit-in-place cost-estimating method is especially well suited to industrial buildings. Because such buildings often vary widely in size, shape, and height, it is difficult to make an accurate estimate of them using comparative square-foot cost calculations.

How It Works

The appraiser refers to one of the various cost-estimating guides available and prices the subject building one component at a time: walls, floors, roof, mechanical, and so on. The figure for each component includes all the necessary costs to fabricate and attach that particular building part to the structure. This means that all the direct and indirect costs of labor, material, design, engineering, and builder's profit are included in the component cost figure.

When applying the unit-in-place method, major structural components are figured first. Floors, walls, and roof structures are typically measured and priced by the square foot of surface area. However, walls can be priced by the linear foot. Costs for interior and exterior extras and roof cover are then added, along with plumbing, electrical, heating and cooling, and other mechanical components. Here is an example.

Example 11.4
Unit-in-Place Cost Estimate for a Small Commercial Building

Floors	5,000 sq ft at $3.50 =	$17,500
Walls	300 linear ft at $80.00 =	24,000
Roof structure	5,000 sq ft at $5.00 =	25,000
Interior partitions	100 linear ft at $30.00 =	3,000
Ceilings	5,000 sq ft at $2.00 =	10,000
Doors and windows		5,000
Roof cover		10,000
Plumbing lines and fixtures		5,500
Electrical system		5,000
Heating and cooling		20,000
Hardware and all other costs		10,000
Total direct and indirect costs		$135,000

The Index Method

The index method is sometimes relied upon to estimate costs for unique or unusual structures when the original or historic costs are known. The method adjusts the original costs to the current cost level by a construction multiplier derived from published cost indexes. Year-by-year construction cost information is accumulated and published nationally by a number of well-known companies. Cost records are cataloged by building design and type of construction, and then indexed to a base year such as 1940 or 1967. Regional or area modifiers are also provided to help account for differences in construction costs that relate to location.

The formula for cost estimating by the index method is as follows:

$$\text{original cost} \times \frac{\text{current-year index}}{\text{historic-year index}} = \text{current cost}$$

To use the index method, follow these steps:

1. Verify that the original cost figure includes all the present building components.
2. Find the applicable cost index figures for the current year (or year of appraisal) and for the original or historic year.
3. Divide the current-year index by the historic-year index to derive an adjustment factor.
4. Multiply the original cost by the adjustment factor.

Assume that you are estimating the current cost of a building that originally cost $80,000 in 1975. You find that no additions or major remodeling have been done since that time. Your cost index chart for this type of building shows a current-year index figure of 1475 and a year 1975 index of 726. Current construction cost would then be estimated as follows:

$$\$80,000 \times \frac{1475}{726} = \$80,000 \times 2.03 = \$162,500 \text{ (rounded)}$$

Some published cost services provide charts of precomputed cost multipliers. In such cases, the factor for the current-year cost update (2.03 in this example) may be taken directly from such a chart.

Although not considered as accurate as other methods of cost estimating, indexing is often used as a secondary value tool. When an estimate of replacement cost new is needed merely to indicate an upper limit of value for a building, indexing can eliminate the time-consuming process of a detailed cost analysis. Indexing is also well adapted to computer-assisted, statistical appraisal programs, where the improvement cost new is often a significant variable in the analysis of market sales. Such programs are common in mass appraisal work such as that done in assessment jurisdictions.

The Quantity Survey Method

The quantity survey method is the most detailed and accurate of the construction cost-estimating methods. It involves the listing and separate pric-

Example 11.5
Chart of Cost Estimating Methods

Method	How It Works	Primary Application	Cost Data Requirements
Comparative square-foot	Uses the average cost per sq ft (or other unit) of a comparable new building. Most useful method.	Universally used and accepted for most buildings.	Base costs from published or known sources; refinements made by unit-in-place method.
Unit-in-place	Prices building components by in-place cost per sq ft surface, lineal foot, or lump-sum amounts. More accurate and more detailed than the comparative sq-ft method.	Primary method for shell-type buildings, unique projects; most often used to refine the comparative sq-ft method.	Component costs from published or known sources.
Index	Trends original (historic) costs to current cost level.	Unique buildings; mass appraisal applications.	Trend factor from construction cost index service.
Quantity survey	A detailed cost breakdown by each category of labor, materials, fees, profit margin, etc. Most accurate; least useful for typical buildings because of detail and knowledge required.	Development of detailed construction bid by a contractor.	Current prices of all building materials, amounts of materials, wage rates, profit margins, etc.

ing of all material and labor components of a project, as well as all of the indirect costs of construction, such as a survey, permits, overhead, and contractors' profit. Written specifications and drawings are required.

Although the quantity survey method is the most precise method of estimating construction costs, it is rarely used by appraisers. Instead, it is used mainly by building contractors when bidding on unique projects. It is a highly specialized method that requires more technical knowledge of construction than most appraisers have. Also, the great amount of time and detail required by the method is seldom warranted (considering that other cost methods produce reasonable answers in less time).

The main features, applications, and requirements of the four methods are listed in Example 11.5.

SECTION 11.3
UNDERSTANDING DIRECT
AND INDIRECT COSTS

Have you ever asked a builder or developer what it would cost to construct a house or some other structure? In all likelihood, the answer you got may have confused you because of the different things that people include when they refer to costs. In appraisals, costs should include all the expenditures required to produce the structure, make it ready for use, and pay for selling costs at the consumer level. These include not only the builder's direct costs spent for labor and materials but also a number of indirect costs. The latter are not always reported in informal cost discussions. Builder's profits and interest and property taxes during construction are examples of indirect costs. Failure to take into account all direct and indirect costs of building construction often results in an understated cost approach in relation to value.

Direct Costs

All the items directly involved with the physical construction of the structure are classified as direct cost elements. These include the following:

1. Labor.
2. Materials and equipment.
3. Design and engineering.
4. Subcontractors' fees.

Labor Costs
Labor costs include all wages and salaries paid for direct work on the construction project. Such expenditures may be paid by either the builder or any of the several subcontractors involved in the project. All costs of labor, skilled or unskilled, must be included.

Materials and Equipment
The material and equipment costs include all the items that eventually become integral parts of the structure, whether purchased directly or included in subcontracts: the concrete, steel, and lumber used in the founda-

FIGURE 11.3
Construction Project and Stored Materials. (Photograph Courtesy of Doug Frost)

tion and framework, as well as the appliances, finish hardware, and paint. (See Figure 11.3.)

Design and Engineering
Engineering and architectural costs are included in the building cost estimate. Soil grading, soil compaction, special soil engineering, and retaining walls, however, are included in the site value.

Some residential structures require little or no engineering, and many are built from standardized plans and specifications. However, design and engineering can involve substantial expense, particularly for custom and unusual construction. This is partly because design specialists are often required to supervise the work.

Subcontractors' Fees
Much of the construction labor is not provided by employees of the contractor. Instead, subcontractors are used. For example, plumbing, heating, and electrical work are commonly performed by subcontractors. Although the amounts paid to subcontractors are not usually broken down between labor, material, and other components, any amount paid for such services is included as one of the four direct construction cost elements.

Indirect Costs

Indirect costs include all the hidden time and money costs involved in a project. Although they are often somewhat proportional to the direct cost of labor and material, indirect costs can vary considerably from one job to another. Here is a list of indirect construction costs to be included in a cost estimate.

1. Legal fees, appraisal fees, and building permits and licenses.
2. Interest and fees for construction financing.
3. Construction liability and casualty insurance.
4. Property taxes during construction.
5. Construction administration and management.
6. Interest on investment and loss in rental.
7. Builder's and entrepreneurial profit.
8. Selling costs.

Some of the items listed need further definition and discussion.

Interest on Construction Financing

Construction loan funds are usually paid to the borrower in "progress payments," based on the work performed each month during construction. As a result, the amount of principal paid out grows each month, as does the monthly interest payment. Calculating the exact interest amount is quite hard to do. As a rule of thumb, however, interest can be based upon one-half the amount borrowed and then calculated for the entire construction time period. For example, at a 10% interest rate, a $100,000 project that takes six months to develop would incur interest charges of

$$\frac{\$100,00}{2} = \$50,000 \text{ at } 5\% \text{ (10\% per year for 6 months)} = \$2,500$$

In addition, the loan fees and points charged for granting the construction financing must be added to the interest charges. For example,

Three points on the loan, or $100,000 × 0.03	=	$3,000
Plus: Progress inspection fee at ½% of the loan		+ 500
Equals: Total fees and points		3,500
Plus: Interest charges (from above)		+ 2,500
Equals: Total loan costs		$6,000

The interest on the construction loan, fees, and points could be paid in cash by the borrower or included as one of the disbursements to be made from the construction loan funds. In either case, it is a valid indirect cost element.

Property Taxes During Construction

Property taxes during the construction period are included in the construction cost estimate. In Texas, improvements that start construction after January 1st are not assessed until the next year. For this reason, property taxes during construction may consist only of taxes on the land itself.

Construction Administration and Management

These costs are generally included in the general contractor's bid and are often referred to as builder's overhead. Office rent, office employee salaries, utilities, and transportation costs are examples of such administrative costs. If the builder's overhead costs have been included in an actual contract cost, they should not be added again.

Interest on Investment and Loss in Rental

The owner's investment in land and buildings is entitled to a fair return during the construction and marketing period. If the owner has a substantial investment beyond the construction loan funds, then some return on that investment must be accounted for here. For example, if the owner had a $100,000 investment in the site, it could be assigned a 5% return rate for a six-month construction period, or $5,000 interest on investment. This represents a 10% annual return. After construction has been completed, sales or rentals provide for a return on investment. However, it often takes from three to six months to sell all the space or to bring a building up to normal occupancy. The lack of return on vacant space during this period is therefore figured as an additional cost.

Builder's and Developer's Profit

These costs are the most variable and difficult to estimate of all the indirect costs of construction. Normal builder's profit represents the payment for professional services paid to the general contractor of a construction job. Typical charges for such services are dependent upon competition, the predicted construction progress, and other conditions not entirely controlled by the builder. Charges vary from one project to the next, but most depend on the specific undertaking. Some information on prevailing contractor profit margins can be obtained from local builders. At one time, 10% of the total hard costs was a common profit margin for the contractor. Now, there is greater variation.

The individual developer who "packages" the project, land, and building, is often referred to as the entrepreneur. The entrepreneurial profit is the amount required to pay for the know-how, incentive, and risk involved in speculative development. The amount to be charged for this element depends on economic conditions and competitive investment opportunities. Many cost manuals try to include a "normal" builder's profit, but very few attempt to suggest actual amounts for entrepreneurial profits. Omitting this amount from a cost approach, however, fails to account for one of the costs that must be paid to get the product into the hands of the consumer.

SECTION 11.4
IMPORTANT DESIGN FACTORS
AFFECTING COST ESTIMATES

When you make an inspection and general analysis of the improvements under appraisal, your field notes or inspection check form should contain the building information needed to estimate the reproduction or replacement cost. This section outlines the design and construction features that have the greatest effect upon the cost of construction. Clearly, these features must be noted in your inspection. This section also explains how to use published cost data when you are applying the comparative square-foot or unit-in-place methods.

Key Construction Cost Variables

In a given location, seven different building characteristics affect the total cost of construction as well as the square-foot cost. These can be identified as:

1. Design or use type (type of occupancy).
2. Type of construction (construction classification).
3. Quality of construction.
4. Size.
5. Shape.
6. Height.
7. Yard or site improvements.

Design or Use Type

The design or use category of a structure (sometimes referred to as type of occupancy) is considered the first cost variable. It defines what features the building is likely to have. For example, single-family homes have entirely different cost characteristics than stores or factories. In most construction cost manuals, suggested costs are grouped into the following design or use types:

Auditoriums	Industrial buildings
Auto showrooms	factories
Banks	warehouses
Bowling alleys	Lumber yards
Car washes	Mobile home parks
Churches	Nursing homes
Farm buildings	Office and professional buildings
Fire stations	Residential buildings
Garages	singles, duplexes, multiples
Government buildings	Restaurants
Hospitals	Rooming houses and fraternities
Hotels and motels	Schools and classrooms
	Stores and markets
	Theaters

Construction Classification

The second cost variable is the type of construction. Buildings are divided into basic cost groups by the type of structural frame (supporting columns and beams), walls, floors, roof structures, and fireproofing. Marshall and Swift (a well-known cost publisher) identifies five such cost groups: A, B, C, D, and S construction. Typical specifications for the major classifications are outlined in Chapter 7 of this book.

Higher construction costs are typical for the A and B (sometimes labeled 1 and 2) classes of construction because of their greater fire protection, better engineering design, and additional component costs. High-rise and institutional buildings usually are designed to meet class A or B specifications.

Class C and D (or Class 3, 4, 5, and S) buildings characteristically cost less to build than Class A or B buildings. Many common residential, commercial, and industrial buildings fit into these categories. The frame, floor, roof, and wall structure of Class C and D buildings are built primarily of wood, masonry, or sheet metal construction.

A certain amount of knowledge and experience is needed in order to tell which construction class a particular building fits in. To assist the inexperienced user, most construction cost manuals define the main characteristics of the building classes. It is important to identify correctly the construction class of a building being appraised because typical cost factors are presented in most cost manuals under the respective construction class headings.

Quality of Construction

For a given use type and construction class, the quality of construction is generally the most important cost variable. In most systems, quality is noted on a scale ranging from low cost to excellent, with typical specifications usually pegged as average.

Rating the quality of construction is perhaps the most subjective part of cost estimating. Experience, good building specifications, and some knowledge of construction are therefore essential in making a valid quality rating.

Size and Shape

When estimating construction costs by the comparative square-foot method, it is important to recognize the effect of the size and shape on the square-foot cost.

First, let us examine the effect of size. Most buildings have a floor, a roof, and outside walls; these we can refer to as the building "shell." The cost per square foot of such a building could easily be calculated by adding up the "in-place" costs of these shell components and dividing by the number of square feet in the building. Now, the effect of the floor area on the square-foot cost can be demonstrated by comparing two building shells of different sizes. Let us assume that for both buildings in Example 11-6 the floors cost $3.00 per square foot, the roof costs $6.00 per square foot, and the walls cost $90.00 per linear (running) foot (all calculated as in-place unit costs).

Example 11.6
The Effect of Size on Square-Foot Costs (Building Shell)

Floor: 2,500 sq ft at $3.00 = $ 7,500
Roof: 2,500 sq ft at   6.00 =   15,000
Walls: 200 linear ft at 90.00 =   18,000
　　　　Total cost　　　　　　　$40,500

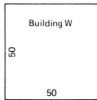

Cost per sq ft: $\dfrac{\$40,500}{2,500} = \$16.20$

Floor: 10,000 sq ft at $3.00 = $ 30,000
Roof: 10,000 sq ft at   6.00 =   60,000
Walls: 400 linear ft at 90.00 =   36,000
　　　　Total cost　　　　　　　$126,000

Cost per sq ft: $\dfrac{\$126,000}{10,000} = \$12.60$

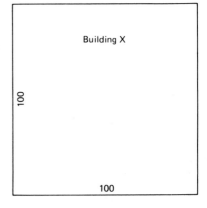

Note that doubling the dimensions of the building decreased the square-foot cost by $3.60, or 22%. In actual practice, the net effect will vary, depending upon roof design requirements and project size. Greater roof spans may increase costs. Generally, however, large projects may often cost less per square foot than smaller ones because of the economies of scale.

In residential buildings (and others that have relatively expensive interior components), the effect of size on square-foot costs may be less predictable than in the examples, but it is still important. The total in-place cost for such things as plumbing, cabinets, and doors is often fairly similar in buildings of different sizes. Consequently, the square-foot cost of such "fixed-cost" components will vary with the size of the building. Thus, increases in floor area tend to reduce the overall square-foot costs, and decreases in floor area generally increase square-foot costs.

The effect of size upon construction cost depends in part upon building shape. This can be seen if we compare a 50×200 foot building with building X in Example 11.6. Let us call the building in Example 11.7 building Y. Note that buildings X and Y have the same square-foot area although they have different dimensions.

Example 11.7
The Effect of Shape on Square-Foot Costs

Floor: 10,000 sq ft at $3.00 = $ 30,000
Roof: 10,000 sq ft at 6.00 =   60,000
Walls: 500 linear ft at 90.00 =   45,000

     Total cost $135,000

Cost per sq ft: $\dfrac{\$135,000}{10,000} = \$13.50$

Contrast:
Cost per sq-ft if dimensions are
  100×100 ft: $12.60

Building Y (200 × 50)

Here, changing the shape from square to long and narrow increases the square-foot cost by $0.90, or about 7.1%. An even more dramatic difference would result if our building Y were scaled down to the square-foot area of building W in Example 11.6.

In residential buildings, the higher costs resulting from changes in shape can be attributed to several factors. These include:

1. *Increase in the number of corners*   Results in increased costs for foundations and wall framing.
2. *Increase in linear feet of the building perimeter*   Causes increased costs for walls, doors, windows, insulation, and weather stripping, as well as wiring and length of plumbing runs and heat ducting.
3. *Increase in roof framing and overhang*   Adds valleys, ridges, flashing, gutters, and downspouts to costs.

Figure 11.4 shows some of the various shapes that are found in single-residence buildings.

Height

The story or wall height of a building also influences its cost. We can see how height changes the square-foot cost of a building if we use the size and shape examples previously discussed. With a 20% increase in wall height, the increase in the square-foot costs of the three buildings, W, X, and Y, would vary from 5.7 to 8.8%.

Yard or Site Improvements

Besides the main building, cost estimates made for appraisal purposes must include any other improvements to the site. This could mean garage or parking structures, walks, driveways, outside lighting, sprinkler systems, fencing, pools, patios, and landscaping. Published cost manuals provide typical unit-in-place costs for many such items, as well as for outbuildings such as detached garages and greenhouses.

Landscaping often varies widely in cost; its contribution to value can vary even more. As a result, most appraisers try to estimate how much landscaping contributes to value rather than what it costs. This is both practical and acceptable in single-residence appraisals.

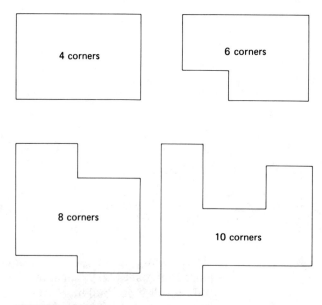

FIGURE   11.4
Common house shapes

Using Published Building Cost Services

As we have already stated, several building cost services are available to the appraiser—by subscription or purchase. These include the *Marshall Valuation Service,* the *Boeckh Appraisal Manual,* the *Dodge Building Cost Calculator and Valuation Guide,* the *National Construction Estimator,* and the *Marshall and Swift Residential Cost Handbook.* Many of the listed services provide both comparative square-foot and unit-in-place costs. Some also include an index of construction cost changes by year and by class of construction. Most are based on national averages but include local adjustment multipliers. They include all direct cost elements but often exclude entrepreneurial profit, property taxes, interest, and investment return during construction.

General Format of Manuals

As a general rule, the published building cost guides are organized and designed around the major cost variables just discussed. These elements are usually handled as follows:

1. *Design or use type*   Usually the main subdivision of the manual. Up to 40 types of buildings may be described with photographs and general specifications.

2. *Construction classification*   Given as a separate cost schedule within each design type; four or five classifications are typical.

3. *Quality of construction*   Interpreted by pictures and typical specifications for each class of construction; includes square-foot cost factors for four to six quality ranges.

4. *Size, shape, and height*   Usually handled by corner count or by floor area-shape multipliers and then story-height factors. These are used to adjust the manual's base costs. In multiple-residence buildings, adjustments are often based upon the average unit size and number of units. Both are significant cost variables in such buildings.

5. *Cost refinements*   Often given as unit-in-place costs for building components; may be broken down into labor and material components (as in the *National Construction Estimator*).

6. *Yard or site improvements*   Referenced in both the main and supplemental cost sections of most guides.

Suggested Costing Procedure

When using any of the mentioned cost services, it is very important to read all introductory notes and instructions; they clearly define what costs are included in the manual and how to adjust for cost variables.

Once you have selected the cost section to be used, be sure to read the footnotes that often appear on the individual base-cost schedules. *Base costs often exclude such things as fireplaces and kitchen built-ins,* making it necessary to add lump-sum amounts to your initial figure.

Here is a general outline of the steps required in estimating construction costs by the comparative square-foot method, as featured in most of the published building cost services:

1. Select the use-type table appropriate for your building and determine the building construction class. Choose the quality range with the

best-fitting specifications. Determine the base cost factor from the table.

2. Calculate any required floor area, shape, corner, story height, or unit size multipliers; multiply (as required) by the base cost factor.

3. Multiply the adjusted base cost by the area of the building.

4. Add the unit-in-place costs for various building components and features.

5. Add lump-sum costs of the various site or yard improvements.

6. Apply a current-cost multiplier and a local multiplier to adjust the published manual costs to the current date and to local costs. Published cost manuals usually provide such multipliers in a supplement or update section.

SUMMARY

In this chapter we discussed construction cost estimates: how they are used in appraisals and how they are made.

Cost estimating plays a significant role in each of the three approaches to value. In appraisals, the concept of cost is related to its economic impact, which means that cost estimates are made at current price levels and reflect the total amount of typical costs passed on to consumers. The cost approach is used primarily to estimate the value of new or special-use properties. It is also an important check against the other value approaches.

There are four methods commonly used to estimate costs. The comparative square-foot method is the most useful because it is the easiest to apply. The unit-in-place method is most often used to refine costs that were estimated by the comparative square-foot method. The index method is useful for costing unique structures or for updating current cost estimates in mass appraisal applications. The quantity survey method is the most accurate method but is too detailed and technical to be of much practical use in appraisals.

When estimating construction costs, it is important to reflect both direct and indirect costs of construction. The contractor's costs for labor and materials are not the only costs involved. Indirect costs such as building permits, interest on loans and on investment, insurance, property taxes, overhead, and profit must also be included.

A number of design and construction features greatly affect construction costs. As reflected in published construction cost manuals, these include:

1. Design or use type.
2. Construction classification.
3. Quality.
4. Size, shape, and height of the building.
5. Yard and site improvements.

IMPORTANT TERMS AND CONCEPTS

Base costs
Comparative square-foot method
Construction class
Cost approach
Design use or type
Direct costs
Financing charges
Historical cost
Index method
Indirect costs

Insurance costs
Lump-sum costs
Multiplier, cost
Quantity survey method
Replacement cost
Reproduction cost
Shape
Size
Unit-in-place method

REVIEWING YOUR UNDERSTANDING

1. The cost estimates used in appraisals are what we describe as generalized economic costs. This means that they should reflect:
   (a) Wholesale costs
   (b) Current cost levels, not book costs or historic costs
   (c) Typical costs to build such a building
   (d) Both (b) and (c)

2. There is an important technical difference between the terms reproduction cost and replacement cost. Replacement cost refers to:
   (a) The cost of constructing an exact replica building
   (b) The cost of constructing a building that would have similar utility to the subject property
   (c) The cost of reproducing the subject building
   (d) None of the above

3. From the appraiser's point of view, replacement cost estimates are preferred over reproduction cost estimates because:
   (a) They provide a direct rating of the market demand for the quality and design of a structure
   (b) They are more detailed
   (c) They are less time-consuming
   (d) Both (a) and (c)

4. The cost approach may be emphasized in a number of appraisal situations. Which is not among them?
   (a) Checking the other value approaches
   (b) Appraising institutional or special-use properties
   (c) Estimating the value of new or nearly new property
   (d) Appraising older homes in an active market

5. The most practical and widely used method of estimating construction costs is:
   (a) The comparative square-foot method
   (b) The unit-in-place method
   (c) The index method
   (d) The quantity survey method

6. The cost-estimating method often used as a supplement to refine the square-foot method is called:
   (a) The quantity survey method
   (b) The index method
   (c) The unit-in-place method
   (d) None of the above

7. Estimating costs by adjusting the original costs to the current cost level with a cost multiplier is a method known as:
   (a) The comparative square-foot method
   (b) The unit-in-place method
   (c) The index method
   (d) The quantity survey method

8. Which method of estimating construction costs is the most precise, yet seldom used by appraisers?
   (a) The index method
   (b) The quantity survey method
   (c) The comparative square-foot method
   (d) The unit-in-place method

9. Failure to take into account the indirect, as well as direct, costs of building construction often results in an understated cost estimate in relation to value. Which of the following choices most suggests indirect-cost elements?
   (a) Materials and equipment
   (b) Interest on investment and loss in rent
   (c) Labor and materials
   (d) Design and engineering

10. Using the unit-in-place cost factors provided in Example 11.6, calculate the square-foot cost of a shell structure that is 25 ft wide and 100 ft long. Compared with the square-foot cost of building W in the Illustration, this represents a square-foot cost that is approximately:
    (a) $2.00 lower
    (b) $1.80 higher
    (c) $2.80 higher
    (d) The same

CHAPTER TWELVE

ESTIMATING LOSS IN VALUE: ACCRUED DEPRECIATION

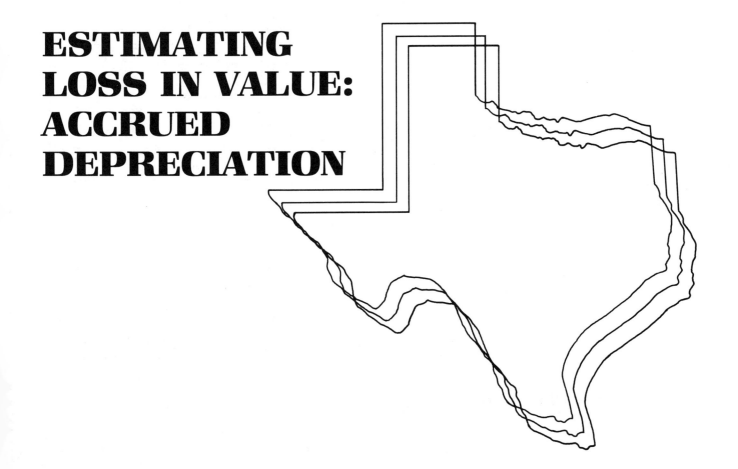

PREVIEW

Estimating the relative loss in the value of improvements compared to their costs is a necessary part of the cost approach. Additionally, an estimate of accrued depreciation is sometimes necessary in the sales comparison and income approaches to value.

What is depreciation? Accountants define it one way, appraisers another. After explaining the difference, this chapter will explore the types and causes of accrued depreciation and explain the major methods appraisers use to measure actual loss in value.

When you have completed this chapter, you should be able to:

1. Distinguish between the concept of depreciation as it is used in accounting from that used in appraisal.

2. Name, and identify the causes of, three types of depreciation.

3. Name four methods of estimating accrued depreciation and describe how they may be applied to an appraisal problem.

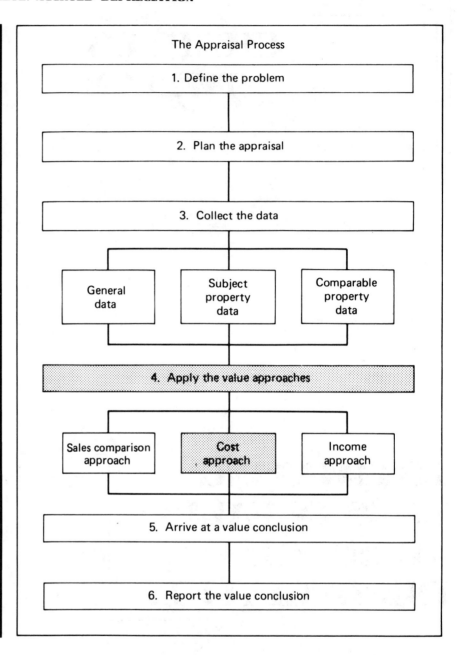

The Appraisal Process

1. Define the problem

2. Plan the appraisal

3. Collect the data

General data | Subject property data | Comparable property data

4. Apply the value approaches

Sales comparison approach | Cost approach | Income approach

5. Arrive at a value conclusion

6. Report the value conclusion

SECTION 12.1
DEPRECIATION DEFINED

Depreciation is a term with two distinctly different meanings, both used by people in real estate. One defines an accounting term used in income tax calculations; the other defines an appraisal term used in the cost approach and elsewhere in the appraisal process.

Depreciation as Used in Accounting

In accounting practice, all capital assets except land are considered to be wasting assets that decline in value over time. These assets may include machinery, vehicles, and other types of equipment, as well as buildings. When calculating income taxes, the owner of such an asset (if it is held to produce revenue) is allowed to deduct an estimate of an annual value loss from income, just as operating expenses are deducted.

Accountants calculate the allowable depreciation deduction by starting with the historic book value of the asset. Book value refers to the original asset cost, plus the cost of any capital additions or improvements, reduced each year by the depreciation deduction taken. Book value is also called cost basis. The important characteristic of income tax depreciation as applied to buildings is that it is determined by the property's cost basis and the allowable depreciation period and does not consider what is actually happening to the building's value. See Example 12.1.

Example 12.1
Accounting Depreciation

Purchase price		$275,000
Less:	Land value	− 65,000
Equals:	Building cost basis	$210,000
Divided by:	Depreciation period	÷ 15 years
Equals:	Annual depreciation claim	$ 14,000

As income tax depreciation deductions are taken, the building cost basis declines. This declining cost basis is also used in reporting the assets of businesses (on balance sheets). When real estate values are increasing, a company with substantial real estate assets can actually have a much higher asset value than that reported to its stockholders. Accountants are now studying ways to handle this problem. Many are using what is called current-value accounting to supplement the more traditional cost-basis accounting procedure.

Accrued Depreciation in Appraisals

The estimate of accrued depreciation used in appraisals is governed by an entirely different set of rules than those used in accounting. In appraisals, a dollar or percentage amount is deducted from the estimated *current* cost of the improvements as if new, rather than from their historical cost basis. Second, the amount of depreciation represents the appraiser's best estimate of the actual *market* loss in value as compared to a new building, whereas accounting depreciation is a theoretical loss. Thus, an appraiser's estimate of depreciation is not dependent in any way on the property's historical cost basis, the owner's depreciation schedule, or the loss in value allowable for income tax purposes.

As used in appraisals, accrued depreciation is the difference between the current cost new of the improvements and the current market value of those improvements on the valuation date. This difference is sometimes referred to as diminished utility, that is, the total loss in value from all causes. As we shall learn in the next section, value loss can be caused by either physical, functional, or economic conditions.

Purpose of Depreciation Estimates in Appraisals

You may recall that the cost approach involves, first, estimating the reproduction or replacement cost new of the improvements; then deducting the total accrued depreciation from this cost; and, last, adding this depreciated improvement value to the land value. An estimate of the total property value is the result. See Example 12.2.

Example 12.2
Appraisal Depreciation

Reproduction cost new		$125,000
Less:	Estimated accrued depreciation (say, 10%)	− 12,500
Equals:	Reproduction cost less accrued depreciation	112,500
Plus:	Land value	+ 50,000
Equals:	Total indicated value of the property	$162,500

When replacement cost estimates are used instead of reproduction cost estimates, note that the amount deducted for accrued depreciation should be only the loss in value *in excess of* any loss in value caused by the loss of utility from antiquated materials, undesirable design features, and the like. The replacement cost estimate would have already adjusted for such factors, whereas production cost estimates would not.

As we learned in the last chapter, estimating accrued depreciation is often the most critical step in the cost approach.

Although depreciation estimates are of the greatest importance in the cost approach to value, they also play an important part in market and income studies. For example, the sales comparison approach calls for comparing properties, and this may involve an analysis of relative loss in value from age or obsolescence. When the comparables vary in age, the adjustment for age differences can be regarded as the difference in accrued depreciation. Also, in the appraisal of land, the abstraction method of calculating land value from improved sales often involves an estimate of accrued depreciation. In this method, the land value is presumed to be equal to the selling price of the property less the depreciated value of all improvements. Last, depreciation estimates sometimes assist the appraiser in the analysis of income properties. When the total net income for the property must be allocated between land and improvements, the value contribution of each of these agents of production becomes important. As we have seen, the value contribution of improvements can be estimated by calculating their current cost as if new, less the total accrued depreciation.

SECTION 12.2
TYPES AND CAUSES OF
ACCRUED DEPRECIATION

Is any one building worth the same as another of the same design type, size, and quality? When the location and site are different, different values should be expected. However, even if the site and location are similar, differences in age, condition, and utility usually result in different values. Once differences in these influences have been identified, they can be used to estimate the relative loss in value that they cause. But what are the precise factors involved?

The appraiser's basic task is to recognize specific conditions or features of the property that cause value losses and then to measure the effect of these conditions upon value. Two steps are involved. First, the loss in value is categorized by the type and probable cause. Second, the depreciation in each category is classified as either curable or incurable. In other words, the questions are:

1. What is the apparent cause?
2. Can the loss be measured by the cost to correct (or "cost-to-cure") the problem?

Accrued depreciation is classified into three types or categories, known as physical deterioration, functional obsolescence, and economic obsolescence. We will discuss the question of whether each is curable as we describe these three types of value loss:

1. Physical deterioration.
2. Functional obsolescence.
3. Economic obsolescence.

Physical Deterioration

Regardless of quality or design, all buildings deteriorate physically over the years. The physical deterioration of a structure describes its wear and tear from use, age, weather, neglect, and vandalism. Since each part of a building is affected differently by these conditions, the loss in value is often analyzed component by component.

Curable Physical Deterioration

Economically, physical deterioration can prove to be either curable or incurable. Curable deterioration refers to conditions that are economically feasible to correct. This means that correcting the defect would add at least as much to the market value as the cost of the repairs would. For example, if it cost $2,000 to repaint the exterior of a house in a neighborhood where buyers appear willing to pay $2,500 more for freshly painted homes, then such repair or renovation would be judged economically feasible. For an otherwise sound building, painting, replacing a worn-out roof or heating system, or simply making the building more presentable by cleaning can often enhance the market value at least as much as the cost of the work. Thus, such examples of needed repair would logically fall in the category of curable physical deterioration. Examples are shown in Figure 12.1.

Incurable Physical Deterioration

Incurable physical deterioration, on the other hand, describes building conditions that are likely to cost more to repair than the value that is added to the structure. Such repairs would be considered economically unfeasible. For example, slight damage to the foundation or structural framework of a building would usually be considered incurable physical deterioration. This is because the repair cost would be substantial and the resulting increase in market value would be relatively small.

Other types of deterioration are also considered incurable. They involve some part of the building that will need to be replaced in the years ahead but is too good to replace at the moment. An example would be an air-conditioning system that will need replacement in five or six years but that has too much useful life left to be retired now. The value loss in such a case is referred to as short-lived incurable deterioration (sometimes called "cur-

FIGURE 12.1
Examples of Curable Physical Deterioration. (Photographs Courtesy of Doug Frost)

able postponed"). In five years, when the remaining economic life of the air-conditioning system has been used up, we would then consider the value loss as curable. Why? Because replacement of the building component will at that time be economically feasible.

Long-Lived Incurable Physical Deterioration
Value losses attributable to the major components of a building, when age is the major contributing factor, are called long-lived, incurable physical deterioration. These nearly always cost more to repair or renew than the value added by the repairs. Gradual reduction of the value of the founda-

FIGURE 12.2
An Older Home May Suffer Incurable Physical Deterioration. (Photograph Courtesy of Doug Frost)

tion, framework, plumbing, fixtures, or electrical wiring because of age are examples of long-lived incurable physical deterioration. (See Figure 12.2).

Functional Obsolescence

Functional obsolescence describes a type of depreciation that is caused by a relative loss of building utility. Loss of utility means that there is some feature of the building that is not as useful as its cost would suggest. This loss of usefulness could be caused by faulty building design, outmoded equipment, or some other design defect within the structure. A poorly arranged floor plan or a house lacking a side yard are examples of functional obsolescence. (See Figure 12.3.)

Functional obsolescence is often associated with original building design features that are not suitable for the location. A building that is out of place—the wrong type or use for that location—is functionally obsolete to a degree and is called a misplaced improvement. A building that is too large or lavish for the neighborhood also has functional obsolescence and is labeled an overimprovement.

Functional obsolescence can be curable or incurable, depending on whether the cost to cure is less or greater than the value benefits. In some cases, a kitchen can be remodeled, a room added, or a wall knocked out at a fairly nominal cost to bring the building up to current market standards. However, the value loss suffered by a misplaced improvement or overimprovement is usually considered incurable functional obsolescence. (See Figure 12.4.)

Economic Obsolescence

Economic obsolescence describes a loss in value caused by factors located outside the subject property. Such loss is also known as locational or envi-

No
Side—yard

FIGURE 12.3
Functional Obsolescence. (Photograph Courtesy of Doug Frost)

ronmental obsolescence. Traffic hazards, changes in the highest and best use, changes in the zoning, inharmonious nearby land uses, dust, and airport noise are examples of conditions that can cause value loss. A new freeway reducing values of abutting residences is another example of economic obsolescence. Generally, economic obsolescence is caused by some event that has occurred in the neighborhood since the property was built.

Economic obsolescence can be curable or incurable in the same way that physical deterioration and functional obsolescence are. However, the cause of the problem is often beyond the control of any one property owner. The cost of repair is also frequently very large. For example, a very

FIGURE 12.4
A Misplaced Improvement: Does It Have Functional Obsolescence?

expensive sound barrier wall might be needed to reduce the effects upon value created by a noisy freeway. As a result, economic obsolescence is nearly always incurable.

Deciding whether to classify a particular loss in building value as functional or economic obsolescence is sometimes difficult. As the demands, wants, and needs of the market change, buildings once considered adequate may no longer measure up to current tastes. For example, in some areas, houses or condominium units with fewer than two baths are now considered out of date. Since the cause of such obsolescence is clearly related to external factors (change in market demand), one might argue that the loss in value should be labeled economic obsolescence. However, the usual practice is to categorize it as functional obsolescence, just as if the defect had been present since the time of construction. Changes in general population needs are credited with causing economic obsolescence (for example, higher density zoning) whereas changes in the specific desires of that same population (one bath or two) are usually explained as causing functional obsolescence. No fine line can really be drawn. However, the appraiser should be careful not to account for the decrease in value twice, by counting it as both functional and economic obsolescence.

SECTION 12.3
METHODS OF MEASURING
ACCRUED DEPRECIATION

There are four basic methods for measuring accrued depreciation. It is important to remember that none are merely abstract mathematical calculations. Rather they are attempts to estimate the actual loss in market value compared to a new building. Note that, in practice, it is common to use them in combination. The four methods are illustrated in Fig. 12.5.

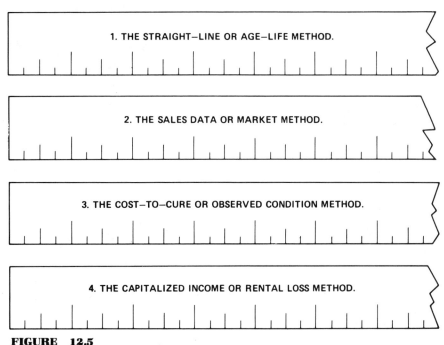

FIGURE 12.5
Methods of Measuring Accrued Depreciation

Straight-Line, or Age-Life, Method

The straight-line, or age-life, method of estimating accrued depreciation is based on the theory that all structures have a total useful life that can be predicted. This is called the economic life of the building. It is defined as "the period over which improvements to real estate contribute to the value of the property."* Therefore, at the end of a building's economic life, the vacant land would sell for as much or more than the improved property. Economic life is rarely as long as the physical life of a structure.

In straight-line depreciation, loss in value due to age is assumed to be directly proportional to the useful life (economic life) of the structure. However, other age-life methods are also in use. With straight-line depreciation, if a residence is considered to have a 100-year economic life but is now 25 years old, it should be allowed 25% depreciation.

Age		25 years
Divided by:	Economic life	÷ 100 years
Equals:	Accrued depreciation	25%

Because buildings of the same age vary greatly in their condition and desirability (due to differences in maintenance, modernization, etc.), many appraisers base depreciation estimates on the "effective age" of the building, rather than the actual age. The effective age of a building is the actual age of other buildings that are in similar condition and of comparable utility and marketability. For example, a 40-year-old building that has been modernized and well maintained may be able to compete directly with 20-year-old buildings. Here, the effective age of the 40-year-old building in question would be 20 years. When effective age is used to estimate accrued depreciation, normal functional and economic value loss, as well as some physical deterioration, has to be accounted for by the effective age adjustment. If actual age is used in figuring depreciation, however, separate adjustments may be necessary to reflect these factors. Note that the effective age adjustment is largely a matter of judgment and is very difficult to prove.

To estimate the loss in value using effective age rather than actual age, you simply divide the effective age of the structure by the total estimated economic life of the structure. Then convert this figure to a percent of accrued depreciation as before. Here is an example: A 40-year-old building with an effective age of 20 years is judged to have a total economic (useful) life of 50 years. Here the accrued depreciation would be 40%, using a straight-line basis (20/50 = 40%).

Many of the published depreciation tables are based on the age-life concept, although they modify the straight-line idea to a more realistic pattern or loss in value. For example, some such tables show a rapid loss of value in the early years and then a more gradual loss with age. To use such tables, simply find the correct column for the type of building under appraisal. Then look up the percent of accrued depreciation for the building's age. Finally, multiply this percent times the building cost new.

Some published cost tables claim to be based in part on studies of actual experience with building demolition or major rehabilitation. Others claim to be based on studies of market sales of old and new buildings. In any

---

* B. N. Boyce, *Real Estate Appraisal Terminology*, rev. ed., Ballinger Publishing Co., Cambridge, Mass., 1981, p. 74.

case, published tables not relating to the specific market conditions surrounding the subject property would give only a generalized result.

There are a few additional drawbacks to the age-life method of estimating depreciation. The economic life of a structure is difficult to predict because the usefulness and value of a building changes, relative to land values, with both market and zoning changes. Neither can be reliably forecast by an appraiser, investor, or broker. Effective age is also subjective. Another disadvantage of the age-life method is that it does not separate curable and incurable loss in value.

Sales Data, or Market, Method

The sales data, or market, method is based on the principle that value loss is determined in the market by buyers and sellers. If old buildings are worth less than new buildings, they will sell for less. In the sales data method, a number of sales are analyzed, subtracting the estimated land value from the selling prices, to obtain the building's contribution to the sale price. In turn, this amount is compared with the current cost of a new building. The difference is the loss in value, or accrued depreciation.

To estimate accrued depreciation of a property by the sales data method, follow these steps:

1. Estimate the reproduction or replacement cost new for the improvements of each comparable sale.

2. Estimate the land value for each comparable, if possible, by using market sales of vacant land.

3. Abstract the building portion of the selling price by subtracting the land value from the selling price.

4. Deduct the abstracted building value from the reproduction/replacement cost new for each sale. The difference is the accrued market depreciation estimated for each comparable sale.

Age differences must be accounted for, however, if we are to compare these data to the subject property. If we divide the accrued depreciation of each property by the estimated cost new for each property, the result is the percentage of value loss for each sale property. Dividing this answer by the age of the improvements translates into an annual percentage loss in value. To complete the analysis, the typical annual percentage loss would be applied to the subject property. Example 12.3 shows how each comparable sale would be analyzed.

Example 12.3
Calculating Depreciation by the Sales Data Method

Reproduction cost new of improvements			$100,000
Less:	Improvement value:		
Sales price		$120,000	
Less:	Land value	− 40,000	
Equals:	Improvement value		− 80,000
Equals:	Accrued depreciation		20,000
Divided by:	Actual age		÷ 20 years
Equals:	Annual value loss		1,000
Divided by:	Cost new		÷ 100,000
Equals:	Annual percent depreciation		1%

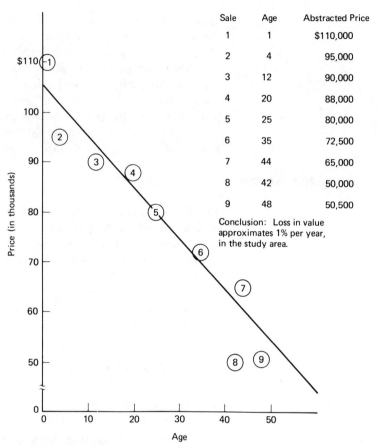

Sale	Age	Abstracted Price
1	1	$110,000
2	4	95,000
3	12	90,000
4	20	88,000
5	25	80,000
6	35	72,500
7	44	65,000
8	42	50,000
9	48	50,500

Conclusion: Loss in value approximates 1% per year, in the study area.

FIGURE   12.6
A Study of Age and Value Loss

The sales data method is the most direct method of estimating accrued depreciation from all causes. If an adequate sample is obtained, the results can be studied by plotting them on a chart or by using a simple regression analysis program available in many desk-top computers. (See Figure 12.6.)

What about the measurement of value loss resulting from unusual property defects or disadvantages? Although it may be difficult to find sale properties with the same defect as the subject, either functional or economic obsolescence can theoretically be measured directly from sales. For example, the loss in value from an obsolete architectural style could be estimated by comparing the sales of two otherwise similar properties in the same neighborhood, one with the same architectural style as the subject and the other with a different style. The difference in price would be the amount of functional obsolescence caused by the obsolete style, as estimated by the sales data method. (See Figure 12.7.)

Cost-to-Cure, or Observed Condition, Method

This method measures the accrued depreciation by the cost to cure or repair any observed building defects. After inspecting the premises, the appraiser tries to identify each building defect, feature, or condition that reduces value. Each is then classified as either physical, functional, or

FIGURE 12.7
Style Difference: Does It Affect Price? (Photograph Courtesy of Doug Frost)

economic. In addition, each defect must be studied to estimate whether it is economically curable or incurable.

First, the curable physical deterioration is estimated. This means adding up the cost of deferred maintenance work and repairs necessary to restore the structure to normal operating condition. Typical items include repainting peeling exterior paint, repairing broken glass, and repairing inoperative building equipment. Larger repairs might include replacing floor coverings or roofs. Dollar estimates for needed repairs can be derived from contractor's estimates or from cost evaluation services available to the appraiser. The total estimate of painting, fix-up, and repair costs is the estimate of the loss in value due to curable physical deterioration.

Next, any incurable physical deterioration is measured. By comparing the condition of both short-lived and long-lived building components with the same components in a new building, the relative loss in value of each component can be estimated. Here is how it works:

1. Estimate the cost new as of the value date for each building component involved.
2. Calculate the percentage of useful life already used up by dividing the actual chronological age of the component by its total estimated life.
3. Multiply the estimated cost new by the percentage of useful life already used up.

The result is an estimate of the loss of value caused by incurable physical deterioration. As you can see, this result will only be as reliable as the estimates of total life and cost of replacement for each component.

Last, curable functional obsolescence is estimated. Usually, such value loss results from outmoded equipment, such as obsolete plumbing, heating, or lighting fixtures. Here the value loss can be estimated by using the cost to replace with modern equipment. This may simply mean the in-place cost of replacing the obsolete items. Such cost estimates may be based on contractor bids or cost manuals. From the cost to replace with modern equipment, you usually deduct the amount included in your cost estimate for the existing equipment. Only the extra cost is deducted.

Curable functional obsolescence can also be caused by major building deficiencies or inadequacies. For example, a three-bedroom house with a single-car garage (or only one bath) may suffer in market appeal compared to one with a two-car garage (or two baths). However, the total added cost for a larger garage (in our example) must not be subtracted as the loss in value because the estimate of current new cost will not have included any costs for the second-car space. The accepted procedure is to compare the present cost of adding the extra garage space (or other market-desired components) with the current new cost as if included in the original building. Remodeling is generally more expensive than new construction (feature by feature). The difference is the measure of curable functional obsolescence in the improvements (see Example 12.4.)

The cost-to-cure method has some obvious practical limitations. First, individual component life spans used to estimate incurable physical deterioration are largely theoretical. Second, unless component costs have already been estimated by using the unit-in-place or quantity survey method to estimate total costs, it is prohibitively time-consuming. Additionally, the cost-to-cure method cannot measure the loss in value from either incurable functional or economic obsolescence. These losses must be measured by the capitalized income method, adding to the complexity.

Example 12.4
Calculating Curable Functional Obsolescence

Estimated current cost of enlarging garage		$6,000
Less:	Estimated current cost new of added garage area if built as part of the original structure	− 4,000
Equals:	Functional obsolescence	$2,000

Capitalized Income, or Rental Loss, Method

The capitalized income method can be used to estimate either the total loss in value from all causes or simply the loss in value from a single cause. To estimate loss in value from all causes, a comparison is made between the economic or market rent of the subject building and the rent of a new or modern building that could take its place. The difference can be called the rental loss attributed to age or obsolescence. In practice, a gross rent multiplier is normally used to capitalize the rental loss. A gross rent multiplier would be the typical ratio found between price and gross scheduled rent for properties in the area.

To illustrate this method, assume that a single-family residence under appraisal suffers from age and functional obsolescence. If its monthly rental is $150 per month less than new competitive properties and a gross rent multiplier of 200 is suggested by a market study, the total accrued depreciation could be estimated by the rental loss method. Here is an example:

Monthly rental of new competitive property		$550
Less:	Monthly rental of subject property	− 400
Equals:	Rental loss amount	$150
Multiplied by:	Gross rent multiplier	× 200
Equals:	Accrued depreciation	$30,000

The amount of value loss attributed to a single cause or factor can also be estimated. The rental or income loss that results from the unique physical, functional, or economic problem with the building is capitalized. For example, if a poor floor plan results in a $50 per month rent reduction, the value loss from that single cause would be $50 × 200, or $10,000 (using the same 200 gross multiplier as before).

When typical income property is under appraisal, the loss in value, or depreciation, can be estimated by a more formal capitalized income method using net income instead of gross income. The first step is to capitalize the net income that can be attributed to the improvements after a return for land is deducted. This provides an estimate of the building value. Subtracting this value from the estimated cost to produce the same building will provide the appraiser with the total amount of accrued depreciation for the building. The capitalized income method is actually part of the income approach to value, to be more fully described in Chapters 13 and 14.

SECTION 12.4
COST APPROACH SUMMARY

The cost approach is completed when the estimate of land value is added to the depreciated improvement costs for the property under appraisal. Conclusions that might result from the application of the cost approach to a single-family residence are given in Example 12.5.

Example 12.5
A. Reproduction Cost of Improvements

Living area	1,800 sq ft × $60 =	$108,000
Covered patio	200 sq ft × $15 =	3,000
Garage	400 sq ft × $20 =	8,000
Yard improvements		+ 5,000
Total reproduction cost as if new		$124,000

B. Accrued Depreciation

Physical deterioration		
Curable	$10,000	
Incurable	5,000	
Functional obsolescence		
Curable (old-style kitchen)	6,000	
Incurable (poor floor plan)	5,000	
Economic obsolescence		
(Adjacent to commercial)	+ 10,000	
Total accrued depreciation		−$36,000

C. Depreciated cost of improvements	$88,000
D. Estimated land value from sales comparables	+ 50,000
E. Total property value indicated by cost approach	$138,000

SUMMARY

In this chapter we defined accrued depreciation for appraisal purposes as the estimated loss in value of the improvements compared to their current cost as if new. Such value losses can be caused by physical deterioration, functional obsolescence, or economic obsolescence. Physical deterioration is caused by wear and tear, age, and the elements. Functional obsolescence occurs when faulty design or other such defects within the property detract from its marketability. Such loss in value can be evident from the first date of construction, or it may appear when building styles change and the structure can no longer meet the needs of the typical consumer. Economic obsolescence is caused by factors outside the property. For example, when rezoning makes existing improvements obsolete because a more intensive land use is in demand, the loss in value is categorized as economic obsolescence.

Accrued depreciation may be curable or incurable, depending upon whether the value increase resulting from the cure is greater than the cost of it. Many types of physical deterioration, such as deferred maintenance, are economic to cure by painting, fixing up, and repair work. However, certain functional and most economic value loss is incurable.

Accrued depreciation may be estimated by the straight-line/age-life method, the sales data method, the cost-to-cure/observed condition method, or the capitalized income method. Sometimes a combination of methods can be used.

The straight-line/age-life method relates the loss in value to the estimated life expectancy of the building. Accrued depreciation caused by physical deterioration and normal functional and economic obsolescence are estimated by comparing the age of the structure, at the time of the appraisal, with its total projected life. Published depreciation tables are usually based upon this method.

The sales data or market method measures accrued depreciation directly from the market. First, the land value is subtracted from the sale price for a comparable property, giving the building value contribution. Next, the building value is subtracted from its estimated reproduction cost, giving the value loss. Dividing the value loss by the cost new gives the total value as a percentage of value loss. In turn, the total percentage loss is divided by the age of the building to calculate the annual straight-line depreciation percentage. Functional or economic obsolescence from a single characteristic of a building may also be measured by the sales data method if sales can be found with the same basic defect as the subject property.

The cost-to-cure method equates the loss in value to the cost of repairs or changes necessary to restore the building to a normal operating condition. Incurable physical deterioration is measured by the observed condition of the components involved. Thus the cost-to-cure method may be used to measure all types of accrued depreciation except incurable functional and economic obsolescence.

Last, the capitalized income method provides an estimate of value loss by relating it to the loss in gross income. A gross rent multiplier is usually used to calculate the value loss. The total loss in value may also be estimated by comparing an income-derived building value with the reproduction cost new. Loss in value because of a single property defect is often estimated by applying a gross rent multiplier to the estimated rent loss attributed to the particular functional or economic factor involved.

When loss in value from all causes has been estimated, the value of the improvements may be estimated by subtracting the total accrued depreciation from the current cost new of the improvements.

IMPORTANT TERMS AND CONCEPTS

Accrued depreciation
Book value
Cost basis
Cost-to-cure method
Curable depreciation
Diminished utility
Economic life
Economic obsolescence

Effective age
Functional obsolescence
Incurable depreciation
Misplaced improvement
Overimprovement
Physical deterioration
Underimprovement

REVIEWING YOUR UNDERSTANDING

1. In accounting practice, depreciation is treated as:
    (a) A theoretical loss in value
    (b) An expense before taxes
    (c) An asset
    (d) Both parts (a) and (b)

2. Accrued depreciation can be defined in appraisal terms as:
    (a) Deduction from value
    (b) Total loss in value from all causes
    (c) Diminished utility
    (d) Both (b) and (c)

3. Accrued depreciation is classified in three types or categories. Which of the following should not be included?
    (a) Functional obsolescence
    (b) Economic obsolescence
    (c) Detrimental obsolescence
    (d) Physical deterioration

4. Each category of depreciation can be classified as curable or incurable. This helps the appraiser determine:
    (a) The economic feasibility to correct the condition
    (b) Whether the value loss can be estimated by the cost of needed repair or remodeling
    (c) Both of the above
    (d) Neither of the above

5. A building that is too large for the neighborhood is an example of functional obsolescence labeled as an overimprovement. Another example of functional obsolescence is:
    (a) A sound building with a worn-out heating system
    (b) A misplaced improvement
    (c) A residence abutting a new highway
    (d) A building that is likely to cost more to repair than the value added to the structure

6. There are four basic methods for measuring accrued depreciation. Which one of the following would probably be used to estimate the value loss from deferred maintenance?

    (a)   The sales data or market method
    (b)   The straight-line, or age-life, method
    (c)   The cost-to-cure, or observed condition, method
    (d)   The capitalized income, or rental, method

7. There is a theory that all structures have a total useful life that can be predicted. The method of estimating accrued depreciation based on this theory is:

    (a)   The capitalized income, or rental, method
    (b)   The sales data, or market, method (abstraction method)
    (c)   The straight-line, or age-life, method
    (d)   The cost-to-cure, or observed condition, method

8. Some appraisers base depreciation estimates on the effective age of the building rather than the actual age. Effective age is best defined as:

    (a)   The average age
    (b)   The actual age divided by the age life
    (c)   The age of other buildings similar in condition and utility
    (d)   The chronological age

9. A 40-year-old building with an effective age of 20 years has a total life expectancy of 50 years. How much depreciation has occurred?

    (a)   20%   **(b)**   50%
    (c)   10%   **(d)**   40%

CHAPTER THIRTEEN

THE INCOME APPROACH

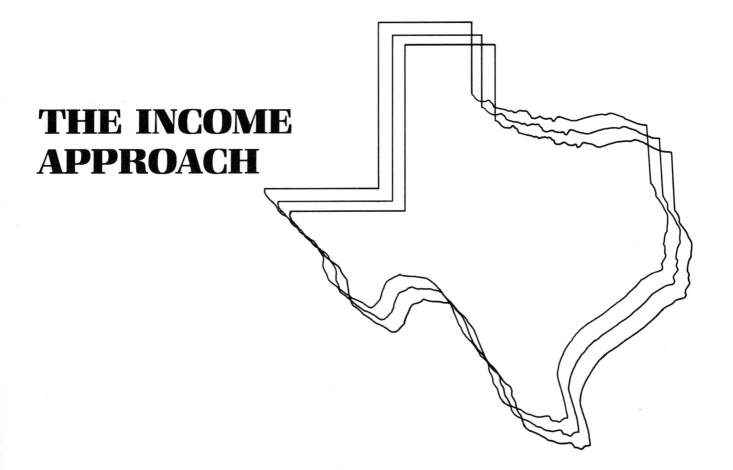

PREVIEW

The income approach to value is a special application of the principle of anticipation. In Chapter 5 that principle was summarized in the statement, "Value is the present worth of future benefits." Very simply, persons who invest in real estate do so to acquire the benefits that will flow from the real estate. The income approach to value consists basically of identifying, quantifying, and valuing those benefits. Note the emphasis on *future* benefits. Only the future is important. This principle is true in all the approaches to value, but it comes more sharply into focus in the income approach. What are "benefits?" Generally, we are speaking of money, in the form of rents or profits. Income tax savings are another form of monetary benefits. But ownership of real estate offers other benefits, as well. In the case of a residence, the benefits include shelter, comfort, and security.

Intangible benefits may include pride of ownership and the pleasure of sharing the home with family and friends—benefits often labeled amenities. Valuing intangible benefits can be very difficult since they are subjective and individual.

This chapter deals primarily with the valuation of tangible benefits—principally the dollars expected from the rental or use of property and its eventual sale at increased value or conversion to other assets. Another key phrase in our introductory statement was "present worth." Money in hand is worth more than the promise of money in the future. Since the future is always uncertain, investors in real estate always take some risk. And they forgo the interest the money could be earning and postpone the pleasures the money could purchase. For these reasons investors discount the future benefits in arriving at a price they are willing to pay for the right to receive those benefits. Thus, the income approach is often spoken of as a discounting process.

This chapter provides an overview of the income approach, focusing particularly on the relationship between income and value. It also deals with methods for accurately identifying and measuring, or quantifying, the benefits—chiefly the estimating of income and expenses. This discussion will be continued in

The Appraisal Process

1. Define the problem

2. Plan the appraisal

3. Collect the data

| General data | Subject property data | Comparable property data |

4. Apply the value approaches

| Sales comparison approach | Cost approach | Income approach |

5. Arrive at a value conclusion

6. Report the value conclusion

Chapter 14, which deals primarily with methods for converting estimates of income into estimates of value, or discounting the benefits.

When you have completed this chapter, you should be able to:

1. Distinguish between tangible and intangible benefits of property ownership.
2. Name the five steps in the income approach to value.
3. Explain the use of gross rent multipliers in the income approach.
4. Define the terms contract rent and economic, or market, rent, as used in appraisals.
5. Name the three main categories of expenses and give examples of items in each.
6. Outline the procedure used for reconstructing the owner's operating statement.

SECTION 13.1
INTRODUCING
INCOME PROPERTY

How is income property distinguished from other types of property? What are the motives and benefits of ownership? These are some of the questions we should consider in order to understand how to apply the income approach properly.

Types of Income Property

Any type of real estate may be purchased for income and investment purposes. One common reason given for buying a single-family home today is that it can easily be converted to a rental property and retained for the possible benefits of long-term value appreciation. However, the term income property is traditionally reserved for property purchased for its income. Figure 13.1 illustrates some good examples of income-producing properties.

FIGURE   13.1
Types of Income Property. (Photographs Courtesy of Doug Frost)

A multiple residential property is the most common type of income property. However, income (or investment) property includes commercial and industrial properties as well. Thus a list of property types usually treated as income property should include the following:

1. Multiple residential, chiefly large and small apartment buildings.
2. Commercial buildings, including stores, offices, medical offices, convalescent hospitals, hotel and motel properties, and shopping centers.
3. Industrial properties, such as warehouses and factories.

Types of Investors

Investors may be classified in three broad categories. First, there is the part-time investor—an individual or family group—who acquires relatively inexpensive investments and provides his or her own management and, sometimes, maintenance services. Such investors usually have other sources of income; hence the label "part-time."

Second, there is the relatively sophisticated investor who may invest fairly large sums of money from family or business funds, supplemented usually by heavy borrowings from real estate lenders. This type of investor may or may not employ professional management but almost certainly will contract with others to do the necessary maintenance and repairs. Sophisticated investors are usually driven in part by a desire to shelter a portion of their earnings from income taxes.

The third category of investors consists of institutions. Pension funds, foundations, banks, and corporations are good examples. The funds for investment come from a variety of sources, including the sale of real estate securities on the open market, the accumulation of savings in a thrift institution, or the cash reserves held by life insurance companies. Institutions usually employ full-time professionals to acquire, manage, and dispose of their income property portfolios.

SECTION 13.2
REAL ESTATE VERSUS
OTHER INVESTMENTS

Why should anyone invest in real estate, as opposed to stocks, bonds, or savings accounts, for example? Investment motivations differ among different individuals and firms, but the objectives shared by most include the following:

Safety They want to be able to get their money back at some future time.

Yield They want an acceptable rate of return on their capital, considering the risk involved as compared with other available investments.

Capital appreciation Some investments offer the opportunity for growth in value. That is, after the asset is held for a few years, it may bring more money than the original sum invested. (Of course, there is a risk that the opposite may be true.)

Liquidity Investments differ in the ease with which they may be converted back to cash in the owner's hands.

Burden of management   The demands on the investor's time and management skills vary widely among investments.

To get an idea of how real estate stacks up according to these five criteria, let's compare it with a savings account at a bank. Safety is no problem for money placed in a savings account in a depository insured by Federal Deposit Insurance Corporation or Federal Savings and Loan Insurance Corporation. The full principal amount is guaranteed (up to certain maximum limits) by an agency of the federal government. Returns on real estate, however, are rarely guaranteed, except in the case of a long-term lease by a creditworthy tenant. Even then, the guarantee is limited to the amount of rent due over the term of the lease.

As for yield, most real estate investments return at least as much as a savings account, although not necessarily in the early life of the investment. Yields vary widely among various kinds of real estate, as they do in other types of investments.

Capital appreciation is one of the strongest motivations for investment in real estate. The principal invested in a savings account cannot grow. Except for the accumulated interest, the balance remains the same. Because of inflation and taxes on interest, the purchasing power of the money invested in a savings account may actually decline over time, even when the interest earned is allowed to accumulate.

Liquidity differs greatly between real estate and a savings account. To convert a savings account to cash, the saver has only to fill out a withdrawal slip. To convert real estate back to cash may require a considerable length of time and some major expense. In certain market periods, liquidity may be gained only at substantial loss to the investor.

The same unfavorable comparison between savings and real estate applies to the burden of management. A savings account imposes no burden at all. Real estate, on the other hand, may involve problems of collecting rent, modernizing and re-leasing vacant space, and a host of other management challenges.

With these drawbacks, one might question why anyone would prefer to invest in real estate. But invest they do! Real estate probably accounts for about two-thirds of our national wealth. The principal forces driving investment in real estate are probably related to inflation and taxes. In times of inflation, real estate normally maintains its value in terms of real purchasing power, while fixed-dollar investments, such as savings accounts and bonds, are eroded. Also, real estate offers distinct advantages to persons in high income tax brackets. A detailed discussion of those advantages is beyond the scope of this book, but they involve chiefly the creation of artificial or "paper" losses through deductions from income for depreciation and for interest on funds borrowed to acquire the property. Secondarily, the capital appreciation of real estate is generally taxed at lower rates than other investment income, such as interest on savings accounts.

Tangible Benefits of Ownership

The tangible, or monetary, benefits of ownership of income property may be divided into two main categories: (1) a return *on* the investment, from rents or profits produced by the real estate, and (2) a return *of* the investment. The latter refers to the conversion of the investment in real estate back to cash or to other valuable assets when the investor chooses to terminate ownership.

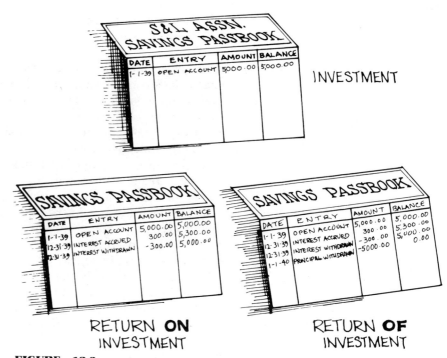

FIGURE 13.2
Return *on* and Return *of* Investment—Savings Account Example

Using the savings account analogy once again, the initial deposit in the account compares with the purchase of the real estate investment. The bank pays rent on the use of the saver's money, called interest. This is a return *on* the investment and compares with rent paid for the use of real estate. The withdrawal of savings at some future time accomplishes a return *of* the investment. (See Figure 13.2.) The real estate investor accomplishes return *of* investment by selling the property for cash or trading it for other valuable assets. Of course, it has already been pointed out that the cash returned from liquidation of real estate may be more or less than the original investment, while the principal held in the savings account is guaranteed to be the original amount plus accrued interest.

Intangible Benefits of Ownership

It has already been stated that the benefits that motivate many investors are intangible, even vague. Often investors—particularly part-time investors—cannot express their motives or are not even completely aware of them. Such intangible benefits as pride of ownership and a sense of security in controlling one's own destiny can play a part in any investment decision. To the extent that these perceived benefits are shared in the marketplace, they have a bearing on value and should not be overlooked by the appraiser. They may help to explain why the apparent yield or return on an investment is lower than might otherwise be expected. In effect, the investors are purchasing these intangible benefits in competition with other investors. They may sacrifice some monetary returns in order to secure equally important non-monetary benefits.

In summary, the benefits of owning income property may be both tangible and intangible. The mixture of benefits depends on the size and type of the investment, the type of investors active in the market, and the nature of the market itself. Prospects of income tax relief and capital appreciation may appear to be intangible, but in the minds of most purchasers they are quite real and impact strongly on the market value of real estate. These aspects of investment will be more fully explored in the next chapter under the heading Investment Criteria.

The Income-Value Relationship

An income approach to value is possible because a demonstrated relationship exists between income and value. In Chapter 5 the concept of utility was introduced. In order to have value, a commodity must have utility, or usefulness. The greater the utility, the greater the value. In income property, utility is best measured by rent. In theory, the rent paid for a parcel of real estate expresses the usefulness of that parcel to the renter, or tenant, for the period of time covered by the rental payment. Of course, supply and demand have a bearing. The tenant will not normally pay more rent than the going, or market, rent paid for comparable properties in the marketplace.

When market rent can be established, the only other ingredient necessary for estimating value is a conversion factor. This is a multiplier or a rate that expresses a relationship between income and value—a relationship applicable to, and valid for, a particular type of property in a particular market. For example, the conversion factors applicable to valuation of roadside motels are not the same as those associated with multistory office buildings. In fact, conversion factors useful in appraising apartment houses in Houston would not necessarily apply to apartments in Lubbock or Tyler. The simplest form of conversion factor is a gross income multiplier (GIM). This concept was introduced in Chapter 9 as a tool in the sales comparison approach. To employ the GIM, the appraiser must first analyze enough sales of similar properties to discover the relationship of gross income to sale prices. Taking into account the differences in the individual properties (comparables and subject), the appraiser decides on a GIM that best represents the property under appraisal. The GIM is then multiplied by the gross income produced (or expected to be produced) by the subject property to develop an indicated market value. For example, if the appropriate GIM is 5 and the estimated gross annual rent of the property is $100,000, then the indicated market value is $500,000.

Rent is usually spoken of as gross income. The landlord must pay certain expenses, such as taxes, insurance, and maintenance of the property. By agreement with the tenant, the landlord may provide other services, such as cleaning, heating, air conditioning, and security. In other cases, the terms of the rental agreement require the tenant to pay most or all of the expenses. When the landlord is relieved of all expenses, the lease is called a net lease.

In the income approach to value the real estate appraiser is interested primarily in the net income to the property. This consists of the gross income as reduced by vacancy or collection losses as well as operating expenses. The preceding paragraphs dealt with gross income with a multiplier as the conversion factor. In dealing with net income, the conversion factor is usually a fraction called a capitalization rate.

The value equation for net income is:

$$\text{value} = \frac{\text{income}}{\text{rate}}$$

For example, if the net income is $100,000 and an appropriate capitalization rate is judged to be 8%, the indicated value of the real estate is:

$$\frac{\$100,000}{.08} = \$1,250,000$$

The appraiser could just as easily use a multiplier (indeed, this is the practice in some European countries). Of course, the multiplier would be the reciprocal of the rate, that is, 1/rate. (In the example above, the multiplier would be 1/.08 or 12.5.) Probably, the practice of using fractional rates has developed in the United States because the capitalization rate is analogous in many ways to interest rates and is usually influenced by interest rates. In effect, the capitalization rate is the rate of return on investment required by typical purchasers of income property similar to that being appraised at the time of valuation.

Examples of Monetary Relationships

The savings account example clearly illustrates the direct relationship between value, income, and rate of return. A savings account of $2,000.00, earning an 8% rate of interest, would earn $160.00 in one year because 8% times $2,000.00 equals $160.00. If someone told us only the annual earnings and the rate of interest, we would still be able to figure out the amount on deposit in the account because of the fixed relationship between the three numbers. The annual income of $160.00, divided by 0.08, equals $2,000.00.

Let us apply the monetary relationship described here to investment real estate. Assume that the only tangible return on investment is in the form of the annual income. For a property earning $10,000 per year, if a 10% annual rate of return is required, the value would be $100,000. Why? Because $10,000 is 10% of $100,000, or $10,000 divided by 0.10 equals $100,000. In both examples, we can again see that value is the relationship between the *amount* of return and the *rate* of return.

Real estate investments are rarely as simple as deposits in a savings account. For example, the benefits available to the real estate investor are not always restricted to annual income, as we pointed out earlier. For this reason, the relationship between amounts and rates of return is often complex. This topic will be discussed under the heading Income Capitalization Techniques in the next chapter.

The Income Capitalization Approach

Mathematically, the income approach is based on the relationship between value, income, and rate of return. A property earning $15,000 per year (net), assuming a rate of return at 10%, can be said to have a value of $150,000. Actually, dividing the net income by an appropriate rate is only one of many methods of applying the income approach. The techniques vary, depending on the nature of the income stream and other variables, which will be discussed in Chapter 14. The simple division method illustrated here is called direct capitalization.

Now we are ready to look at the six basic steps in the income approach:

1. Estimate the gross annual income the property is capable of producing.
2. Estimate typical vacancy and collection or rent losses.
3. Subtract vacancy and collection losses from gross income to arrive at the effective gross income.
4. Subtract annual expenses to arrive at estimated net income.
5. Select the method of capitalization appropriate to the valuation problem, and derive the applicable capitalization rates from market analysis.
6. Capitalize the net income into an indicated value by the income approach.

Let us assume that we are appraising a 20-unit apartment house. It has a projected annual gross income of $80,000 and a predicted vacancy and rent loss amounting to $4,000 per year. Annual expenses of $28,000 can be expected. Our analyses indicate that an 8% rate of return is appropriate, and we decide to use the capitalization method already discussed. (Other capitalization methods will be explained in Chapter 14). Our calculations are shown in Example 13.1.

Example 13.1
Direct Capitalization

Projected gross income		$80,000
Less:	Vacancy and collection loss	− 4,000
Equals:	Effective gross income	76,000
Less:	Annual expenses	−28,000
Equals:	Net income	48,000
Divided by:	Capitalization rate	÷ .08
Equals:	Value estimate	$600,000

Real estate appraisal by income capitalization depends upon a careful estimate of income and expenses, to be discussed in the last two sections of this chapter.

SECTION 13.3
ESTIMATING GROSS INCOME

The first step in the income approach is to estimate the gross income. This will define the property's potential production, measured in rent dollars. That is why the gross income estimate is sometimes referred to as an income forecast.

The gross income of a property refers to the total income generated, assuming 100% occupancy. Such income is often composed of two parts: (1) rent for tenant space and (2) service or miscellaneous income. The rent for tenant space is the sum total of all the scheduled rental amounts, including tenant parking space. It is sometimes referred to as the rent roll in properties with multiple tenants. Service income refers to money collected for laundry facilities, vending machines, utilities sold to tenants, and other incidental amounts.

Contract Versus Market Rent

Income property is often sold subject to existing leases and other contractual arrangements between the landlord and tenant. Thus, the price may be influenced by the terms of the lease, going up if terms are favorable to the landlord or down if favorable to the tenant. In other words, the price tends to reflect the property rights being sold.

In most appraisals, the property is valued as if it were free from all encumbrances, except for public controls and deed restrictions shown in public records. The procedure is first to estimate the value of all the property rights and then to make any adjustments relevant to the specific rights being appraised. Appraisal of leased property will be discussed further in Chapter 17.

Market Rent Defined

Market rent is the rental income the property could command if placed for rent on the open market as of the effective date of the appraisal. Market rent may or may not be the same as the rent currently being paid. If not based on a net lease, market rent means the gross rent. This potential gross rent is the most common rent used in appraisals. It assumes not only that the subject property is available for rent, that is, unencumbered by any lease, but also that it is being efficiently managed so as to realize its full potential income. Market rent is sometimes referred to as economic rent.

Understanding Contract Rent

Technically, contract rent means rent being paid under contractual commitments binding owners and tenants. Such rental agreements range from simple verbal contracts to complex leases beyond the scope of this book. The appraiser's task of seeking out rental information requires a general understanding of common types of rental arrangements.

A tenant's right to occupy space may result from a month-to-month occupancy, short-term lease, or long-term lease agreement. Multiple-residential and commercial tenants most commonly occupy their space under month-to-month agreements or short-term leases ranging from three to five years. Tenants of more specialized properties, such as chain restaurants, office buildings, and department stores, are often willing to sign long-term leases of 10 years or more.

The most common types of leases encountered by appraisers are the straight lease, the step-up lease, and the percentage lease, shown in Figure 13.3. Combinations of these lease forms are common. The straight, or flat, lease is one in which the monthly or annual rent is a fixed amount that stays the same over the entire lease term. The step-up, or graduated, lease is a more popular type of lease today because it provides a way to keep up with inflation. Such a lease agreement establishes progressively higher rental amounts for different segments of the lease terms. For example, a lease might call for a rental of $750 per month for the first two years, then $850 per month for the third and fourth year, and $950 per month for the fifth and sixth year. Sometimes, the rentals step up with the Consumer Price Index or some other general economic measure of inflation.

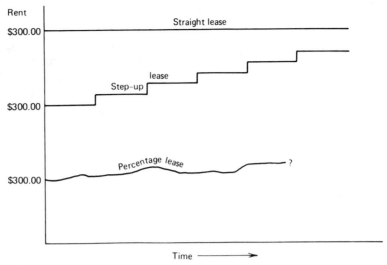

FIGURE 13.3
Types of Leases

The percentage lease fixes the rent as a stipulated percentage, usually of the gross sales of goods and services offered by the tenant. Most percentage leases require a certain base rent, regardless of sales volume. Typically, this minimum rent is credited against the percentage rent due. The actual percentage rate generally follows standardized guidelines for each type of tenant, depending on typical profit margins and the volume of business. Percentage rentals range from 1½% of gross sales, for large-volume department store retailers, to as high as 50 to 75% for parking lot operators. Most common retail tenancies pay from 2¼ to 10% of gross sales under percentage lease agreements.

When existing leases are analyzed and compared with past rent payments, appraisers use special terms to describe the various types of rent payments. Minimum rent describes the base rent that is the minimum amount paid under a percentage lease, overage rent describes the amounts paid over and above the base rent, and excess rent is the amount by which the total contract rent exceeds market rent. Most of these terms are of concern only to appraisers specializing in commercial and industrial appraisals.

When analyzing a lease, it is important to determine who is responsible for paying the various expenses. In apartment rentals, the usual lease terms hold the landlord responsible for all expenses except for water, electricity, and gas bills on the tenant's space. However, in commercial and industrial leases, the landlord and tenant may share many expense costs. The trend is to have the tenants pay the building expenses directly. Operating costs such as maintenance, insurance, and taxes will be discussed later in this chapter.

How to Make a Rent Survey

An estimate of market rent should be based upon a survey of the rent charged by competing properties in the immediate neighborhood. When possible, the appraiser should choose buildings of the same age, general design, services, and amenities as the subject so that the rentals can be directly compared with those charged for the subject property's space. For many appraisals, the rental schedules of the sale properties used in the market approach can be incorporated into the rental study. For each property surveyed, the appraiser should record the location and building description, along with the schedule of existing rents and the vacancy history. The number of units and their size, age, condition, and quality should be noted, along with the specific amenities offered to tenants. For multiple-residential properties, it is important to note any units subject to rent control. Also, such features as parking and recreation facilities are important to note and describe. See Figure 13.4.

As shown on the sample rent survey form, apartment units are usually

---

Rental Survey

Project Name   Brookvale Manor   Person Contacted   Grace Schnider

Number of Units   150   Position   Assistant Manager

Address   36163 N. Marcus Blvd.   Person Surveying   B. Neale

          Dallas   Date of Survey   7-4-81

PROPERTY DATA:

Age 5 yrs.   Condition Avg.   No. of Stories 2   No. of Bldgs. 1

Construction   Lathe and plaster   Land Area Avg.

No. of Units 150   Density Avg.   View Fair to Good

Parking one covered; extra open parking assigned

AMENITIES: View some   Pool(s) one   Recreation Room large

             Sauna none   Other Rec. Features None

APARTMENT FEATURES: Utilities All electric--tenant pays

    Furniture none   Carpets x   Drapes x   Patio none

    Refrigerator x   Dishwasher none   Air Cond. none   Balcony x

    Range & Oven x   Fireplace none   Other Features

RENTAL DATA:

No. of Units	Apartment Type	Area Sq. Ft.	Rental Total	per Sq. Ft.
80	1-BR, 1-Ba	575	$235	$0.35
70	2-BR, 1-Ba	980	$300	0.30

Concessions no pets; six months lease

Deposits   1st & last months rent, plus $135 1-BR or $150 2-BR, Security deposit

OCCUPANCY

    TYPE   Adult---some family   Date Opened 1976

    Total Units 150   No. Occupied 147   % Occupancy 98%

FIGURE 13.4

listed by the number of bedrooms and baths, specifying whether each unit is rented furnished or unfurnished. The dates that the spaces were first occupied by the current tenants, and the last date of rent adjustment may also be noted. In a rapidly changing market, this information is needed to suggest when a rental increase might be practical. If deposits and leases are required, record this data too. Of course, tenant obligations to pay utilities and any rent concessions or free rent agreements made by the landlord have a direct effect on the rent schedule and must not be overlooked.

In commercial properties, tenant improvements can have a notable effect on the rent schedules of properties surveyed, as well as on the market rent estimate for the subject property. The original rent often depends upon who pays the costs of items such as floor covering, lighting, and air conditioning. When these have been installed by the tenant of the surveyed property, the rent may need adjustment before comparing it to a space in the subject property that is ready to occupy.

Industry standards for pricing tenant space usually depend upon the type of property. As already indicated, apartment units are usually priced or compared by the number of bedrooms and baths but may be compared by the monthly rent per square foot of living area. Office rents are calculated by a monthly or annual price for each square foot of the net rentable area. Net rentable area is sometimes distinguished from net usable area, which excludes stairways, mechanical areas, restrooms, and other space shared in common with other tenants in a multitenanted building. It is now the practice of many building owners to prorate such areas among the tenants so that rent is paid on every square foot of the building. The term net rentable, then, pertains to the number of square feet for which the tenant is actually paying rent, regardless of what is usable.

Assigning the Market Rent

In most cases, the market rent estimated for the subject property is derived from an analysis of the rentals found in the rent survey and a comparison of those amounts with the existing rent schedule for the property being appraised. In determining what is usable and what is rentable, the appraiser should be guided by customary practices of landlords and tenants in the area. Consistency of treatment is the rule, with the same criteria applied to the subject and to the comparables.

Analysis of Survey Rentals

The rental survey provides data on competitive rental rates. After these rates have been analyzed to estimate what factors cause rents to vary, they should then be adjusted to represent rental space more like that of the subject property. The following factors should be considered:

1. *Time* Based on the date the lease was signed or the occupancy began and the observed trend in rental prices.

2. *Location* If differences are significant.

3. *Physical features* Size, age, quality, appeal, amenities offered, and building condition.

4. *Services, utilities, and personalty (personal property) included in the rent* Note that furnished apartments should not be compared with unfurnished without adjusting. Any furniture or personal property involved in the property under appraisal should be described and the rent allocated separately between real and personal property.

5. *Vacancy rates*   Abnormally high vacancy, indicating overpricing; low vacancy rates, suggesting underpricing of units.

6. *Limitations of any rent control regulations in effect*   Imposing artificial limits on tenant rents. Since market rent is commonly understood as the potential *legal* income of the property, some readers may view a market rent survey as an academic exercise in a rent control situation. However, most rent control ordinances offer some legal opportunity for landlords to appeal rent schedules that are grossly out of line with competing properties. The rent survey might be necessary, therefore, to prepare the appraiser to consider such possibilities.

Construction of Market Rent Schedule

The appraiser's final unit-by-unit rent schedule and gross income estimate should result from the analysis of competing property rentals and the history of rentals for the subject property. However, if the existing management is competent and aggressive in pricing and marketing units, the appraiser might well conclude that the current rent schedule represents market rents. On the other hand, any part of the existing rent schedule that appears to be noticeably higher or lower than the competition should be given a second look and then either adjusted or fully explained.

Current rent schedules may have other defects. For example, rent for the owner's or manager's unit, as well as income from such building services as laundry facilities, are commonly omitted. The appraiser's gross income projection should make corrections for such omissions. If the manager is to be provided free rent, it is more appropriate to include the rent from that unit in the gross income and then deduct the rental amount as part of the management expenses. Example 13.4 shows how to format a market rent schedule.

Example 13.4
Gross Rent Schedule for a Six-Unit Apartment

Unit Number	Type	Current Rent	Market Rent
101	Two-bedroom	$275	$325
102	One-bedroom	180	275
103	Bachelor	160	200
201	Two-bedroom	285	340
202	One-bedroom	Manager	280
203	One-bedroom	220	+ 260
Total monthly rent roll			$1,680
Total annual rent roll ($1,680 × 12)			$20,160
Plus: Laundry and miscellaneous income			+ 870
Equals: Total potential gross income			$21,030

The appraiser should consider the past history of vacancy rates for the subject property. Unless there are specific problems with the property or its management, abnormal vacancy rates suggest that a rent adjustment is needed. In an area not affected by rent control, the building with the lowest vacancy rates often has the lowest rents. Efficient management can maximize gross receipts by increasing rental rates to achieve normal vacancy. For example, an apartment building that has a zero vacancy factor could increase actual (effective) gross receipts if rents were increased, say, from \$300 to \$335 per month (across the board), as long as only a 10% vacancy factor were to result.

Effective Gross Rent

The effective gross rent is defined as the market rent minus the allowance for vacancy and credit losses. It is a projection of the potential income receipts of the property before normal operating costs and capital recovery.

Vacancy rates should always be considered separately for each type of unit. Consider the appraisal of a 20-unit apartment building composed entirely of two-bedroom units. Your rent survey reveals that buildings in the area with one-bedroom units have much lower vacancy rates than those with two- and three-bedroom units. You would conclude that an appropriate vacancy factor for your building would be higher than that of the typical one-bedroom building.

The allowance for rent or credit losses is estimated next to provide for rents not collected because of nonpayment. In making this calculation, we again assume efficient management of the property and follow the typical experience of the neighborhood.

In summary, the estimate of effective gross income should result from a carefully worked-out rent schedule reflecting the rental and vacancy experience of competing properties in its neighborhood. This estimate should *not* be a mere reflection of the existing operation of the property but should be a realistic prediction of what maximum income the property could reasonably produce in the current market under competent management.

SECTION 13.4 ANNUAL EXPENSES

Annual expenses are deducted from the effective annual gross income to calculate the net income. In turn, annual net income is used in the capitalization process to develop an indicated value of the property.

Expenses to Be Included

For appraisal purposes, expenses are limited generally to current operating costs. Therefore, loan or interest payments, income taxes, and depreciation deductions are not included. Although such outlays are important to the owner, and significant for accounting and income tax purposes, they relate solely to the debt or tax position of one particular owner rather than to the real estate in question. One exception occurs in equity residual capitalization, where loan payments are deducted to discover the cash flow return on the equity down payment. This procedure is described in Chapter 14.

Categories of Expenses

Regardless of the type of investment property, expenses are formally classified as (1) operating expenses, (2) fixed expenses, or (3) reserves for replacement. There is no requirement that you must separate them in this way, but the categories serve as useful reminders.

Operating Expenses

Operating expenses are the day-to-day out-of-pocket expenses required to run the building. These usually include administration and management, maintenance and repairs, and utility costs. Building expenses may be incurred either as payroll items or as contracted services.

In economics, management is considered to be one of the four agents of production. Management cost varies greatly with the type and size of the property. For small apartment buildings, management is often accomplished by the services of a resident manager. Costs vary with the number of units. The resident manager usually collects the rent and takes care of minor maintenance and repair work. Often the manager's compensation is in the form of free rent and perhaps a small salary.

In larger apartment complexes and commercial properties, professional management companies are often needed in order to oversee the on-site property manager and perform all administrative services for the owner. When all legal, accounting, and supervisory costs are included, such companies usually charge from 3 to 7% of the rent collected. In some cases, this includes the payment to the resident manager.

Maintenance and repair costs include all building and grounds upkeep, except for the replacement of major building components or equipment. In apartment buildings, monthly maintenance and repair work includes grounds and pool maintenance, cleaning, interior painting and decorating, and minor plumbing repairs. Elevator and major equipment maintenance is included and is usually covered by annual service contracts. Outside painting and major building repair is performed at irregular intervals over the years; hence, average annual costs should usually be estimated from the building's history or from industry standards.

Utility costs include water and power, gas, garbage collection, and so on. In most properties, the owner pays for all garbage collection as well as water, power, and gas for the common areas, which include parking lots, recreation and laundry facilities, as well as central water and space heating. When the rental units have separate meters, tenants usually pay all metered utilities. Appraisers should compare the actual utility costs of a property to those typically experienced by owners of similar buildings. However, it is important to remember that each building is unique. The amount of electricity, gas, and water used, and garbage generated varies with the building design and tenant needs. Utility rates also vary from place to place. Also, leases vary concerning who—landlord or tenant—will pay the utility bill. So, utility cost information from competitive buildings must be used cautiously when being compared to the subject property.

Fixed Expenses

These expenses are paid on a fairly regular basis and are relatively stable from year to year. Insurance premiums and property taxes are the most common examples.

Insurance coverage on income property usually includes fire, extended coverage, and public liability. Special coverages may also apply. Special coverage could include insurance against rent loss, with one type covering rent loss resulting from fires and similar events, and another type insuring or guaranteeing a specified lease (as for a commercial store). Another type of special coverage is flood insurance. Rates depend in part on the specific coverages. They also vary with the type of occupancy and with the construction classification of the buildings (discussed in Chapter 11). Appraisers often rely on the past costs from the property operating statement to project insurance costs; however, it is a good idea to compare such figures with quotations from local insurance carriers. Note that premiums are sometimes quoted on terms of payment other than on an annual basis, and such amounts should be prorated to a yearly cost.

Real property taxes are usually assessed by an ad valorem, or according-to-value, formula. The appraiser most often projects taxes as a property expense based on the present taxes unless a revaluation by the assessor seems likely. It is important to remember that in market value appraisals, the property tax expense used in the income approach should be the amount a new owner would probably be charged under the local tax laws. Also, unless rent for personal property, such as furniture and equipment, is included in the rent projected for the property, personal property taxes should not be included in the appraiser's expense estimate.

Reserves for Replacement

Certain property components wear out from age and usage and must be replaced from time to time. Although inexpensive replacements may be accounted for under maintenance expense, larger costs are most often capitalized (i.e., listed as "capital" improvements). This is why they do not show on building expense statements. An annual reserve allowance is considered a valid way of accounting for these costs, particularly when the items have shorter useful lives than the main structure.

Reserves for replacement usually include roof and floor coverings, built-in kitchen equipment, water heaters and boilers, heating and air conditioning units, and other operating machinery and equipment. In furnished offices and apartments, replacement reserves would also be set up to pay for new furnishings as the old ones wear out. However, the expense of furniture reserves is appropriate only if the projected rent includes rent for the furnishings or equipment.

Major capital additions to the structure, such as major remodeling and facility enlargement/expansion, do not properly belong under replacement reserves. This is because such work generally alters (increases) the income potential of the property. Replacement reserves are intended only to maintain the property's condition and income.

How are the dollar amounts for reserves for replacements estimated? First, of course, the appraiser must determine what components of the property are eligible for such treatment. It should be borne in mind that most investors in income property do not hold the property for its entire useful life. It has become common practice for owners to dispose of property through sale or trade when its special tax advantages have been exhausted. Therefore, as a general rule, reserves should be established only for those components that will normally be replaced within a typical ownership cycle. Suppose, in the appraisal of a new six-unit apartment house, the refrigerators are chosen as items to be covered by a reserve. The first step is to determine the probable cost (at current prices) of replacing the refrigerators. Then the appraiser must estimate the useful life of the units under normal use. The replacement cost is then divided by the useful life to arrive at an annual allocation to reserves. For example, if the refrigerators cost $500 each to replace and are estimated to have a ten-year life, the reserve for replacements would be set at 6 × $500 divided by 10, or $300 per annum. A similar calculation is made for each of the items involved, and the sum of the individual allocations is obtained.

The practice of establishing a reserve for replacements is not followed by all appraisers. It was commonly practiced before tax laws favored frequent disposition of properties, when it was not uncommon for an investment property to remain under the same ownership for generations. While this still happens, it is now the exception. Some appraisers set up a typical term of ownership—say, 10 years—and establish reserves for only those items they believe will actually be replaced during that term.

Once again, consistency is the primary goal. It would be misguided practice for an appraiser to establish reserves for replacements in arriving at a net income estimate for the subject property, then derive capitalization rates from the sales of other properties in which the owners did not maintain such reserves. The appraiser should either estimate proper reserves for the comparable properties before arriving at net income or disregard reserves for the subject as well as the comparables.

SECTION 13.5
RECONSTRUCTION OF
THE OPERATING STATEMENT

In written reports, appraisers often include a reconstructed operating statement in the income approach. This statement shows the appraiser's estimate of stabilized income and expenses for the property, listed category by category. By stabilized, we mean under current economic conditions but adjusted to show current market rents, average collection losses, and normal expenses for this location.

Why We Reconstruct the Statement

The owner's actual operating statement for prior years is important because it is the actual history of the property and usually helps develop good estimates of many elements of operating income and expenses. (See Example 13.5). However, owners' statements may contain some items that are improper or that are irrelevant to the appraisal of the property. Quite often, the operating statement is simply an income tax report, reflecting the personal income and expenses of the owner rather than strictly those of the property.

The purpose of reconstructing the operating statement in an appraisal, then, is to set forth an estimate of the current market rents, the typical long-term vacancy and collection losses in this location with good manage-

Example 13.5
An Owner's Operating Statement

Receipts

Rent	$72,350	
Other	+ 1,039	
Total		$73,389

Expenses

Management	$3,000	
Utilities	3,817	
Pool service	900	
Landscape service	850	
Depreciation	8,713	
Building maintenance	1,050	
Property taxes ($\frac{1}{2}$ year)	5,000	
Interest	+ 16,721	
Total		− 40,051
Net		$33,338

ment, and the normal annual expenses to operate this property efficiently on a continuing basis.

The appraiser should be aware that some advanced capitalization techniques require a year-by-year projection of income, vacancy and collection loss, and expenses. Such a year-by-year series of numbers would probably use different figures from those used in a stabilized statement. As examples, vacancy rates for a new building might be selected to reflect a declining vacancy rate, and replacement reserve deductions could be estimates of the actual replacement amounts for the specific year in which the replacement is anticipated.

Typical Rental and Vacancy Adjustment

Reconstruction of the owner's operating statement must incorporate the findings of the income and expense study already described. Reconstruction nearly always involves some rental adjustments. Example 13.6 is a

Example 13.6
Example of Reconstructed Operating Statement

Scheduled Gross Income

10 units at $300 per month	$3,000	
10 units at $375 per month	+ 3,750	
Total Annual Rents	$6,750 × 12 = $81,000	

Service Income

Laundry facilities	+ 1,000
	$82,000
Vacancy and credit loss (2.5%)	− 2,050
Effective gross income	$79,950

Expenses

Operating		
Management (6%)	$4,800	
Utilities	4,000	
Pool service	900	
Landscape service	850	
Building maintenance	+ 3,950	
Total operating expenses	$14,500	
Fixed		
Insurance	$1,500	
Real estate taxes	+ 10,000	
Total fixed expenses	$11,500	
Reserves for replacement		
Carpets and drapes	$2,000	
Kitchen built-ins	750	
Roof	950	
Other building components	+ 400	
Total reserves for replacement	+ $4,100	
Total expenses		− $30,100
Net Income Projection		$49,850

reconstructed statement based upon the owner's statement presented in Example 13.5. One common adjustment arises because owners' statements often fail to list the manager's unit in the rent schedule whereas, in a reconstructed statement, all units would be included. Next, the rental rates usually must be adjusted to market rent levels.

Estimation of an appropriate vacancy and credit loss is the next step. The appraiser will lean heavily, in this step, on the information gained in the rental survey. Usually, this estimate will reflect vacancy rates actually experienced by the subject property, as well as those generally prevailing in the area for similar properties. However, unusual swings in the local market may be caused by temporary business recessions or booms. Or increased competition may be in the offing because of construction under way. In such cases it is the responsibility of the appraiser to apply common sense to the vacancy estimate. Also, if the reconstructed operating statement is based on market rentals significantly higher than the current rents being charged, vacancy will probably increase over the current level.

Reconstructing Expenses

As noted, there are two typical problems with actual expense statements. The first is the inclusion of expense categories that reflect the owner's particular financing and income tax costs. These expenses must be deleted. Examples include loan interest, loan principal, income taxes, and depreciation.

The second major problem with actual expense statements is the frequent need to adjust the actual expenses reported. One adjustment is to add for expenses not yet paid, such as delinquent taxes. Another adjustment is to prorate any actual payments for insurance premiums or service contracts for more than a year's coverage. Still another reason is to add dollar amounts for expenses that do not involve any dollars in this particular owner's operations. One example is the cost of any free living units provided for the resident manager, mentioned earlier. Another example occurs when the owner performs all the maintenance personally so that the only historical maintenance expense was for materials.

Comparing Expenses with Industry Standards

As reasonable as the owner-reported expenses may seem, it is still advisable to compare them, category by category, with amounts reported for similar properties in the area and with industry norms. Industry experiences are usually reported either as a percentage of the gross income or as a cost per square foot of rentable area. Published expense reports are available from the Institute of Real Estate Management, the Building Owners and Managers Association (BOMA), the Urban Land Institute, and other management groups. After comparing the actual building expenses with industry experience, the appraiser will make an effort to project realistic expenses for the subject property. The final estimate should not only reflect the prices of labor, material, services, utilities, and taxes in the area, but also the unique characteristics of the property under appraisal.

SUMMARY

The income approach is designed to measure the income-production capability of a property or to find what we refer to as the present worth of future benefits. Since the benefits of owning income property may be both tangible and intangible, the method to be used may depend upon the size and type of property.

Larger residential-income properties and most commercial or industrial properties are bought primarily for their income-producing ability. In such properties the income approach is relied upon heavily. The principal ingredients of the income approach are a reliable estimate of income accruing to the property and a tool for converting that estimate to an indication of value for the property. The simplest form of an income approach is use of a gross income multiplier (GIM). Sales of comparable properties are examined to derive multiples of gross income at which the properties were exchanged. By a process of comparison, an appropriate estimated GIM is developed for the subject property. The estimated gross income for the subject property is multiplied by its GIM to derive an indication of value. Since it deals with gross income, the GIM technique belongs in the sales comparison approach to value. The income approach, in contrast, deals primarily with net income—the dollars remaining to the owner after paying all charges associated with operating and owning the property. The net income is converted to an indication of market value by a process of capitalization. In its simplest form, called direct capitalization, the net income is divided by a capitalization rate. The capitalization rate is developed by the appraiser through the analysis of market data, principally the sales of income-producing properties similar to the one being appraised. Some capitalization methods involve more than one rate, as will be shown in Chapter 14.

The income approach consists of the following steps:

1. Estimate the gross annual income the property is capable of producing.
2. Estimate typical vacancy and collection or rent losses.
3. Subtract vacancy and collection losses from gross income to arrive at the effective gross income.
4. Subtract annual expenses to arrive at estimated net income.
5. Select the method of capitalization appropriate to the valuation problem, and derive the applicable capitalization rates from market analysis.
6. Capitalize the net income into an indicated value by the income approach.

Property expenses are customarily estimated in three categories: operating expenses, fixed expenses, and reserves for replacement. Operating expenses include such familiar items as management costs, cost of services and utilities, and building and grounds maintenance. Since major building repairs occur at uneven intervals, average rather than actual annual expenditures are projected under building maintenance. Insurance premiums and property taxes usually make up what are known as fixed expenses. Reserve for replacements is the category to cover annual allocations for the eventual cost to replace short-lived building components such as floor coverings, roof, and mechanical building equipment.

In written appraisal reports, a reconstructed operating statement is often included to support the income approach conclusion. Actual historical numbers for both income and expense may need correcting. The projected rental schedule should reflect the rent level of competing properties in the area, with rent assigned to all units, including the owner's or manager's apartment. Expenses must be limited to those necessary to operate the property. Personal expenses, such as interest and depreciation, are deleted for appraisal purposes. In appraisals, expense estimates should be checked against the amounts reported for similar properties in the area or against known industry standards.

IMPORTANT TERMS AND CONCEPTS

Contract rent	Operating expenses
Economic rent	Overage rent
Effective gross rent	Percentage lease
Excess rent	Reconstructed operating statement
Fixed expenses	Rent roll
Gross income	Reserves for replacement
Gross rent, or income, multiplier	Return of investment
Income capitalization	Return on investment
Income forecast	Service income
Intangible benefits	Step-up, or graduated, lease
Market rent	Straight, or flat, lease
Minimum or base rent	Tangible benefits

REVIEWING YOUR UNDERSTANDING

1. Which of the following might be classified as tangible rather than intangible amenities?
    (a) Pride of ownership
    (b) A sense of security
    (c) Free rent
    (d) Work satisfaction

2. Tom Smith has a savings account that just paid a $700 annual dividend. If the declared interest rate was 7%, which of the following represents the amount of the deposit?
    (a) $1,000   (b) $10,000
    (c) $17,000   (d) None of the above

3. An income property renting for $10,000 per year before expenses just sold for $100,000 cash. What was the gross income multiplier?
    (a) $\frac{1}{10}$ or 10%   (b) 5
    (c) 10   (d) None of the above

4. Market rent can be defined as:
    (a) The potential gross rent
    (b) The contract rent
    (c) The average rent
    (d) None of the above

5. Which of the following is an example of a specific expense item rather than a basic expense category?

(a) Reserve for replacement
(b) Property taxes
(c) Operating expenses
(d) Fixed charges or expenses

6. The property under appraisal has a 100% occupancy. What conclusion would you most likely draw if the typical occupancy rate in the area were only 85%?

(a) Advertising is superior
(b) The rents are too high
(c) The rents are too low
(d) Management is better

7. A rent survey reveals that buildings offering one-bedroom units have a considerably lower vacancy factor than those with two-bedroom units. If the subject property includes only units with two bedrooms, the appraisal should probably project:

(a) An average of the vacancy factors for all units surveyed
(b) A higher factor than found in the one-bedroom units
(c) A lower factor than found in the one-bedroom units
(d) The same factor as found in the one-bedroom units

8. An apartment owner spent $2,500 last year to replace five built-in stoves. In a 10-unit apartment house, what annual expense would be projected for replacement if all the units had stoves? Assume a 10-year life for all replacements.

(a) $500.00 (b) $2,500
(c) $10,000 (d) $1,000

9. If market rent is less than contract rent, the difference is known as:

(a) Overage rent
(b) Excess rent
(c) Percentage rent
(d) Capital gain

10. In market value appraisals, which of the following items should be excluded from the expense statement?

(a) Loan interest payments
(b) Necessary current expenses
(c) Projected expenses
(d) None of the above

11. Painting and redecorating of units is an expense that appraisers normally treat as:

(a) An operating expense
(b) A fixed expense
(c) Unnecessary if you have 100% occupancy
(d) Overhead

CHAPTER FOURTEEN

INCOME CAPITALIZATION: RATES AND TECHNIQUES

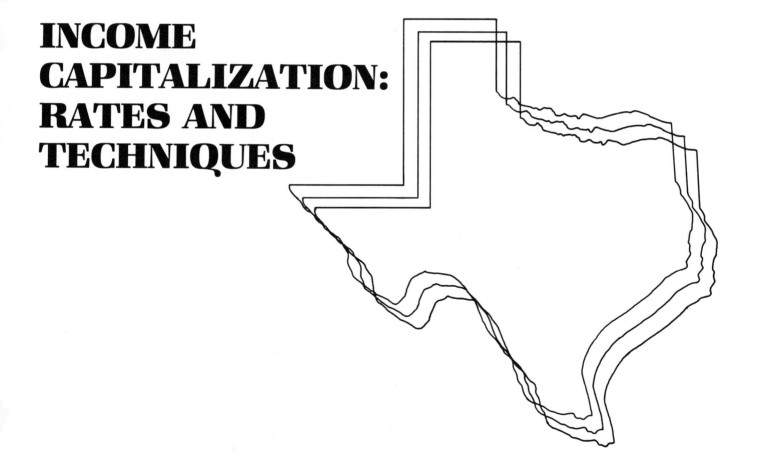

PREVIEW
In the last chapter we outlined the basic steps in the income approach and covered the methods used to estimate income and expenses for investment property. This chapter completes our discussion of the income approach by describing the techniques of income capitalization most widely used today.

When you have completed this chapter, you should be able to:

1. Define income capitalization.

2. List the three primary aspects of an income stream.

3. Define and illustrate direct capitalization.

4. Name and describe at least three methods for developing capitalization rates or discount rates.

5. Understand the principle of discounting future benefits to reflect present value.

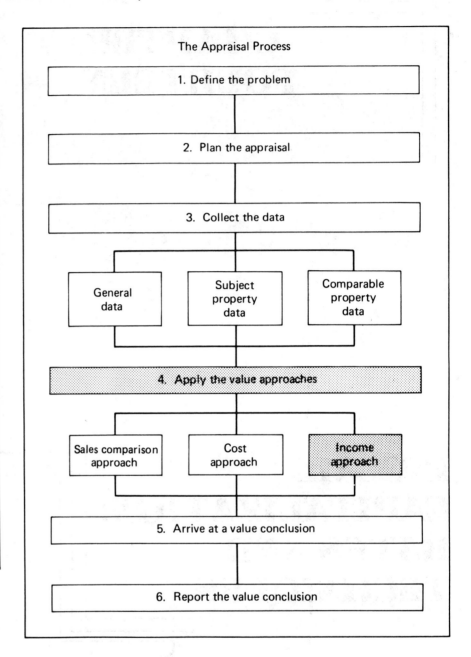

The Appraisal Process

1. Define the problem

2. Plan the appraisal

3. Collect the data

| General data | Subject property data | Comparable property data |

4. Apply the value approaches

| Sales comparison approach | Cost approach | Income approach |

5. Arrive at a value conclusion

6. Report the value conclusion

SECTION 14.1
PURPOSE AND
THEORY OF CAPITALIZATION

We can estimate the value of income property by studying the economic relationship between income and value. Income capitalization is the broad term used to describe this process. A number of income capitalization techniques are available to the appraiser. Some are relatively simple and direct while others are more complex. In actual practice, the preferred technique depends on the nature of the appraisal problem and the specific kinds of market data available.

Simply stated, capitalization is the process of converting a projected stream of income into a lump-sum value on the date of appraisal. We know that a promised future dollar is worth less than a dollar in hand. It follows that income to be received over a number of years is worth less today than the simple total of the dollars to be received. This recognizes a principle known as the time value of money. The capitalization process reflects the time value of money by reducing or discounting future income to its present worth.

All income capitalization techniques focus on the three primary aspects of a projected stream of income (see Fig. 14.1):

Quantity   Amount of income expected to be received.

Quality   Relative risk of the income projection.

Timing   Duration and frequency of the income installments.

The quantity of income is the NOI developed from analysis of income and expenses, which is covered in Chapter 13.

The quality of income refers to the relative desirability of the property in question as compared with other investments. It has particular reference to the reliability of the income stream, or the degree of probability that the expected income will materialize. Frequently it is described as the relative risk of ownership of a given property as compared to other investment opportunities. Other aspects are involved, however. The size and structural quality of the building influences the desirability of the investment. Look at Figure 14.2 and decide which of these possible investments is of higher quality. The interest rate used to discount future benefits to present value is a function of the quality of the investment.

Timing encompasses two important aspects of an income stream: the duration of time over which the income is likely to be received, and the time intervals between the date of investment (or appraisal) and the dates on which the income installments will be received.

As an illustration of the influence of these three aspects on an income stream, consider the following illustration based on a hypothetical income-producing property. Assume that all incomes are to be received at the end of the year, with investment (purchase of the property) occurring at the beginning of year 1. At the end of year 5, the property will be sold for cash, so that the income at that time will consist of *both* periodic income *and*

FIGURE 14.1

return of capital. (The return of capital through sale is called the reversion.) Assume further that the quality of, or risk associated with, the income stream indicates 10% per annum as an appropriate rate of return on invested capital. Discount factors associated with a 10% annual interest rate may be obtained from standard compound interest tables (see Table 14.3) in the column headed "Present Worth of $1".

Table 14.1 is a simple discounted cash flow (DCF) valuation.

TABLE 14.1
Discounted Cash Flow

Year No.	Amount of Income	Discount Factor	Present Value
1	$ 1,000	.9091	$ 909.10
2	1,000	.8264	826.40
3	1,200	.7513	901.56
4	1,300	.6830	887.90
5	14,000	.6209	8,692.60
Totals	$18,500		$12,217.56

Discount factors will be explained more fully a little later. Briefly, the factor of .9091 means that $909.10 is the amount that, deposited today at 10% interest, will be worth $1,000 at the end of one year. Conversely, the right to receive $1,000 after one year has a present value of only $909.10. The farther away we move from the present day, the lower the present value, as reflected by the reducing discount factor. Thus, in the preceding example, the right to receive total proceeds of $18,500 over a five-year period is worth only $12,217.56 today.

Suppose the total proceeds remained unchanged, but the entire amount was receivable at the end of the period. Would the present value be the same? No. It would be $18,500 × .6209, or $11,486.65 ($730.91 less than under the prior schedule). Why? Because receipt of some of the funds is postponed longer, exposing it to the more severe discount associated with time. Thus, not only the *duration* of the income stream, but the *timing* of the income stream is highly significant. What would have been the effect on present value if the rate of return were reduced to 8%? Or increased to 12%? Obviously, the *quality* of the income stream (as reflected in the interest rate) has a major influence on value. Notice in Table 14.2 that as the interest rate goes up, the discount factor goes down.

TABLE 14.2
Interest Rate vs Discount Factor

Year No.	Interest Rate	Discount Factor
5	.08	.6806
5	.09	.6499
5	.10	.6209

In the preceding chapter, income capitalization was introduced with a brief illustration of the direct capitalization method. This method is based on the equation

$$\text{value} = \text{income divided by rate, or } V = \frac{I}{R}$$

Can this method be applied to the problem illustrated above? In looking at the equation, the question immediately arises, "What income?" because five different annual incomes were presented (or five periodic incomes, plus the reversion). Where, in the valuation equation, is the provision for timing of the income stream?

The answers are not difficult. In direct capitalization, only one income amount is used. It is usually the current year's income (although it may be the previous year's, the next year's, or a stabilized average over some period of time). Timing of the income is assumed to be identical to the period contemplated by the rate. That is, if the rate is expressed as per annum, then the income is stated on an annual basis. The duration is an implied infinity. Direct capitalization is sometimes called capitalization in perpetuity because the equation assumes that the income continues forever. Is that unrealistic? Of course it is. But that doesn't invalidate the method.

Investors know that each projected use of real estate will come to an end, but it will be replaced by some other use. In capitalizing into perpetuity, the appraiser is simply saying, "For the foreseeable future, the property is expected to produce approximately x dollars per annum. At some point in the future, the property will be converted to some other use, and that use will probably produce an income comparable to the current projection," and so on. Because of the steep discounts applied to future incomes, the amount of error in such an assumption tends to become negligible. For example, any published compound interest table will reveal that the discount factor applied to the 20th year at 12% per annum is .1037; at the 30th year, .0334; and at the 50th year, .0035.

Capitalization Rate Defined

In the illustration of the DCF method on the preceding page, we used a rate of 10%, or .10, per annum. We called that a rate of return, or a discount rate, not a capitalization rate. (For all practical purposes, terms such as interest rate, risk rate, discount rate, yield rate, and rate of return are synonymous—the distinctions lie in the uses to which the rates are put or the sources from which they are derived.) The discount rate was applied separately to different amounts of income, each occurring at a different time. A capitalization rate (frequently abbreviated as "cap" rate) is generally defined as a single rate that blends all aspects of the property into one fraction, which relates value to income. Because the capitalization rate incorporates into one rate all the elements affecting value of the property, it is frequently called the overall rate (OAR) and is calculated by:

$$\text{overall rate} = \frac{\text{income}}{\text{value}}$$

For example, if an income property producing a current income of $100,000 per year sold for $1,250,000, we could say it sold at "an 8% cap rate based on current earnings." If a new hotel were sold on the day it opened, there would be no data from which to derive current earnings. An investor might predict that the hotel would achieve stabilized income by the end of the third year of $250,000 per annum. If the investor then paid $2 million for the property, the sale could be reported at "a 12.5% cap rate, based on stabilized earnings." What is the cap rate indicated by the data in Table 14.1? If the property sold at the value indicated by the DCF analysis, the cap rate may be calculated as follows, using the first year's income as the criterion:

$$\text{rate} = \frac{\text{income}}{\text{value}}$$

or

$$\text{OAR} = \frac{\$1,000}{12,217.56} = .08185$$

The indicated capitalization rate is 8.19%.

Capitalization rates have become a popular and useful tool for reporting sale prices and comparing properties and transactions. But, as the illustrations in this chapter have demonstrated, the cap rate may serve simply to mask or hide some of the highly significant facts about a given property. As a tool to rank various possible investments or to observe trends in a particular type of property, cap rates can be highly useful, *provided* the properties analyzed are of similar type with comparable patterns of income and subject to similar external market conditions.

It is now time to give closer consideration to the basic components of real property income so as to understand their impact on capitalization rates.

FIGURE 14.2

The Size of the Investment Affects Its Desirability. (a) Courtesy of Doug Frost) (b) Photograph by Carlos Carpenter, courtesy of Tenneco, Inc.

SECTION 14.2 COMPONENTS OF REAL PROPERTY INCOME

Current and Future Returns

In investment properties, current return is the periodic (usually annual) flow of net earnings that we refer to in appraisals as the income stream. Future, or deferred, return is postponed income; the term usually refers to the proceeds available when an investment is resold (the reversion). When real estate is owned free of any debt, the owner's current income consists of the total net income produced by the real property. However, when real estate is mortgaged, the current earnings available to the owner are reduced by the required interest and principal payments to the lender (called debt service). The residue is called cash flow, or cash return to equity (equity is the difference between the total value of the real estate and the total indebtedness against it). "Cash-on-cash" is still another term used to designate this portion of the income stream, since it is the cash return on the owner's cash investment in the property, as distinguished from return on borrowed funds.

The amount of the reversion is also influenced by the mortgage debt. If the property is mortgaged, the proceeds to the owner at reversion are reduced by the balance(s), if any, remaining on the loan(s) secured by the property. If the reversion (net of loans) is greater than the investor's original equity investment, the difference is called equity buildup. Equity buildup results from a combination of appreciation in the property value as a whole, plus the principal payments, if any, made on the loan. Of course, the equity buildup could be negative if the property declined in value and the amount of the decline is more than enough to offset any reduction in the loan principal.

The opportunity to raise part of the funds to purchase real estate through debt is another advantage of real estate over other types of investments. This advantage is called leverage. The term is based on the investor's ability to raise his/her overall rate of return through using the lender's money. A good example of how leverage works is its effect on the reversion. Assume an investor purchases an income property for $1 million, paying 20% cash and mortgaging 80% of the purchase price. In five years the property has appreciated 20%. No principal payments are made on the loan. The investor's equity appreciation is 20% of $1 million or 100% of the original equity investment. The loan balance is unchanged. Thus, a 20%

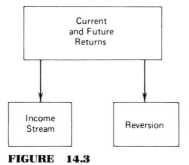

FIGURE 14.3

increase in the total value of the property translates into 100% increase in the equity investor's position.

	Original Purchase	Sale After 5 Years
Total price	$1,000,000	$1,200,000
Less loan	800,000	800,000
Value of equity	200,000	400,000

Of course, leverage can work both ways. If the net income from the property is not sufficient to pay debt service, the equity investor will suffer negative cash flow. In some cases this could wipe out the anticipated gains.

The preceding comments and illustrations ignored the potential effect of federal income taxes. The impact of these taxes can greatly alter the profitability of a real estate investment, for better or for worse. Taxes affect different investors in different ways, and different tax rules apply to different kinds of properties. Therefore, the appraiser must be careful to state clearly any assumptions in the appraisal based on tax considerations. Normally, unless the client has requested analysis of tax impact, the appraisal is made on a before-tax basis. An after-tax analysis, because it must be based on the tax status of some individual or class of individuals, is usually considered a counseling assignment rather than an appraisal.

The analysis of income tax rules and their effect on real property investments is beyond the scope of this book, and the rules are constantly being changed by legislation, regulation, and court rulings. Suffice it to say that the after-tax analysis of income may turn an apparently mediocre investment into a very attractive one for people in high tax brackets.

Yield Versus Recapture

So far, we have pointed out that the financial returns from investments consist of both current income and future reversions, as shown in Fig. 14.4. In the previous chapter we also demonstrated that returns from real estate can be divided into return *on* the investment (called interest) and return *of* the investment (called reversion). Now we must add yet another observation: Cash returns from real estate, whether from current income or reversion, may consist of either return of, or return on, investment, or both at the same time. Figure 14.4 shows the various terms used to describe these two types of investment returns. It should be noted that the term yield is

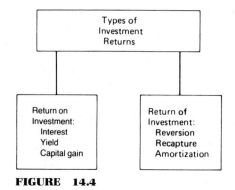

FIGURE   14.4

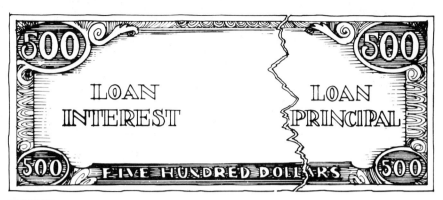

FIGURE 14.5
Where the Loan Payment Goes

generally understood to mean the investor's total net profit on invested capital (comparable to the yield-to-maturity, as applied to bonds). The yield is a weighted average return over an entire ownership term or projection period (called the investment horizon).

The return *of* (or recapture of) investment capital out of current income can best be illustrated in the field of finance. A mortgage loan is a form of real estate investment. In an amortized loan the debt service includes payments of both principal and interest (see Fig. 14.5). The lender's outstanding investment is recovered through the principal portion of the mortgage payments. This accomplishes return *of* the investment. The interest portion of the payments accomplishes return *on* the investment. If the loan is paid off with a lump-sum principal payment, this compares with the reversion that occurs when a real estate investment is sold.

In a conventional real estate investment, the major part of recapture is generally accomplished through the sale of the investment. In some cases, however, it is appropriate to think of part of the recapture as occurring through periodic income earned by the investment. (See Figure 14.6.) It is not necessary to isolate recapture from other proceeds in order to understand it. It is necessary to point out, however, that yield, or profit, on real estate cannot occur until recapture has been accomplished.

SECTION 14.3
INCOME
CAPITALIZATION TECHNIQUES

Four types of income capitalization are presented in this section. The first is a family of techniques called the residual techniques. They are of more historic interest than current usefulness. The second is direct capitaliza-

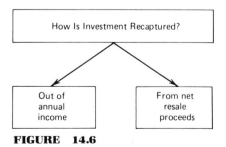

FIGURE 14.6

tion, and the third is discounted cash flow, both of which have already been introduced. The fourth type of income capitalization is annuity capitalization, a special kind of discounted cash flow.

Residual Techniques of Capitalization

Payments to lenders arising from the terms of mortgages can clearly be allocated between principal (return of investment) and interest (return on investment). Unfortunately, the returns on real estate cannot be so clearly distinguished. Appraisers formerly tried to isolate interest from recapture in real estate revenues, developing so-called residual techniques of capitalization.

The land residual technique, for instance, isolated the dollar return allocable to land (or residual to the land). This return was called interest and was capitalized into a presumed value of the land. The theory underlying the residual techniques held that recapture was not necessary for money invested in land because land does not depreciate. Recapture could be accomplished through sale of the land. The value of the land was presumed to remain constant.

The building residual technique worked in the reverse way. Income presumed to be attributable to the building was separated out of net income and capitalized into an implied value of the building. Dollar returns attributable to the building included both interest and recapture because the theory held that the building was a "wasting asset." That is, the value of the building was steadily declining because of deterioration and obsolescence. Allocating a part of the income to recapture permitted the investor to recover the funds invested in the building before its value had declined to zero.

The residual techniques were developed during periods of market stability and little or no inflation—conditions that have not been observed for many years. These techniques were based on assumptions no longer held valid by most observers, such as the notion that land held its value constant over long periods of time. Another assumption held that typical investors expected to recover their investment in buildings over a rather long investment horizon, corresponding to the estimated physical or economic life of the improvements—say, 30 to 50 years. While such assumptions were always questionable on logical grounds, they have been rendered untenable by the constraints of contemporary income tax laws. Recent research indicates that most investments in income-producing real estate are recycled through sale or exchange every eight to ten years. The reason: most of the income tax advantages of holding real estate are consumed during the early years of investment. Therefore, it pays investors to sell, take their gains, and move into a new investment cycle.

A simple illustration of the residual techniques will serve to illustrate the methodology and rationale behind them, as well as to expose their weakness in contemporary practice. The following facts are assumed:

Market value of land as vacant	$ 200,000
Depreciated value of improvements	800,000
Total value of property	1,000,000
Interest rate	7.5%
Economic life of improvements (years)	40
Recapture rate (1/40)	2.5%
Net operating income (NOI)	$ 95,000

To apply the land residual technique, the appraiser was required to know (or believe that he or she knew) all the preceding information except the land value. For the building residual, the same requirement held, except that the appraiser "knew" the value of the land but not of the improvements. The calculations are shown in Examples 14.1 and 14.2.

Example 14.1
Land Residual Technique

NOI	$ 95,000
Less Capital Requirements of Building:	
$800,000 @10% (7.5% Interest +	
2.5% Recapture)	80,000
Income Residual to Land	$ 15,000
Capitalized @ Interest Rate of 7.5%	
$15,000/.075 = Value of Land	200,000
Add Value of Improvements	800,000
Indicated Value of Property	$1,000,000

Example 14.2
Building Residual Technique

NOI	$ 95,000
Less Capital Requirements of Land:	
$200,000 @7.5%	15,000
Income Residual to Building	$ 80,000
Capitalized @ Building Capitalization	
Rate of 10% (7.5%+2.5%)	
80,000/.10 = Value of Building	800,000
Add Value of Land	200,000
Indicated Value of Property	$1,000,000

Note that the land capitalization rate was the interest rate without provision for recapture. The building capitalization rate was the sum of the interest rate and the building recapture rate which, in turn, was the reciprocal of the economic life of the building.

While these techniques are of historic interest, and they do tend to illustrate the principle that returns to real estate are composed of different components, they are no longer in common use. In addition to the problems already raised, the techniques rely on still more unsupportable assumptions, such as:

1. Net operating income is constant and level. (Mathematically, the assumption is that income declines each year in an amount precisely equal to the product of interest rate × recapture installment.)

2. Depreciation of buildings is inevitable and occurs at a constant and level rate for all buildings of similar types, while land value remains constant.

Many years of monetary inflation (accompanied by rapidly rising real estate values and building costs), a shrinking supply of choice land, and other factors have taught us how obsolete such assumptions are. During most of the past 20 years, building costs have risen at a faster rate than the rate at which building values have declined due to deterioration and obsolescence. That is, the net values of most buildings have risen with the passage of time, even though deterioration was occurring. What's more, incomes are anything but stable. Landlords now prefer short-term leases so that they can keep ahead of inflation. Incomes can vary widely from year to year because of such factors as percentage rents, adjustments based on the Consumer Price Index, expense pass-throughs, and other variables.

In addition to these conditions, simplistic equations do not allow for such real-life variables as fluctuating income and expenses, occasional capital replacements, and the effect of financing or refinancing.

Mortgage/Equity Technique of Capitalization

To deal with the failure to consider effects of financing, a new type of residual technique came into wide use during the 1960s and early 1970s—the mortgage/equity technique. Special tables based on complex mathematical equations were developed by L. W. ("Pete") Ellwood, chief appraiser for New York Life Insurance Company. These tables permitted the appraiser to separate the overall capitalization rate into the following components:

1. Debt service
2. Impact of appreciation/depreciation
3. Return on equity

This method could be called an equity residual technique since it isolated the return on equity as a separate component of property income. The cash flow after debt service was treated as the residual. This residual was capitalized by an equity capitalization rate to arrive at the implied value of the equity. When the mortgage debt was added back to the equity, the value of the property was accounted for.

In its simplest form, the mortgage/equity technique can be illustrated as follows. Assume that a property has an NOI of $50,000. The property is subject to a mortgage loan with an unpaid balance of $385,000 and an annual debt service of $38,770. This leaves a residual to equity of $11,230. Research indicates that an appropriate equity capitalization rate is 9%. Following the universal capitalization equation, we achieve the following results:

$$\text{value} = \frac{\text{income}}{\text{rate}}$$

Substituting,

$$\text{value of equity} = \frac{\text{equity residual}}{\text{equity cap rate}}$$

or

$$\text{value of equity} = \frac{\$11,230}{.09} = \$124,778$$

The value of the equity is $124,778. Adding back the mortgage balance of $385,000, we get an indicated property value of $509,778, which we might round to $510,000.

Alternatively, we can compute directly an overall capitalization rate by blending the mortgage and equity components, using a technique called the band of investment. Think of the components of the capitalization rate as layers of a cake. The whole cake is composed of different layers, or bands. If lenders are typically lending 75% of value, then the layer of the cap rate representing debt is 75% of the cake. The equity portion is 25%. We speak of these portions as weights.

The overall capitalization rate consists of two weighted components under the theory of the mortgage/equity technique: the equity capitalization rate and the mortgage capitalization rate. The mortgage cap rate is actually the loan constant, which is the annual fraction of the loan required to repay the loan under the lender's terms. For example, to repay a loan over 25 years at 9% interest, the monthly constant, as derived from financial tables or from a financial calculator, is .00839196. Multiplying this constant by 12 gives an annual constant of .100704. This means that for each dollar loaned, the annual payment is a little more than 10 cents (we are actually speaking of the sum of 12 monthly payments—constants are stated in annual terms because net income and return to equity are normally stated in annual terms).

Each band of the investment is then weighted and the weighted components are added to produce the capitalization rate. Example 14.3 illustrates the development of an overall cap rate under the mortgage/equity theory, using the band of investment method. The assumptions are the same as those used in the equity residual technique.

Example 14.3
Mortgage/Equity Technique

Component	Weight	Required Return	Weighted Rate
Equity	.25	.090000	.022500
Loan	.75	.100704	.075528
Total	1.00		.098028

The indicated overall rate is .097728, which we might round to .098. The value of the property is then calculated by means of direct capitalization, using the familiar equation:

$$\text{value} = \frac{\text{income}}{\text{rate}}$$

Substituting,

$$\text{value of the property} = \frac{\text{total net income}}{\text{overall cap rate}}$$

or

$$\text{value of the property} = \frac{50,000}{.098} = \$510,204$$

Note the difference between this example and the preceding one. In the first instance, the value of the equity was independently estimated, applying an equity capitalization rate to the income residual to equity. The mortgage balance was added to obtain an estimate of property value. In the second example, an overall capitalization rate was applied to the total property income to obtain an estimate of value for the total property, consisting of both debt and equity.

Further refinements in the mortgage/equity technique involved adding additional weighted components into the overall rate to allow for equity buildup through loan amortization, as well as change in value of the reversion through appreciation or depreciation. These advanced methodologies are widely known as the Ellwood techniques because they were popularized by Pete Ellwood through his published tables and frequent lectures and articles on the subject. Ellwood developed the concepts and tables primarily as analytical tools to aid him and his staff in reviewing loan applications submitted to his company. His formulations also permitted explicit weightings in the cap rate for changes in periodic income through complex J factors.

The mortgage/equity techniques were a considerable advancement over the older residual techniques. They were much more realistic in terms of their ability to account for fluctuating income. During the period of roughly 1960 to 1975, long-term mortgages with fixed interest rates and level amortized payments were widely available. Correspondingly, the Ellwood techniques were adopted by thousands of appraisers and mortgage bankers. Incomes were more stable and inflation rates were relatively modest compared to the era that followed. Sophisticated mortgage/equity analysis was particularly well suited to that period.

But problems remained. The mortgage equity techniques still presume some sort of pattern to income, either level or increasing/decreasing at constant ratios or by constant amounts. No provision is made for changes in the underlying asset base, such as the replacement of a roof or a partial sale of the property five years into the ownership period. The method presumes an equity investment coupled with a mortgage debt. In the current investment era, many investments are made on an all-cash basis, particularly by pension funds and foreign investors. Joint ventures are arranged in which a financial partner (such as a life insurance company) provides all the cash while the development partner receives an equity interest for providing development expertise. Ellwood's mathematics ignores the effect of federal income tax and makes no provision for such modern financing innovations as "equity kickers" (participation in the developer's profits by the lender) or "bullet loans" (nonamortizing loans that fall due before the end of the normal investment cycle). These shortcomings, emphasized by rapid changes occurring in real estate finance techniques and federal income tax laws, have led many appraisers to rely on a combination of two income capitalization techniques: direct capitalization and discounted cash flow (DCF) analysis.

Direct capitalization was introduced in Chapter 13 and was touched on earlier in this chapter. A simple illustration of DCF analysis was presented in Table 14.1; the methodology of DCF is not new, but the availability of high-speed computers has made it more practical, as well as more responsive to current needs. Detailed presentations of both techniques follow.

Direct Capitalization

For quick analysis and preliminary valuation opinions, many appraisers and investors utilize direct capitalization with an overall rate (OAR). The OAR is derived from familiarity with, or continuing analysis of, transactions occurring daily in the real estate market. It is similar to rates relied on by securities dealers, such as price/earnings ratios, dividend yields, and yield-to-maturity. Methods of computing the OAR will be discussed in Section 14.4.

Direct capitalization is the simplest form of capitalization, based on the now-familiar equation,

$$\text{value} = \frac{\text{income}}{\text{rate}}$$

Income in the equation is the NOI for the current year. Rate is an OAR derived from the market. All the variables in the property, including financing or the lack of it, age and obsolescence of the improvements, probability of appreciation or depreciation, are presumed to be reflected in the NOI and the OAR.

Advantages of direct capitalization include its simplicity and its wide use among both sophisticated and novice investors and appraisers. Applied to large numbers of properties or transactions, the method yields discernible patterns of investor behavior and affords a generally reliable guide to value. When the OAR is derived from highly reliable and consistent sources, and when accurate projections of NOI can be made, the direct capitalization technique may be as accurate as any other.

The chief disadvantage of direct capitalization is also its simplicity. Although the rate reflects every individual variation in a given property or transaction, the influence of any individual factor, such as financing or expectation of capital appreciation, is not separately measurable. Therefore, in the hands of unqualified analysts, direct capitalization can develop highly misleading results.

As an example of direct capitalization, suppose you are appraising a 50-unit apartment property. Occupancy is stable at about 92%, which is typical for the neighborhood. Your analysis of recent income and expense statements on the property, confirmed by discussions with experienced property managers, has helped you project an NOI for the coming year of $150,000. Market research has turned up three recent sales of similar properties in the area, with the following statistics:

Sale Property Number	Annual NOI	Sale Price	Cap Rate
1	$180,000	$2,010,000	.0896
2	167,500	1,850,000	.0905
3	160,000	1,750,000	.0914

The capitalization rates were derived from the sales using the following variation of the universal valuation equation:

$$\text{rate} = \frac{\text{income}}{\text{value}}$$

For example, in sale No. 1, the

$$\text{rate} = \frac{\$180,000}{\$2,010,000} = .0896$$

Notice that the cap rates run from .0896 to .0914 but they cluster around .0900, or 9%. You conclude that an overall capitalization rate of 9% is a reasonable expression of the market for the property being appraised. Substituting in the value equation (value = income/rate),

$$\text{value} = \frac{\$150,000}{.09} = \$1,666,667$$

which you may round to $1,675,000, or $33,500 per unit.

Discounted Cash Flow Technique

When value or investment decisions must be based on the most precise data available, and when the complexities of the property defy a simple analysis, the discounted cash flow, or DCF, technique is a requirement.

DCF is based on the mathematics of compound interest. All appraisers should be thoroughly familiar with those mathematics. They begin with the equation:

$$S^n = (1+i)^n$$

where S is the future value of 1 invested for n periods at the effective interest rate i. For example, what is the future value of $1 invested for 5 years at an interest rate of 10%, compounded annually? The solution is:

$$S^n = (1 + .10)^5$$

or

$$1.10 \times 1.10 \times 1.10 \times 1.10 \times 1.10 = 1.61051$$

To know the future value of any sum so invested, the amount invested should be multiplied by S^n. Thus, the future value of $1,000 invested for 5 years at 10% per annum is $1,000 × 1.61051, or $1,610.51.

To find the present value of $1, with receipt postponed for 5 years, assuming a 10% annual compounding rate, we need only take the reciprocal of S^n, or $1/S^n$, which, in this illustration is $1/1.61051$ or .620921. Thus, the promise of $1,000 to be received at the end of 5 years is worth only $620.92. Obviously, the future value is influenced by the magnitude of the interest rate i and the length of time n. The higher the rate is and the longer the time, the more the future value is and, conversely, the less the present value of a future receipt.

The interest rate is a function of two factors: risk and the time value of money. Risk includes consideration of such factors as inflation and the probability of the expected amount being returned. For real estate, risk includes such considerations as the credit rating of the tenants in shopping centers and office buildings. For a motel, it could include the risk of future competition or a rerouting of a major highway.

The effective interest rate is the nominal annual interest rate divided by the number of compounding periods in a year. For example, if interest is to be compounded quarterly at 12% per annum, the effective rate is one-fourth of 12% or 3%. In practice, most appraisers treat income as being received annually (at the end of the year). While some receipts may come in monthly, or even daily, many of the expenses are paid annually, and the true annual NOI can be known only at the end of the year.

The Six Functions of the Dollar

The appraiser is not required to know the formulas or compute the mathematics every time a compound interest problem is encountered. Modern pocket calculators can quickly compute the appropriate factors. In addition, standard reference works publish tables for a wide range of rates and time periods. Such tables are often arranged in six columns, displaying factors associated with "the six functions of the dollar," or the six most commonly used compound interest functions. The six functions are:

1. *Future worth of $1*   The amount to which $1 will accumulate.

2. *Future worth of $1 per period*   The amount to which periodic installments of $1 each will accumulate.

3. *Sinking fund factor*   The amount that, deposited at the end of each period, will accumulate to $1.

4. *Present worth of $1*   The present value of $1, with receipt postponed to the end of a future period.

5. *Present worth of $1 per period*   The present value of a series of future payments.

6. *Installment to amortize*   The amount that, paid at the end of each period, will pay off $1, with interest on the unpaid balance.

A sample set of tables follows (see Table 14.3); it gives factors for the six functions at a 10% interest rate for 1 through 40 periods.

TABLE 14.3
Compound Interest Tables: Six Functions of the Dollar

	1	2	3	4	5	6
Number of Periods	Future Worth of $1	Future Worth of $1 per Period	Sinking Fund Factor	Present Worth of $1	Present Worth of $1 per Period	Installment to Amortize
1	1.100000	1.000000	1.000000	0.909091	0.909091	1.100000
2	1.210000	2.100000	0.476190	0.826446	1.735537	0.576190
3	1.331000	3.310000	0.302115	0.751315	2.486852	0.402115
4	1.464100	4.641000	0.215471	0.683013	3.169865	0.315471
5	1.610510	6.105100	0.163797	0.620921	3.790787	0.263797
6	1.771561	7.715610	0.129607	0.564474	4.355261	0.229607
7	1.948717	9.487171	0.105405	0.513158	4.868419	0.205405
8	2.143589	11.435888	0.087444	0.466507	5.334926	0.187444
9	2.357948	13.579477	0.073641	0.424098	5.759024	0.173641
10	2.593742	15.937425	0.062745	0.385543	6.144567	0.162745
11	2.853117	18.531167	0.053963	0.350494	6.495061	0.153963
12	3.138428	21.384284	0.046763	0.318631	6.813692	0.146763
13	3.452271	24.522712	0.040779	0.289664	7.103356	0.140779
14	3.797498	27.974983	0.035746	0.263331	7.366687	0.135746
15	4.177248	31.772482	0.031474	0.239392	7.606080	0.131474
16	4.594973	35.949730	0.027817	0.217629	7.823709	0.127817
17	5.054470	40.544703	0.024664	0.197845	8.021553	0.124664
18	5.559917	45.599173	0.021930	0.179859	8.201412	0.121930
19	6.115909	51.159090	0.019547	0.163508	8.364920	0.119547
20	6.727500	57.274999	0.017460	0.148644	8.513564	0.117460
21	7.400250	64.002499	0.015624	0.135131	8.648694	0.115624
22	8.140275	71.402749	0.014005	0.122846	8.771540	0.114005
23	8.954302	79.543024	0.012572	0.111678	8.883218	0.112572
24	9.849733	88.497327	0.011300	0.101526	8.984744	0.111300
25	10.834706	98.347059	0.010168	0.092296	9.077040	0.110168
26	11.918177	109.181765	0.009159	0.083905	9.160945	0.109159
27	13.109994	121.099942	0.008258	0.076278	9.237223	0.108258
28	14.420994	134.209936	0.007451	0.069343	9.306567	0.107451
29	15.863093	148.630930	0.006728	0.063039	9.369606	0.106728
30	17.449402	164.494023	0.006079	0.057309	9.426914	0.106079
31	19.194342	181.943425	0.005496	0.052099	9.479013	0.105496
32	21.113777	201.137767	0.004972	0.047362	9.526376	0.104972
33	23.225154	222.251544	0.004499	0.043057	9.569432	0.104499
34	25.547670	245.476699	0.004074	0.039143	9.608575	0.104074
35	28.102437	271.024368	0.003690	0.035584	9.644159	0.103690
36	30.912681	299.126805	0.003343	0.032349	9.676508	0.103343
37	34.003949	330.039486	0.003030	0.029408	9.705917	0.103030
38	37.404343	364.043434	0.002747	0.026735	9.732651	0.102747
39	41.144778	401.447778	0.002491	0.024304	9.756956	0.102491
40	45.259256	442.592556	0.002259	0.022095	9.779051	0.102259

Note: Interest rate: 10% compounded annually.

Application of the DCF Technique

The first step in applying DCF is to forecast the expected income over the time period of the analysis. This may involve sophisticated analysis of leases, imputing renewal rates as of future dates, and allowing for turnover vacancy, as well as redecorating expense and possible leasing commissions. Or the appraiser may be satisfied that an average annual increase in net income of, say, 5% will be an adequate form of forecast. In any event, projections are made for each element of income and expense for each year in the projection period.

For purposes of DCF analysis, income means cash received; expense means cash disbursed. Conventional accounting distinctions between operating expenses and capital expenditures do not apply. Expenses may include capital additions or replacements. Income may include sale of partial interests, such as surplus land. If the property is financed, cash outlays would include principal and interest payments. If the analysis applies on an after-tax basis, the expenses include federal income taxes. These, in turn, would depend on such variable factors as the mortgage interest, allowable depreciation write-off, and the investor's marginal tax rate (the rate paid on the last dollar added to taxable income).

Example 14.4
Calculation of Cash Flow

Gross Rents		$100,000
Less Operating Expenses		−35,000
Net Operating Income (NOI)		65,000
Less Mortgage Payments (Principal and Interest)		−23,000
Net Cash Flow Before Taxes		42,000
Less Federal Income Taxes:		
NOI	65,000	
Less:		
Mortgage Interest	−21,000	
Depreciation	−35,000	
Taxable Income	9,000	
Taxes Due @ 40%		−3,600
Cash Flow After Taxes		38,400

If the property shows a net loss for income tax purposes, the analysis will reflect tax savings as an additional cash flow. This assumes that the investor has other taxable income against which to offset the losses on the property being analyzed, thus reducing the investor's overall tax burden. The final net cash remaining (whether positive or negative) is referred to as the cash flow for the year in question. To distinguish it from cash generated by a sale of the property, it might be called cash flow from operations.

Obviously, a detailed DCF analysis can be quite sophisticated and demanding. Frequently, special computer programs will be required to analyze future income properly. Several days or even weeks may be involved in assembling the pertinent information and testing it for accuracy and reasonableness.

The second step in DCF analysis is estimating the cash proceeds generated by a sale of the property and the expected time of sale. That is, the appraiser must form an opinion as to the likely selling price of the property and the most probable time of sale. (Some DCF techniques permit an assumption of sale at the end of each year of the projection so that the various alternatives can be compared). The future resale value is usually based on a simple valuation formula associated with the purchase of the property. For example, if the property was purchased at a multiple of 6 times gross income, the future estimated price might be based on the same multiple of future expected income. Or, if income is projected to increase at 5% per year, perhaps the property will also grow in value by 5% per year. Many appraisers will feel it wise to dampen future expectations to give weight to the advancing age and obsolescence of the property. For example, if the property were purchased at an overall rate of 9%, perhaps the resale in 10 years should be projected on the basis of a 10% OAR.

At any rate, the future resale value of the property should be reduced by selling expenses, remaining balance due on loans, and capital gains taxes, if appropriate. The resulting estimate of net proceeds may be referred to as cash flow from disposition and should be added to the cash flow from operations for the year of the sale to arrive at total cash flow for that year.

The final step in applying DCF technique is to estimate the appropriate interest, or discount rate. Methods for this will be discussed in a later part of the chapter. The value of the property, under DCF theory, is the sum of the discounted cash flows for the projection period. The equation is:

$$\text{value} = \left(CF_1 \times \frac{1}{S^1}\right) + \left(CF_2 \times \frac{1}{S^2}\right) + \ldots \left(CF_n \times \frac{1}{S^n}\right)$$

Example 14.5
Property Value Under DCF Theory

Let's consider an example. Assume that a DCF analysis is to be conducted on a single-tenant property on a pretax basis. The tenant's rent will escalate each year at the same rate as the Consumer Price Index. The property is subject to an interest-only mortgage, which will be paid off when the property is sold. The basic facts are:

Income Year 1	$100,000
Operating Expenses, Year 1	20,000
Estimated Annual Increase in CPI	5%
Estimated Annual Increase in Expenses	5%
Projection Period in Years	5
Amount of Mortgage	600,000
Annual Mortgage Interest Rate	11%
Discount Rate	10%

The DCF projection is laid out in rows or columns corresponding to the number of years in the projection. Each item to be included is projected for each year, based on the appraiser's forecast. Outlays are subtracted from incomes to arrive at the net cash flow for each year. The net cash flow is then discounted to the date of the appraisal (sometimes called "time zero"). The indicated value of the real estate is the sum of the discounted cash flows (see Table 14.4).

Note that for year 5 the discount factor was applied to the sum of the cash flow from operations and the cash flow from disposition. Since all proceeds were net of the loan requirements, the preliminary discounted value of $316,414 pertained to the equity interest only. By adding back the mortgage amount, we arrived at the total value of the property. What was

TABLE 14.4
Discounted Cash Flow Analysis

	Year 1	Year 2	Year 3	Year 4	Year 5
Gross Income	100,000	105,000	110,250	115,763	121,551
Expenses	20,000	21,000	22,050	23,152	24,310
NOI	80,000	84,000	88,200	92,611	97,241
Interest	66,000	66,000	66,000	66,000	66,000
Cash Flow from Operations	14,000	18,000	22,200	26,611	31,241
Proceeds of Sale					972,410
Less Balance of Mortgage					600,000
Cash Flow from Disposition					372,410
Total Cash Flow for Year	14,000	18,000	22,200	26,611	403,651
Discount Factor	.90909	.82645	.75131	.68301	.62092
Present Value	12,727	14,876	16,679	18,175	250,635
Total Present Value (Columns 1–5)					313,093
Plus Mortgage					600,000
Total Indicated Market Value of Property					913,093
				Rounded to	915,000

the overall rate indicated by the DCF calculation? To find out, we simply divide the *first* year's NOI by the value developed by the DCF analysis:

$$\text{rate} = \frac{\text{income}}{\text{value}}$$

or

$$\text{OAR} = \frac{80,000}{915,000} = .08743 \text{ or, say, } 8.75\%.$$

One might ask why the OAR of 8.75% differed from the interest rate of 10%. The interest rate reflected today's value of a specific cash flow postponed to a future date. The OAR is a composite rate. It includes the weighted effect of future increases in cash flows and sales proceeds. An investor might reason as follows: "I want a 10% average return on my investment. Looking at this particular investment, I expect the income to rise each year for five years, at which time I intend to sell the property at a profit. Pricing the property to yield slightly less than 9% on current income should produce the 10% yield I am looking for over a five-year holding period."

What would have been the effect on the OAR of a higher mortgage interest rate? Of a higher annual increase in income—or of expenses? By thinking through the implications of these questions, one can begin to appreciate the marvelous sensitivity of the DCF technique to a variety of real-world conditions. By the same token, one can appreciate the absolute necessity of making sound, reliable forecasts based on convincing market data and research.

Annuity Capitalization

An annuity is a constant payment over a certain period of time, such as the rent paid under a long-term lease agreement. Each payment may be identical, or the payments may change by a fixed amount or a fixed ratio. In such cases, a DCF analysis may be done by a shortcut method, using compound interest tables or a financial calculator. In annuity capitalization, the components of a real estate investment are separated into the income stream and the reversion. The owner of a property under a long-term lease has basically two benefits to be valued:

1. The flow of rental payments over the term of the lease.
2. The right to receive the leased property back at the end of the lease period.

The valuation problem could readily be solved by employing the DCF technique to ascertain the present discounted value of each rental payment (cash flow), plus the monetary equivalent of the value of the reversion. The appraiser could compute the present value of each separate rental payment, multiplying the payment by $1/S^n$. Or the appraiser could consult a compound interest table and extract the factor for $1/S^n$ from the column titled Present Worth of $1. However, if the rental payments are uniform, the appraiser may save time with a financial calculator or a set of compound interest tables. The latter will include a column of factors under the heading Present Worth of $1 per Period. (See Table 14.5.) The shortcut formula for valuation of a stream of income with the characteristics of an annuity is:

$$value = income \times factor$$

The second part of the problem is to compute the value of the reversion. The reversion is valued by multiplying the estimated future value of the property (at expiration of the lease) by $1/S^n$ or by a factor taken from a compound interest table under the column Present Worth of $1. The two products (present value of the income stream and present value of the reversion) are added to produce the indicated present value of the property subject to the lease.

Exercise

Compute the value of a five-year lease at $20,000 per year, payable at the end of each year, assuming that the reversion has a future value of

TABLE 14.5
Compound Interest Tables: "Six Functions of the Dollar"

	1	2	3	4	5	6
Number of Periods	Future Worth of $1	Future Worth of $1 per Period	Sinking Fund Factor	Present Worth of $1	Present Worth of $1 per Period	Installment to Amortize
1	1.100000	1.000000	1.000000	0.909091	0.909091	1.100000
2	1.210000	2.100000	0.476190	0.826446	1.735537	0.576190
3	1.331000	3.310000	0.302115	0.751315	2.486852	0.402115
4	1.464100	4.641000	0.215471	0.683013	3.169865	0.315471
5	1.610510	6.105100	0.163797	0.620921	3.790787	0.263797
6	1.771561	7.715610	0.129607	0.564474	4.355261	0.229607

Note: Interest rate: 10% compounded annually.

$210,000 and that the discount rate is 10%. Use the compound interest table (Table 14.5).

Solution
In Table 14.5, look under column 5 and opposite year 5. The factor for the present worth of $1 per period is 3.790787. The present worth of the income stream is $20,000 × 3.790787, or $75,815.74. Now, look under column 4 opposite year 5 to find the present worth of $1 factor, which is .620921. Multiplying the factor by the future reversion value of $210,000 yields a present reversion value of $130,393.41. Adding the two components produces a capitalized value of the leased property equal to $206,209.15, which we might round to $205,000.

SECTION 14.4
SOURCES OF
CAPITALIZATION RATES

Overall Capitalization Rates

As explained in Chapter 13, overall capitalization rates, or OARs, can be derived from actual sales transactions. The appraiser obtains data concerning recent sales of comparable properties and applies the following equation:

$$\text{rate} = \frac{\text{income}}{\text{value}}$$

or, substituting terms to fit the situation,

$$\text{overall rate} = \frac{\text{NOI}}{\text{sale price}}$$

(Section 14.3 contained three examples of this calculation.)

Sometimes buyers and sellers are reluctant to release information concerning net income but will disclose gross income figures. When gross income information is available, a shortcut method may be used. If the appraiser is familiar with typical gross income multiples (GIMs) and net income ratios for the property type involved, the following equation will produce approximate overall rates:

$$\text{OAR} = \frac{\text{net income ratio}}{\text{gross income multiple}}$$

For example, suppose that, for multifamily properties of the type being appraised, GIMs are typically 6.4 and net income is typically 60% of gross. The indicated OAR is calculated as follows:

$$\text{OAR} = \frac{.6}{6.4} = .09375 \text{ or, say, } 9.4\%$$

The appraiser must be careful not to use such shortcuts unless the properties from which the data are derived are similar to each other and to the subject property. It is particularly important that they have similar operating expense patterns, vacancy rates, terms of financing, and ratio of land-to-building values, as well as age and condition.

Band of Investment

In Section 14.3, the concept of weighted layers or bands of investment was introduced. Usually, the layers are those represented by debt and equity. This can be a useful concept in estimating OARs if the property type under appraisal is generally bought and sold through conventional mortgage financing and if investors demonstrate a consistent pattern of yield requirements.

For example, assume that mortgage loans are generally available in the amount of 65% of value at 13% interest with a mortgage constant of .13275. Your research indicates that equity investors are requiring a cash-on-cash return of 9%. An OAR can be estimated as follows:

Component	Constant	Weight	Weighted Rate
Mortgage	.13275	.65	.08629
Equity	.09000	.35	.03150
Total			.11779

Overall rate indicated is, say, 11.8%.

Comparison with Alternative Investments

If other market data are not available or are deemed unreliable or inconsistent, the appraiser may resort to analysis of competing forms of investment, such as stocks, bonds, and other money market media. For example, earnings from stocks of corporations or shares of trusts investing principally in real estate are considered analogous to real estate yields if the property portfolio of the investment firm is not too dissimilar from the property being appraised. Particularly useful is information concerning the earnings of real estate investment trusts (REITs). The REIT is a special investment vehicle designed by Congress to make the advantages of investing in real estate available to large numbers of small investors. The REIT is required to invest most of its assets directly in real estate and to distribute at least 90% of its net earnings directly to the shareholders. Statistics on REIT earnings are available from the National Association of Real Estate Investment Trusts in Washington, D.C.

Other sources of overall rate comparisons include published results of pension funds invested in real estate (such as Prudential Insurance Company of America's PRISA fund and First National Bank of Chicago's Fund F. Periodic reports are available from these funds and others). The American Council of Life Insurance also publishes capitalization rates gleaned from statistics on real estate loans made by the major life insurance companies in the country. These rates are categorized by property types, ages, geographical regions, purpose of loan, and other criteria.

Interest Rates

To use the DCF method, the appraiser must estimate the appropriate interest or discount rate (the terms are interchangeable). This rate should be a pure monetary return rate. Inflation, if any, is provided for in the scheduled cash flows and reversion. Therefore, if the DCF analysis is realistically performed, it should reflect the monetary returns on real estate as compared with other investments, such as corporate or government bonds. Many investors feel that financial returns on high-grade real estate investments should compete on a par with yields on corporate bonds of comparable quality and reliability. Some appraisers like to follow corporate bond rates on a select group of stable corporations like AT&T or General Motors. Based on their "feel" for the market, they fine-tune their estimates of real estate discount rates in line with the movements of such securities. A major advantage of such methodology is the availability of daily rate quotations in financial publications.

For example, assume that AT&T bonds with 15-year maturities are selling to yield 11% per annum. For an appraiser using this methodology, a DCF analysis of a new office building in a large city with a stable office space market might be based on an 11.5% discount rate. At the same time, a small shopping center in a medium-size city with a static economy might be subject to a 13% rate.

In the final analysis, any method used for selecting rates must bear the test of market relevance. Appraisal methodologies should never be so sophisticated that they are out of touch with the real world of buyers and sellers. Appraisers must constantly compare their results with actual transactions and adjust their perceptions as needed. Indeed, the DCF technique can be used to discover rates apparently being realized in actual market transactions. Instead of solving for value by discounting each cash flow at a given rate, the analyst experiments with different rates until the sum of the discounted cash flows equals the price paid for the property. This is accomplished through a tedious process of iteration, or successive trials, until the precise rate is discovered (usually with the aid of a computer). The rate so computed is called the internal rate of return (IRR). Many investors rank investment opportunities by calculating and comparing their respective IRRs.

SUMMARY

Income capitalization is a process of converting anticipated incomes from a parcel of, or interest in, real estate into an indication of the market value of the property. A variety of techniques and procedures are available to the appraiser, although many that were formerly in common use are considered obsolete today. The principle of change is continuously working in real estate markets, requiring appraisers to adapt to new methods of financing and new ways to structure deals.

The former practice of attempting to isolate income into separate components attributable to land and improvements is now considered arbitrary and misguided. Components of debt and equity are still subject to some separate analysis because the terms of debt financing are readily ascertainable (although equity return rates are more difficult to pin down). The Ellwood techniques of mortgage/equity capitalization are suitable for some appraisal problems, particularly where net incomes are highly predictable and debt requirements are consistent over the term of the investment horizon.

The two most common and useful income capitalization techniques today are direct capitalization and discounted cash flow (DCF). The former is the simplest method available, the latter the most complex. Direct capitalization is often employed for quick comparative analysis when precise results are not needed. In those situations in which sales transactions are abundant, accurate information is available, and the sold properties are closely similar to each other and to the subject, direct capitalization may be as reliable as any form of capitalization or, indeed, any approach to value.

In today's highly complex and sophisticated real estate market, dominated in large part by financial institutions and professional investors, discounted cash flow is an essential tool, both for appraisals and analysis of investment opportunities. DCF isolates each component of cash receipts and disbursements over the life of the investment, including the proceeds from final sale of the property. The net cash flow for each year (positive or negative) is then discounted to its present value by the appropriate compound interest factor.

Annuity capitalization is a shortcut method of DCF analysis, utilizing compound interest tables or financial calculators. It is used when incomes follow consistent patterns, permitting the cash flows to be grouped instead of treated individually, as in normal DCF. Formulas and tables are available to process annuities that change at constant amounts or constant ratios, as well as those that remain level. The annuity method is used primarily in valuing property interests associated with long-term leases.

A capitalization rate is a blended rate expressing the direct relationship between income and value. It may be impacted by a number of separate components or influences, including financing, expectations of changing income, and probability of a gain or loss in the reversion. It includes expectation of both return *on* and return *of* investment. An interest rate or discount rate refers only to financial return (return *on* investment). Matters of financing, capital recapture, gain or loss in future value, and income taxes (if applicable) are handled explicitly in DCF analysis.

Capitalization rates may be estimated by analysis of actual market transactions or returns on certain types of securities, by bands of investment, or by Ellwood-type formulations. Direct comparison of market transactions is the most reliable source. Interest rates may be derived by comparison with alternative investment opportunities, such as yields on corporate bonds. They may also be derived from DCF-type analysis of actual properties and transactions, solving for the internal rate of return (IRR).

IMPORTANT TERMS AND CONCEPTS

Annuity capitalization	Discount rate
Band-of-investment method	Ellwood method
Building residual technique	Equity
Capital gains	Interest rate
Cash flow	Internal rate of return
Compound interest	Mortgage constant
Debt service	Overall rate
Direct capitalization	Recapture rate
Discounted cash flow	Reversion

REVIEWING YOUR UNDERSTANDING

1. Income capitalization is the broad term used to describe the process of estimating the value of income property by studying the economic relationship between income and value. This process:

(a) Converts the net income of a property into its equivalent capital value
(b) Reflects the time value of money by reducing or discounting future income to its present worth
(c) Focuses on the present worth of future benefits
(d) All of the above

2. The appraiser's choice of a capitalization technique should be based in part on the nature of the appraisal problem and the type of data available. Which of the following factors would indicate direct capitalization as a good choice?

(a) Complex leases with different expiration dates and renewal terms
(b) An abundance of sales transactions with reliable data on income and expenses
(c) Comparable sales with widely differing ratios of land to building values
(d) A level stream of income from a major national corporation as tenant

3. Assuming ample available data, which of the following methods of estimating a capitalization rate (OAR) is the most reliable?

(a) Band of investment
(b) Stock quotations in the newspaper
(c) Analysis of actual sale of real estate
(d) Compound interest tables

4. How is return *of* the investment accomplished if the investment is a mortgage?

(a) Principle and interest payments
(b) Reversions
(c) Principal payments only
(d) NOI

5. Which of the following capitalization techniques would explicitly recognize the effect on value of an expenditure to resurface the parking lot during the third year of ownership?

(a) DCF
(b) Ellwood
(c) Direct capitalization
(d) Annuity capitalization

6. Which of the methods listed in question 5 would be most appropriate in estimating the value of the landlord's interest in a property leased for 20 years to IBM with the rent increasing 3% per year?

7. An investor has located a shopping center she wants to buy. She has arranged for a long-term mortgage loan in the amount of 60% of the purchase price. The loan constant is .11234. The investor desires a cash-on-cash return of 8%. What is the OAR that reflects what she is willing to pay for the property?

8. A property sold recently for $900,000. Its annual gross income at the time of sale was $150,000. You cannot learn the NOI, but you know that buildings of that sort generally net about 65% of gross income. What is your estimate of the effective OAR at which the property sold?

CHAPTER
FIFTEEN

RECONCILING
THE VALUE
ESTIMATES

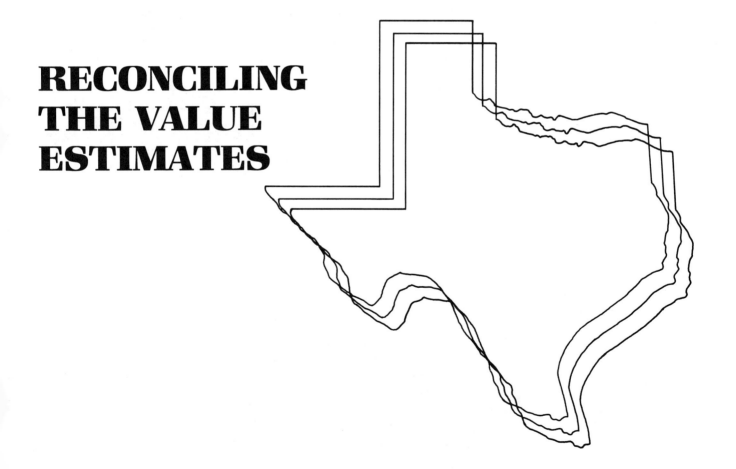

PREVIEW

After the appraiser has processed each of the three approaches, the three value indications that have been developed must be reduced to a single opinion of value. The process that the appraiser follows to do this is called reconciliation. This chapter will explain that process.

When you have completed this chapter, you should be able to:

1. Define the term reconciliation.
2. Explain why the appraiser must review each value approach that has been used.
3. Explain why the appraiser reviews the data used in each approach.
4. Round the final answer.

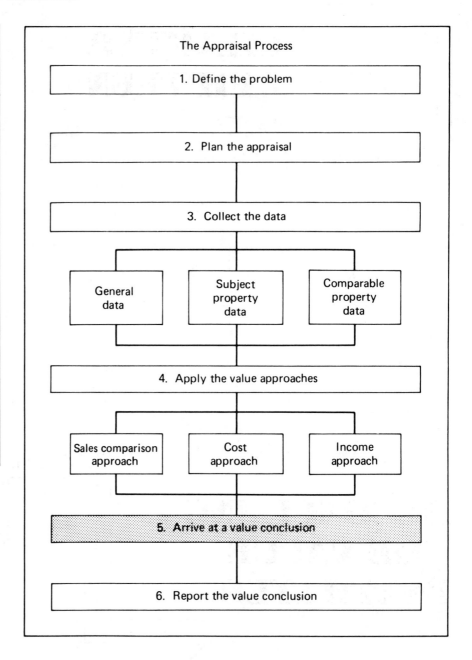

The Appraisal Process

1. Define the problem

2. Plan the appraisal

3. Collect the data

| General data | Subject property data | Comparable property data |

4. Apply the value approaches

| Sales comparison approach | Cost approach | Income approach |

5. Arrive at a value conclusion

6. Report the value conclusion

**SECTION 15.1
GENERAL REVIEW
OF THE APPRAISAL**

In order to arrive at a value conclusion, the appraiser must review the appraisal itself. The appraiser must be satisfied that an adequate appraisal was performed *before* reconciliation begins. This review can be divided into two steps.

1. Review the overall appraisal process.
2. Review for technical accuracy.

Reviewing the Appraisal Process

The first step is to reconsider the overall appraisal assignment. What was the appraisal to accomplish? Have you (1) precisely located and identified the property, (2) clearly stated the property rights to be appraised, (3) pinpointed the date as of which the value estimate applies, and (4) given a formal definition of the type of value stated as the purpose of the appraisal? Also, is the length of your report appropriate for its intended use? In reviewing the data collected and analyzed, have you considered (1) the type of property being appraised, (2) the purpose of the appraisal, and (3) the type of report required. Depending upon the property type and the purpose of the appraisal, one or another of the value approaches may be most relevant. The appraiser should now go back and apply any important approach that might have been omitted.

Technical Review

The next step in this review process is a clerical check for possible errors. First, all calculations should be checked for accuracy. All critical measurements should be reviewed as well. Second, all data should be checked for completeness and accuracy. Were the data complete and adequate for the purpose for which they were used? Third, the appraiser should check for consistency. Was the highest and best use of the site used as the basis for its value? Is the property age used in the sales comparison approach the same in the cost approach? Were the desirable features rated in the sales comparison approach also considered in estimating rents for the income approach? Was any economic or functional obsolescence in the cost approach also adjusted for in the sales comparison and income approaches? A positive answer to these and similar questions will assure that the data in the appraisal have been processed consistently.

Finally, the last step in this technical review is to reconsider any assumptions made during the appraisal. Now that the appraisal has been completed and the appraiser has the benefit of added insight into the market gained from the various approaches used, do the adjustments, judgment, or assumptions used in each approach appear as appropriate, reasonable, and sensible as they did when first employed? This is another way of checking for consistency.

SECTION 15.2 RECONCILING THE VALUE APPROACHES

Reconciliation has been defined as:

The process by which the appraiser evaluates, chooses, and selects from among two or more alternative conclusions or indications to reach a single answer (final value estimate). Preferable terminology to the traditional term correlation.*

Appraising the Appraisal

Once an overall review of the appraisal has been made, the process of reconciliation then requires an evaluation of each value approach to esti-

---

* B. N. Boyce, *Real Estate Appraisal Terminology*, rev. ed., Ballinger Publishing Co., Cambridge, Mass., 1981.

mate its overall relevance and accuracy. The key questions in this evaluation are

1.   How appropriate is this approach in this case?
2.   How many data were used and how reliable were they?
3.   What range of values do the three approaches suggest and what does the value indication of each tell you about the others?

How Appropriate Is the Approach?

Having completed the approaches, ask yourself how accurate and relevant each is. What does each tell you about the importance of the others? The validity or relevance of each approach to value depends, first, upon the purpose of the appraisal. In this book, our emphasis has been on using appraisals to estimate market value. However, there can be a number of purposes for an appraisal other than estimating market value. For example, appraisals for insurance purposes may call for an emphasis upon the cost approach.

The *type* of property plays a role in determining which value approach is used. It usually makes little sense to use an income approach when you are appraising an individual vacant lot. The sales comparison approach would be more logical. Similarly, you would normally use the sales comparison approach when appraising a single-family residence or, for that matter, any property in an area where good comparable sales are in ample supply.

The use of the appropriate approaches can also depend upon the state of the market. In some markets, for example, single-family homes are rarely bought and sold for their income characteristics. In such markets, an income approach would not be appropriate. In other markets, however, single-family homes may be sought for their income advantages; here the income approach might be appropriate.

Finally, you must consider the characteristics of each approach. Each has its strengths; each has its weaknesses. In a particular case, the strength of one approach may be important; the weakness of another may disqualify it. Your intent throughout is to form an opinion on the relative reliability of this approach in each case.

Evaluating the Data

The next step in the reconciliation process is to consider how many data were used in each approach and how reliable they were. This step takes you further toward an overall conclusion about the probable reliability of each approach. Each approach must be based on evidence that is both appropriate for that approach and also reliable enough to support the overall validity of the approach. Finally, the quantity of data must be adequate to provide reasonable support for the conclusions of the approach. An old appraisal saying is that "One swallow doesn't make a spring, nor does one sale make a market."

As part of this review of the data used, the appraiser should consider how comparable or how relevant was the evidence used in each approach. Did the sales require larger amounts of adjustment? Are the adjustments well supported? Are the replacement costs based on costs adjusted to the particular location? Have the comparative costs been derived from types of property similar to the property being appraised? All of these are examples of the kinds of questions the appraiser must ask. In the end, the approach that is the more reliable in this circumstance and/or has the more adequate and reliable data, gets the greater weight when you make your final conclusion of value.

The Value Range

The last step in reviewing the approaches is to develop a range of values. It is important to note that each approach to value tells you something about the reliability of the other two approaches. A common error is the belief that the cost approach sets the upper limit of value. Most appraisal theoreticians agree that depreciated replacement cost does *not* set the upper limit. Depending upon the types of judgment errors made in the cost approach, it is just as conceivable that in a particular circumstance, the cost approach will be at the lower limit.

In any one appraisal, the appraiser may have a hunch that one or another approach is likely to result in a value that is high or low. For example, in appraising a home in an area that is primarily owner-occupied, it is possible (but not certain) that the income approach would produce a lower estimate of value than the other approaches. This could depend on how the appraiser developed the gross rent multiplier, among other possibilities. Similarly, in appraising a house that may have some economic obsolescence, the cost approach could be higher than the sales comparison approach, particularly if an economic obsolescence deduction had not been calculated. Here is where the appraiser relies upon the economic principles that were developed in Chapter 5. By applying these principles to the region, city, and neighborhood, with facts relevant to a particular appraisal, the appraiser can better judge the reliability of each of the three approaches to determine whether they have established a reasonable range of value.

After a review of the three preliminary conclusions, you will see that there is a highest number and a lowest number. This suggests the probable range of minimum-maximum value. The reliability of each approach influences the reliability of this range. Sometimes, you may conclude that the approach with the lowest figure probably *is* a low estimate of value. So, your own evaluation of an approach suggests whether it is high or low. Comparing its value conclusion to the conclusion from the other two approaches gives you a cross-check. In addition, if two of the three approaches cluster at one end of the range, that could lead you to pick a value toward that end of the range. At this point, then, the appraiser reviews (1) the reliability of each approach, (2) what value each one indicates, and (3) which values are high and which are low.

Reviewing the Theory of the Approaches

Each approach has its own characteristic strengths and weaknesses. Depending upon the type of property and the quality and quantity of evidence considered, a particular approach may deserve more weight or less weight in arriving at a value conclusion. See Figure 15.1.

The sales comparison approach, for example, is often considered to be the most direct approach. Because of the usually ample sales data, it often should receive the greatest weight in valuing residences. Depending upon the quality of the comparable sales, it is also considered the best evidence in an appraisal performed for condemnation or eminent domain. However, the sales comparison approach requires that there be comparable

RECONCILIATION AND VALUE CONCLUSION

Indicated Value by the Cost Approach . . . . $ 82,500

Indicated Value by the Sales Comparison Approach . . . . . $ 80,000

Indicated Value by the Income Approach . . . . $ 76,500

FINAL RECONCILIATION: In this appraisal, the income approach deserves the least weight because very few homes in the area are rented. While the cost and sales comparison indications are fairly close together, the sales comparison is the more reliable because of the large depreciation estimate.

As a result of my investigation and analysis, my estimate of market value of the subject property as of _____7/14_____ 19_84_ is . . . . . .

$ 80,000

Date _7/20/84_   Appraiser _John Thomas_

FIGURE   15.1

sales, that reasonable numbers of sales be available, and that the adjustments to the sales be relatively minor or else fairly well supported.

The cost approach is often cited as being especially useful when new buildings are being appraised. In addition, it is considered the only way to appraise building types that do not rent *and* are rarely bought or sold. Examples could include special-purpose or public buildings, certain factories, churches, and so on. Major problems with the cost approach include the difficulty in estimating indirect costs, such as the developer's and builder's profit and overhead allowance.

Another problem arises in estimating the amount of accrued depreciation, especially with an older building. Depreciation is also difficult to estimate for misplaced improvements or for buildings suffering from other forms of unusual obsolescence. However, even with its weaknesses, the cost approach is still useful as a check on the other approaches.

The income approach is particularly useful when appraising types of properties usually purchased as investments, based on their ability to generate income. However, the income approach requires adequate and reliable market data on such factors as rents, expenses, and capitalization rates and techniques. For example, adjusting the capitalization rate for differences between the comparables and the subject property may require documenting changes in rates over time. Other difficult adjustments may be involved. Small errors in the data used in the income approach can cause large errors in the final value conclusion.

Reaching a Final Value Estimate

At the end of this entire process, the appraiser normally reaches a single estimate of value. In a few appraisal assignments, however, a range of value will suffice if specifically called for by the appraisal assignment and the agreement with the client. There is no magic method to reach a final value conclusion. It is rarely a mathematical average of the three value

VALUATION SECTION

Purpose of Appraisal is to estimate Market Value as defined in Certification & Statement of Limiting Conditions (FHLMC Form 439/FNMA Form 1004B). If submitted for FNMA, the appraiser must attach (1) sketch or map showing location of subject, street names, distance from nearest intersection, and any detrimental conditions and (2) exterior building sketch of improvements showing dimensions.

COST APPROACH

Measurements		No. Stories		Sq. Ft.	
x ___	x ___	___	=		
x ___	x ___	___	=		
x ___	x ___	___	=		
x ___	x ___	___	=		
x ___	x ___	___	=		

ESTIMATED REPRODUCTION COST – NEW – OF IMPROVEMENTS:

Dwelling ___970___ Sq. Ft. @ $ _60.82_	=	$ _59,000_
___ Sq. Ft. @ $ ___ /	=	
Extras _Kitchen Equipment_	=	_4,000_
___	=	
Special Energy Efficient Items ___	=	
Porches, Patios, etc. ___	=	_2,400_
Garage/Car Port _200_ Sq. Ft. @ $ _8.00_	=	_1,600_
Site Improvements (driveway, landscaping, etc.)	=	_2,500_
Total Estimated Cost New	=	$ _68,500_

Total Gross Living Area (List in Market Data Analysis below) ___

Comment on functional and economic obsolescence: ___
Old-fashioned floor furnace

	Physical	Functional	Economic		
Less Depreciation $ _33,000_	$ _3,000_	$ _0_	=	$(_36,000_)
Depreciated value of improvements			=	$ _30,500_
ESTIMATED LAND VALUE			=	$ _50,000_
(If leasehold, show only leasehold value)				
INDICATED VALUE BY COST APPROACH				$ _82,500_

The undersigned has recited three recent sales of properties most similar and proximate to subject and has considered these in the market analysis. The description includes a dollar adjustment, reflecting market reaction to those items of significant variation between the subject and comparable properties. If a significant item in the comparable property is superior to, or more favorable than, the subject property, a minus (-) adjustment is made, thus reducing the indicated value of subject; if a significant item in the comparable is inferior to, or less favorable than, the subject property, a plus (+) adjustment is made, thus increasing the indicated value of the subject.

MARKET DATA ANALYSIS

ITEM	Subject Property	COMPARABLE NO. 1	Adjustment	COMPARABLE NO. 2	Adjustment	COMPARABLE NO. 3	Adjustment
Address	XXXX Acton St	XXXX Sacramento St.		XXXX Acton St.		XXXX Channing St.	
Proximity to Subj.		2 blocks		9 blocks		4 blocks	
Sales Price	$ 79,500	$ 75,000		$ 75,000		$ 86,000	
Price/Living area	$ 81.96	$ 62.50		$ 65.79		$ 80.45	
Data Source	Inspection	M.L.S. & Broker		S.R.E.A.		S.R.E.A.	
Date of Sale and Time Adjustment	7/80	3/80	3,000	6/80	1,000	2/80	4,500
Location	Average	Inferior	4,000	Equal		Superior	(3,000)
Site/View	Typical/none	Superior	(1,000)	Superior	(3,000)	Equal	
Design and Appeal	Average	Equal		Equal		Equal	
Quality of Const.	Average	Equal		Equal		Equal	
Age	1925	1930		1920		1930	
Condition	Good	Equal		Inferior	3,000	Inferior	2,000
Living Area Room Count and Total	Total 5 B-rms 2 Baths 1	Total 5 B-rms 2 Baths 1	(1,000)	Total 6 B-rms 3 Baths 1		Total 5 B-rms 2 Baths 1	
Gross Living Area	970 Sq.Ft.	1,200 (E) Sq.Ft.	(3,000)	1,140 Sq.Ft.	(3,000)	1,069 Sq.Ft.	(2,000)
Basement & Bsmt. Finished Rooms	None	None		None		10% Fin.	(5,000)
Functional Utility	Average	Average		Average		Average	
Air Conditioning	None	None		None		None	
Garage/Car Port	1 Car	1 Car		Open	2,500	1 Car	
Porches, Patio, Pools, etc.	Deck	Equal		Equal		Equal	
Special Energy Efficient Items	Average	Average		Average		Average	
Other (e.g. fireplaces, kitchen equip., remodeling)	Comp. remod. Fireplace Floor furn.	Comp. remod. Fireplace Floor furn.		No remod. Fireplace Floor furn.	5,000	Comp. remod. Fireplace Floor furn.	
Sales or Financing Concessions	Conv.	Conv.		Conv.		Conv.	
Net Adj. (Total)		☒ Plus; ☐ Minus	$ 3,000	☒ Plus; ☐ Minus	$ 4,500	☒ Plus; ☐ Minus	$ 3,500
Indicated Value of Subject			$ 78,000		$ 79,500		$ 82,500

Comments on Market Data ___All of the comparables are felt to be equally valid and are therefore given equal weight.___

INDICATED VALUE BY MARKET DATA APPROACH		$ _80,000_
INDICATED VALUE BY INCOME APPROACH (If applicable) Economic Market Rent $ _450_ /Mo. x Gross Rent Multiplier _170_	=	$ _76,500_

This appraisal is made ☐ "as is" ☐ subject to the repairs, alterations, or conditions listed below ☐ completion per plans and specifications.

Comments and Conditions of Appraisal: ___

Final Reconciliation: _The income approach is given the least weight, as few properties in the area are rented. The cost and market indications are quite similar, however, market is the more reliable, given the large depreciation estimate._

Construction Warranty ☐ Yes ☒ No   Name of Warranty Program ___   Warranty Coverage Expires ___

This appraisal is based upon the above requirements, the certification, contingent and limiting conditions, and Market Value definition that are stated in

☐ FHLMC Form 439 (Rev. 10/78)/FNMA Form 1004B (Rev. 10/78) filed with client ___ 19 ___ ☐ attached.

I ESTIMATE THE MARKET VALUE, AS DEFINED, OF SUBJECT PROPERTY AS OF _July 14_ 19 _84_ to be $ _80,000_

Appraiser(s) _John Thomas_
John Thomas

Review Appraiser (If applicable) ___
☐ Did   ☐ Did Not Physically Inspect Property

FHLMC Form 70 Rev. 7/79   Forms and Worms Incorporated 315 Whitney Ave. New Haven, CT 06511   REVERSE   FNMA Form 1004 Rev. 7/79

FIGURE 15.2

indications but is sometimes justifiably a weighted average of the three. This means that the three indications are averaged, allotting, for example, twice as much weight to one approach, an average weight to the second approach, and half a weight to the third approach. However, this often implies a mathematical accuracy that is probably not warranted. In particular, there may be subjective questions that cannot be handled by any weighting process. (See Figure 15.2, page 317.)

Of all the steps in the appraisal process, arriving at and explaining the final value conclusion may be one of the most difficult and subjective. However, if the reconciliation process that we have outlined above is carefully followed, the appraiser will have developed a factual basis from which to draw a reliable value opinion. The appraiser will then be able to report the factors that were considered, such as the strengths and weaknesses of the approaches and the data that were developed.

SECTION 15.3
ROUNDING THE ANSWER

Throughout the appraisal process, we work with numbers, from defining the square footage of an area to estimating the value of a subject property. One of the characteristics of a number is how many significant digits it has. The significant digits are those that go from the first numeral on the left over to the last figure on the right that is not a zero. For example, 10 has only one significant digit, while 111 has three. A number calculated in an appraisal might contain all significant digits, for example $85,319.27. However, a final value conclusion might be presented with differing numbers of significant digits, depending upon the appraisal process and the data used. Thus, one appraiser's reconciliation process could lead to a value conclusion of $130,000 (two significant digits). On the same property, another appraiser, perhaps relying on another technique, might conclude a value of $133,495 (six significant digits.) To the layman, this difference might suggest that the second appraisal conclusion is more accurate than the first. In fact, the two appraisals may be of *equal* accuracy. Accordingly, it can be misleading for the appraiser to use a larger number of significant digits in the final answer than is warranted. In other words, should that second figure, $133,495, be rounded to $133,500, or to $134,000, or to $135,000, or to $130,000, or even to $150,000?

The General Rule

There is a general rule that the appraiser should follow: the answer to any mathematical step should not be reported with any more significant digits than the smallest number of significant digits occurring in any number used. If $36,312.67 is multiplied by 8.7, the answer, $315,920.22, is only *mathematically* accurate as $320,000. If accrued depreciation in the cost approach is estimated to be 20%, this is a number with one significant digit. It follows that carrying the cost approach conclusion to four significant digits implies greater accuracy than is really there.

In the reconciliation process, however, we are analyzing alternate value indications, usually of differing precision. The cost approach might have only two significant digits, whereas the income approach might have three. Because these can be argued to be independent of each other, it is acceptable to round the final value conclusion to an intermediate accuracy.

General Practice

There are no standards of practice for rounding. However, few appraisers report their final conclusion rounded to just one significant digit, for example, $100,000 or $200,000. Instead, appraisers generally round their conclusion to either two, two and one-half, or three significant digits. An answer rounded to two significant digits could be $52,000, $140,000, and so on. When an answer is rounded to two and one-half significant digits, the third digit is either a zero or a five, and no other number. Examples of answers rounded to two and one-half digits would be $145,000, $97,500, and even $120,000. (The latter number was rounded from $122,000. Here $120,000 is closer than $125,000.) Answers to three significant digits might be $322,000 or $37,600. Usually, appraisers carry out intermediate answers to more digits than the final answer. Depending on the accuracy of the data, then, appraisers might just round the indicated value of each approach to three or four digits.

SUMMARY

After a value indication has been reached for each of the three approaches, the appraiser must then reduce these values to a single estimate. This process is called reconciliation.

Before reconciliation begins, a review of the overall appraisal process should be made. Such factors as the purpose of the appraisal, the approaches used, and the data collected should be reevaluated. The question is: Was the appraisal correctly performed? A check for technical accuracy should also be made. Are your figures, sources, data, and other information correct? Now that the appraisal is completed, do you feel that your initial assumptions, adjustments, and use of judgment are still accurate? These are just a few of the questions you could ask yourself before actual reconciliation begins.

The first step in the reconciliation process is to evaluate the reliability of each approach. Carefully review the purpose of the appraisal—perhaps, the intent of the report naturally calls for greater weight to be placed upon one approach over others. Such factors as the type of property can determine if one approach should be considered over others. It is important to understand the strengths and weaknesses of each approach in order to decide which approach is likely to give the more reliable answer.

The next step in the reconciliation process is to consider if the data used were adequate and reliable. Since each approach is based in part upon data, it is the accuracy of each approach that plays a major part in how you select the final value conclusion. Were enough sales used to provide reasonable support for the conclusion of the approach? The approach that has the most accurate and adequate data should have the greatest influence on the final value conclusion.

The last step in reconciliation is to develop a range of values. After reviewing all the approaches, you will probably find a high number and a low number. These two figures can *usually* be considered as the maximum-minimum range of value. However, many factors, such as the accuracy of the data collected, can influence these maximum-minimum figures.

At the end of this process, a final value conclusion is normally reached. Arriving at a final conclusion involves many considerations. It usually is not the averaging of the three approaches. It requires the use of judgment:

reflection on all the factors involved in the appraisal and on subjective or intuitive experience. Combined, these factors should result in a final conclusion.

Once your conclusion has been reached, you may then want to round your answer. There are no set standards for rounding. Most appraisers usually round to either two, two and a half, or three significant digits. However, the answer for each appraisal assignment should be rounded according to the limits of the data found in that appraisal.

IMPORTANT TERMS AND CONCEPTS

Appropriate approach data	Judgment errors Range of values
Consistency	Reconciliation
Evaluating data	Rounding numbers
Final conclusion of value	Significant digit
	Technical review

REVIEWING YOUR UNDERSTANDING

1. Before reconciliation is made, the appraiser should:
   (a) Reinspect the subject property
   (b) Evaluate the reliability of each approach
   (c) Review the overall appraisal process and check it for technical accuracy

2. Briefly, reconciliation is:
   (a) An estimate of value
   (b) One of the three approaches
   (c) A process of reevaluation, which leads to the final value estimate

3. Reconciliation is important because:
   (a) It is intended to find any possible errors in your appraisal that you may have overlooked
   (b) It can help you to see if the appraisal is accurate and reliable
   (c) It produces the final value conclusion of the appraisal
   (d) All of the above
   (e) Two of the above

4. A key question that should be answered during the reconciliation process is:
   (a) How appropriate is the approach?
   (b) How adequate are the data?
   (c) What range of values do the approaches suggest?
   (d) Two of the above
   (e) All of the above

5. In the review of the approaches, the type of property is:
   (a) Not an important factor
   (b) An important factor
   (c) Only important to the income approach
   (d) Two of the above

6. Since each value approach has its own strengths and weaknesses, in arriving at a final value conclusion, you should:

   (a) Choose the approach that is the most popular

   (b) Choose the approach that has the most available data

   (c) Weigh the strengths and weaknesses of each and, by using your judgment and the data collected, choose the figure you think is most accurate

7. In evaluating the data that you used to arrive at a value, it is important to check to see if:

   (a) You have collected enough data

   (b) You have used the best comparables available

   (c) The data are reliable

   (d) Two of the above

   (e) All of the above

8. How many significant digits are there in $135,000?

   (a) 5 (b) 3 (c) 6 (d) 4

9. Which is the correctly rounded answer to $16,280 divided by 11.3%?

   (a) 144,071 (b) 144,070.79

   (c) 144,100 (d) 144,000

10. In rounding an answer, the number of significant digits to use depends upon:

    (a) The purpose of the appraisal

    (b) The range of values

    (c) The numbers used

    (d) All of the above

    (e) Two of the above

CHAPTER
SIXTEEN

REPORTING
APPRAISAL
OPINIONS

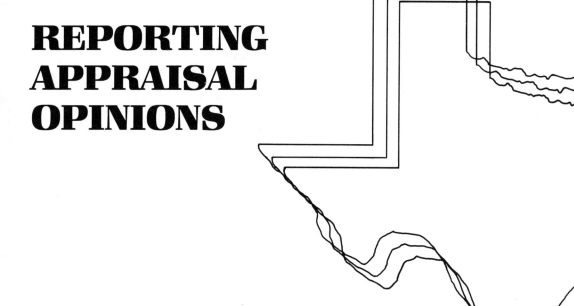

PREVIEW

The appraisal report is a formal communication that details the investigation the appraiser has made on behalf of the client. Whether delivered orally or in writing, as a letter, form, or narrative document, the appraisal report must contain certain minimum elements required for practical and professional reasons, which have evolved over 50 years of appraisal theory and practice.

In this chapter we will cover the basic elements of appraisal reports and describe the three types of written reports most commonly used.

When you have completed this chapter, you should be able to:

1. List the 10 basic elements of a written appraisal report.

2. Understand the use for, and the contents of, the three types of written appraisal reports.

3. Outline the contents of a narrative appraisal report.

4. Discuss the assumptions and limiting conditions that should accompany an appraisal report.

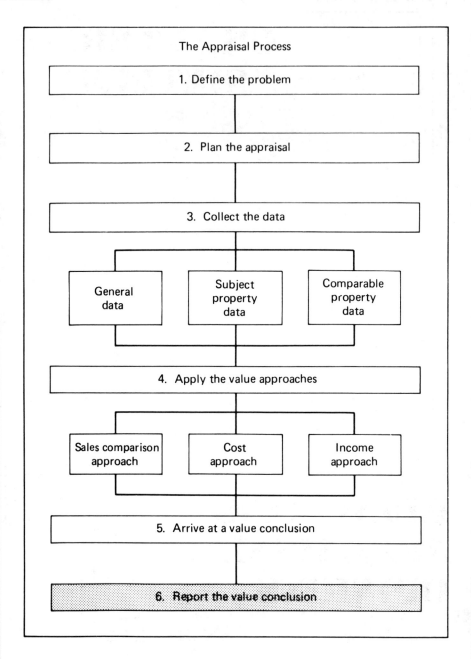

The Appraisal Process

1. Define the problem

2. Plan the appraisal

3. Collect the data

General data | Subject property data | Comparable property data

4. Apply the value approaches

Sales comparison approach | Cost approach | Income approach

5. Arrive at a value conclusion

6. Report the value conclusion

SECTION 16.1
ESSENTIAL ELEMENTS
OF APPRAISAL REPORTS

The form and content of appraisal reports are generally governed by good business practice and appraisal tradition. Even if the client contracts for a verbal (or oral) report of value, notes concerning the essential elements of the appraisal should be maintained in the appraiser's file.

**Practical and
Professional Considerations**

Written appraisal reports are a form of business communication; they should, above all, be practical. This means that every report should be concise, well organized, and easy to read. In particular, the writer must consider the knowledge level of the probable readers and define technical terms as necessary to assure comprehension.

All written appraisals should contain only information that relates to the appraisal problem, yet should be adequate enough in scope to meet the client's needs. Extraneous data should be omitted and all pertinent data incorporated into the report in logical order and nontechnical terms.

Professional standards of some appraisal groups require that appraisal reports contain all the facts and elements necessary to support the value opinion. Others, including the American Institute of Real Estate Appraisers, permit, as a minimum, a reasonably complete summary of salient facts. Such requirements are intended to ensure that the services of the member-appraiser can always be relied upon to demonstrate the best efforts of an investigative reporter, and nothing less.

Outline of Essential Elements

In order to accomplish the practical and professional goals of written appraisal reports, the following elements should be included in every appraisal report:

1. The name of the client requesting the appraisal.
2. An adequate identification and description of the property.
3. A statement of the rights being appraised.
4. The purpose of the appraisal and the intended use of the report.
5. The date of valuation.
6. A formal definition of the type of value sought.
7. A summary of the factual data used to make the appraisal; interpretation and analysis as appropriate.
8. The final estimate of value.
9. The assumptions and limiting conditions under which the appraisal was made.
10. The appraiser's certification and signature.

In summary, the necessary elements of appraisal reports should define the appraisal problem and present at least a summary of both the factual data revealed by the study and the analysis that supports the stated opinion of value.

**SECTION 16.2
TYPES OF WRITTEN
APPRAISAL REPORTS**

The type of appraisal report to be used should be agreed upon in advance by the client and the appraiser. As a general rule, the type of report depends upon the amount of background information and detail required by the client and the written format that best serves the intended use of the report itself. There are three general types of written reports: the letter, the form, and the narrative report.

The Letter Report

The letter appraisal report is a short business letter, generally defining the appraisal assignment and providing a brief summary of the nature and scope of the investigation made by the appraiser and an opinion of value for the property in question. Its length is likely to be three to six pages.

A letter report should contain *all* the essential elements of an appraisal report. Usually, however, the description of the subject property is brief, and only a summary of the factual data and its analysis is presented. Exhibits, such as a plot plan, a floor plan, and pictures, may be attached to the report if desired.

In most cases, supporting data are included in the letter report only by reference. For example, comparable sales data are usually summarized in the report itself, with the specific details about each transaction retained in the appraiser's files. However, the assumptions, limiting conditions, and appraiser's value certification must always be included because they define the appraisal itself. (Section 16.3 will provide examples.)

The Form (or Short-Form) Report

Institutions and agencies that regularly contract for appraisals usually require the use of a standard form appraisal report. Forms are preferred because they are usually designed in a checklist format on a printed page. The types of data commonly required are also presented in a sequence that is easy to review. Most appraisal forms also provide blank spaces for the appraiser to use for additional analysis and comment.

Although designed along similar guidelines, many variations of the form report are available today. Some agencies and appraisal services develop their own forms for each property type. Written instructions for completion are sometimes prepared. Single-family residential, condominium, multifamily residential, and commercial are examples of standard forms currently available.

The most common form report in use today for loan appraisals is the FHLMC Form 70, also referred to as the FNMA Form 1004. Often simply called Form 70s, these forms (shown in Figure 16.1) are required by the Federal Home Loan Mortgage Corporation and the Federal National Mortgage Association for single-family appraisals. Most savings and loan associations have adopted this form in order to be able to sell mortgages in the secondary mortgage market.

Form 70 contains all the basic elements of an appraisal report. The form defines the appraisal problem, presents factual data revealed in the appraisal, and demonstrates evidence of value through the cost, sales comparison, and income approaches. Most commonly, FHLMC Form 439 (or FNMA Form 1004B), shown in Figure 16.2, is attached to the Form 70 report. The attachment contains a formal definition of market value, the appraiser's certification, and a statement of contingent and limiting conditions.

The Federal National Mortgage Association publishes about 18 pages of written guidelines on how to complete Form 70. The appraiser should review these guidelines before attempting to fill out the form. For example,

J.B. FEATHERSTON & ASSOCIATES, INC.
1 Parker Square, Suite 406   817/723-6615   Wichita Falls, Texas 76308

RESIDENTIAL APPRAISAL REPORT

File No. _____

To be completed by Lender

Borrower Owner: Terry M. Davenhauer	Census Tract 437.02 Map Reference KM528G
Property Address 1311 Agarita Lane	
City Wichita Falls County Wichita State Texas Zip Code 79788	
Legal Description Lot 31, Block 5, Braewood Glen, Section 6,	
Sale Price $ N/A Date of Sale _____ Loan Term _____ yrs Property Rights Appraised [X] Fee [ ] Leasehold [ ] DeMinimis PUD	
Actual Real Estate Taxes $ 1313 (82) (yr) Loan charges to be paid by seller $ N/A Other sales concessions _____	
Lender/Client Fairchild Camera & Instrument Corp. Address P. O. Drawer 7283, Mountain View, CA 94043	
Occupant Mr. & Mrs. Terry Appraiser J. Don Jones Instructions to Appraiser Estimate Fair Market Value	
Davenhauer	

NEIGHBORHOOD

Location	[ ] Urban	[X] Suburban	[ ] Rural
Built Up	[X] Over 75%	[ ] 25% to 75%	[ ] Under 25%
Growth Rate	[X] Fully Dev. [ ] Rapid	[ ] Steady	[ ] Slow
Property Values	[ ] Increasing	[ ] Stable	[X] Declining
Demand/Supply	[ ] Shortage	[ ] In Balance	[X] Over Supply
Marketing Time	[ ] Under 3 Mos.	[X] 4-6 Mos.	[ ] Over 6 Mos.

Present Land Use 97% 1 Family 0 % 2 4 Family 0 % Apts. 0 % Condo 0 % Commercial
 0 % Industrial 3 % Vacant ____ %

Change in Present Land Use	[X] Not Likely	[ ] Likely (*)	[ ] Taking Place (*)
	(*) From _____	To _____	
Predominant Occupancy	[X] Owner	[ ] Tenant	____ % Vacant
Single Family Price Range	$ 80,000 to $ 95,000	Predominant Value $ 90,000	
Single Family Age	new yrs to 6 yrs	Predominant Age 3 yrs	

	Good	Avg.	Fair	Poor
Employment Stability	[X]			
Convenience to Employment		[X]		
Convenience to Shopping	[X]			
Convenience to Schools	[X]			
Adequacy of Public Transportation		[X]		
Recreational Facilities	[X]			
Adequacy of Utilities	[X]			
Property Compatibility	[X]			
Protection from Detrimental Conditions	[X]			
Police and Fire Protection	[X]			
General Appearance of Properties	[X]			
Appeal to Market	[X]			

Note: FHLMC/FNMA do not consider race or the racial composition of the neighborhood to be reliable appraisal factors.

Comments including those factors, favorable or unfavorable, affecting marketability (e.g. public parks, schools, view, noise) Subdivision is located about 15 miles southwest of Wichita Falls. There is good access to all support facilities and schools. shopping and recreational facilities are within a mile radius. The neighborhood consists of 1, 1 1/2, & 2 story dwellings, most of which are well cared for. Subject property is on typical 65-ft. lot. There were no adverse market factors observed.

SITE

Dimensions   65 ft x 115 ft.   = 7,475   Sq. Ft. or Acres   [ ] Corner Lot

Zoning classification deed restrictions-residential   Present improvements [X] do [ ] do not conform to zoning regulations

Highest and best use [X] Present use [ ] Other (specify) _____

	Public	Other (Describe)	OFF SITE IMPROVEMENTS	Topo _____
Elec.	[X]		Street Access [X] Public [ ] Private	Size _____
Gas	[X]		Surface concrete	Shape _____
Water	[X]		Maintenance: [X] Public [ ] Private	View _____
San. Sewer	[X]		[X] Storm Sewer [X] Curb/Gutter	Drainage _____
	[X] Underground Elect. & Tel.	[ ] Sidewalk	[X] Street Lights	Is the property located in a HUD Identified Special Flood Hazard Area [ ] No [ ] Yes

Comments (favorable or unfavorable including any apparent adverse easements, encroachments or other adverse conditions) No adverse easements or encroachments were apparent. Lot is typical interior site with usual utility easements. Subject dwelling was located on cul-d-sac street.

IMPROVEMENTS

[X] Existing [ ] Proposed [ ] Under Constr. No. Units 1 | Type (det, duplex, semi/det, etc.) detached | Design (rambler, split level, etc.) rambler | Exterior Walls BV & Frame
Yrs. Age: Actual 2 Effective 1 to 2 No. Stories 1

Roof Material Wood Shingles	Gutters & Downspouts [ ] None Aluminum	Window (Type) Aluminum [ ] Storm Sash [ ] Screens [ ] Combination	Insulation [ ] None [ ] Floor [X] Ceiling [ ] Roof [X] Walls

[ ] Manufactured Housing	BSMT	[ ] 0 % Basement	[ ] Floor Drain	Finished Ceiling _____
Foundation Walls		[ ] Outside Entrance	[ ] Sump Pump	Finished Walls _____
Concrete Walls		[ ] Concrete Floor	___ % Finished	Finished Floor _____
[X] Slab on Grade [ ] Crawl Space		Evidence of: [ ] Dampness [ ] Termites	[ ] Settlement	

Comments The condition of subject dwelling was good

ROOM LIST

Room List	Foyer	Living	Dining	Kitchen	Den	Family Rm.	Rec. Rm.	Bedrooms	No. Baths	Laundry	Other
Basement											
1st Level	1	1	1	1				4	2	1	brfst. room
2nd Level											

Finished area above grade contains a total of 7 rooms 4 bedrooms 2 baths. Gross Living Area 2,050 sq. ft. Bsmt Area 0 sq. ft.

INTERIOR FINISH & EQUIPMENT

Kitchen Equipment [ ] Refrigerator [X] Range/Oven [X] Disposal [X] Dishwasher [X] Fan/Hood [ ] Compactor [ ] Washer [ ] Dryer
HEAT Type Central Fuel gas Cond. good   AIR COND. [X] Central [ ] Other [X] Adequate [ ] Inadequate

Floors	[ ] Hardwood [X] Carpet Over concrete vinyl	
Walls	[X] Drywall [ ] Plaster _____	
Trim/Finish	[X] Good [ ] Average [ ] Fair [ ] Poor	
Bath Floor	[X] Ceramic [X] Carpet	
Bath Wainscot	[X] Ceramic around shower & tub	

Special Features (including energy efficient items) built in micro-wave Oven, ceiling fan & intercom system

ATTIC [X] Yes [ ] No [ ] Stairway [ ] Drop-stair [ ] Scuttle [ ] Floored
Finished (Describe) storage area   [ ] Heated
CAR STORAGE [X] Garage [ ] Built-in [ ] Attached [ ] Detached [ ] Car Port
No. Cars 2 [X] Adequate [ ] Inadequate Condition _____

PROPERTY RATING

	Good	Avg	Fair	Poor
Quality of Construction (Materials & Finish)		[X]		
Condition of Improvements		[X]		
Room sizes and layout		[X]		
Closets and Storage		[X]		
Insulation—adequacy		[X]		
Plumbing—adequacy and condition		[X]		
Electrical—adequacy and condition		[X]		
Kitchen Cabinets—adequacy and condition		[X]		
Compatibility to Neighborhood		[X]		
Overall Livability		[X]		
Appeal and Marketability		[X]		

Yrs Est Remaining Economic Life 45 to 50 Explain if less than Loan Term

FIREPLACES, PATIOS, POOL, FENCES, etc. (describe) 6 ft. cedar fence in back, driveway & patio, fireplace, normal landscaping. NOTE: above-ground pool in back was treated as personal property.

COMMENTS (including functional or physical inadequacies, repairs needed, modernization, etc.) There were no functional or physical inadequacies observed. Interior & exterior condition of house was in good condition at time of inspection.

FHLMC Form 70 Rev. 7/79   ATTACH DESCRIPTIVE PHOTOGRAPHS OF SUBJECT PROPERTY AND STREET SCENE   U   FNMA Form 1004 Rev. 7/79

FIGURE 16.1

VALUATION SECTION

Purpose of Appraisal is to estimate Market Value as defined in Certification & Statement of Limiting Conditions (FHLMC Form 439/FNMA Form 1004B). If submitted for FNMA, the appraiser must attach (1) sketch or map showing location of subject, street names, distance from nearest intersection, and any detrimental conditions and (2) exterior building sketch of improvements showing dimensions.

COST APPROACH

Measurements		No. Stories		Sq. Ft.
46.4 x 30	x 1	=	1,392.00
28.4 x 23	x 1	=	653.20
12.6 x 2	x 1	=	25.20
3.4 x 6	x 1	=	(20.40)
x	x	=	
x	x	=	

Total Gross Living Area (List in Market Data Analysis below) _____

Comment on functional and economic obsolescence: _____

ESTIMATED REPRODUCTION COST — NEW — OF IMPROVEMENTS:

Dwelling 2,050 Sq. Ft. @ $ 35.00	=	$ 71,750.00
Sq. Ft. @ $ _____	=	
Extras _____	=	
Special Energy Efficient Items ceiling fans	=	100.00
Porches, Patios, etc. front porch, patio	=	2,000.00
Garage/Car Port 484 Sq. Ft. @ $ 10.00	=	4,840.00
Site Improvements (driveway, landscaping, etc.)	=	4,000.00
Total Estimated Cost New	=	$ 82,690.00
Less — Physical / Functional / Economic		
Depreciation $ 1,000 $	$	= $ (1,000.00)
Depreciated value of improvements	=	$ 81,690.00
ESTIMATED LAND VALUE . . . . (If leasehold, show only leasehold value)	=	$ 15,000.00
		96,690.00
INDICATED VALUE BY COST APPROACH . . .	$	

The undersigned has recited three recent sales of properties most similar and proximate to subject and has considered these in the market analysis. The description includes a dollar adjustment, reflecting market reaction to those items of significant variation between the subject and comparable properties. If a significant item in the comparable property is superior to, or more favorable than, the subject property, a minus (-) adjustment is made, thus reducing the indicated value of subject; if a significant item in the comparable is inferior to, or less favorable than, the subject property, a plus (+) adjustment is made, thus increasing the indicated value of the subject.

MARKET DATA ANALYSIS

ITEM	Subject Property	COMPARABLE NO. 1		COMPARABLE NO. 2		COMPARABLE NO. 3	
Address	13311 Argarita Lane	13326 Agarita Lane		13326 Rain Lily		13207 Agarita Lane	
Proximity to Subj.		Same block		3 blocks north		1 block east	
Sales Price	$ N/A	$ 90,500		$ 95,000		$103,000	
Price/Living area	$ N/A	$ 44.15		$ 37.80		$ 50.50	
Data Source	inspection	MLS		MLS		MLS	
		DESCRIPTION	Adjustment +(-)$	DESCRIPTION	Adjustment +(-)$	DESCRIPTION	Adjustment +(-)$
Date of Sale and Time Adjustment	N/A	12-83		8-83		7-83	
Location	MK528G	KM528G		KM528G		KM528G	
Site/View	Average	equal		Equal/inferior	+2,000	equal	
Design and Appeal	Average	inferior	+1,000	equal		equal	
Quality of Const.	Average	equal		equal		equal	
Age	2 years	2 years		2 years		new	-2,000
Condition	good	inferior	+2,000	inferior	+2,000	new	-2,500
Living Area Room Count and Total	Total 7 / B-rms 4 / Baths 2	Total 7 / B-rms 4 / Baths 2		Total 8 / B-rms 4 / Baths 2.5		Total 7 / B-rms 4 / Baths 2	
Gross Living Area	2,050 Sq.Ft.	2,050 Sq.Ft.		2,390 Sq.Ft.		2,040 Sq.Ft.	
Basement & Bsmt. Finished Rooms	none	equal		equal		equal	
Functional Utility	good	equal		equal		equal	
Air Conditioning	central	equal		equal		equal	
Garage/Car Port	2-car garage	equal		equal		equal	
Porches, Patio, Pools, etc.	front porch patio	equal		equal		equal	
Special Energy Efficient Items	wall & ceiling insulation fan in FR	equal		equal		equal	
Other (e.g. fireplaces, kitchen equip., remodeling)	Kitchen BIs fireplace	Kitchen BIs no fireplace		equal		equal	
Sales or Financing Concessions	cash or equivalent	assumption	-3,000	conventional		conventional	5,000
Net Adj. (Total)		Minus $	-3,000	Plus $	3,000	Minus $	98,000
Indicated Value of Subject		$	92,000	$	92,000	$	

Comments on Market Data __All three sales are located in the same subdivision and are comparable in features, location, utility, market appeal and construction. Values range from $92,000 to $98,000. Comp. No. 1 is considered to be most similar.__

INDICATED VALUE BY MARKET DATA APPROACH . . . . $ 92,000.00

INDICATED VALUE BY INCOME APPROACH (If applicable) Economic Market Rent $ N/A /Mo. x Gross Rent Multiplier N/A = $ N/A

This appraisal is made [X] "as is" [ ] subject to the repairs, alterations, or conditions listed below [ ] completion per plans and specifications

Comments and Conditions of Appraisal: __Comp. No. 1 is given more weight because it was listed for $92,500 on September 15, 1983, and sold on October 15, 1983.__

Final Reconciliation: __The Market Data Approach is given the most weight as it best reflects the action of buyers and sellers in the market. The income approach is not considered applicable in this area because very few of the houses are rented.__

Construction Warranty [ ] Yes [ ] No Name of Warranty Program _____ Warranty Coverage Expires _____

This appraisal is based upon the above requirements, the certification, contingent and limiting conditions, and Market Value definition that are stated in

[ ] FHLMC Form 439 (Rev. 10/78)/FNMA Form 1004B (Rev. 10/78) filed with client _____ 19___ [ ] attached

I ESTIMATE THE MARKET VALUE, AS DEFINED, OF SUBJECT PROPERTY AS OF December 22, 1983 to be $ 92,000

Appraiser(s) _J. Don Jones_ _____ Review Appraiser (If applicable) _____
[ ] Did [ ] Did Not Physically Inspect Property

FHLMC Form 70 Rev. 7/79   Forms and Worms, Inc. 315 Whitney Ave. New Haven, CT 06511   REVERSE   U   FNMA Form 1004 Rev. 7/79

FIGURE 16.1
(continued)

DEFINITION OF MARKET VALUE: The highest price in terms of money which a property will bring in a competitive and open market under all conditions requisite to a fair sale, the buyer and seller, each acting prudently, knowledgeably and assuming the price is not affected by undue stimulus. Implicit in this definition is the consummation of a sale as of a specified date and the passing of title from seller to buyer under conditions whereby: (1) buyer and seller are typically motivated; (2) both parties are well informed or well advised, and each acting in what he considers his own best interest; (3) a reasonable time is allowed for exposure in the open market; (4) payment is made in cash or its equivalent; (5) financing, if any, is on terms generally available at the specified date and typical for the property type in its locale; (6) the price represents a normal consideration for the property sold unaffected by special financing amounts and/or terms, services, fees, costs, or credits incurred in the transaction. ("Real Estate Appraisal Terminology," published 1975.)

CERTIFICATION AND STATEMENT OF LIMITING CONDITIONS

CERTIFICATION: The Appraiser certifies and agrees that:

1. The Appraiser has no present or contemplated future interest in the property appraised; and neither the employment to make the appraisal, nor the compensation for it, is contingent upon the appraised value of the property.

2. The Appraiser has no personal interest in or bias with respect to the subject matter of the appraisal report or the participants to the sale. The "Estimate of Market Value" in the appraisal report is not based in whole or in part upon the race, color, or national origin of the prospective owners or occupants of the property appraised, or upon the race, color or national origin of the present owners or occupants of the properties in the vicinity of the property appraised.

3. The Appraiser has personally inspected the property, both inside and out, and has made an exterior inspection of all comparable sales listed in the report. To the best of the Appraiser's knowledge and belief, all statements and information in this report are true and correct, and the Appraiser has not knowingly withheld any significant information.

4. All contingent and limiting conditions are contained herein (imposed by the terms of the assignment or by the undersigned affecting the analyses, opinions, and conclusions contained in the report).

5. This appraisal report has been made in conformity with and is subject to the requirements of the Code of Professional Ethics and Standards of Professional Conduct of the appraisal organizations with which the Appraiser is affiliated.

6. All conclusions and opinions concerning the real estate that are set forth in the appraisal report were prepared by the Appraiser whose signature appears on the appraisal report, unless indicated as "Review Appraiser." No change of any item in the appraisal report shall be made by anyone other than the Appraiser, and the Appraiser shall have no responsibility for any such unauthorized change.

CONTINGENT AND LIMITING CONDITIONS: The certification of the Appraiser appearing in the appraisal report is subject to the following conditions and to such other specific and limiting conditions as are set forth by the Appraiser in the report.

1. The Appraiser assumes no responsibility for matters of a legal nature affecting the property appraised or the title thereto, nor does the Appraiser render any opinion as to the title, which is assumed to be good and marketable. The property is appraised as though under responsible ownership.

2. Any sketch in the report may show approximate dimensions and is included to assist the reader in visualizing the property. The Appraiser has made no survey of the property.

3. The Appraiser is not required to give testimony or appear in court because of having made the appraisal with reference to the property in question, unless arrangements have been previously made therefor.

4. Any distribution of the valuation in the report between land and improvements applies only under the existing program of utilization. The separate valuations for land and building must not be used in conjunction with any other appraisal and are invalid if so used.

5. The Appraiser assumes that there are no hidden or unapparent conditions of the property, subsoil, or structures, which would render it more or less valuable. The Appraiser assumes no responsibility for such conditions, or for engineering which might be required to discover such factors.

6. Information, estimates, and opinions furnished to the Appraiser, and contained in the report, were obtained from sources considered reliable and believed to be true and correct. However, no responsibility for accuracy of such items furnished the Appraiser can be assumed by the Appraiser.

7. Disclosure of the contents of the appraisal report is governed by the Bylaws and Regulations of the professional appraisal organizations with which the Appraiser is affiliated.

8. Neither all, nor any part of the content of the report, or copy thereof (including conclusions as to the property value, the identity of the Appraiser, professional designations, reference to any professional appraisal organizations, or the firm with which the Appraiser is connected), shall be used for any purposes by anyone but the client specified in the report, the mortgagee or its successors and assigns, mortgage insurers, consultants, professional appraisal organizations, any state or federally approved financial institution, any department, agency, or instrumentality of the United States or any state or the District of Columbia, without the previous written consent of the Appraiser; nor shall it be conveyed by anyone to the public through advertising, public relations, news, sales, or other media, without the written consent and approval of the Appraiser.

9. On all appraisals, subject to satisfactory completion, repairs, or alterations, the appraisal report and value conclusion are contingent upon completion of the improvements in a workmanlike manner.

Date:... *july 5/1985* .... Appraiser(s) ... *John Smith* ....

FHLMC FORM 439 REV. 9/75
FDL 179 (Rev. 1-76) Page 3

FNMA FORM 1004B

FIGURE 16.2
FHLMC Form 439 or FNMA Form 1004B

under the Neighborhood description, the term employment stability must be rated good, average, fair, or poor. The guidelines suggest appropriate ratings in this manner:

Consideration should be given to the number of employment opportunities and the variety and type of industries in the community. One-industry or cyclical industry areas would not normally be rated as favorably as those having a broader variety of employment with greater stability.

Under Site, the term zoning classification appears. The guidelines direct the appraiser to "state the zoning category as designated by the local zoning code, and the major permitted uses." In comments on the Improvements section, the guidelines state that "the appraiser should here describe any physical deterioration or functional inadequacy found in the basic structure. Such conditions should then be reflected in the estimate of depreciation in the cost approach."

These examples demonstrate that the FNMA guidelines present rather definite and concrete information for completing Form 70s. Changes in statutes, case law, market conditions, technology, and appraisal theory will, of course, necessitate periodic revisions in the guidelines.

The Narrative Appraisal Report

The narrative appraisal report is the most formal of the written appraisal reports. Ranging from a dozen to a hundred pages or more in length, this type of appraisal is most often required by large corporations and government agencies. It is preferred when the report user needs a self-contained document, in which all the pertinent facts discovered in the investigation are presented under one cover.

Because of the high standards expected of this type of report, the preparation of a narrative report is often required as a test of competence for the appraiser seeking a professional designation.

What to Include

Over the years, users of narrative reports have developed rather definite ideas of what they want in these reports. For example, the General Services Administration of the Federal Government has an 82-point outline that must be followed. Most state highway departments also have specifications on report content. Perhaps the most detailed specifications on narrative format are those issued by the appraisal societies for demonstration appraisals. These are available to the general public in outline form at nominal cost.

Outline of the Narrative Report

One very acceptable format for narrative appraisal reports divides the report into the three main sections that follow. Some appraisers further subdivide the middle section into two parts, separating description from analyses and conclusion.

1. Introduction.
2. Description, analyses, and conclusion.
3. Addenda.

The three main subdivisions of the narrative appraisal report include the following items and features:

A. Introduction
　　1. Title page
　　2. Letter of transmittal
　　3. Table of contents
　　4. Photograph of the subject
　　5. Summary of salient facts and conclusions
B. Description, Analyses, and Conclusion
　　1. Identification of the property
　　2. Objectives of the appraisal
　　　　(a) Property rights appraised
　　　　(b) Date of value estimate
　　　　(c) Purpose of appraisal and definition of value sought
　　　　(d) Intended use of the appraisal report
　　3. Description of neighborhood and community
　　4. Description of land, zoning, community services, and taxes
　　5. Description of improvements
　　6. Highest and best use analysis
　　7. Analysis of data by the value approaches
　　　　(a) The cost approach
　　　　(b) The sales comparison approach
　　　　(c) The income approach
　　8. Reconciliation and final conclusion of value
　　9. Qualifying and limiting conditions
　　10. Certification of value opinion, with signature of the appraiser
　　11. Qualifications of the appraiser
C. Addenda or Supporting Material
　　1. Maps, plats, and photographs
　　2. Plot plan of subject property
　　3. Diagram of improvements
　　4. Statistical data
　　5. Sales data sheets and sale location maps

Specific guidelines for expanding the narrative appraisal report outline will be provided in the next section of this chapter.

Variations

In actual practice, appraisal reports often mix the features of the three types of reports we have described. For example, letter reports sometimes extend in length to become what could be called short narrative-type reports. Other written appraisal reports will often mix the features of the letter, form, and narrative appraisal reports to best suit the needs of the client or the style of the appraisal.

SECTION 16.3
WRITING THE
NARRATIVE APPRAISAL REPORT

Because of the detail and formality characteristic of the narrative appraisal report, it should have the appearance of a professionally prepared document. It is customarily typed on quality paper and bound in a durable cover. A carelessly prepared report suggests inferior effort put into the appraisal itself.

The style of writing, though formal, can be interesting if the writing is succinct and without redundancies. Information on a given topic should not be scattered throughout the report but should be confined to the pertinent subject area. To help the client understand, visualize, and remember, topical paragraphs should be sequenced logically. For example, when describing a residential neighborhood, you would cover: the location of the subject; a brief history of the general area; identification of the immediate neighborhood; residential quality; land uses; convenience of the subject property to commercial facilities; and proximity to schools, churches, and parks, in this approximate order.

The contents of the narrative appraisal report should communicate to the client what the appraiser has done, in a step-by-step, logical sequence, describing the data gathered and analyzed, and explaining the reasoning that leads to the value conclusion.

In this section, we shall cover the major subdivisions of the narrative appraisal report and the recommended content for each section.

Introductory Material

Title Page

The first page of the introductory material is the title page. A sample is shown in Figure 16.3. Typically a title page specifies: property address, type of property, date of value, for whom the property was appraised, and by whom it was appraised.

Letter of Transmittal

The second page of the introductory material is the letter of transmittal. The letter should be typed in standard business correspondence format and is usually addressed to the client. The purpose of the letter is to formally present the appraisal report to the client. The following elements should be included:

1. Date of the letter.
2. Identification of the person requesting the appraisal.
3. Identification of the subject property.
4. The purpose of the appraisal and the property rights being appraised.
5. A statement that the appraiser has made an investigation and analysis to arrive at a value conclusion.
6. A statement that the letter is transmitting the appraisal report, often with the number of pages indicated.
7. Clear statement of any unusual assumptions or limiting conditions.
8. Reference to other assumptions and limiting conditions set forth in the report.
9. The date of value.
10. The value estimate.
11. The signature of the appraiser.

```
┌─────────────────────────────────────┐
│                                      │
│              APPRAISAL               │
│                 OF                   │
│        RESIDENTIAL PROPERTY          │
│            LOCATED AT                │
│                                      │
│          127 JEFFERSON AVE.          │
│          SAN ANGELO, TEXAS           │
│                                      │
│            DATE OF VALUE             │
│           January 13, 1933           │
│                For                   │
│                                      │
│        Jack Taylor & Associates      │
│                                      │
│                 By                   │
│          Andrew L. Cochran           │
│            MAI SRPA ASA              │
│                                      │
└─────────────────────────────────────┘
```

FIGURE   16.3
Title Page of an Appraisal Report

Figure 16.4 is a sample letter, with the 11 elements identified by number. Other pertinent data may be included in the letter of transmittal such as a brief description of the property.

Table of Contents

The third page of the introductory material is the table of contents. This lists the major topics as they appear in the report and supplies page numbers. Some report writers recommend that major tables and exhibits also be referenced here.

Photograph of Subject

Often, the introductory material next contains a photograph of the subject property or perhaps a map or aerial photograph showing its location.

Summary of Salient Facts and Conclusions

The last page of the introductory material contains a summary of salient facts and conclusions. Items often included are

1. Location of the property.
2. Present ownership of the property.
3. Date of appraisal.
4. Date of value.
5. Type of property.
6. Land size.
7. Improvement size.
8. Age of improvements.
9. Zoning.
10. Present use.
11. Highest and best use.
12. Site value.
13. Value indicated by the cost approach.
14. Value indicated by the sales comparison approach.

January 19, 1985

Mr. Donald English
Executive Vice President
Jack Taylor and Associates
4919 Bruckner Blvd.
Garland, TX 75024

③ Re: 127 Jefferson Ave.
        San Angelo, Texas

② Pursuant to your request of December 11, 1984, I have inspected the above-
④ captioned property for the purpose of estimating its market value. It is
understood that this appraisal is to be used in connection with pending
litigation. The property is appraised as if free of any leases, mortgages,
or other liens.

⑧ As in all such appraisals, damage from wood destroying organisms, <u>if any</u>, is
assumed to be corrected by seller or the repair cost deducted from the stated
figure.

⑥ As you requested, the attached report is summary in nature. For your infor-
⑤ mation, supporting data and analyses are retained in my files.

⑦ It is my opinion, subject to the standard and special conditions contained
in the attached report, that the fair market value of the property commonly
⑨ known as 127 Jefferson Ave., San Angelo, Texas, and further described herein,
as of January 13, 1933, is the sum of

⑩   EIGHTY-TWO THOUSAND DOLLARS   ($82,000)

                                    Respectfully submitted,

⑪
                                    Andrew L. Cochran
                                    ANDREW L. COCHRAN

ALC:sas

FIGURE 16.4
Letter of Transmittal

15.   Value indicated by the income approach.

16.   Market value estimate.

The appraiser may include in this summary whatever additional information is considered important such as any special conditions affecting
value.

Description, Analyses, and Conclusion

This section follows the introductory material and contains the body of the
report. Essentially, it outlines the appraisal process from start to conclusion.

Identification of the Property

The subject parcel should be clearly identified by street address and legal description. If the legal description is lengthy, it may be included in the addenda and simply referred to at this point. A map of the property is desirable if the legal description is hard to follow.

Objectives of the Appraisal

The statement of objectives should include the following parts:

1. Property rights appraised.
2. Date of value estimate.
3. Purpose of the appraisal and definition of value sought.
4. Intended use of the appraisal report.

Description of Neighborhood and Community

Neighborhood and community data should include a brief history of the area and the prominent physical, social, and economic factors. The intent is to draw a clear picture of the neighborhood for the reader. Usually, the quality and general appearance of the homes, main community interests, and sources of employment for the residents are included. Other nearby land uses, and convenience to shopping, schools, cultural centers, and transportation routes, are also described. When important observations and conclusions are made, they should always be accompanied by supporting facts. For example, neighborhood improvement or decline, if asserted, should be documented by reference to specific examples of improved or deteriorated property, or by reference to factual studies.

The amount and kind of detail included in this section depends upon the purpose it will serve. For example, if industrial property is being appraised, statistics on the economic base of a community are of more significance than the number of churches and schools in the area.

Land Data, Zoning, Services, and Taxes

Land site data, as discussed in Chapter 6, should present the physical characteristics, site location elements, and private and public restrictions of the subject property. Lot size and shape, street improvements, topography, and soil conditions should be described, with reference to any maps, plats, and photographs included either in the report or the addenda.

The precise zoning classification of the parcel needs to be identified, as well as the municipality that has jurisdiction over the property. (Figure 16.5 is an example of a zoning map.) Also, any special building restrictions or regulations must be described.

The availability of public utilities should be noted, as well as any problems regarding their reliability. If a septic tank is used to dispose of sewage, it should be made known to the client. If there are questions about adequate drainage, they should be referred to the appropriate expert for study, with the client's approval and at his or her expense.

Based on the latest information available from the assessment roll, relevant property tax information should also be included in this section. When the appraiser has reason to expect a significant change in property taxes, information on the probable change should be provided here. For example, in some states, property is reassessed upon property transfer or upon long-term lease agreement.

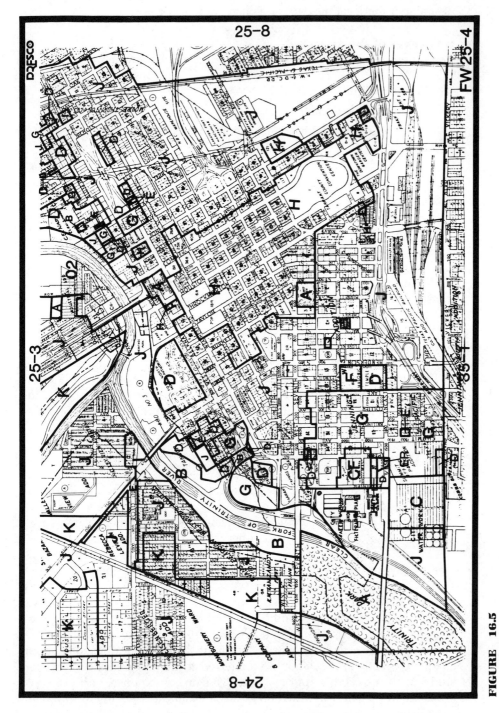

FIGURE 16.5
Example of a Zoning Map. (Courtesy of DRESCO, Inc., Roddy Publications)

Description of Improvements

Following the inspection guidelines covered in Chapter 7, the description of the improvements should include their physical features and also their condition, general marketability, and appeal. However, if detailed improvement specifications, blueprints, and photographs are to be included, they should probably be placed in the addenda of the report. Any deferred maintenance or structural defects noted during the improvement inspection must be described carefully in the body of the report.

Highest and Best Use

The appraiser's opinion of highest and best use must be stated here. If any other use than the present use is suggested, supporting evidence for such a conclusion should be discussed in detail in the report. The highest and best use statement should cover the highest and best use of the site, as if vacant, and then the highest and best use of the improved property.

Analysis of Data by the Value Approaches

It is helpful to introduce the value approaches used in the appraisal with a brief description of these methods. Their general strengths and weaknesses, as well as their applicability in the appraisal, should be briefly explained. Some appraisers label this subsection Methodology.

The Cost Approach

If structural improvements are included in the appraisal, the cost approach may be presented early or late in the value analysis, depending upon its relative importance. The priority of sequence is sometimes interpreted to suggest emphasis.

Land or site value should be based on one of the recognized methods of appraisal described in Chapter 10, with a full exposition of the market data leading to the conclusion.

Improvement value should be demonstrated by an analysis of reproduction or replacement cost new, less the estimated total value loss as compared with the improvement as if it were new. A clear explanation of any deferred maintenance, as well as any functional or economic obsolescence allowance, should be provided.

The Sales Comparison Approach

The basic data to be included in the sales comparison approach are the pertinent facts about each comparable sale. In the appraisal of single-family residential properties, these facts usually include:

1. Name of buyer and seller.
2. Date of sale and date of recordation.
3. Sales price and terms of sale.
4. Lot size and shape.
5. Description of residence, including square-foot size, number of rooms, bedrooms and baths, age and condition, type of construction, and character of outside improvements, such as garage and swimming pool.

Most narrative appraisal reports present comparable sales in an abbreviated chart form (see Example 16.1), in the body of the report. All the details about the sales are recited in separate sales data sheets in the addenda. A sample sheet is presented in Figure 16.6

Example 16.1
Comparable Sales Chart

Address	Price	Date	Quality	Condition	Lot (sq ft)	Building (sq ft)	Age
(1) 718 Stonewall	$375,000	1/85	Excellent	Good	8,850	4,811	1978
(2) 3921 Rose	300,000	7/84	Good	Good	7,250	3,830	1910
(3) 331 Oakridge	462,000	2/85	Good	Good	28,793	3,461	1952
(4) 7792 Crestor	318,000	2/85	Good	Average	15,000	3,136	1937
(5) 1864 Walnut	335,000	10/84	Excellent	Excellent	3,960	2,323	1925
(6) 8274 Alvarado	390,000	11/85	Excellent	Good	9,200	5,137	1914
(7) Subject	—	2/86	Excellent	Very good	8,292	5,409	1907

The appraiser should include the following additional data for multiple-family residence sales:

6. Number and type of units.

7. Sale price per unit, per room, and/or per square foot.

8. Gross scheduled rent.

9. Gross rent multiplier.

```
                           SALES DATA

    ADDRESS:  248 Park St.            PARCEL:  62-2872-xx

    CITY:     Waco

    GRANTOR:  John E. Thomas

    GRANTEE:  James T. Stoms

    DATE SOLD: 1/85                   DATE RECORDED: 2/9/85

    VOLUME: 2784        PAGE: 26      DOCUMENT:  81-149

    SALE PRICE: $125,000

    SALE TERMS: $117,000 mortgage by      CONFIRMED BY: Seller's
     seller, market rate, 10 year payoff    attorney and by buyer.
    ZONE: Single        LOT AREA: 6225 sq. ft.  LOT SIZE:  Rectangle, 65 F.F.,
         family                                  diagonal rear line.
    IMPROVEMENTS:      STORIES: 1      AGE:  new 1926
      Wood frame residence, 2200 square feet

    ANALYSIS:
     -Paid $56.82/S.F. of building.
     -Rent was $500 at sale, raised to $630.
     Another $10 rent increase will go into effect next
     month because of increased taxes.
     -At current rents, sold for 198 times monthly
     gross income.
```

FIGURE 16.6

The Income Approach

In the case of income and investment properties, this section in the appraisal report should outline and summarize the investigation made to determine market rent, suggest appropriate capitalization methods, and show how rates of return for the subject property were derived. Specific properties studied should be cited. Then a reconstructed operating statement should be provided, along with a discussion presenting the basis for the expense projections. It is preferred that the income capitalization procedure be clearly demonstrated in formula form, with the process itself also explained in a narrative fashion.

Reconciliation and Final Conclusion of Value

This section should review for the reader the findings of each value approach explored and describe their relevance in this appraisal. Therefore, the appraiser should discuss the reliability of the data used and the applicability of each approach and, finally, should provide an argument to justify the final conclusion of value rendered.

Qualifying and Limiting Conditions

The statement of qualifying and limiting conditions serves to clarify the assumptions made by the appraiser, limit his or her legal liability, and define the rights of disclosure of information contained in the report. A typical statement includes provisions as follows:

1. The appraiser assumes no responsibility for matters of a legal nature affecting the property.

2. Any sketch in the report may show approximate dimensions; the appraiser has made no survey of the property.

3. The appraiser is not required to give testimony or appear in court regarding the appraisal unless arrangements have been previously made.

4. Any distribution of values in the report between land and improvements applies only under the existing program of utilization and may not apply in other contexts.

5. The appraiser assumes that there are no hidden or unapparent conditions of the property, subsoil, or structures that would render it more or less valuable.

6. Information, estimates, and opinions furnished by others were obtained from sources considered reliable and believed to be true and correct, but no responsibility for the accuracy of such items is assumed by the appraiser.

7. Disclosure of the contents of the appraisal report is governed by the bylaws and regulations of the professional appraisal organizations with which the appraiser is affiliated.

8. Neither all nor any part of the content of the report, or copy thereof, shall be used for any purposes other than the purpose specified in the report without the previous written consent of the appraiser.

Certification of Value Opinion

This is a signed statement that gives assurance of the appraiser's neutrality and responsibility. It typically includes the following assertions:

1. The appraiser has no present or contemplated future interest in the property appraised; and neither the employment to make the appraisal nor the compensation for it is contingent upon the appraised value of the property.

2. The appraiser has no personal interest in or bias with respect to the subject matter of the appraisal report or the participants in the sale.

3. The appraiser has personally inspected the property, both inside and out, and has made an exterior inspection of all comparable sales listed in the report. To the best of the appraiser's knowledge and belief, all statements and information in this report are true and correct and the appraiser has not knowingly withheld any significant information.

4. All contingent and limiting conditions that are imposed by the terms of the assignment, or by the undersigned, affecting the analyses, opinions, and conclusions contained in the report are presented herein.

5. This appraisal report has been made in conformity with, and is subject to, the requirements of the Code of Professional Ethics and Standards of Professional Conduct of the appraisal organizations with which the appraiser is affiliated.

QUALIFICATIONS OF SAMUEL GEORGE

EDUCATION — ACADEMIC
  Bachelor of Business Administration Degree, Major: Real Estate
  University of Texas, Austin, Texas, 1975.

EDUCATION — PROFESSIONAL
  Education Seminars and Conferences: Richland Community College Extension;
  American Institute of Real Estate Appraisers, including AIREA exams or
  courses 1, 2, 4 & 8; Texas Real Estate License.

PROFESSIONAL AFFILIATIONS
  Member, American Institute of Real Estate Appraisers (MAI #CD40)
  Senior Member, American Society of Appraisers (ASA), in Real Estate.

PROFESSIONAL ACTIVITY
  AIREA: Texas Chapter Admissions Committee, 1980-82 and other committee
  memberships
  Instructor: Real Estate subjects, Richland Community College Extension
  Richardson, Texas

APPRAISAL EXPERIENCE
  Since 1963, appraisals in excess of $100,000,000.
  Expert Witness - Testimony in Dallas, Rockwall and Hunt Counties.
  Property tax appeals, eminent domain, bankruptcy, income tax, and
  damage lawsuits.

CLIENTS
  Either individually or in association with other appraisers including:
      Foster City; Bank of Dallas; Union Bank; North Central Bank;
      First National Bank; Singer Company; SCM Corporation; Newhall
      Land and Farming Company; Coopers and Lybrand, CPAs; Homequity,
      Inc.; Executrans; U.S. National Park Service; and numerous
      private clients.

FIGURE 16.7

6. All conclusions and opinions concerning the real estate that are set forth in the appraisal report were prepared by the signing appraiser (unless otherwise indicated in the appraisal report).

Qualifications of the Appraiser

This is usually a one- or two-page biosketch of the appraiser, outlining his or her education and experience. It often cites important appraisals that he

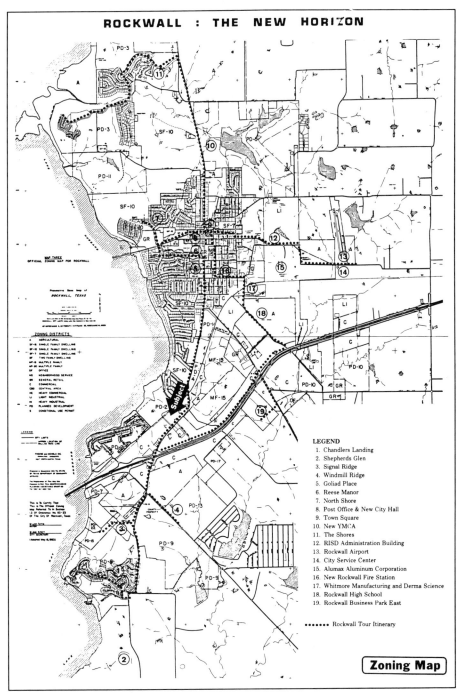

FIGURE 16.8
Maps Are Often Used as Supporting Material. (Courtesy of Jeff Potter)

or she has made. Professional designations, leadership activity, real estate teaching experience, and titles of any published writings are also suitable topics to include. The appraiser's qualifications not only serve to suggest the level of confidence to be placed in the value investigation but also indicate whether the appraiser would probably be considered by a judge as qualified to testify as an expert witness if such service is ever required. A sample qualifications sheet is shown in Figure 16.7.

Addenda or Supporting Material

The addenda should contain any relevant data not included in the body of the report. Examples include:

1. Maps (Figure 16.8, page 341) or photographs.
2. Plot plan of the subject property (see Figure 16.9).
3. Floor plan or diagram of improvements (see Figure 16.10).
4. Statistical data.
5. Sales data sheets and maps.

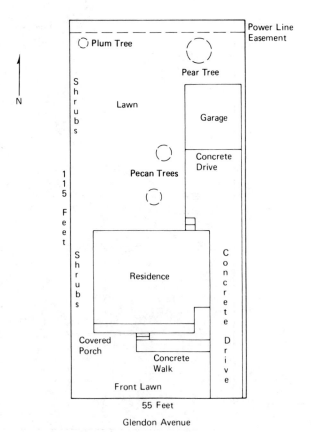

FIGURE   16.9
Plot Plan of the Subject Property

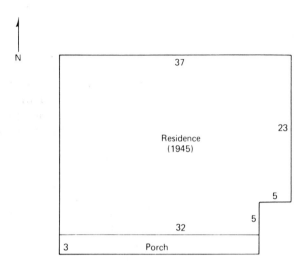

Area Computations
Residence: 23 × 37 =   851
                5 × 32 =   160
                       1,011 Square feet
Porch: 3 × 32 =   96 Square feet
Garage: 20 × 18 = 360 Square feet

FIGURE 16.10
Building Diagram of the Subject Property

SUMMARY

The written appraisal report is a formal business communication from the appraiser to the client. In the tradition of good business standards and appraisal practice, the report should be concise, well organized, and easy to read.

All written appraisals should contain only the information necessary to define the appraisal problem, present the factual data found by the study, and show support for the stated opinion of value.

The essential elements included in every appraisal report, whether written or oral, are:

1. The name of the client requesting the appraisal.
2. An adequate identification and description of the property.
3. A statement of the rights being appraised.
4. The purpose of the appraisal and the intended use of the report.
5. The date of valuation.
6. A formal definition of the type of value sought.
7. A summary of the factual data used to make the appraisal, and interpretation and analysis as appropriate.

8. The final estimate of value.

9. The assumptions or limiting conditions under which the appraisal was made.

10. The appraiser's certification and signature.

The three main types of written appraisal reports are the letter report, the form (or short form) report, and the narrative report. The letter report is a short business letter containing all the essential elements but abbreviating the supporting data, often referring to some facts in the appraiser's files. The conditions, assumptions, and appraiser's value certification, however, should be included or attached, no matter how short the letter report.

There are many variations of the form (or short-form) report. The most commonly used short-form report is the FHLMC Form, or FNMA Form 1004, simply referred to as the Form 70. This form is required by the Federal Home Loan Mortgage Corporation, the Federal National Mortgage Association, and most savings and loan associations. It contains all the basic elements of an appraisal report and is accompanied by FHLMC Form 439 (or FNMA Form 1004B), which provides a formal definition of value and furnishes the appraiser's certification and statement of contingent and limiting conditions.

The most detailed, formal, and lengthy appraisal report is the narrative report. This report is preferred when the client wants to follow the appraiser's step-by-step logic in arriving at the value conclusion and needs to have documentation of all the pertinent facts revealed in the investigation performed.

Various government agencies and appraisal organizations have developed rather rigid requirements for the form and content of narrative appraisal reports. Because of the high standards required, a demonstration narrative appraisal report is often used as a test for the appraiser seeking a professional designation.

The narrative appraisal report requires very high standards. The actual writing of this report includes three basic considerations: appearance, form, and content. Obviously, the appearance must be formal, neat, and professional. Narrative appraisal reports should follow a carefully planned outline and form. The format presented in this chapter is not only traditional but also makes it easier for the client to follow, visualize, and remember the facts and conclusions of the appraisal report. Of course, the content is the most important of the three considerations. The facts, analyses, and opinions set forth in a narrative report should show the appraiser's best efforts to "leave no stone unturned" in carrying out the appraisal assignment. Thus, the narrative appraisal report enables the appraiser to utilize all the knowledge, skill, or training at his or her command, and present to the client the information required in a succinct, convincing, and interesting manner.

IMPORTANT TERMS AND CONCEPTS

Assumptions	Letter of transmittal
Certification	Letter report
FHLMC Form 70	Limiting conditions
FHLMC Form 439	Narrative report
Form (or short-form) report	Qualifications of the appraiser

REVIEWING YOUR UNDERSTANDING

1. Written appraisal reports are a form of business communication. Every report should be:

   (a) Concise
   (b) Well organized
   (c) Easy to read
   (d) All of the above

2. The essential elements of appraisal reports:

   (a) Usually follow the outlines of the appraisal process
   (b) Vary according to the type of report
   (c) Are dependent upon the requirements of the client
   (d) None of the above

3. The type of appraisal report depends upon the amount of background information and detail required by the client. Which of the following types is the longest and most detailed?

   (a) The letter report
   (b) The form report
   (c) The narrative report
   (d) The subdivision report

4. There are three main subdivisions in the typical narrative appraisal report. Which of the following is not one of these subdivisions?

   (a) Introduction
   (b) Letter of transmittal
   (c) Description, analyses, and conclusion
   (d) Addenda

5. Which type of appraisal report requires a statement of the rights being appraised?

   (a) The letter report
   (b) The form report
   (c) The narrative report
   (d) All of the above

6. The letter report usually:

   (a) Contains only a brief description of the subject property
   (b) Does not contain the assumptions, limiting conditions, and the appraiser's value certification
   (c) Is the most formal written report
   (d) Is required by institutions and agencies

7. In the form report, it is not usually necessary for the appraiser to:

   (a) Demonstrate evidence of value through one or more approaches
   (b) Describe any physical deterioration or functional inadequacy found in the structure
   (c) Rate the neighborhood employment stability
   (d) Write a letter of transmittal to the client

8. Sales data sheets in the addenda of a narrative appraisal report contain:

   (a) Details about each comparable sale

(b) An analysis of the data by the value approaches

(c) An outline of the investigation made to determine market rent

(d) All of the above

9. In the reconciliation and final conclusion of value, the appraiser should:

(a) Describe the relevance of each value approach explored

(b) Discuss the reliability of the data used

(c) Provide arguments to justify the final conclusion of value rendered

(d) All of the above

10. The statement of limiting conditions in the appraisal report:

(a) Serves to clarify the assumptions made by the appraiser

(b) Limits the appraiser's legal liability

(c) Obligates the appraiser to appear in court regarding the appraisal at any future time

(d) Both parts (a) and (b) are correct

CHAPTER
SEVENTEEN

APPRAISING
SPECIAL
OWNERSHIPS
AND INTERESTS

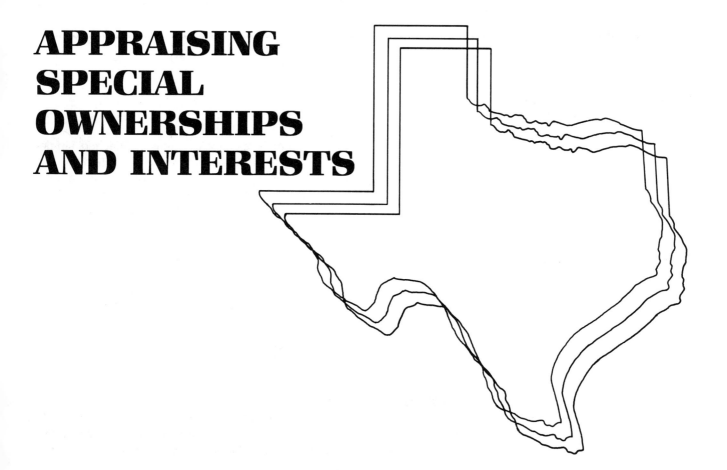

Increasingly, new ownership concepts and unique types of residential properties have presented new appraisal problems. This chapter provides an introduction to some unusual types of housing—from town houses to mobile homes.

Next, we review the appraisal of partial interests in real estate. A partial interest consists of an ownership interest that includes less than the unencumbered fee title. The most common example of this is property subject to a lease.

Finally, we introduce you to the appraisal of property for purposes of condemnation under the power of eminent domain. This is one of the most specialized, technical areas of appraisal practice. The intent of this section is to point out the areas of similarity to other appraisals, as well as the major differences. Performing satisfactory eminent domain appraisals is difficult and generally requires years of appraisal experience and education.

When you have finished this chapter, you should be able to:

1. List at least four less common types of homes, define each, and explain what special problems each presents to the appraiser.

2. Explain the difference between a condominium, a real estate cooperative, and a planned unit development.

3. Define the several commonly marketed types of partial interests in housing and explain how to value each.

4. Explain three ways in which the appraisal process is different for eminent domain appraisals.

SECTION 17.1
CONDOMINIUMS AND
OTHER SPECIALIZED HOUSING

The typical appraisal assignment is usually to value a detached single-family home on a fee-simple lot. More and more frequently, however, appraisers are working with varied and unusual types of housing. Some of these new types of appraisal assignments involve property types that are centuries old; others involve new ideas in housing. A variety of unusual homes will be discussed in this section.

Variations in Housing Design

Several new types of housing are characterized by the lack of side yards. Eliminating side yards reduces the amount of land required per housing unit and lowers the cost of land. The smaller lot also reduces the per-lot costs for roads, street lights, utility mains, and so on, because the frontage per lot is less. Row houses, town houses, planned unit developments, and zero-lot-line homes are typical of this type of housing.

Row Houses

What is a row house? It is a house on an individual lot, which is nearly always owned in fee simple, built without side yards between adjoining houses. Common walls are an essential characteristic. The concept of row housing is centuries old and was the tradition in urban housing of the early 1800s in the eastern United States. In some areas, lots have been developed with widths of as little as 11 feet. Lot depths of 70 to 100 feet are typical in row house development.

Because of the close proximity of row houses, several housing problems must be given more attention by the appraiser in valuing row houses. One common urban housing problem is obtaining a degree of personal privacy and protection from fire. The limited spacing between neighbors allows row houses less visual privacy than in conventional houses because there is no room for foliage. Fire can be a threat because there is no side yard to function as a firebreak. With row houses, the type of wall between the units may determine the extent of sound insulation and fire resistance. Most commonly, problems arise when two units share a common wall structure, called a party wall, instead of two separate walls. This type of construction is now used less frequently because it is harder to design satisfactorily. In addition, the use of a party wall imposes legal obligations on each owner concerning maintenance and repairs that can sometimes lead to conflicts between neighbors.

Town Houses

The town house is essentially a modern name for the row house. However, most town houses are in larger projects built since 1970. They are typically designed as two-story units, on fee lots, without side yards. Town houses are sometimes built in clusters of four or more, creating end units that are separated from the next cluster of units by side yards. A current trend is toward the small town house project (as few as three units) on an existing city lot. These are frequently referred to as ''in-fill'' developments, since they are filling in bypassed vacant lots.

The most noticeable town house projects are the large ones, which are popular in many parts of the country. Often designed as retirement communities, these developments offer a type of self-contained living environment, complete with elaborate recreation facilities such as tennis courts and golf courses. Most commonly, the yard areas and recreation facilities are owned by all the unit owners. Normally, town house projects have a homeowners' association, which takes care of the commonly owned areas and exterior maintenance of the buildings. Homeowners pay association fees to cover common expenses. Effectively, the owners' association is a local government, complete with rules, taxing power, and occasional member conflicts.

Notice that each homeowner usually owns the individual lot on which the home sits. Such ownership is considerably different from condominium ownership (condominiums will be discussed later in this section). In different areas of the country, town house projects are called by different names. In Texas, for example, this type of ownership is usually called a planned unit development, and the label town house refers only to the architectural styling that is featured.

Planned Unit Development

The planned unit development, or PUD, is a zoning concept that became popular in the late 1960s. Planned unit development zoning allows flexibility in lot size, density, and variety, creating better project designs. Many PUD projects have been built with town house styling so that the two terms PUD and town house are often used together, as noted earlier. Some newer housing developments mix the types of units: detached houses, town houses, zero-lot-line homes (discussed below), condominiums, and sometimes rental housing. Commercial buildings can even be a part of the plan.

The unique problems in the appraisal of town houses and planned unit developments often revolve around handling the recreation facilities and other common areas and recognizing the effects of a good or bad home-owners' association. For example, the cost approach must allocate a proportional part of the total cost of all common area improvements to the unit under appraisal. This cost may add proportionately more to the value of some units than to others. Land value is usually allocated as a percentage of the total property value or abstracted from sales. The sales comparison approach may be difficult because of a shortage of adequate recent sales of similar-sized units within the same project. Sales from nearby projects may not be helpful either, if recreation or other amenities are so different that each project forms a different "neighborhood."

Zero-Lot-Line (Patio) or Courtyard Homes

A zero-lot-line home, also called a patio or courtyard home, is based upon design concepts developed in California in the 1970s. Adjacent homes are built without side yards, as in the row house style. Normally, they are one-story. Instead of being rectangular-shaped, as row houses or town houses often are, the homes usually are L-shaped. Each L wraps around a courtyard or patio, as shown in Figure 17.1, forming two of the courtyard's four sides. The side wall of the adjacent house forms the third side of the patio.

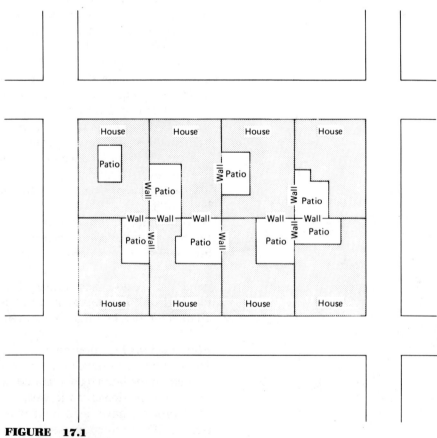

FIGURE 17.1
Zero-Lot-Line Homes

This wall is usually windowless to assure the privacy of the patio. The back of the patio may be the windowless rear wall of the house behind or a high fence or wall. The patio home provides privacy and open space on a very small lot.

In the appraisal of patio homes, it is important to note whether the project design has addressed the sound and fire problems typical of row houses. The appraiser should examine and note the visual privacy of the outdoor patio, since such privacy is often a major factor to buyers. The appraiser must consider how it will sell on the local market, usually by comparing the sales prices of patio homes to those of town houses or detached houses of similar size and amenities.

Varying the Type of Ownership

The second unique housing concept entails a different legal form of ownership. In the regular detached home, the owner's title includes the building and the land under it. Both building and land are owned in fee simple, that is, owned outright. Of course, such title is subject to the four government restrictions discussed in Chapter 2, as well as to any existing loans, leases, and so on. In the forms of ownership discussed in this section, however, the person who "owns" the dwelling unit holds a type of title or ownership right different from that of a conventional detached home.

Condominiums

What is a condominium? It is a form of real estate ownership. The dwelling unit itself, or the airspace it occupies, is separately owned, and the land underneath is owned in common with the owners of the other dwelling units. The common example of a condominium is a multistory complex of units, similar to an apartment building. With a three-story building, there could be three identical dwelling units, one on each floor. Obviously, each of the three owners cannot own the land underneath, so they must share its ownership. Besides sharing the ownership of the land, condominium owners share the ownership of the lobby, halls, parking spaces, recreation facilities, and other common areas. Since the individual units extend between interior wall surfaces, the structural walls are also owned in common. (See Figure 17.2.)

The legal description of a condominium unit, accordingly, is not restricted to two dimensions on a horizontal plane. Rather, it describes the space as a three-dimensional outline of airspace to include the height of the unit from some reference point, as well as its length and width. This explains the term airspace condominium—each unit consists of a "block" of airspace. The legal description also describes the percentage ownership of the common areas and *their* descriptions.

The condominium dates back to ancient Rome. Its active use in the United States is recent, starting with enabling laws passed in the early 1960s. The condominium idea has since been applied both to new construction and to existing buildings. In both cases, a developer must subdivide the airspace and offer for sale the right to own individual units separately.

A condominium is usually run by a homeowner's association, similar to that of a PUD or town house project. The basic authority given to the association is set forth in the recorded conditions, covenants, and restrictions (CC&Rs) document that is binding upon each owner. The association normally runs the project, maintains the exterior and common areas, and

FIGURE   17.2
A Condominium Project. (Photograph Courtesy of Doug Frost)

adopts rules to minimize conflicts between owners. Some associations also set up recreation, child-care, and education programs.

In appraising an individual condominium, the appraiser most commonly emphasizes the sales comparison approach. There are four important aspects to the sales comparison of condominiums. The first is the market itself: Have condominiums sold well in this market area? In some areas, neighborhoods, and price ranges, the condominium concept has sold poorly. In others, market reception has been very good. If the appraiser can identify recent market sales of units in the same project, these sales may provide the best comparables. The second aspect is the unit itself: What size, condition, quality, and amenities are offered? As in the appraisal of town houses, the appraiser must consider how adequate the sound insulation is, especially in condominium conversions. The third aspect is the scope of recreation facilities, parking, and other common areas. Projects vary greatly. In some states, these common facilities may be owned by the developer and leased to the homeowners' association; it pays to double-check the ownership of all common areas. These facilities must be reviewed for their quality, condition, and features. In addition, the appraiser must consider whether they are adequate. A single 10 × 20 foot swimming pool may add little to the value of a 500-unit project in a summer resort area because the pool is far too small for the demand.

A fourth aspect for the appraiser to consider is the homeowners' association. How much is the annual assessment? How does the assessment compare to that of nearby similar projects? Is the budget adequate to maintain the project? Does the association appear competently managed? How stable are the relationships between the association and its members? These questions relate to the continued ability of the project to provide a comfortable place to live.

As you can see, appraisals of condominium projects require first a good understanding of the ownership rights and then a knowledge of the differences that are typical from unit to unit as well as from project to project.

Cooperatives

There are many different types of cooperative ventures in our society. Here, we are interested in the stock cooperative form of ownership for a multiple-unit housing project, somewhat similar to the condominium concept. In a stock cooperative, each owner holds a stated percentage ownership in the cooperative association. The association owns the land and buildings and grants the individual owner the permanent right to occupy the specified dwelling unit, as well as the right to the joint use of the common areas.

Cooperative ownership of real estate has existed in the United States for some years. For example, numbers of cooperative apartment buildings were built in New York City during the 1950s and 1960s. A major flaw with the cooperative concept at that time was the method of financing. One master mortgage covered the entire building. When an individual cooperative unit resold, the buyer had to pay for the seller's equity interest (the total unit value, less the unit's proportionate share of the current balance on the master mortgage) in cash or with an unsecured note to the seller. It was *not* possible to refinance, unless a majority of the owners of all of the units agreed to refinance the entire master mortgage. When condominium legislation of the 1960s offered condominiums and other partial ownerships that could be separately financed, the cooperative ownership concept fell into disfavor.

Mobile Homes and Prefabs

Another special type of housing consists of structures that are of unusual construction. Of course, what is unusual construction at any one time may become common a few years later. Two types of similar but unusual construction are of particular interest to the appraiser. One is the mobile home; the other, the prefabricated home. The number of each has increased considerably over the past decade. This increased popularity is due to cost advantages but is restrained by some special problems that appraisers need to understand.

Mobile Homes

What is a mobile home? It is a housing unit that is capable of being moved on the highway. The mobile home is different from a travel trailer, which is much smaller and designed for part-time living and frequent moving. A mobile home is also different from a modular home, although both might have the same floor plan and be built at the same factory. Both are described by the label "manufactured housing." However, the modular home has no wheels, undercarriage, or towing arrangement, and is designed to be permanently placed on a lot.

Mobile homes are sold in various lengths and widths. Generally, state laws limit the maximum width and length. For many states, 12 feet wide by 60 feet long is a practical maximum. Such units are called a "twelve-wide." Often, the mobile home consists of several units, transported separately and fastened together at the site. Each unit might be the maximum 12 × 60 feet. "Double-wide" units, 24 × 60 feet, are common, and some "triple-wide" mobile homes can be found. Figure 17.3 displays an older "single-wide."

Over the past decade, the number of mobile homes built each year has increased substantially. Mobile homes are built in a factory, which means a

FIGURE 17.3
An Older Mobile Home. (Photograph Courtesy of Doug Frost)

major saving to the buyer. This advantage has been somewhat ignored because of the poor past image of mobile-home communities, relatively unattractive exterior design, and the inability to obtain zoning for new mobile-home parks.

The appraisal of mobile homes offers some special problems. As with other housing, the appraiser should consider the age, condition, quality, and features of the mobile home. However, *location* takes on added importance in the appraisal of homes located within rental mobile-home parks. In some areas, there are special laws regarding rental rates and occupancy rights in these parks. In addition, most areas have a shortage of spaces, and waiting lists are common. Some park owners also sell new mobile homes and try to reserve vacant spaces for their new customers. As a result, sales prices of used mobile homes can vary, according to whether or not the buyer gets to rent the space at the park or must move the mobile home. The appraiser must examine sales and try to estimate how much of the total price was paid for the mobile home and how much was paid for the right to occupy the space at the park. A third important element of location is to consider the different features of the particular mobile-home park.

Whether the mobile home is located in a mobile-home park or situated on a privately owned lot, its appraisal is most commonly based upon the sales comparison process. The income capitalization approach is rarely used because very few mobile homes are purchased as income-generating investments. The cost approach is difficult to apply because (1) open market sales of lots zoned for mobile homes are infrequent in most areas, (2) the estimate of accrued depreciation is often more difficult than in conventional homes, and (3) the influence of location upon value is difficult to measure when the home is located in a mobile-home park.

How is the sales comparison approach applied in the appraisal of mobile homes? When the home is on a privately owned lot, whether in a conventional subdivision or a mobile-home park condominium, the process is the same as that used in any appraisal relying upon sales of similar homes on similar sites. However, when a mobile home is located in a *rental* mobile-home park, and site value is not a factor, some appraisers rely on national publications that list average prices for particular models of mobile homes. This is less accurate than relying on local sales prices but may be adequate for loan purposes because the national data involve a large number of sales. The national publications are also able to present actual average market price adjustments for awnings, utility sheds, and other common mobile-home extras.

Prefabricated and Modular Homes

A major portion of the money spent to build a conventional house goes for labor. Traditionally, each board is cut to the desired length at the house site. The use of prefabrication in housing attempts to lower this cost by transferring work from the construction job site to a factory-style operation. See Figure 17.4. The advantages of a factory operation include the use of machines to increase the production per person, as well as an assembly-line style of construction that operates with a less expensive work force. The influence of the factory-style process upon housing has been noticeable in the design of both modular homes and prefabricated components for conventional houses.

Most modular homes are essentially of mobile-home design but without the running gear and towing assembly. However, some two-story designs have been offered. The biggest handicaps have been public acceptance, the tendency toward a boxy look, problems getting building code approval, and the high cost of transporting units any great distance from the factory. The advantages are the considerable cost reductions and the reduced con-

FIGURE 17.4
Modular Homes. (Courtesy of the U.S. Department of Housing and Urban Development)

struction period compared with other methods. Within the past few years, more attractive designs of modular and prefabricated homes have reduced resistance to modular homes among building officials as well as buyers. Thus, expansion of modular home construction is anticipated in the years ahead.

Modular homes, based upon mobile home designs, are not the only form of factory housing. A second category is often labeled prefabricated housing. Prefabricated houses are similar to conventionally built homes except that many of the component parts of the house are pre-assembled in a factory and shipped to the job site for assembly. Unfortunately, the savings in labor costs are usually offset by the high capital costs of the factory. Also, buyers have often reacted to such homes as being either too boxy, too repetitious, or too unconventional.

Market acceptance is the biggest question facing the appraiser of modular and prefabricated housing. Of course, the design must be evaluated to consider unit size, features, and especially layout. The interior and exterior finish materials and the unit's appearance must then be compared with units selling in the local area. When the units are quite different from housing sold locally, the appraiser might want to get a consumer panel's reaction to the units if presale appraisals are being made.

As noted earlier, the use of prefabricated components is the second major component of factory-built housing. Roof trusses were an early prefabricated component. As a form of prefabrication, many larger homebuilders now precut and package all the lumber needed for a particular model of a home. Some fireplace-chimney units are prefabricated. Plastic tub and shower combinations are now common; full prefabricated plastic bathrooms are available but less common. Some builders now preassemble nearly all the complex plumbing, drain, and vent pipes into one wall section. Increasing numbers of firms supply preassembled wall panels. Precast concrete floor or wall assemblies are especially common. The use of prefabricated components is clearly a growing element in construction, spurred on by high costs of on-site labor and the appeal of some new energy-saving wall assemblies now being offered.

SECTION 17.2 VALUATION OF PARTIAL INTERESTS

Appraisals can involve many types of partial interests (or subdivisions of the fee interest) in real estate. For example, appraisals are often made to divide the value of the fee interest between the owner and tenant; in legal terms, the lessor and lessee. Less common, partial-interest appraisals include those found between the life estate and the remainder estate, the interest between lender and borrower, and the valuation of time-share ownerships.

In this section, each of these types of partial ownership will be described. In addition, the appraisal process for each will be outlined. Note, however, that this section is only an introduction to these complex subjects.

Leased Property

The most common appraisal situation involving a partial interest is the leased property. Any lease of real estate subdivides the rights to the property because the tenant gains possession of the property in return for agreeing to pay the owner the contracted rent. If the contract rent is less than the market rent (which can happen in a rising market), the tenant keeps the difference. The benefit of such a rent difference creates a value that belongs to the tenant. The amount of this leasehold value depends on the size of the rent differences, as well as the remaining period of the lease.

Defining Leased Property Interests

As you can see, the difference between the contract rent and the market rent divides a leased property into two partial interests. The first is the owner's interest (lessor's interest, or leased fee), and the second is the tenant's interest (lessee's interest, or leasehold). Theoretically, each can be sold; therefore, each can be valued. In the appraisal of partial interests, the combined values of the two interests generally add up to equal the value of the fee-simple interest, although there is some question as to whether this is an exact and constant rule. Note that leased property interests may involve any type of real property, not just commercial or income property. For our examples, however, we will talk about an income-generating property (such as a store) because we can more easily show how the benefits of ownership are split up by using dollars of income.

Who Gets What?

The primary question in appraising leased property (and every other partial-interest situation) is "Who gets what?" How are the rights to the property split up? What are the obligations of owner and tenant? The lease conveys possession of the property for a limited time in return for a rental. Thus, it is essential to know what property is conveyed. Is the basement included? Does the owner retain use of a locked storeroom? Was the furniture included in the lease?

We must also know what the time period is, that is, the time remaining until the lease expires. This means we must know the exact expiration date of the lease. Many leases give the tenant an option to extend or renew the lease, when the expiration date arrives. Such options sometimes are at a different rent or even at a rent "to be agreed upon." Thus, we must read lease option clauses carefully in order to understand their real effect upon the owner's and tenant's respective rights.

Finally, we must know what rent terms have been agreed upon. The rent could be "flat"—the same amount throughout the lease; or the rent might be projected to vary, as in a "step-up" lease, where the rent increases by a stated amount each period. Some leases set the rent as a percentage of the tenant's business, usually in terms of the gross volume of sales. Percentage rent may be combined with a minimum flat rent, or it may be calculated only on sales volumes over a stated amount. Sometimes, percentage rent is reduced by stated categories of expenses paid by the tenant. More and more, we see leases in which the rent is increased as the consumer price index increases. The index used could be the national index or the index for a particular city. The rent increase, resulting from increases in the index, is sometimes calculated annually, although every five years is also common. There could also be a maximum to the allowable cost-of-living rent increase. In short, terms agreed upon between owner and tenant can be almost as varied and complex as the human mind can make them.

The tenant's responsibility for expenses is another factor in the analysis of leased property interests. This is significant because the rental alone may not completely define what amount the tenant pays. Each lease may vary, from a "gross" lease, in which the landlord must pay all operating expenses, to a truly "net" lease, in which the tenant pays everything. Indeed, in shopping centers, leases often require the tenants to pay operating expenses, *plus* a contribution toward a center promotion budget, *plus* separate payment for all the special partitions, storefronts, and so forth, in the store. As a result, the question the appraiser must answer about lease compensation is "Who pays what?"

Valuing Interests in Leased Property

The lessor's and the lessee's interests in leased property usually are appraised by the income approach. Separate valuations of the two interests are typically required. The cost approach provides no way to separate the interests. When market sales of leased property are available, the sales comparison approach may be used; however, an income analysis is generally required to interpret the sale and apply it to the property being appraised.

The value of the leasehold (the lessee's interest) can be estimated or measured by capitalizing the favorable rent difference over the life of the lease. By favorable rent difference, we mean the difference between the contract rent and market rent. This difference is a net annual benefit, similar to annual incomes from other real estate, and can be capitalized and converted into an estimate of value today. In contrast to other real estate income flows, however, this income benefit is scheduled to end at a known time in the future. For this reason, the capitalization procedure is more complex.

If leasehold estates were commonly bought and sold, the income to the lessee (the net rent savings) could be capitalized by using an overall capitalization rate derived from an analysis of sales. However, only those sales of similar tenant interests would be relevant. In practice, appraisers use annuity capitalization, a technique mentioned but not fully explained in Chapter 14 (the annuity capitalization techniques are more fully covered in advanced appraisal courses). Briefly, annuity capitalization makes use of special factors, or multipliers, usually listed in books of financial tables. The length of the lease and the relevant interest (discount) rate determine the factor selected. The appropriate factor is then multiplied by the annual income to calculate the current value. If the tenant's rent saving is not the same each year, more complex methods can be used.

The more common appraisal problem involves the appraisal of the landlord's interest, the leased fee, which could also be labeled the value of the property subject to a lease. The lessor's interest also involves an annual income for a known time period, the term of the lease. The present value of this income is estimated in the same manner as is the present value of the lessee's income. However, in addition to the lease income, the lessor gets back possession of the property when the lease is up and the right to sell the fee interest or rent it at full market rents. The return of the full ownership rights is called the reversion. Note that when studying *any* comparable sale, the appraiser should determine if the sale was of the full fee interest or if only a leased fee interest was sold. If the sale is of the leased fee, the appraiser must compare the contract rent with the market rent. For an appraisal of fee-simple interest in a property, a sale of a property that is subject to a poor lease is not the best comparable.

The economic benefits that the lessor obtains from the lease can then be described in terms of these two types of dollar flows, the annual income from the lease and the market value of the fee-simple rights at the end of the lease. In other words, the current value of the leased fee equals the present value of the income from the lease plus the present value of the reversion of the fee-simple rights.

How is the present value of the reversion calculated? The first step is to estimate what the fee-simple value of the property will be at the time the lease ends. This future value is translated into an estimate of present value, using another form of discount factor called the reversion factor. This entails looking up the proper factor in the financial tables, using the lease length and the relevant interest/discount rate. Then, the factor is multiplied by the appraiser's estimate of the future value of the reversion. The answer is the present value of the reversion. It is added to the present value of the income stream, and the total is the estimated value of the lessor's interest.

Since the combined value of the lessor and lessee interests usually equals the value of the undivided fee, some appraisers prefer to value the lessor's interest merely by subtracting the value of the lessee's interest from an estimate of the undivided fee value.

Valuing Other Partial Interests

Life Estates

Another way of breaking up the fee-simple interest is to split it into the life estate and the remainder estate. This unusual breakdown nearly always involves a residence. The owner of the life estate controls the right of possession and use of the property during the lifetime of some specifically named person. The named person usually owns the life estate but need not. The named person need not occupy the property either, since the owner of the life estate could sell or rent the property. The life estate owner must pay all the operating expenses but does not pay rent. A life estate is different from a lease in that no rent is paid and the term is not a fixed number of years. The owner of the remainder of the estate has *no* rights to the real property, except the right to gain full fee-simple ownership upon the death of the named person by whose life the estate is defined.

No one can reliably forecast when a named individual will die. However, there are studies of the *average* remaining life for people of various ages. These are called actuarial studies and were developed to calculate necessary life insurance premiums. From the actuarial studies, the appraiser calculates the breakdown of a property's total value into the life estate and the remainder, based upon the age of the person holding the life estate. These calculations are a form of annuity capitalization, dividing the present worth of $1 per year for the remaining life estimate of the holder of the life estate at an appropriate discount rate, by the present worth of $1 per year forever, calculated at the same discount rate. The answer is the total value represented by the life estate.

Figure 17.5 shows an IRS table for a female, using a 6% discount rate. The age of the owner of the life estate is in column 1, and column 4 shows the value of the remainder interest as a percent of the total market value.

Mortgaged Property

When someone borrows money and signs a mortgage or deed of trust on real property as security for the loan, he or she has split up the fee-simple interest into two parts. The lender's interest in the real property is the right to have the real property as security for the amount owing on the promissory note. The borrower's interest is the right to full use of the property less the obligation to make the payments.

Table, single life female, 6 percent, showing the present worth of an annuity; of a life interest; and of a remainder interest

(1) Age	(2) Annuity	(3) Life estate	(4) Remainder	(1) Age	(2) Annuity	(3) Life estate	(4) Remainder
0	15.8972	0.95383	0.04617	55	11.6432	.69859	.30141
1	16.2284	.97370	.02630	56	11.4353	.68612	.31388
2	16.2287	.97372	.02628	57	11.2200	.67320	.32680
3	16.2180	.97308	.02692	58	10.9980	.65988	.34012
4	16.2029	.97217	.02783	59	10.7703	.64622	.35378
5	16.1850	.97110	.02890	60	10.5376	.63226	.36774
6	16.1648	.96989	.03011	61	10.3005	.61803	.38197
7	16.1421	.96853	.03147	62	10.0587	.60352	.39648
8	16.1172	.96703	.03297	63	9.8118	.58871	.41129
9	16.0901	.96541	.03459	64	9.5592	.57355	.42645
10	16.0608	.96365	.03635	65	9.3005	.55803	.44197
11	16.0293	.96176	.03824	66	9.0352	.54211	.45789
12	15.9958	.95975	.04025	67	8.7639	.52583	.47417
13	15.9607	.95764	.04236	68	8.4874	.50924	.49076
	15.9239			69	8.2068	.49241	.50759

FIGURE 17.5
U.S. Treasury Valuation Table A(2), Internal Revenue Service

In one sense, the current value of the mortgage is its principal balance, or the amount owed. However, if current mortgage interest rates for new loans are considerably different from the interest rate being paid on an existing note and mortgage, then there is a problem. No one would buy the promissory note at its current balance because the interest return they receive would differ from the going rate of interest. Thus the current value of the note is a price that will yield for the buyer of the mortgage the current market interest rate, given the dollar payments the borrower has promised to make. Calculating this value involves another aspect of annuity capitalization. First, the annuity factor for the required yield rate and time is determined. Note that if the loan payments are received monthly, a monthly-payment factor must be used. The factor is then multiplied by the payment amount to find the present value of the promissory note. The value of the note can differ from the value of the lender's interest in the real estate itself. This topic is explored more fully in advanced appraisal courses.

The value of the borrower's interest in the real estate (also called the equity interest) is calculated most accurately by capitalizing the net income that the owner will have left after making loan payments. A number of capitalization techniques are available; one, described as the equity residual technique, is discussed in Chapter 14 of this text.

Time-Shared Ownership

Time-shared ownership is a new example of the increasing complexity of real estate. Most often applied to resort or vacation housing, it is a subdivision of the fee interest into blocks of time, with each time block owned by a different owner. The usual division is made by weeks. Thus, owner A might own the right to occupy the property during the second and third week of July. Owner J might purchase the last three weeks of the year, and so on. Most commonly, the project developer not only sells the units but manages them as well. Unoccupied units are rented out, and the unit owners are credited with the revenue after deducting expenses.

The individual time blocks sell for varying prices. In or near ski areas, the Christmas and Easter blocks sell at a large premium, but the summer periods may sell at a discount. The developer's most critical decision is to select a sale price for each block, with these premiums and discounts carefully balanced. The goal is to generate the maximum total revenue *and* most rapid sellout of all the time blocks. Prices for the individual units usually vary as well because of differences in views, exposure, and other locational influences. As a result, there is no fixed formula for valuing each unit time block. Valuation of the time-block ownership basically involves estimating (1) the value of the unit in fee simple, and then (2) the bonus/discount for each time block. The appraiser must carefully study the locational differences of each unit and the seasonal bonus/discounts found in the market for time-block projects that can be compared with the subject. Only by doing such research can the appraiser hope to value these interesting partial rights in real property.

SECTION 17.3 VALUATION FOR EMINENT DOMAIN

Defining Eminent Domain

We have said earlier that valuation for condemnation actions under the power of eminent domain is one of the most specialized areas of appraisal practice. The power of eminent domain is one of the four rights to real estate that are retained by the government (see Chapter 2). Eminent domain refers to the government's right to take private property from its owners for public use (whether the owners want to sell or not) upon payment of just compensation. This term, just compensation, has been interpreted by the courts to mean the fair market value of the property. The appraiser's primary role in eminent domain suits, then, is to estimate market value.

From this introduction, you can see that appraisal for eminent domain has the same general purpose as most other appraisals: the estimation of market value. There are other similarities, as well as some differences. Valuation for eminent domain is a complex subject; this section is intended as an introduction.

The Appraisal Process

Eminent domain valuation involves the same appraisal process as detailed in Chapter 3. The six steps of the appraisal process were listed as:

1. Defining the appraisal problem.
2. Planning the appraisal.
3. Collecting and analyzing the data.
4. Applying the appropriate value approaches.
5. Arriving at a value conclusion.
6. Reporting the appraisal conclusion.

Let us explore these steps as they apply to eminent domain appraising. We will not discuss step 2, planning the appraisal, because the information would be essentially the same as in Chapter 3.

Defining the Appraisal Problem
In Chapter 3 we listed the five essential elements necessary to define the appraisal problem:

1. Identify the property to be appraised.
2. Define the property rights to be appraised.
3. Establish the date of value.
4. Define the purpose of the appraisal and the value definition.
5. Identify the intended use of the report.

These same elements are essential to condemnation appraisal.

1. Identifying the property to be appraised can be a special problem, because the government does not always acquire the entire property. However, the appraiser must consider the concept of the "larger parcel," even if only a portion of the property is acquired. The ownership and value of fixtures is also a common problem in condemnation. We will explore these two topics later.

2. The property rights to be appraised in condemnation are most commonly the fee-simple rights. On occasion, however, the governmental agency could be condemning only an easement, a leasehold estate, or some other partial interest. The appraiser will usually be provided with a clear statement of the rights to be taken.

3. The date of value can be a significant problem in condemnation appraisals. It will usually be the date on which the formal court documents are filed, but it can also be a different date. The appraiser may have to rely on the client's attorney to indicate the date of value. Sometimes, too, the appraiser will have to reappraise the property as of a later date such as the trial date.

4. The purpose of the appraisal is always the estimation of market value. Various states and the federal courts follow slightly different legal definitions of value, however, so the appraiser must use the definition appropriate for the court hearing the case.

5. Finally, the intended use of the report could be for the condemnor (the public agency) or the condemnee (the owner). In the former case, the report usually will be the basis for the offer to the property owner. Often the condemnor will furnish the property owner with a copy or a summary of the appraisal report. When the appraisal report is for the condemnee (the property owner), it is most commonly for use in challenging the value assigned by the condemnor.

Collecting and Analyzing the Data

In the third step of the appraisal process, collecting and analyzing the data, there is a major difference between condemnation appraisal assignments and others. The difference is that the courts, rather than the appraiser, make the final decision as to what types of data are admissible, that is, can be used in testimony. Indeed, some jurisdictions by law exclude some types of market data that an appraiser might otherwise consider relevant to a particular appraisal. For example, listings and offers are not admissible in some courts. Sometimes a court will establish its own definition of comparability, limiting the date of sale or distance from the subject property for comparable sales instead of leaving such matters to the appraiser's judgment. However, the great majority of condemnation appraisals rely on the same kinds of sales, rents, costs, overall rates, and so on, that are required for loan appraisals or other common appraisal purposes.

Applying the Value Approaches

Special rules in condemnation appraisal also affect the fourth step in the appraisal process, applying the appropriate value approaches. Certain possible methods of analysis, such as the development method of land appraisal, may not be allowable in some jurisdictions or are given less weight by the courts. The appraiser will want to know this in planning the appraisal, in order not to rely on a method that the court will exclude. However, there are no special approaches to value, just the time-tested sales comparison, cost, and income approaches you have met before. Thus, most condemnation appraisals will rely on the same appraisal techniques and methods you would use for any other appraisal assignment.

Arriving at a Value Conclusion

This is the fifth step in the appraisal process. It is no different for eminent domain appraisal than appraising for other purposes, except that the value conclusion may have to be given in several parts, as detailed later.

Reporting the Conclusion

The sixth step in the appraisal process, reporting the value conclusion, is also modified for eminent domain appraisals. The major difference between condemnation and other appraisals is that the format for such appraisal reports varies greatly. In some cases, as in appraisals made for the condemnee, you might be asked to prepare only an oral report, leaving the expense of preparing a written report for a time closer to trial. If the parties can settle the case without a trial, the written report will not be needed.

In preparing an appraisal for the condemnor, however, a written appraisal report is usually required. The report will often be a long, documented narrative. The condemnee will sometimes be given a copy. A well-written report may play a key part in convincing the property owner to accept the government's offer.

Problems in Condemnation Appraisals

Condemnation law is different for real and personal property. Thus, for condemnation appraisals, it is often necessary to identify and appraise *only* the real property.

Fixtures

The problem area is fixtures: objects that were once personal property but have been joined to the real property and may now be either real or personal, depending on a series of complex rules. You may want to review the earlier coverage of this topic in Chapter 2. On occasion, the appraiser will have to prepare sets of values including and excluding particular fixtures and have the court decide which are real property and which are personal property.

The Legal Setting

Appraisals for condemnation are always prepared in close cooperation with an attorney who is skilled in the law of eminent domain. The appraiser may be employed by either the condemnor or the condemnee. The client will make his attorney available to assist the appraiser in understanding the legal requirements of the appraisal. But the appraiser must resist the tendency of either the client or attorney to influence the appraiser's professional judgment in order to produce a result more favorable to the client.

In condemnation appraisal work, the appraiser may end up as an expert witness, testifying to the judge and jury and being cross-examined about qualifications, comparables, and methods. The appraiser must be aware of this possibility and prepare for it from the first moment of working on an appraisal of this kind. The fixture issue discussed above is one of a number of issues that are decided by the rules of the courts. Eminent domain appraisal is different from most other appraisal work precisely because it is prepared for, and presented to, the courts, and performed according to the special rules established by the courts and legislature.

Often, the appraiser will have to rely on an attorney hired by the client (whether condemnor or condemnee) to provide needed legal advice concerning both the appraisal and the testimony. This could involve many issues, such as establishing the probability of rezoning, what value date to use, what property to appraise, which data and approaches will be admissible in this court, and so on. If the attorney for the other side has a different view of the law, and prevails, your appraisal and your testimony could be tossed out. It is prudent to try to understand the basis for any legal advice and to ask the attorney again if the advice is not understood. A letter detailing any vital issues is often desirable.

The Partial Taking

Perhaps the most unusual aspects of appraising for eminent domain are those that stem from a partial taking: when the government agency is acquiring only a portion of the property, called the "part taken." The owner is to be left the rest, called the "remainder" parcel. The total parcel is called the "whole property" or "larger parcel." Figure 17.6 portrays such a partial taking.

The Larger Parcel

The appraiser must first determine what the larger parcel is. What if the same owner owns the two adjacent houses? What if he or she has a 99-year lease on the warehouse behind? What if she and her brother jointly own the property across the street? This issue is important in evaluating whether the remainder parcel has been hurt (lost value) as a result of the taking. The courts have evolved three tests to determine which parcels make up the larger parcel, based upon the theory that the larger parcel consists of a coherent functional economic grouping.

First, the parcels must be contiguous. Increasingly, the courts have interpreted this to include across the street, or even up the street, if economically joined together. Second, they must be under the same ownership. The appraiser may need to review the many court cases examining this issue or explore the issue with the attorney. Third, the parcels must be put to the same use. The courts have tended to interpret this rule rather strictly. Again, it may be wise for the appraiser to ask an attorney's opinion on this legal issue.

Taking, Damages, and Benefits

The courts have interpreted just compensation in a partial taking to include the three elements to be discussed. Some courts require that each element

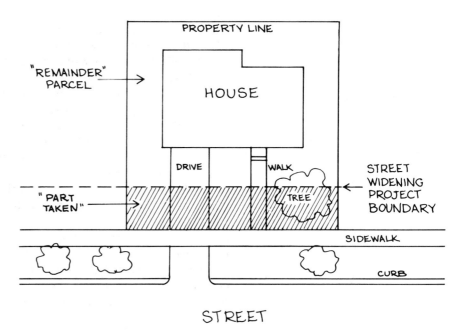

FIGURE 17.6
A Partial Taking

be calculated in turn. Other courts combine all three elements, appraising the value of the larger parcel and subtracting the value of the remainder parcel. The key is to use the procedure approved by the court involved.

The first element to consider is the value of the part to be taken. In Texas courts, the part to be taken is valued as if it were a separate parcel. In some cases, it is valued as a fraction; by area, for example, of the larger parcel.

The second element is the possible damage to the remainder parcel as a result of the government project, called severance damage. For instance, a parcel may no longer front on a road so that the owner must build a $100,000 bridge over an irrigation canal in order to regain access to the property. The $100,000 cost might be a measure of the damages. A government project could harm property in many other ways. However, not all damages are compensated for under the power of eminent domain. Some damages are the result of actions legally authorized under the government's police power, and no compensation or payment to property owners is required. For example, the government, in widening a commercial boulevard from two to four lanes, could also install a center barrier or median. This would prevent drivers from turning left in the middle of the block and into shopping area driveways. Customers would have to drive to the next intersection, make a U-turn and come back. They might shift their business to another store on that side of the street, hurting the business, and value, of stores on this side of the street. Contrary to certain logic, such limited "circuity of travel" is rarely ruled as a "compensable damage." In many partial-taking appraisals, the appraiser will need to research carefully which damages are compensable and which are not. A legal opinion will often be necessary.

The third element of just compensation in a partial taking is the possible benefit of the government project to the remainder parcel. The courts have defined two kinds of benefits, general and special. Only special benefits affect the calculation of just compensation. General benefits are those that are shared by the community at large or at least by more than a few adjacent property owners. Special benefits, on the other hand, are those that benefit only the remainder parcel (or perhaps only a few more parcels). An example of a special benefit could arise when a larger parcel is swampy land and too wet to build on. As part of a government project, the low corner of the parcel is taken and extensive drainage put in. After the project, the remainder parcel is well drained, habitable, and much more valuable. If other land in the area has not similarly benefited, the remainder parcel has obtained a special benefit.

The courts differ on how to apply the value of special benefits. Some courts simply value the larger parcel and then deduct the value of the remainder parcel in its improved state. In this case, extensive special benefits could reduce the total payment by the condemnor to zero. Under Texas law, courts allow recognition of special benefits only to the degree that they offset damages. Thus, the appraiser must first decide if the benefits to the remainder exist. Next, are they special benefits? Third, how are they to be appraised? And, fourth, how are they to be applied in calculating the final estimate of just compensation?

SUMMARY

Today, appraisers are faced with a growing variety of appraisal assignments. Many of these assignments now involve unusual house design and new concepts in ownership. Such types of housing include:

Cooperatives
Mobile homes
Modular homes
Planned unit developments (PUDs)
Row houses
Town houses
Zero-lot-line (patio or courtyard) homes

The common walls between some of these housing types, such as the town house, cause special problems with which appraisers should be familiar. One is the greater possibility of fire spreading from one unit to another. Another is the increased lack of privacy. New trends in ownership should also be noted. New legal forms of ownership, such as the condominium and cooperative, have different ownership rights than the conventional detached residence.

There are many appraisal assignments that involve the appraisal of partial interests or the dividing of the fee-simple title. A common appraisal situation involves establishing the current market value of the lessor's and lessee's interests in a given property. Other partial-interest appraisals include those studying the life estate and the remainder estate, as well as the property interests of lender and borrower and the valuation of time-shared ownerships.

One of the most specialized areas of appraisal practice involves valuing property for eminent domain. This type of appraisal follows the same steps as the standard appraisal process; however, a few areas need special attention. For instance, unlike the regular appraisal process, eminent domain cases often require the appraiser to testify as an expert witness before the courts. Therefore, the data collected and analyzed should be well prepared and documented for such testimony. Eminent domain cases also differ in that the value definition, date of value, and methodology are defined by the courts. The classification of property fixtures is also much more critical.

Finally, eminent domain often involves acquisition of only a portion of the property, called a partial taking. Here, the appraiser must consider the concepts of the larger parcel, the remainder parcel, severance damages, and general and special benefits, in order to reach a final value conclusion.

IMPORTANT TERMS AND CONCEPTS

Airspace
Conditions, covenants and restrictions
Condominiums
Cooperative
Eminent domain
Homeowners' association
Just compensation
Leased property interest
Life estates
Mobile homes
Modular homes

Mortgaged property
Partial interest
Partial taking
Planned unit development (PUD)
Prefabricated homes
Remainder estate
Row house
Seasonal discount
Time-shared ownership
Town house
Zero-lot-line home

REVIEWING YOUR UNDERSTANDING

1. Which of the various forms of detached housing are characterized by the lack of side yards?

   (a) Mobile homes, standard detached single-family residential
   (b) Apartment buildings, condominiums
   (c) Row houses, town houses

2. A condominium is:

   (a) A type of real estate description
   (b) Like a cooperative
   (c) A legal concept of ownership
   (d) A type of physical design of a building

3. A zero-lot-line home is also known as:

   (a) A duplex
   (b) A modular home
   (c) A patio or courtyard home
   (d) A condominium

4. Homeowners' associations are usually found in:

   (a) PUDs
   (b) Condominiums
   (c) None of the above
   (d) Both (a) and (b)

5. The most common type of partial-interest appraisal involves:

   (a) A leased property
   (b) A time-share residence

    (c) A row house

    (d) None of the above

6. A gross lease is:

    (a) A lease under which the tenant pays for all expenses

    (b) A lease under which the landlord pays for all operating expenses

    (c) A lease that applies only to commercial properties

7. The lessor's interest in leased property is referred to as the:

    (a) Leasehold

    (b) Leased fee

    (c) Fee simple

    (d) Remainder

8. An example of a partial interest is:

    (a) A life estate

    (b) Mortgaged property

    (c) Both (a) and (b)

    (d) None of the above

9. In eminent domain cases, the courts have determined "just compensation" to mean:

    (a) The fair market value of the property rights taken

    (b) Current market value plus compensation for anticipated future benefits

    (c) The market value at the time the property was bought by the current owner

    (d) All of the above

10. Eminent domain cases are commonly referred to as:

    (a) Condemnation

    (b) A taking

    (c) Both (a) and (b)

    (d) None of the above

CHAPTER
EIGHTEEN

THE
PROFESSIONAL
APPRAISER

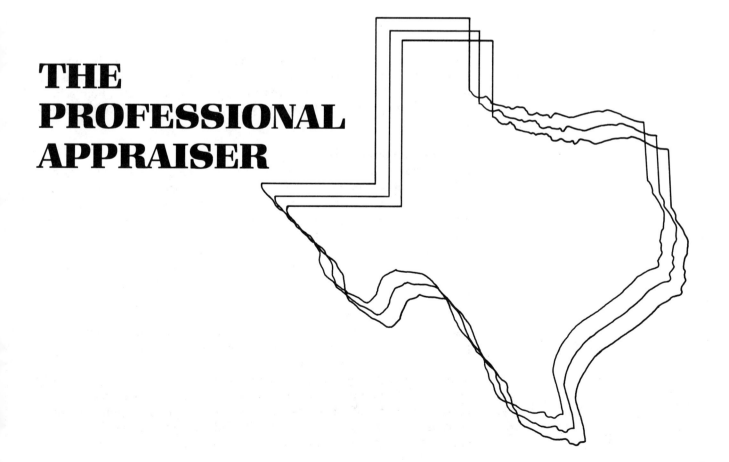

PREVIEW

In this last chapter, you meet the appraisers, the people whose craft you have been studying. The first section looks at their education and experience. The second section covers the major professional organizations appraisers belong to, explaining their purposes, membership criteria, and professional designations. In the third and fourth sections, we examine the code of ethics that appraisers follow and appraising as an occupation.

When you have completed this chapter, you should be able to:

1. List at least four important courses for an appraiser to take.
2. List the three major professional groups.
3. Understand the code of ethics.
4. Define the two occupational areas for an appraiser and know in which area trainee jobs usually occur.

SECTION 18.1
THE APPRAISER'S BACKGROUND

What are the backgrounds of people who do appraising? What kind of training is necessary? Are there minimum educational requirements? The qualifications of appraisers vary widely; however, most of the people who have recently become appraisers have had somewhat similar preparation for the job.

Education

There are no set educational requirements one must pass to become an appraiser. Most appraisers now have some college-level courses, and a few have Ph.D.s. There are also successful appraisers who lack a high school diploma. To appraise in Texas, however, one must be a licensed salesperson.

Reasons for Education

Formal education helps the appraiser gain valuable general knowledge and skills. Education can help an appraiser learn to reason clearly, which is an aid in figuring out appraisal problems. The appraiser must also learn to write clearly. The appraisal report, even if on a form, must communicate the appraiser's findings succinctly. Mathematics is also an important skill to master since all three approaches involve working with numbers. Algebra is helpful in handling formulas in the income approach. Plane geometry is helpful in calculating areas of odd-shaped parcels. These are some of the general skills used by appraisers.

Appraisers also need to have a good understanding of the many factors that affect real estate. Taking courses in finance, economics, taxation, city planning, city and county government, and economic and urban geography is helpful in expanding one's understanding of real estate. The series of real estate courses taught at many community colleges is particularly helpful in expanding the appraiser's knowledge of real estate markets and brokerage practice. Sometimes, too, appraisers find other courses helpful, such as beginning geology, blueprint reading, architectural history, accounting, transportation, geography, and statistics.

The third area in which appraisers seek formal education is in their own field. Theories, ideas, and techniques learned in an accredited appraisal course will enable later on-the-job training to be much more meaningful.

And, finally, an appraiser must hold a real estate license to appraise in Texas. Specific educational requirements must be met. The Texas Real Estate License Act (TRELA) describes in detail the requirements for both a salesperson's and broker's licensure. The following is a brief summary of these requirements.

For a salesperson's license:

1. Sponsorship by a broker.
2. U.S. citizenship or legally admitted alien status.
3. Age minimum of 18 years.
4. Texas residency (at least 60 days prior to application).
5. Satisfactory evidence of honesty and trustworthiness.
6. Educational requirements.
7. Fees.
8. License examination.

For a broker's license:

1. Satisfactory evidence of not less than two years' active real estate salesperson experience in Texas during the 36-month period preceding application for licensure.
2. Educational requirements.
3. Fees.
4. License examination.

FIGURE 18.1
Photo by Ken Karp

Educational requirements for real estate licensure in Texas are as follows:

For salespersons
Prelicensure
Twelve semester hours, at least 6 of which must be in core real estate courses. All 12 may be core courses. Core real estate courses must include Principles of Real Estate (or equivalent).

Three classroom hours on federal, state, and local laws governing housing discrimination, housing credit discrimination, and community reinvestment *or* at least 3 semester hours on constitutional law.
Postlicensure
First annual recertification
At least 2 additional semester hours with cumulative total of 8 semester hours of core real estate courses.

Second annual recertification
At least 2 additional semester hours with cumulative total of 10 semester hours of core real estate courses.

Third annual recertification
At least 2 additional semester hours with cumulative total of 12 semester hours of core real estate courses.

For Brokers
60 semester hours, at least 12 of which must be in core real estate courses, balance must be in related courses.

General Educational Trends

Increasing numbers of appraisers hold college degrees. The two largest professional appraisal groups, the American Institute of Real Estate Appraisers (AIREA) and the Society of Real Estate Appraisers (SREA), now require a college degree or equivalent for full professional membership. The Institute requires an earned degree. The number of employers requiring college degrees also appears to be growing, although some will waive the degree requirement if the appraiser has several years of satisfactory work experience. Certainly, the more formal education an applicant has, together with specialized courses in real estate and/or real estate appraisal, the more favorably most employers will consider his or her application.

More appraisers are earning college degrees in real estate now as more and more colleges and universities offer real estate majors or concentrations. For many years, only a handful of major schools maintained full real estate departments. Today, the University of Texas, Indiana University, the University of Wisconsin, Southern Methodist University, and Texas A & M University, as well as a number of other outstanding institutions, offer degrees in real estate. Most colleges with strong emphasis on economics and finance now offer at least introductory courses in real estate. There is a growing perception that business and financial executives need a strong foundation in real estate because of the dominant role of real estate in corporate balance sheets. Some schools integrate such courses as architecture, urban geography and city planning into their real estate curriculum, recognizing the social responsibility of real estate owners and developers.

Real Estate Courses

Many appraisers have taken the series of real estate courses offered by many community colleges. Although most of these courses were originally designed to supplement the education of real estate brokers, they include many elements valuable for appraisers. Typically, such curricula include courses in real estate principles and practice, finance, law, appraisal and economics. Advanced courses may cover real estate investment analysis, exchanging, rehabilitation, escrow/title law, and other specialized topics.

Generally, the appraisal courses sponsored by the various professional societies are more specialized and intense than the community college appraisal courses. Some appraisers take the community college appraisal course at the very start of their career and the first course of AIREA or SREA after six months or a year on the job. The second course of AIREA or SREA might be taken six months or a year after that, depending upon the course availability and the appraiser's work experience.

Appraisers may also rely on professional societies for specialized education. These include courses on such subjects as appraising industrial property or seminars on condominiums and money markets. In addition, there are numerous workshops, special seminars, and dinner speeches from which the appraiser learns of current trends and ideas.

FIGURE 18.2
Photo by Bruce Roberts/Rapho-Photo Researchers

Do-It-Yourself

By nature, appraisers have to be inquisitive. As a result, casual meetings between appraisers are often filled with shoptalk about this or that new house design, theory, trend, and so on. It is a form of self-improvement.

The body of appraisal theory could be learned in the same way. There are numerous texts, journals, and books of case studies. However, there is more to an appraisal class than the theories. For example, various members of advanced classes hold different jobs in real estate appraising and have different experiences to share. These form a significant part of the learning experience, as well as resources for continued learning after the class is finished.

Experience

Education alone will not create a competent appraiser. The second element is applying the ideas and skills learned in class. You will not really know if you understand an idea—the sales comparison approach, for example—until you have tried to use it a number of times. Because real estate appraisal involves so many bits of knowledge, experience gives you the added knowledge that is missing. Information not covered by classes is learned in the field; rating the quality and condition of houses is one such area. Despite what we have said on these subjects in this book, you will find that most of your skills in these areas will be gained in the field.

Do not expect to be able to make good appraisals upon completing this book. It usually takes six months of full-time experience before an appraisal trainee is producing reliable appraisals of homes without close supervision.

More complicated appraisals require variety as well as years of experience. The appraiser learns from working with each new type of property and appraisal purpose. This accumulated experience is helpful in preparing complex appraisals.

Knowledge

One measure of an appraiser's qualifications is the extent of his or her knowledge. The general areas of knowledge most important to an appraiser are real estate markets, property operations, and market data.

Markets

Real estate appraisers try to understand how real estate markets function, from the role of the broker to the interaction of supply and demand. This means that appraisers try to be aware of the forces that affect prices and current trends and activity. A practical understanding of markets can be extremely valuable to the appraiser.

Operations

Appraisers have to be somewhat familiar with the characteristics and management procedures of the various types of real estate they appraise. For instance, what are the day-to-day problems of convalescent hospital buildings? What is the current practice in writing tax escalation clauses in office leases? Which lenders customarily loan on retail store buildings? How common are net-net-net leases on office space? What is the typical depth of an office space from center hall to outside windows? In what locations are three-story walk-up apartments feasible?

FIGURE 18.3
Appraisal Judgment

Market Data

One reason for hiring appraisers is that they know how to find market data. On occasion, a client will hire an appraiser solely to work up a list of relevant sales or rents. Market information is not widely circulated. The knowledgeable appraiser has developed sources for particular kinds of data. Few people realize the amount and variety of data the expert appraiser can uncover.

Judgment

An extremely important component of the appraiser's art is judgment, an elusive concept. One definition is

. . . the operation of the mind, involving comparison and discrimination, by which knowledge and values and relationships are mentally formulated.*

Note that this definition uses the word discrimination to mean recognition of differences. The essential elements in this definition of judgment are to (1) compare, (2) distinguish differences, (3) recognize relationships, and (4) arrive at conclusions. Such a description is so general, it almost describes the appraisal process itself. What makes the use of judgment different from the overall process that appraisers follow?

Judgment for an appraiser means the ability to develop an understanding of the relationships between causes and effects on value. It is the ability of human intuition to process a mass of data and draw reliable conclusions from it. A knowledgeable broker, working in a well-known sales territory with which he or she is familiar, is using judgment when, after quickly walking through a home, he or she can judge what it will probably sell for. In short, judgment is what gets us from the market data, and any mathematical or graphic analysis of it, to an opinion about market value.

There is no simple method for developing good judgment. Taking classes can show what factors to consider. Experience gives you practice at applying analytical techniques to practical situations. Developing good judgment, however, may require a third step: self-review. You may need to follow up on your appraisal to see if your opinions turned out to be true.

* Webster's Collegiate, 5th ed., G. C. Merriam.

If not, why not? You may also want to see what others think of your opinion, and what reasons they offer for their differences. In a broker's open-house tour, for example, how do your estimates of probable selling price compare to those of others, and equally important, to the final price? Summarizing, good judgment is developed by education, experience, reviewing one's mistakes, and considering the comments of others.

Integrity

In addition to education, experience, knowledge and judgment, the professional appraiser must have integrity. In fact, because of the great responsibility placed on appraisers by society, integrity is possibly the greatest need. Appraisers are frequently pressured by parties with opposing interests to make their value estimates higher or lower, depending on their interest. For example, a borrower may want the appraisal to be high in order to get the maximum loan. On the other hand, in a tax dispute, the owner may want a low appraisal to keep taxes to a minimum. The appraiser must recognize that, regardless of who pays his or her fee, the interests of the public as a whole must come first.

The word "integrity" comes from the same root as "integer," meaning a whole number—not a fraction. So the appraiser with integrity is a person with high standards of character and conduct. Such an appraiser will not permit his or her standards to be compromised (fractionalized) in order to accommodate the special interests of any party. Because of the paramount importance of ethical conduct, professional appraisal organizations came into being. They were born in the dark days of the early 1930s, when the nation was in the grips of depression, an economic collapse without precedent. Billions of dollars in the hands of financial institutions were lost, partly because the officers of those institutions did not have reliable information concerning the value of their securities backed by real estate. We will now look at some of those organizations and the part they play today in the education, training, and discipline of the appraisal profession.

SECTION 18.2
APPRAISAL GROUPS

The great majority of appraisers are either members or member candidates of one of the various appraisal organizations. Many nonmembers regularly attend appraisal group meetings. What do appraisers gain from being associated with such groups?

Purpose

One benefit is that most groups award professional designations to their members who have achieved the required standards. These designations provide a means for the general public to rate the competency of appraisers. Licenses are not required for appraisers in most states. When licenses are required, the sole requirement often is a real estate broker's license. As a result, the public has come to rely upon the better-known professional designations as an aid in selecting appraisers. (See Figure 18.4.)

A second benefit is that these groups provide a major source of formal and informal training for appraisers. As already mentioned, these groups sponsor regular courses, one-day seminars, afternoon workshops, and

FIGURE 18.4
A Professional Designation Logo.
(Reproduced with Permission of the
American Institute of Real Estate Ap-
praisers)

dinner speakers for the benefit of members. The various groups also publish periodic journals, texts, research monographs, and newsletters. Beyond this type of formal education, the group's meetings offer informal education. People ask their peers how to handle a particular problem. They ask who may have recently researched a particular type of property sale. They may ask the group's leaders to arrange for a speaker on some troublesome new problem (for example, mini-warehouses when such types of property were first developed).

Major Organizations

There are three nationally recognized appraisal organizations with a membership encompassing all areas of real estate appraising. All three (or their legal predecessors) were founded in the 1930s and now have chapters throughout the country. All three offer more than one professional designation. A summary of these designations, and their requirements, is presented here.

American Institute of Real Estate Appraisers

The Institute, also known as AIREA, is affiliated with the National Association of Realtors (NAR) and is headquartered in Chicago. The original members, in the 1930s, were all licensed real estate brokers, but membership now includes real estate appraisers of every occupational background. Appraisers first apply and are then accepted as candidates for a professional designation. Candidates must then complete courses (or successfully challenge the course exam), submit written demonstration appraisal reports for grading, and have samples of their actual appraisals reviewed for experience rating.

The Institute has an extensive educational program involving many course titles taught at locations across the country. Courses are either intensive, lasting for one to three weeks, or are taught one or two nights a week. Courses may be either nationally sponsored or local chapter-sponsored. AIREA's publishing program includes the major reference text *The Appraisal of Real Estate,* as well as a number of other texts, research monographs, and the quarterly *Appraisal Journal.*

Member, Appraisal Institute (MAI), is the designation granted by AIREA to an appraiser qualified to appraise income property, complex realty, and all real estate interests generally. The requirements for this designation include at least five years' experience in real estate, five years or more of real estate appraisal experience, and three years' experience appraising various types of income-generating properties. There are approximately 4,000 active holders of the MAI designation. Each designee is given a certificate number. This designation probably has the widest public recognition.

Currently, people who want to receive the MAI designation must attend at least eight weeks of full-time classes (or successfully challenge the related examinations) and pass eight half-day examinations. Most submit two narrative demonstration appraisal reports, each around 100 pages in length and quite thorough in coverage. At least two interviews are required. At the second interview, samples of the candidate's actual work are submitted and critiqued. A college degree or equivalent is required.

Residential Member (RM) is the designation granted by AIREA to an appraiser qualified to appraise one- to four-family buildings. The RM designation was established in 1968. The RM must have a minimum of three years in the real estate field generally and at least two years' experience appraising residences. At the time of this writing, a high school diploma or equivalent is required. There are 1,500 active holders of the RM designation, each with a serially assigned certificate number.

The special education requirements for the RM designation currently call for either: (1) attending four week-long classes, each followed by a half-day examination; or (2) successfully passing the exams. A narrative demonstration appraisal report on a home or an alternate report must be submitted. The alternate can be combinations of actual appraisal reports, plus a demonstration report prepared on an expanded version of the FNMA/FHLMC appraisal form.

Society of Real Estate Appraisers

The Society of Real Estate Appraisers (SREA) is an independent group, also based in Chicago. It was founded in the 1930s as the Society of Residential Appraisers, a spin-off from the Savings and Loan League. The original members all worked for residential lenders. Today there are still numbers of savings and loan and bank appraisers as members, but also many fee appraisers, county assessment staff, and other governmental appraisers. The Society also has an extensive educational program. Three courses are taught nationwide on both the intensive or solid-week scheduling, and also on the extension or once-a-week scheduling. In addition, the Society sponsors a series of one- and two-day seminars that are offered throughout the country. The Society's publishing program includes an extensive series of audio cassettes on appraisal topics, course reference materials, research monographs, and the bimonthly journal *The Real Estate Appraiser and Analyst*. The Society also sponsors the SREA Market Data Center, Inc., a nonprofit sales data center that publishes books of tabulated sales and also provides computer terminal access to these sales and programs for computer sales analyses.

The first step toward a professional designation with SREA is to be admitted as an Associate Member/Applicant. The applicant then completes the courses, demonstration appraisal report, and experience rating required for the particular designation sought. The SREA offers three professional designations, appealing to appraisers with differing types of work experience.

Senior Real Estate Analyst (SREA) is the designation granted by the Society to an appraiser with substantial experience in two areas. One is the appraisal of income-generating real property and complex realty. The other is in real estate analysis and consulting work, which involves questions other than the value of property. Requirements are those for the SRPA designation detailed below, plus completion of an additional advanced course (Course 301), 8 to 12 years' experience in income-property appraising, both written and oral examinations, inspection of office operations, and review of actual appraisals. For those currently seeking an SREA designation, a college degree or equivalent is now required.

The SREA designation is relatively new, having been instituted in 1963. Because of its newness and the substantial experience needed to qualify, only some 400 persons hold the SREA designation. The designation has been well received, however. Each holder of the SREA designation must apply for recertification every five years and must submit evidence of integrity, continued technical training, experience, and professional leadership during that five-year period. Otherwise, the application is denied and the designation withdrawn. This is the first appraisal designation to require recertification. The favorable reaction has led to requirements for recertification by some other designations.

Senior Real Property Appraiser (SRPA) is the designation granted by the Society to an appraiser qualified to appraise income-generating real property and complex realty. At present, the appraiser must complete at least four weeks of full-time classes (or successfully challenge the related exams) and pass two eight-hour written examinations and one five-hour written examination. In addition, he or she must submit a narrative demonstration appraisal report on income-producing property.

Finally, the appraiser must submit a number of actual reports for a review of his or her work experience. The applicant must obtain 100 points of credit for work experience. Five points are awarded for each income-property appraisal report, three for special-purpose property or subdivisions, and one for homes. A maximum of 50 points out of 100 can be from single-family appraisals. All the reports must be complete and of good quality. In any one calendar year, there must be at least 10 points of satisfactory work before any of the work can be counted. The maximum number of points from any one calendar year is 50. From this, the minimum number of years of experience is two. For those currently seeking an SRPA designation, a college degree or equivalent is now required. Point systems are subject to change because experience evaluation methods may change. The SRPA designation was first granted in 1971, so it also is comparatively new. There are approximately 2500 SRPAs, but the designation is not yet well known to the general public.

Senior Residential Appraiser (SRA) is the designation granted by the Society of Real Estate Appraisers to an appraiser who has demonstrated his or her qualifications to appraise single-family homes and small apartments. The appraiser must complete at least two weeks of full-time classes (or successfully challenge the related exams) and pass one eight-hour and one five-hour written examination. In addition, the applicant must submit a demonstration appraisal report of a single-family residence, usually one full narrative report of approximately 100 pages.

The SRA candidate must submit actual reports in order to have his or her experience rated. A total of 50 experience credits is currently needed. One credit is awarded for each satisfactory home appraisal, and three for each subdivision. Reports must all be complete and of good quality. As with the SRPA, there is a minimum of 10 points in any calendar year and a maximum of 50 points. Also, a college degree or equivalent is currently required.

The SRA designation is well known in banking/home finance circles. It has been granted since the mid-1930s and was the only designation granted by the Society for many years. There are approximately 3900 active SRAs.

American Society of Appraisers

The ASA differs from SREA and AIREA in one primary aspect: Membership encompasses the appraising of all types of property, not just real property. The membership of ASA is composed of appraisers whose individual specialities range from ceramics to chemical plants. The group is headquartered in Washington, D.C. It is the successor, by merger in 1952, of two earlier groups, the American Society of Technical Appraisers and the Technical Valuation Society, which were both founded in the 1930s.

The educational program of ASA features a college-degree program developed by ASA and jointly sponsored with various accredited colleges around the country. In addition, ASA publishes a large collection of technical monographs via audio cassettes, as well as the major reference work *The Bibliography of Appraisal Literature,* published in 1974, and the monthly journal *Valuation.*

The ASA awards its professional designations based upon competency to appraise a specified type of property; the holder of the designation *must* indicate the property type, in parentheses, on any qualifications list. The three major property headings used are real estate, personal property, and machinery and equipment. There are many possible subheadings. Under personal property are found appraisers of silverware, porcelain, oil paintings, books, antiques, furs, jewelry, household contents, antique automobiles, intangibles, and so on. Under machinery and equipment, appraisers may specialize in sand or asphalt batch plants, in machine tools, or in construction rolling stock. Many "M and E" appraisers do not specialize in a particular type of machinery but generalize, as most real estate appraisers do. The ASA awards three levels of designation.

1. *Member* is the first professional designation or level. There is no abbreviation of this designation to place after one's name. The designation is awarded to appraisers who have a college degree or its equivalent and two years of full-time appraisal experience. An interview and an examination are also required.

2. *ASA,* or Senior Member, is the designation awarded to appraisers who have met the requirements for Member and also have five years of appraisal experience. In addition, an applicant for Senior Membership must take a written exam and submit two appraisal reports.

3. *FASA* stands for Fellow of the American Society of Appraisers. It is awarded to holders of the ASA designation who have distinguished themselves in their appraisal activities through teaching or writing or by activity as a National Officer.

Specialized Groups

A large number of other appraisal groups exist: some are nationwide; others are regional or local. The national groups tend to have a particular area of interest, as opposed to the three general groups summarized earlier. Of the large number, four will be mentioned here.

American Right of Way Association

This group, usually abbreviated as AR/WA, is headquartered in Los Angeles and was founded in 1934. As its name indicates, membership orientation is toward those involved in the appraisal and acquisition of rights of way. This includes utility company power lines, oil company pipelines, and public highways. All three involve the acquisition of property by condemnation under the power of eminent domain. As a result, other appraisers active in condemnation appraisals may also join AR/WA. Examples include County Public Works department employees, City Real Estate officers, Flood Control District land representatives, and so on. Fee appraisers who do contract work for all of these organizations also join. The AR/WA awards several professional designations.

American Society of Farm Managers and Rural Appraisers

This society is headquartered in Chicago. Founded in 1929, it awards professional designations for farm managers and for rural appraisers. There are area chapters in most major farming regions.

International Association of Assessing Officers

Membership in IAAO is made up of governmental property tax appraisal and assessment staff, private firms who contract to do periodic reappraisals in many states, and private tax representatives for major retailers and manufacturers. The group is headquartered in Chicago and was founded in 1934. There are local chapters in some parts of the country. The IAAO awards three designations: CAE (Certified Assessment Evaluator) for government-employed real estate assessment appraisers; CPE (Certified Personalty Evaluator) for government-employed personalty assessment appraisers; and AAE for assessment appraisers, either realty or personalty, not government employed.

Association of Governmental Appraisers

In January of 1980, the Society of Governmental Appraisers and the Association of Federal Appraisers merged with the Association of Governmental Appraisers. As its name indicates, AGA members work for the government. Some are federal employees, others state and county. The Association is located in Annandale, Virginia.

SECTION 18.3
STANDARDS OF PRACTICE

Each professional group sets standards of acceptable appraisal practice for its members. These are called a code of ethics, standards of professional conduct, and/or standards of professional practice. Many of the provisions are quite similar from one organization to the next, but there are some differences.

In general, the purpose is to lay out the desirable and undesirable rules of practice and conduct in appraisal. Most important, these rules protect the interest of the public at large. Second, they specify actions to protect the interests of the appraiser's clients. Third, they establish standards to protect the interests of other appraisers and the profession in general. These three groups are all interested parties in a discussion of the ethical conduct of an appraiser.

The Public

Impartiality

The appraiser should have no financial interest or undisclosed interest in the results of the appraisal assignment. This has three subcategories:

1. The appraiser should not have an undisclosed interest in the property being appraised.

2. The appraisal fee should not be contingent upon the amount of value concluded.

3. The appraiser should neither pay nor receive referral fees so that referrals will be objectively considered.

Disclosure and Methodology

The appraiser should report his or her findings in full or else in a nondeceptive form. In particular, every report should fully disclose any assumptions relied upon, a summary of the value methodology used, a statement as to whether the property was inspected, and identification of who takes the responsibility for the conclusions in the report.

Some codes of practice say the appraisal report should include all the data and reasoning used to reach the value conclusion. Today, the more common view is that the report can be a summary of the total appraisal effort as long as the report meets minimum disclosure content.

Support for Conclusions

The appraisal conclusions that are reported should be based on data and analyses rather than solely on judgment or intuition. Supporting data and analyses should be contained in the report or retained for a reasonable time in the appraiser's file.

The Client

Competency

The appraiser should take on only those appraisal assignments that are within his or her ability. If necessary, the appraiser should enlist the aid of a more experienced colleague to be sure that a competent job is being performed. The appraiser should only agree to prepare appraisals that he or she anticipates can be completed within the agreed-upon time period.

Finally, once an appraiser accepts an assignment, he or she should perform it competently and adequately, regardless of whether the agreed fee will cover the necessary time. Unexpected problems with property, personality differences, and overtime pressures do not waive this standard, unless clearly covered by the agreement with the client.

Confidentiality

The appraisal report is not a public document. Therefore, the appraiser should keep the value conclusion completely confidential from everyone, except as directed by the client or required by order of a court. Confidential information provided by the client, or by others, in the course of the appraisal investigation should also be held confidential.

The Profession

Competitive Activity

The appraiser may compete for business with other appraisers but should do so in a professional manner. This precludes trying to block others from practicing as appraisers or attempting to take business away from other appraisers by casting unsupported doubts on their capabilities.

Cooperative Activity

The appraiser should work with other appraisers to establish a code of behavior agreed to by all. Once established, each appraiser should try to comply with the code. The appraiser should also support and assist any investigation of possible violations of the code of behavior.

The appraiser should share available market data with other appraisers to the degree legally possible in adversary cases. At the least, the appraiser should not try to hide important market data or misinform other appraisers about the particulars. The appraiser should also indicate when others have played a part in the value analysis of a particular report.

SECTION 18.4
APPRAISING AS AN OCCUPATION

There are various ways to look at the occupation of appraisal. For example, we could compare people with professional designations to those without, or compare beginning appraisers to experienced appraisers. However, the major breakdown within the industry seems to be (1) those who work for a salary, and (2) those who work for themselves and are paid a fee by the job.

Working for a Salary

The majority of appraisers work for a salary. Nearly all salaried appraisal jobs are with large government or private institutions. As a result, salaried appraisers are commonly referred to as institutional appraisers. The number of salaried appraisers working for private appraisal firms is quite small but is growing.

Starting Out

Most appraisers start with a salaried job in an institution. The industry rule of thumb is that the first six months of employment are a net loss. After that, the trainee can work alone well enough so that supervision falls off and appraisal production and quality climb. Only larger institutions can usually afford this cost burden for an appraisal trainee.

Another avenue into appraising is to work in a related area and gain enough experience to bypass most of the trainee stage. One example is the person who works as an appraisal secretary and gradually learns research skills. Over a period of years, a researcher who is intelligent and interested can develop good appraisal skills. A second example is the real estate broker or salesperson who gradually works into an appraisal career over a number of years.

The Institutional Job

There are many institutions that hire salaried appraisers. Some may have only one or two appraisers on their staff, while others have hundreds.

Those with small staffs are usually less known to the public. Nearly all appraisers have worked for an institution at some point of their careers.

Among the public institutions with appraisal departments, county or district property tax appraisal offices are well known. County appraisal districts in each county have appraisal staffs paid on a salary basis. Salaried appraisal staffs are also part of state water, parks, and general services departments, along with state banks and savings and loan regulatory bodies. Regional park and transportation districts may have an appraisal staff. At the Federal level, appraisal staffs are located in the Corps of Engineers, Navy Department, National Park Service, U.S. Forest Service, Bureau of Land Management, Bureau of Public Roads, Internal Revenue Service, Department of Housing and Urban Development, Federal National Mortgage Association, U.S. Postal Service, General Services Administration, and others.

The role of the appraiser in a public institution varies. Establishment of property tax values is the role of the tax appraiser. Another institutional role is to estimate market value of parcels to be acquired by condemnation under the power of eminent domain. This function involves the second-largest group of governmental appraisers, after property tax assessment valuation. A third role is to review or audit appraisals made by private parties or institutions such as banks or savings and loans, lenders who submit loans to FHA and FNMA, and individuals making income tax or estate claims based on private appraisals, and so on. In some cases, public institution appraisers value surplus publicly owned parcels for the purpose of estimating a listing price and probable selling price.

A number of private institutions have appraisal staffs. Banks, savings and loans, life insurance companies, mortgage brokers, mortgage bankers, and similar lenders are among the best known. But many appraisers also work for real estate investment trusts (REITs), large pension funds, and real estate investment management firms.

Some appraisers work as real estate managers for large developers, real estate departments of large national corporations, and national franchise firms. Major oil companies have appraisal staffs, as do pipeline firms; railroads, electric, gas, water, and telephone and utility companies; and major mining companies. Often, these personnel will perform related real estate functions as well, from market research to site acquisition negotiations, construction supervision, and property management.

What is it like to be an institutional appraiser? The varied list of institutions and functions reveals that the jobs themselves vary. The majority of the jobs have hours from 8 to 5, five days a week. Because you spend much of your time on the road inspecting properties and sales and interviewing zoning staff and lenders, it is an out-of-doors job with unpredictable working conditions. Some of these jobs have substantial overtime and travel; this is usually understood at the start.

Salaries for institutional appraisers tend to be midlevel in the total range of salaried jobs. Jobs with longer hours and/or more travel tend to be more highly paid. Starting salaries for novice appraisers are considerably lower than for experienced persons, and the salary increase for experience is greater than for many other salaried jobs.

The greatest demand is for salaried workers with one to three years of experience. Beginning or trainee positions are relatively few. Such positions are usually with banks or savings and loans. Trainees are usually hired when the lender's work load is expanding. Occasionally, however, trainees are hired to eventually replace appraisers who have retired or resigned, especially if there are few experienced appraisers looking for jobs.

Where Does It Lead?

Appraisal jobs are relatively secure, although savings and loan institutions tend to hire and fire with changes in the volume of loans. Recently, salaried appraisers have been changing jobs more frequently than in the past. Many leave institutional employment and open their own appraisal businesses. This usually happens after they have accumulated substantial knowledge and industry contacts. Often, they wait to obtain a professional designation or to make arrangements to contract for appraisal assignments. Some wait for retirement and open a part-time practice to supplement retirement income.

The Fee Appraiser

The term fee appraiser is used to refer to an independent businessperson who performs appraisals for a number of clients and is paid on a per-job basis. A few institutional appraisal employees are paid on a fee or commission basis, but this is now a rare practice and is not considered to be "fee appraising."

Fee appraisers are also commonly referred to as independent appraisers. However, this description is offensive to some salaried appraisers because it implies to them that only fee appraisers arrive at an independent conclusion, that is, one that is not imposed by the employer.

The fee appraiser, to be successful, must be competent both in making appraisals and also in running a small business. This includes managing files, keeping financial records, marketing one's skills effectively, making proposals, collecting money owed, hiring and firing, arranging for space and equipment, and training a staff.

Fee appraisal offices are fairly small. Many consist of just the appraiser and a part-time typist. A small office may be operated out of the appraiser's home, with typing hired out or performed by the appraiser. Offices of three or four people (appraiser, assistant, and secretary) are also common. Few offices are much larger. An office of 20 people is currently considered very large. Offices of this size are found in large metropolitan areas. Currently, there are probably less than 50 such offices of this size in the country.

What Is It Like to Be an Appraiser?

The previous discussion has focused on some of the objective aspects of appraisal as a profession. However, the work of appraisers is enjoyable enough for us to offer the reader some additional thoughts about the occupation.

1. Our work is varied. We meet people of all ages and backgrounds. We see the varied and interesting ways that people live, and how they invest their money.

2. Our work is challenging, since no two properties are alike. There are stimulating problems to solve, even when studying routine properties. The more difficult assignments often require a high degree of professional skill and determined effort.

3. Our work involves us with what is going on in our town. We may be making the construction loan appraisal on the large new store in town or an acquisition appraisal for a new redevelopment project. Our education in real estate economics strengthens our ability to understand these events. As a result, we often have a good grasp of current trends.

4. For some of us, appraisal work can be done, to an extent, at our own convenience. Some clients want inspections performed in the evenings or weekends, so we can work extra hours if we want to. Because our knowledge will continue to grow as we get older, there will be no mandatory retirement.

5. We know that there are a number of related areas in real estate where our knowledge is also useful. While some appraisers go on to other fields, such as property development, mortgage banking, and brokerage, most of us continue to enjoy the challenge and stimulation of professional appraisal work.

SUMMARY

Although there are no set educational requirements needed to become an appraiser, getting an education will help you gain valuable knowledge. Having a formal education in real estate can only improve your career options as well as your income. Many employers in real estate prefer employees who have a college degree. Since only a handful of universities offer a degree program in real estate, you can usually do just as well with a degree in a field related to real estate such as economics, finance, or business administration. Many community colleges and appraisal societies offer courses in real estate.

Becoming a competent appraiser requires many different skills. Besides pursuing a formal education, you need to develop your knowledge of markets and real estate operations. This kind of knowledge is more often gained in the field than in the classroom. Having sound judgment is also an important skill for an appraiser. Developing good judgment usually comes from a combination of experience in the field and in education and, most important, as a result of self-review.

There are a multitude of appraisal organizations, societies, and groups. Many, such as the American Society of Farm Managers and Rural Appraisers, specialize in particular appraisal areas. Joining such a group can offer many advantages: the chance to meet and talk to other people in your field, special courses and workshops on important appraisal topics, and professional designations.

The three main appraisal organizations are the American Institute of Real Estate Appraisers (AIREA), the Society of Real Estate Appraisers (SREA), and the American Society of Appraisers (ASA). Each group offers several designations.

Because integrity is another requirement of appraisers, a code of ethics has been established by each of these professional groups to encourage and enforce a high standard of appraisal practice. These codes seek to protect the general public, the client, and the appraisal profession.

Appraisers may be divided into two categories: those who work for a salary and those who work on a per-job basis. Many appraisers begin in a salaried position with an institution. Many private and public institutions hire appraisers. Fee appraisers, on the other hand, usually work for themselves in a small office. Fee appraisers must have a good sense of business management to be successful.

Appraising is an interesting and varied profession. It is a field that can offer many benefits to those who enjoy its variety and challenge.

IMPORTANT TERMS AND CONCEPTS

Competency	Formal training
Competition	Impartiality
Confidentiality	Informal training
Designations	Institutional appraiser
Disclosure	Integrity
Fee appraiser	Professional societies

REVIEWING YOUR UNDERSTANDING

1. To become an appraiser, you must have:

   (a) A college degree
   (b) A high school diploma
   (c) There are no specific educational requirements

2. People who seek a professional designation from the AIREA or SREA:

   (a) Do not need a high school diploma
   (b) Need a high school diploma
   (c) May need a college degree

3. The three areas that appraisers must be knowledgeable about are:

   (a) Market data, real estate operations, and markets
   (b) Market data, appraisals, and value in use
   (c) Appraisal theory, market data, and real estate brokerage

4. Joining an appraisal group or society has many advantages. These include:

   (a) The chance to meet other people in the field
   (b) Educational seminars and workshops
   (c) Professional designations
   (d) All of the above

5. The three largest nationally recognized appraisal organizations are:

   (a) AIREA, SREA, and MAI
   (b) MAI, RM, and ASA
   (c) AIREA, SREA, and ASA
   (d) SRPA, ASA, and MAI

6. Of the several smaller groups mentioned, which one specializes in appraising property for the government?

   (a) Association of Governmental Appraisers
   (b) Society of Real Estate Appraisers
   (c) American Right of Way Association
   (d) None of the above

7. The American Society of Appraisers differs from the AIREA and the SREA in what important aspect?

   (a) ASA members appraise all types of property, not just real property

   (b) ASA members appraise real property exclusively

   (c) ASA members work primarily for the government

8. Which society offers the Member, Appraisal Institute (MAI) designation?

   (a) American Institute of Real Estate Appraisers

   (b) Society of Real Estate Appraisers

   (c) American Society of Appraisers

9. To improve the quality of appraising, many professional appraisal groups require members to follow a code of ethics. One of the code of ethics requirements is:

   (a) The appraiser should have no financial interest or undisclosed interest in the results of the appraisal

   (b) The appraiser should keep the value conclusions confidential from everyone, except the client, or if required, the courts

   (c) The appraiser must reveal all data and the value conclusion of an appraisal to members of the press

   (d) All of the above

   (e) Two of the above

10. A fee appraiser is:

   (a) An appraiser who works for an institution for a fixed salary

   (b) An appraiser who is paid on a per-job basis

   (c) An appraiser who works for a percentage commission

   (d) An appraiser who specializes in the appraisal of leased fee estates

ANSWERS TO REVIEWING YOUR UNDERSTANDING QUESTIONS

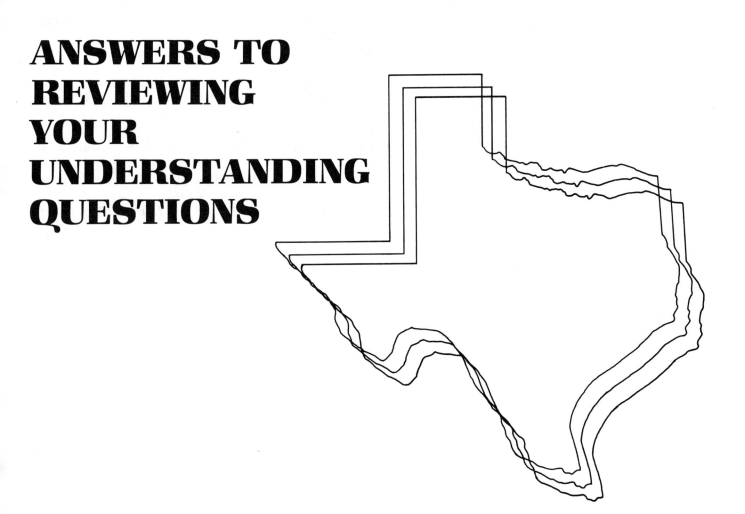

Chapter 1 1. (c). 2. (b). 3. (a). 4. (c). 5. (a). 6. (c). 7. (a). 8. (e). 9. (e). 10. (c).

Chapter 2 1. (a). 2. (b). 3. intent, annexation, adaptation, agreement, relationship of parties. 4. (b). 5. (c). 6. building codes, coastal preservation zones, master plans, rent control, subdivision requirements, zoning ordinances (for examples). 7. (a). 8. one square mile, 640 acres. 9. square of six miles per side, 36 sections of 640 acres each. 10. (b).

Chapter 3 1. (a). 2. (b). 3. (b). 4. (b). 5. (d). 6. (b). 7. (b). 8. (d). 9. (c). 10. (c).

Chapter 4 1. (d). 2. (d, e). 3. (e). 4. (a). 5. (b). 6. (b). 7. (e). 8. (b). 9. (b). 10. (d).

Chapter 5 1. (b). 2. (c). 3. (b). 4. (c). 5. (c). 6. (d). 7. (d). 8. (d). 9. (b). 10. (b).

Chapter 6 1. (d). 2. (a). 3. (b). 4. (a). 5. (c). 6. (b). 7. (c). 8. (b). 9. (b). 10. (a).

Chapter 7 1. (c). 2. (d). 3. (c). 4. (d). 5. (d). 6. (d). 7. (c). 8. (a). 9. (b). 10. (d). 11. (b). 12. (c).

Chapter 8 1. (c). 2. (a). 3. (b). 4. (b). 5. (e). 6. (e). 7. (e). 8. (e—no precise critera exist). 9. (c). 10. (e).

Chapter 9 1. (b). 2. (c). 3. (c). 4. (b). 5. (a). 6. (b). 7. (a). 8. (c). 9. (a). 10. (e).

Chapter 10 1. (e). 2. (b). 3. (d). 4. (c). 5. (c). 6. (d). 7. (d). 8. (d). 9. (d). 10. $35,340, $42,000, $37,450, $38,700. Answer is (a), but median value around $38,000 may be preferred.

Chapter 11 1. (d). 2. (b). 3. (d). 4. (d). 5. (a). 6. (c). 7. (c). 8. (b). 9. (b). 10. (b).

Chapter 12 1. (d). 2. (d). 3. (c). 4. (c). 5. (b). 6. (c). 7. (c). 8. (c). 9. (d).

Chapter 13 1. (c). 2. (b). 3. (c). 4. (a). 5. (b). 6. (c). 7. (b). 8. (a). 9. (b). 10. (a). 11. (a).

Chapter 14 1. (d). 2. (b). 3. (c). 4. (c). 5. (a). 6. (d). 7. 9.94%. 8. 10.83%.

Chapter 15 1. (c). 2. (c). 3. (d). 4. (e). 5. (b). 6. (c). 7. (e). 8. (b). 9. (d). 10. (d).

Chapter 16 1. (d). 2. (a). 3. (c). 4. (b). 5. (d). 6. (a). 7. (d). 8. (a). 9. (d). 10. (d).

Chapter 17 1. (c). 2. (c). 3. (c). 4. (d). 5. (a). 6. (b). 7. (b). 8. (c). 9. (a). 10. (a).

Chapter 18 1. (c). 2. (c). 3. (a). 4. (d). 5. (c). 6. (a). 7. (a). 8. (a). 9. (e). 10. (b).

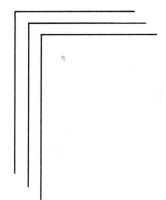

GLOSSARY

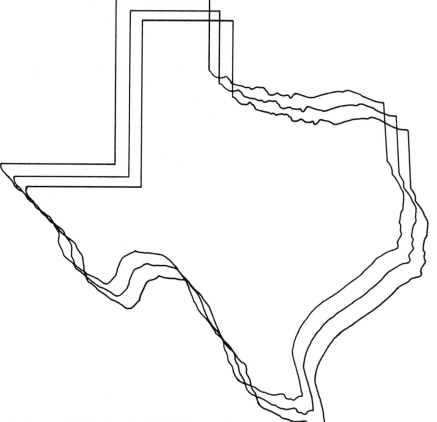

Abstraction Method   Method of appraising vacant land; allocation of the appraised total value or sale price of the property between land and building either on a ratio basis or by subtracting a figure representing building value or price from the total appraised value or price of the property. Also called Allocation Method.

Access   The right of a property owner to have a means of entry and exit from his or her property to a public street.

Accrued Depreciation   The difference between the current cost of replacement new as of the date of the appraisal and the present appraised value; estimate of actual market loss in value as compared with a new building; diminished utility.

Ad Valorem Tax   A real estate tax based on value.

Adjustment   Increase or decrease in the market value of a comparable property to account for a feature that the property has or does not have, which differentiates it from the subject property.

Age-Life Method of Depreciation   *See* Straight-Line Method of Depreciation.

Agents of Production   Four factors that must be combined to produce income: labor, coordination, capital, and land.

Allocation Method   Method of appraising vacant land; allocation of the appraised total value or sale price of the property between land and building either on a ratio basis or by subtracting a figure representing building value or price from the total value or price of the property.

Amenities   Qualities that are pleasing and agreeable; generally intangible benefits of property ownership.

Amortization   The liquidation of a financial obligation on an installment basis; also, recovery, over a period, of cost or value.

Annuity   A series of assured equal or nearly equal payments to be made over a period of time.

Annuity Capitalization   Income capitalization technique; method of valuing interests in leased property; annual income multiplied by an appropriate factor; provides for return on and return of investment capital.

Appraisal   An estimate or opinion of value as of a certain date.

Appraisal Report   Communication of a formal appraisal.

Appraiser   One qualified by education, training, and experience who is hired to estimate the value of real or personal property based on experience, judgment, facts, and use of formal appraisal processes.

Appreciation   Increase in the value of property.

Appurtenance   That which has been added or appended to a property and which becomes an inherent part of same.

Appurtenant Right   A right that belongs to the owners of one property that gives them the right to use another property (which they do not own) in a specific way that benefits their property (e.g., an easement).

Area   Space or size of a surface within a set of boundaries.

Assessment   The valuation of property for the purpose of levying a tax; assessed value. Also, a single charge levied against real estate to defray the cost of public improvements that serve it.

Association Agreement   Set of private conditions, covenants, and restrictions applying to all properties in a planned unit development or condominium project.

Assumption of Mortgage   The taking of title to property wherein the buyer assumes liability for payment of an existing note secured by a mortgage against the property.

Band of Investment   Method of estimating interest and capitalization rates based on the rate of mortgage interest available and the rate of return on equity required.

Base Costs   Average or typical costs of similar buildings, usually obtained from published cost manuals; used in the comparative square foot method of estimating cost of construction.

Base Rent   *See* Minimum Rent.

Book Value   The capital amount at which property is shown for accounting purposes; cost basis.

Bracketing   When using the sales comparison approach, selection of market data such that the subject is contained within a range of data.

Building Code   Municipal regulations concerning the type and quality of building materials and methods of construction established by ordinance.

Building Residual Technique   Technique of income capitalization; net income remaining to the building after interest on the land has been deducted and is capitalized into a value for the building.

Bundle of Rights   The rights that make up the ownership of real estate.

Capital   An agent of production; construction and equipment costs; investment money.

Capital Gains   Profit on the sale of a property.

Capitalization Rate (Cap Rate)   A single rate that blends all aspects of the property into one fraction that relates value to income.

Capitalized Income Approach   *See* Income Approach.

Capitalized Income Method of Depreciation   Method for estimating depreciation by comparing the subject's market rent and rent on a new building.

Cash Flow   Net operating income minus debt service (can be calculated before or after income tax).

Cash-on-Cash   Return based on actual cash invested; cash flow as a percentage or ratio to equity.

Cash Return to Equity   Equity dividend; cash flow.

Central Town   A town that performs a variety of services for the surrounding area.

Comparable Sales   Property sales used for purposes of comparison in the appraisal process; ideally competitive, open market transactions, and recent in time of sale.

Comparative Square Foot Method   Method of estimating construction costs using typical square foot cost manuals or other factual data.

Compound Interest   Interest paid on principal and also on the accrued and unpaid interest.

Condemnation   The taking of property by a governmental agency through the power of eminent domain.

Conditions, Covenants, and Restrictions   Recorded deed restrictions that run with the land, usually initiated by the original subdivider.

Condominium   A form of legal ownership; each individual owns the airspace in his unit in fee simple plus an undivided interest in the structural supports, building systems, and all common areas.

Construction Classification   Type of construction.

Contract Rent   Amount of rent being paid under contractual commitments binding owners and tenants.

Cooperative   A form of legal ownership; each owner holds a stated percentage ownership in the cooperative association, which owns the land and buildings and grants each owner the permanent right to occupy the specified dwelling unit, as well as the right to the joint use of the common areas.

Coordination   An agent of production; management.

Corner Lot   Lot with frontage on two intersecting streets.

Correlation   *See* Reconciliation.

Cost Approach   A method in the appraisal process; an analysis in which a value estimate of a property is derived by estimating the replacement cost of the improvements, deducting the estimated accrued depreciation, then adding the market value of the land.

Cost Basis   Original price paid for a property plus capital improvements less depreciation.

Cost Multiplier   Factor used in adjusting published cost figures in estimating construction costs.

Cost-to-Cure Method of Depreciation   Method of computing depreciation in which the appraiser estimates loss in value as the cost to cure or repair observed building defects.

Courtyard Home   *See* Zero-Lot-Line Home.

Cul-De-Sac Lot   Lot located at the end of a dead-end street.

Curable Depreciation   Items of physical deterioration or functional obsolescence that if repaired, would add as much to the market value of the property as the cost of repairs.

Curbstone Appraisal   An informal valuation of a property based on observation and experience.

Debt Service   The periodic interest and/or principal payments required in a loan agreement.

Decline Phase   Third phase in the cycle of a neighborhood, generally marked by delayed repairs and deterioration of buildings.

Dedication   A voluntary giving of private property to some public use by the owner, as in the dedication of land for streets in a subdivision.

Deed Restrictions   Private limitations in the deed to a property that dictate certain uses that may or may not be made of the property.

Demand   Desire to possess plus the ability to buy; an essential element of value.

Depreciated Cost Method   Method for adjusting comparable sales; adjustments are calculated from an analysis of the depreciated replacement cost for each differentiating feature.

Depreciation   Loss of value in property brought about by age, physical deterioration, or functional or economic obsolescence.

Depth   Distance from the frontage to the rear lot line.

Design Type   Classification based on the use for which a structure is designed.

Development Method   Method of vacant land valuation; development costs and profits are subtracted from estimated gross sales to determine land value.

Development Phase   First phase in the life cycle of a neighborhood, consisting of the initial construction on vacant land.

Diminished Utility   *See* Accrued Depreciation.

Direct Capitalization Method   Income capitalization technique; value is estimated by dividing net operating income by the overall capitalization rate.

Direct Costs   All of the costs that are directly involved with the physical construction of the structure, including labor, materials and equipment, design and engineering, and subcontractors' fees.

Direct Market Comparison Approach   *See* Sales Comparison Approach.

Direct Market Method   Method of adjusting comparable sales; two comparable properties with one differing feature are used to estimate the amount of the adjustment for that feature (also called the matched pair method).

Discounted Cash Flow (DCF)   Technique of income capitalization; estimated future income is discounted to a present value.

Easement   Right, privilege, or interest that one party has in the land of another, created by grant, agreement, or necessity for a specific purpose.

Economic Life   Total number of years of useful life that may be expected from a building.

Economic Obsolescence   Loss in value that is often caused by factors located outside the subject property; locational or environmental obsolescence.

Economic Rent   *See* Market Rent.

Economic Trend   Pattern of related changes in some aspect of the economy.

Effective Age   Relative age of a structure considering its physical condition and marketability.

Effective Gross Rent   Market rent minus an allowance for vacancy and credit losses.

Effective Interest Rate   Nominal annual interest rate divided by the number of compounding periods in a year.

Elements of Comparison   Four categories of information about sales: terms of sale, time of sale, location elements, and physical elements.

Elements of Value   Four prerequisites that must be present for an object to have value: utility, scarcity, demand, and transferability.

Ellwood Technique   A mortgage/equity method of capitalization.

Eminent Domain   The power of a government to acquire property for a public purpose by paying just or reasonable compensation.

Equity   Interest or value that an owner has in real estate over and above the liens against it.

Equity Buildup   Increase in the investor's share of the total property value from reduction of debt through regular installment payments of principal and interest and/or through property appreciation.

Equity Capitalization Rate   Factor used to estimate the value of the equity in the mortgage/equity technique of capitalization.

Equity Residual Technique   *See* Mortgage/Equity Technique of Capitalization.

Escheat   The right of the state to take back title to property if the owner dies or disappears and leaves no relatives or heirs.

Estate   A person's ownership interest in real property.

Excess Rent   The amount by which the total contract rent exceeds market rent.

Export Production   Goods and services produced for sale or use outside of the town in which they are produced.

Farmers Home Administration (FHmA)   An agency of the Department of Agriculture which is primarily responsible for providing financial assistance for farmers and others living in rural areas where financing is not available on reasonable terms from private sources.

Federal Home Loan Mortgage Corporation (FHLMC)   A federal agency known as Freddie Mac, which provides a secondary market for savings and loan associations.

Federal Housing Administration (FHA)   An agency of the federal government that insures mortgage loans.

Federal National Mortgage Association (FNMA)   A quasi-public agency converted into a private corporation known as Fannie Mae, whose primary function is to buy and sell FHA and VA mortgages in the secondary market.

Fee Absolute   *See* Fee Simple.

Fee Simple   An estate in real property by which the owner has title without limitation or end.

Fiscal Policy   Programs by the federal government that are intended to influence economic activity by making changes in government expenditures and taxation.

Fixed Expenses   Costs that are more or less permanent, and vary little from year to year.

Fixture   Personal property that has become attached to real estate and converted into real estate.

Flag Lot   Rear lot, behind other houses or lots, with a long narrow access.

Flat Lease   *See* Straight Lease.

Form Report   Written report of the appraisal value conclusion presented on a standardized form or checklist.

Formal Appraisal   A written estimate of value that is reached by the collection and analysis of data.

Frontage   Boundary line or lot side that faces a street.

Functional Obsolescence   Loss in value that is caused by a relative loss of building utility; the cost to repair or replace would be more than the return.

Functional Utility   The combination of the usefulness and attractiveness of a property.

Future Value   The estimated lump-sum value of money or property at a date in the future.

Government National Mortgage Association (GNMA)   A federal corporation known as Ginnie Mae, mainly involved in the administration of the mortgage-backed securities program and in the secondary mortgage market.

Government Survey System   *See* Rectangular Survey System.

Graduated Lease   *See* Step-Up Lease.

Gross Area   Total space or size of a surface within a set of boundaries.

Gross Income   Total income from property before any expenses are deducted.

Gross Income Multiplier   Figure multiplied by the gross rental income of a property to produce an estimate of the property's value.

Gross Lease   Rental agreement under which the landlord pays all expenses.

Gross Rent Multiplier   *See* Gross Income Multiplier.

Highest and Best Use   The reasonable and probable use of a property that will support the highest present value.

Historic Cost   Cost of a property at the time it was constructed.

Improvement   Permanent structure or other development that becomes part of the land.

Income Approach   Method in the appraisal process; an analysis in which the estimated net income from property is capitalized into a value estimate.

Income Forecast   Gross or net income estimate.

Income Property   Property that is purchased for its income-producing capabilities.

Income Stream   Current periodic flow of net earnings.

Incurable Depreciation   Building defects that would cost more to repair than the value the repair would add to the structure.

Index Method   Method for estimating construction costs; adjusts original costs to the current cost level by a construction multiplier obtained from a published cost index.

Indicated Value   Value estimate determined by an appraisal approach.

Indirect Costs   All of the time and money costs involved in a project that are not directly involved with construction. Examples are accounting, legal fees, and advertising costs.

Informal Appraisal   An estimate of value that is reached by using intuition, past experience, and general knowledge; a verbal appraisal.

Intangible Property   Rights to something other than physical property.

Interest   Charge for the use of money for a period of time.

Interest Rate   Charge made for a loan of money expressed as a percentage of the principal.

Interior Lot   Lot with frontage on only one street.

Internal Rate of Return   Discount rate that discounts the future cash flows to equal the value of investment.

Just Compensation   Payment for private property obtained by condemnation through the power of eminent domain.

Key Lot   Lot that has several other lots backing onto its sideyard.

Labor   An agent of production; cost of all operating expenses and wages except management.

Land   The surface, the soil and rocks beneath, and the airspace above which the landowner can reasonably use and enjoy.

Land Residual Technique   Technique of income capitalization; net income remaining to the land after income attributable to the building has been deducted is capitalized into a value for the land.

Landlord   Property owner who rents property to another.

Larger Parcel   Total parcel of property of which a governmental body is only acquiring a portion through condemnation.

Law of Fixtures   Five tests to determine whether an object is a fixture or personal property.

Lease   A contract between the owner and the tenant, setting forth conditions on which the tenant may occupy and use the property, and the term of the occupancy.

Leased Fee   Property owner's interest in leased property.

Leasehold   Tenant's interest in leased property.

Lessee   Tenant; one who rents property under a lease contract.

Lessor   Landlord; owner who enters into a lease with a tenant.

Letter Report   One- to five-page written report of the appraisal conclusion.

Leverage   Use of borrowed funds to purchase property, with the expectation of increasing the rate of return to equity; trading on the equity.

Life Estate   Holder controls the right of possession and use of a property during the lifetime of some specifically named person.

Linear Regression   Statistical technique for calculating sales adjustment; line of "best fit" for two variables.

Liquidity   The ease with which property can be converted into cash.

Local Production   Goods and services produced for sale or use in the town in which they are produced.

Long-Lived, Incurable Physical Deterioration   Loss in value attributable to the major components of a building, when age is the major contributing factor and the cost of repair would exceed the value that is added to the structure by the repair.

Lump-Sum Dollar Adjustment   Type of sales adjustment; specific dollar amount is added or subtracted for each differing feature.

Market Approach   *See* Sales Comparison Approach.

Market Exposure   Making the potential buyers of a property aware that the property is available for sale.

Market Method of Depreciation   *See* Sales Data Method of Depreciation.

Market Rent   The rental income the property could command if placed for rent on the open market as of the effective date of the appraisal.

Market Value   The most probable price in terms of money which a property should bring in a competitive and open market under all conditions requisite to a fair sale, the buyer and seller each acting prudently and knowledgeably, and assuming the price is not affected by undue stimulus.

Mature Phase   *See* Stable Phase.

Metes and Bounds Description   Legal description of land that describes the boundary lines together with their terminal points and angles.

Minimum Rent   Base rent that is the minimum amount paid under a percentage lease.

Misplaced Improvement   A building that is functionally obsolete because it is the wrong type or use for its location; an example of functional obsolescence.

Mobile Home   A housing unit that is capable of being moved on the highway.

Modular Home   Building composed of modules constructed on an assembly line in a factory.

Monetary Policy   Programs by the Federal Reserve System that increase or decrease the supply of money in an effort to achieve designated economic goals.

Mortgage   Instrument by which property is used to secure the payment of a debt or obligation.

Mortgage/Equity Technique of Capitalization   Income capitalization technique; value is estimated by capitalizing the cash flow to value the equity, then adding the amount of total debt. The result is an estimated total property value.

Motive   Stimulus that causes a person to act.

Multiple Listing Service (MLS)   Organization of real estate brokers wherein all members have the opportunity to find an interested client for any listing taken by a member.

Multiple Regression   Statistical technique for calculating sales adjustments for more than one feature.

Narrative Report   A detailed formal written report of the appraisal value conclusion.

Neighborhood   An area whose occupants and users share some common ties or characteristics.

Neighborhood Cycle   Period during which most of the properties in a neighborhood go through four phases: development, maturity, decline, and renaissance.

Net Area   *See* Useful Area.

Net Income   Gross annual income less lost income for vacancies and uncollectible rents minus all operating expenses.

Net Income Ratio   Net income divided by gross income.

Net Lease   Lease under which the lessee pays all property expenses.

Net Operating Income   *See* Net Income.

Nominal Interest Rate   Percentage of interest stated in loan documents.

Observed Condition Method of Depreciation   *See* Cost-to-Cure Method of Depreciation.

Obsolescence   Loss in value due to reduced desirability and usefulness of a structure.

Open Market Transaction   Transaction in which both buyer and seller act willingly, with full knowledge of all details of the transaction, and under no pressure.

Operating Expenses   Day-to-day, out-of-pocket expenses required to run a property.

Operating Statement   Written record of a property's gross income, expenses, and resultant net income.

Overage Rent   Amounts paid over and above the base rent under a percentage lease.

Overall Rate (OAR)   *See* Capitalization Rate.

Overimprovement   A building that is functionally obsolete because it is too large or lavish for its neighborhood.

Partial Taking   Governmental agency acquiring only a portion of a property through condemnation.

Patio Home   *See* Zero-Lot-Line Home.

Percentage Adjustment   Type of sales adjustment; difference between the comparable sale and the subject is calculated as a percentage of the sale price.

Percentage Lease   Lease agreement by which the tenant pays a stipulated percentage, usually of the gross sales of goods and services offered by the tenant; most percentage leases require a certain base rent regardless of sales volume.

Personal Property Property that is movable; any property that is not real property.

Physical Deterioration Wear and tear from use, age, the weather, neglect, lack of maintenance, and vandalism.

Planned Unit Development (PUD) Zoning designation for mixed use and/or innovative developments.

Plottage Increase in unit value created by joining smaller ownerships into one large single ownership.

Points Amounts paid by the borrower or the seller that increase the effective yield for a lender; each point equals 1% of the loan amount.

Police Power Power of a governmental body to regulate property for the health, safety, morals, and general welfare of the public.

Prefabricated Home House manufactured and sometimes partly assembled before delivery to the building site.

Present Value Current lump-sum value of some future income.

Principle of Anticipation Value is the present worth of future benefits, both income and intangible amenities.

Principle of Change The concept that real estate values are constantly changed by social, economic, and political forces in society.

Principle of Competition The concept that market demand generates profits and profits generate competition; competition stabilizes profits.

Principle of Conformity The concept that maximum value results when properties in a neighborhood are relatively similar in size, style, quality, use and/or type.

Principle of Highest and Best Use The concept that maximum market value of a given parcel of land, vacant or improved, is created by development or utilization at its highest and best use.

Principle of Increasing and Decreasing Returns Income and other benefits available from real estate may be increased by adding capital improvements only up to the point of balance in the agents of production, beyond which the increase in value tends to be less than the increase in costs.

Principle of Progression and Regression Lower-valued properties generally benefit from close proximity to many properties of higher value and higher-valued properties tend to suffer when placed in close proximity with lower-valued properties.

Principle of Substitution When a property can be easily replaced by another, the value of such property tends to be set by the cost of acquiring an equally desirable substitute property.

Principle of Supply and Demand Prices and rent levels increase when demand is greater than supply and tend to decrease when supply exceeds demand.

Principle of Surplus Productivity, Balance and Contribution Income that is available to land, after the other economic agents have been paid for, is known as the surplus of productivity; a proper balance of the agents maximizes the income available to land; the value of any agent is determined by its contribution to the whole.

Promissory Note An agreement signed by the borrower, promising to repay the loan under stipulated terms.

Quality of Construction Classification or rating based on basic structural integrity, materials, finishes, and special features.

Quantity Survey Method Process for arriving at cost estimate of new construction, involving a detailed estimate of the quantities of raw materials used, the current price of the material, and installation costs.

Real Estate The land and everything that is permanently fastened to the land; real property.

Real Estate Cycle Periodic pattern of changes in the amount of construction and volume of sales in the real estate market.

Real Property Real estate.

Recapture Capital out of current income; return of investment.

Reconciliation The process by which the appraiser reviews and considers the indicated values developed by the applied approaches to arrive at a final value conclusion.

Recorded Lot, Block and Tract Legal description of a parcel of land by means of reference to a recorded plat of a subdivision.

Rectangular Survey System System for legal description of property based on principal meridians, baselines, and a grid system.

Remainder Estate An estate that takes effect after the termination of a life estate.

Remainder Parcel The portion of a property left to the owner in a partial taking by condemnation.

Renaissance Fourth phase in the cycle of a neighborhood, the transition to a new cycle through the demolition, relocation, or major renovation of existing buildings.

Rent Consideration paid for the use of real property.

Rent Multiplier *See* Gross Income Multiplier.

Rent Roll Total of all scheduled rental amounts for tenant space and parking.

Rental Loss Method of Depreciation   *See* Capitalized Income Method of Depreciation.

Replacement Cost   Cost of constructing a building or structure that would have a similar utility to the subject improvement, but constructed with modern materials, and according to current standards, design, and layout.

Reproduction Cost   Cost of a near duplicate or replica structure.

Reserves for Replacement   Annual allowances set up for replacement of building components and equipment.

Residual Techniques of Capitalization   Income approach to valuation methods that separate income attributed to land, building, or equity for purposes of analysis.

Return of Investment   Conversion of the investment in real estate to cash or other valuable assets.

Return on Investment   Rents or profits produced by the real estate.

Reversion   Return of capital through sale or return of rights in real estate to a lessor at the expiration of a lease.

Row House   *See* Townhouse.

Sales Analysis Grid   Table of sales data on comparable properties.

Sales Comparison Approach   Method in the appraisal process; means of comparing similar type properties, which have recently sold, to the subject property.

Sales Data Method of Depreciation   Method of estimating depreciation; sales data are compared to current reproduction cost.

Scarcity   In relatively short supply.

Severance Damage   Damage to the remainder parcel as a result of a partial taking by condemnation.

Special-Function Town   A town that concentrates on one special service or purpose.

Stable Phase   Second phase in the cycle of a neighborhood, marked by stability of the existing buildings and occupants.

Step-Up Lease   Lease agreement that establishes progressively higher rental amounts for different segments of the lease term; graduated lease.

Straight Lease   Lease agreement in which rent is a fixed amount that stays the same over the entire lease term.

Straight-Line Method of Depreciation   Method of computing depreciation in which the value of a building is divided for expense purposes evenly over its economic life.

Subdivision   A tract of land divided by the owner into blocks, lots, and streets and recorded in compliance with local regulations.

Summation Approach   *See* Cost Approach.

T-Intersection Lot   Lot at the end of a T-intersection of streets.

Take Parcel   The portion of a property acquired by a governmental agency in a partial taking by condemnation.

Tangible Property   Physical objects and/or the rights thereto.

Tax   A levy under legal auspices for governmental purposes.

Tenant   One who occupies and/or leases property.

Terms of Sale   Financing arrangements and conditions of a sale.

Time-Shared Ownership   Subdivision of the fee interest of a property into blocks of time, with each time block owned by a different owner.

Time-Value of Money   A dollar in the present is worth more than a dollar in the future because of its interest-earning capability.

Topography   Nature of the surface of land.

Townhouse   Rowhouse; a house on an individual lot, which is owned in fee, usually built without sideyards between adjoining houses; an architectural style.

Transferability   Capable of change in ownership or use.

Transportation Service Town   A town that is selected to provide services along a transportation route, usually located at transportation nodes.

Turn-Key Costs   Costs that include all of the charges to the consumer, not just the costs to the developer or builder.

Type of Construction   Classification based on a structure's basic frame, wall, and floor construction.

Type of Occupancy   *See* Design Type.

Unit-in-Place Method   Method of estimating the reproduction cost of a building by estimating the installed cost of each component part.

Unit of Comparison Adjustment   Sales analysis tool; sales prices are converted to price per appropriate unit.

Use Type   *See* Design Type.

Useful Area   That portion of the gross area of a site that can be built on.

Value   The worth, usefulness, or utility of an object to someone for some purpose.

Value Conclusion   The final estimate of value in an appraisal.

Value in Exchange   The value of an item or object to the general public.

Value in Use   The value of an item or object to a particular user.

Veterans Administration (VA)   A federal agency that guarantees approved lenders against loss on loans made to eligible veterans.

Volume   Measurement of the content of the space within a three-dimensional object.

Yield   Total net profit earned by an investor on invested capital.

Zero-Lot-Line Home   House built without a sideyard; may be wrapped around two or more sides of a courtyard or patio.

Zoning   Governmental regulations specifying the type of use to which property may be put in specific areas.

INDEX